PRINCIPLES *of*
LANGUAGE LEARNING
AND TEACHING

FOURTH EDITION

H. DOUGLAS BROWN
San Francisco State University

Principles of Language Learning and Teaching, Fourth Edition

Pearson Education, 10 Bank Street, White Plains, NY 10606

Editorial director: Allen Ascher
Executive editor: Louisa Hellegers
Development manager: Penny Laporte
Development editor: Janet Johnston
Director of design and production: Rhea Banker
Associate director of electronic production: Aliza Greenblatt
Managing editor: Linda Moser
Production manager: Ray Keating
Production editor: Christine Lauricella
Electronic production editor: Lisa Ghiozzi
Senior manufacturing manager: Patrice Fraccio
Manufacturing supervisor: Edie Pullman
Cover design: Tracy Cataldo
Text design adaptation: Steven Greydanus

Library of Congress Cataloging-in-Publication Data

Brown, H. Douglas,
    Principles of language learning and teaching / H. Douglas Brown. – 4th ed.
      p. cm.
    Includes bibliographical references and index.
    ISBN 0-13-017816-0 (alk. paper)
    1. Language and languages–Study and teaching. 2. Language acquisition. I. Title.

P51.B775 2000
418'.0071–dc21

                                            99-058205

8 9 10–DOH–05

CONTENTS

Preface to the Fourth Edition, ix

1 Language, Learning, and Teaching   1

Current Issues in Second Language Acquisition, 2
Language, 4
Learning and Teaching, 7
Schools of Thought in Second Language Acquisition, 8
     Structuralism/Behaviorism, 8
     Rationalism and Cognitive Psychology, 9
     Constructivism, 11
Language Teaching Methodology, 13
In the Classroom: The Grammar Translation Method, 15
Topics and Questions for Study and Discussion, 16
Suggested Readings, 17
Language Learning Experience: Journal Entry 1, 18

2 First Language Acquisition   20

Theories of First Language Acquisition, 21
     Behavioristic Approaches, 22
     The Nativist Approach, 24
     Functional Approaches, 27
          Cognition and Language Development, 28
          Social Interaction and Language Development, 29
Issues in First Language Acquisition, 30
     Competence and Performance, 30
     Comprehension and Production, 33
     Nature or Nurture?, 34
     Universals, 35
     Systematicity and Variability, 37
     Language and Thought, 37
     Imitation, 38
     Practice, 40

Input, 41
Discourse, 42
In the Classrom: Gouin and Berlitz—The First Reformers, 43
Topics and Questions for Study and Discussion, 46
Suggested Readings, 47
Language Learning Experience: Journal Entry 2, 48

3 Age and Acquisition   49

Dispelling Myths, 50
Types of Comparison and Contrast, 52
The Critical Period Hypothesis, 53
Neurological Considerations, 54
      Hemispheric Lateralization, 54
      Biological Timetables, 55
      Right-Hemispheric Participation, 56
      Anthropological Evidence, 57
The Significance of Accent, 58
Cognitive Considerations, 61
Affective Considerations, 63
Linguisitic Considerations, 66
      Bilingualism, 67
      Interference Between First and Second Languages, 67
      Interference in Adults, 68
      Order of Acquisition, 68
Issues in First Language Acquisition Revisited, 70
In the Classroom: The Audiolingual Method, 73
Topics and Questions for Study and Discussion, 75
Suggested Readings, 76
Language Learning Experience: Journal Entry 3, 77

4 Human Learning   78

Learning and Training, 78
Pavlov's Classical Behaviorism, 80
Skinner's Operant Conditioning, 80
Ausubel's Meaningful Learning Theory, 83
      Systematic Forgetting, 86
Rogers's Humanistic Psychology, 89
Types of Learning, 91
Transfer, Interference, and Overgeneralization, 94
Inductive and Deductive Reasoning, 97
Aptitude and Intelligence, 98
In the Classroom: The "Designer" Methods of the 1970s, 103

Topics and Questions for Study and Discussion, 109
Suggested Readings, 110
Language Learning Experience: Journal Entry 4, 111

5 Styles and Strategies   **112**

Process, Style, and Strategy, 112
Learning Styles, 113
      Field Independence, 114
      Left- and Right-Brain Functioning, 118
      Ambiguity Tolerance, 119
      Reflectivity and Impulsivity, 121
      Visual and Auditory Styles, 122
Strategies, 122
      Learning Strategies, 124
      Communication Strategies, 127
          Avoidance Strategies, 129
          Compensatory Strategies, 129
Strategies-Based Instruction, 130
In the Classroom: Styles and Strategies in Practice, 135
Topics and Questions for Study and Discussion, 139
Suggested Readings, 140
Language Learning Experience: Journal Entry 5, 141

6 Personality Factors   **142**

The Affective Domain, 143
      Self-Esteem, 145
      Inhibition, 147
      Risk-Taking, 149
      Anxiety, 150
      Empathy, 152
      Extroversion, 154
Myers-Briggs Character Types, 156
Motivation, 160
      Instrumental and Integrative Orientations, 162
      Intrinsic and Extrinsic Motivation, 164
The Neurobiology of Affect, 166
Measuring Affective Factors, 167
In the Classroom: Putting Methods into Perspective, 169
Topics and Questions for Study and Discussion, 172
Suggested Readings, 174
Language Learning Experience: Journal Entry 6, 175

7 Sociocultural Factors   176

From Stereotypes to Generalizations, 178
Attitudes, 180
Second Culture Acquisition, 182
Social Distance, 185
Culture in the Classroom, 189
Language Policy and Politics, 191
    World Englishes, 192
    ESL and EFL, 193
    Linguistic Imperialism and Language Rights, 194
    Language Policy and the "English Only" Debate, 195
Language, Thought, and Culture, 196
In the Classroom: Toward a Principled Approach to Language Pedagogy, 201
Topics and Questions for Study and Discussion, 203
Suggested Readings, 204
Language Learning Experience: Journal Entry 7, 206

8 Cross-Linguistic Influence and Learner Language   207

The Contrastive Analysis Hypothesis, 207
From the CAH to CLI (Cross-Linguistic Influence), 211
Markedness and Universal Grammar, 213
Learner Language, 215
Error Analysis, 216
    Mistakes and Errors, 217
    Errors in Error Analysis, 218
    Identifying and Describing Errors, 220
    Sources of Error, 223
        Interlingual Transfer, 224
        Intralingual Transfer, 224
        Context of Learning, 226
        Communication Strategies, 227
Stages of Learner Language Development, 227
Variability in Learner Language, 229
Fossilization, 231
Form-Focused Instruction, 233
Error Treatment, 235
In the Classroom: A Model for Error Treatment, 239
Topics and Questions for Study and Discussion, 242
Suggested Readings, 243
Language Learning Experience: Journal Entry 8, 244

9 Communicative Competence 245

Defining Communicative Competence, 246
Language Functions, 248
Functional Syllabuses, 252
Discourse Analysis, 253
       Conversation Analysis, 255
Pragmatics, 257
       Language and Gender, 259
Styles and Registers, 260
Nonverbal Communication, 262
       Kinesics, 262
       Eye Contact, 263
       Proxemics, 264
       Artifacts, 264
       Kinesthetics, 264
       Olfactory Dimensions, 265
In the Classroom: Communicative Language Teaching, 266
Topics and Questions for Study and Discussion, 267
Suggested Readings, 269
Language Learning Experience: Journal Entry 9, 270

10 Theories of Second Language Acquisition 271

Building a Theory of SLA, 272
       Domains and Generalizations, 272
       Hypotheses and Claims, 274
       Criteria for a Viable Theory, 276
An Innatist Model: Krashen's Input Hypothesis, 277
Cognitive Models, 281
       McLaughlin's Attention-Processing Model, 282
       Implicit and Explicit Models, 285
A Social-Constructivist Model: Long's Interaction Hypothesis, 286
From Theory to Practice, 288
Out on a Limb: The Ecology of Language Acquisition, 294
Topics and Questions for Study and Discussion, 296
Suggested Readings, 298
Language Learning Experience: Final Journal Entry, 299

Bibliography, 301
Index, 343

PREFACE TO THE

FOURTH EDITION

WHEN THE first edition of *Principles of Language Learning and Teaching* appeared in 1980, the field of second language acquisition (SLA) was relatively manageable. We had a handful of professional journals devoted to SLA, a good collection of anthologies and conference proceedings, and a small but respectable number of books on SLA and teaching. Today the field of SLA has so many branches and subfields and specializations that it is virtually impossible to "manage"!

In the December 1997 issue of the semi-annually published *Second Language Instruction/Acquisition Abstracts*, 180 periodicals were surveyed and 240 book reviews cited. Some thirty major subject matter areas included child language acquisition, non-native language pedagogy, testing, literacy studies, reading processes and instruction, writing, bilingualism, bilingual education, translation, pragmatics, discourse analysis, specific languages, lexicology, interpersonal behavior and communication, sociolinguistics, language planning, nonverbal language, and more. And several major fields were subsumed into other topics: psycholinguistics, intercultural communication, world Englishes, curriculum design, and critical pedagogy, among others. Incidentally, the December 1997 issue of the above mentioned abstracting journal was the last issue that was printed in hard copy; now, the material has to be electronically downloaded because there is more information than print media can handle!

Today we can see that the manageable stockpile of research of just a few decades ago has been replaced by a coordinated, systematic storehouse of information. Subfields have been defined and explored. Researchers around the world are meeting, talking, exchanging findings, comparing data, and arriving at some mutually acceptable explanations. A remarkable number of respectable, refereed journals are printing the best and most interesting of this research. Our research miscarriages are fewer as we have collectively learned how to conceive the right questions.

At the same time, we should not be too smug. The wonderful intricacy of complex facets of human behavior will be very much with us for some time. Roger Brown's (1966: 326) wry remark of a number of decades ago still applies:

> Psychologists find it exciting when a complex mental phenomenon—something intelligent and slippery—seems about to be captured by a mechanical model. We yearn to see the model succeed. But when, at the last minute, the phenomenon proves too much for the model and darts off on some uncapturable tangent, there is something in us that rejoices at the defeat.

We can rejoice in our defeats because we know that it is the very elusiveness of this phenomenon of SLA that makes the quest for answers so exciting. Our field of inquiry is no simple, unidimensional reality. It is "slippery" in every way.

PURPOSE AND AUDIENCE

Principles of Language Learning and Teaching is designed to give you a picture of both the slipperiness of SLA and the systematic storehouse of reliable knowledge that is now available to us. As you consider the issues, chapter by chapter, you are led on a quest for your own personal, integrated understanding of how people learn—and sometimes fail to learn—a second language. That quest is eclectic: no single theory or hypothesis will provide a magic formula for all learners in all contexts. And the quest is cautious: you will be urged to be as critical as you can in considering the merit of various models and theories and research findings. By the end of the final chapter, you will no doubt surprise yourself on how many pieces of this giant puzzle you can actually put together!

In its first three editions, this book has served a number of purposes for many audiences around the world. For graduates or advanced undergraduates in language-teacher education programs, it is a textbook on the theoretical foundations of language teaching. For a surprising number of people it has become a book that Master's degree candidates pore over in preparation for comprehensive examinations! For experienced teachers, it has become a handbook that provides an overview of current issues in the field.

For the most part, you do not need to have prior technical knowledge of linguistics or psychology in order to comprehend this book. An attempt has been made to build, from the beginning, on what an educated person knows about the world, life, people, and communication. And the book can be used in programs for educating teachers of any foreign language, even though many illustrative examples here are in English since that is the language common to all readers.

CHANGES IN THE FOURTH EDITION

The first question people ask me when they hear that a new edition is about to appear is:"What changes will you make?" In anticipation of these questions about the Fourth Edition, I offer the following highlights:

1. **Updated topics and references.** In a field growing as rapidly as ours, a period of six or seven years sees many advances. The current edition features some new topics: constructivist approaches to SLA, new data on the critical period hypothesis, emotional intelligence, language aptitude, strategies-based instruction (SBI), the neurobiology of affect, language policy and politics, intercultural communication, cross-linguistic influence, form-focused instruction, and Long's Interaction Hypothesis, to name a few. Other topics have been updated to reflect current work in the field. And out of literally thousands of new articles, books, and chapters that have appeared since the last edition, I have added a selection of some 200 new bibliographic references that report the latest work in SLA.

2. **Reorganized chapters.** If you were just getting used to the Third Edition, be prepared to look carefully at the new edition. The process of revising has involved a reorganization of a substantial proportion of the material.

3. **Deletion of the chapter on Language Testing (10).** An overwhelming number of readers and reviewers have stated that the Testing chapter cannot be covered within the scope of a term of coursework. I have therefore deleted that chapter and placed it, in revised form, into the new Second Edition of my companion textbook, *Teaching by Principles*. What was Chapter 11 in the Third Edition has become Chapter 10 here.

4. **Redesigned teacher-friendly end-of-chapter exercises.** In previous editions, the end-of-chapter exercises were designed for individual contemplation and possibly for teachers to adapt to classroom discussion. In this edition, new and improved classroom-tested exercises are explicitly designed for in-class group work, pair work, whole-class discussion, and individual work.

5. **More accessible suggestions for further reading.** In this edition the suggestions for further reading now more effectively target an audience of students just beginning in the field of SLA. Few esoteric, technical articles are listed, and instead students are led to more reader-friendly material.

6. **Journal guidelines for a language learning experience.** I have always recommended that the information in a book like this is best internalized if the reader is concurrently taking a course in a foreign language. At the end of each chapter in this edition is a new section that offers classroom-tested journal-writing guidelines for the reader either to reflect on a current experience learning another language or to take a retrospective look at a previous foreign language learning experience. In both cases, the reader is asked to apply concepts and constructs and models to a personal experience learning a foreign language.

7. **Revised end-of-chapter "In the Classroom" vignettes.** As in the Third Edition, these vignettes provide information on various pedagogical applications and implications of second language research. The first four vignettes describe a historical progression of language-teaching methods; the other chapters deal with related classroom implications of the information in the chapter itself. A new vignette—a model for classroom error treatment—has been added to Chapter 8.

ACKNOWLEDGMENTS

This book has grown out of graduate courses in second language acquisition that I have taught at San Francisco State University, the University of Illinois, and the University of Michigan. My first debt of gratitude is therefore to my students—for their insights, enthusiasm, and support. They offered invaluable comments on the first three editions of the book, and I have attempted to incorporate those insights into this Fourth Edition. I always learn so much from my students!

I am also grateful to faculty colleagues both here at San Francisco State University and around the world for offering verbal commentary, informal written opinion, and formal published reviews, all of which were useful in fashioning this Fourth Edition. I especially want to thank Tom Scovel, May Shih, Jim Kohn, Aysegül Daloglu, and the publisher's anonymous reviewers for feedback and encouragement. Further, I wish to acknowledge the staff and the resources of the American Language Institute for support in the time-consuming task of this revision. I am particularly grateful to Kathy Sherak for assuming the ALI directorship duties while I took a leave to complete this revision.

Finally, to Mary—my wife, lifetime companion, and best friend—thanks once again for believing in me way back when I embarked on this career, and for letting me take over two rooms of the house for this project!

H. Douglas Brown
San Francisco, California

CHAPTER 1

LANGUAGE,

LEARNING,

AND TEACHING

L EARNING A second language is a long and complex undertaking. Your whole person is affected as you struggle to reach beyond the confines of your first language and into a new language, a new culture, a new way of thinking, feeling, and acting. Total commitment, total involvement, a total physical, intellectual, and emotional response are necessary to successfully send and receive messages in a second language. Many variables are involved in the acquisition process. Language learning is not a set of easy steps that can be programmed in a quick do-it-yourself kit. So much is at stake that courses in foreign languages are often inadequate training grounds, in and of themselves, for the successful learning of a second language. Few if any people achieve fluency in a foreign language solely within the confines of the classroom.

It may appear contradictory, then, that this book is about both learning and teaching. But some of the contradiction is removed if you look at the teaching process as the facilitation of learning, in which you can teach a foreign language successfully if, among other things, you know something about that intricate web of variables that are spun together to affect how and why one learns or fails to learn a second language. Where does a teacher begin the quest for an understanding of the principles of language learning and teaching? By first considering some of the issues.

CURRENT ISSUES IN SECOND LANGUAGE ACQUISITION

Current issues in second language acquisition (SLA) may be initially approached as a multitude of questions that are being asked about this complex process. Let's look at some of those questions.

Who?

Who does the learning and teaching? Obviously, learners and teachers. But who are these learners? Where do they come from? What are their native languages? levels of education? socioeconomic levels? Who are their parents? What are their intellectual capacities? What sorts of personalities do they have? These questions focus attention on some of the crucial variables affecting both learners' successes in acquiring a foreign language and teachers' capacities to enable learners to achieve that acquisition. The chapters that follow will help to tease out those variables.

In the case of the teacher, another set of questions emerges. What is the teacher's native language? experience and/or training? knowledge of the second language and its culture? philosophy of education? personality characteristics? Most important, how do the teacher and the student interact with each other?

What?

No simpler a question is one that probes the nature of the subject matter itself. What is it that the learner must learn and the teacher teach? What is communication? What is language? What does it mean when we say someone knows how to *use* a language? How can both the first and the second language be described adequately? What are the linguistic differences between the first and the second language? These profound questions are of course central to the discipline of linguistics. The language teacher needs to understand the system and functioning of the second language and the differences between the first and second language of the learner. It is one thing for a teacher to speak and understand a language and yet another matter to attain the technical knowledge required to understand and explain the system of that language—its phonemes and morphemes and words and sentences and discourse structures.

How?

How does learning take place? How can a person ensure success in language learning? What cognitive processes are utilized in second language learning? What kinds of strategies does the learner use? What is the optimal interrelationship of cognitive, affective, and physical domains for successful language learning?

When?

When does second language learning take place? One of the key issues in second language research and teaching is the differential success of children and adults in learning a second language. Common observation tells us that children are "better" language learners than adults. Is this true? If so, why does the age of learning make a difference? How do the cognitive and emotional developmental changes of childhood and young adulthood affect language acquisition? Other "when" questions center around the amount of time spent in the activity of learning the second language. Is the learner exposed to three or five or ten hours a week in the classroom? Or a seven-hour day in an immersion program? Or twenty-four hours a day totally submerged in the culture?

Where?

Are the learners attempting to acquire the second language within the cultural and linguistic milieu of the second language, that is, in a "second" language situation in the technical sense of the term? Or are they focusing on a "foreign" language context in which the second language is heard and spoken only in an artificial environment, such as the modern language classroom in an American university or high school? How might the sociopolitical conditions of a particular country affect the outcome of a learner's mastery of the language? How do general intercultural contrasts and similarities affect the learning process?

Why?

Finally, the most encompassing of all questions: Why are learners attempting to acquire the second language? What are their purposes? Are they motivated by the achievement of a successful career? by passing a foreign language requirement? or by wishing to identify closely with the culture and people of the target language? Beyond these categories, what other affective, emotional, personal, or intellectual reasons do learners have for pursuing this gigantic task of learning another language?

These questions have been posed, in very global terms, to give you an inkling of the diversity of issues involved in the quest for understanding the principles of language learning and teaching. And while you cannot hope to find final answers to all the questions, you can begin to achieve a surprising number of answers as you move through the chapters of this book.

And you can hone the global questions into finer, subtler questions, which in itself is an important task, for often being able to ask the right questions is more valuable than possessing storehouses of knowledge.

Thomas Kuhn (1970) referred to "normal science" as a process of puzzle solving in which part of the task of the scientist, in this case the teacher, is to discover the pieces and then to fit the pieces together. Some of the pieces of the language learning puzzle have become well established. Others are not yet discovered, and the careful defining of questions will lead to finding those pieces. We can then undertake the task of fitting the pieces together into a "paradigm"—an interlocking design, a theory of second language acquisition.

That theory, like a jigsaw puzzle, needs to be coherent and unified. If only one point of view is taken—if you look at only one facet of second language learning and teaching—you will derive an incomplete, partial theory. The second language teacher, with eyes wide open to the total picture, needs to form an integrated understanding of the many aspects of the process of second language learning.

In order to begin to ask further questions and to find answers to some of those questions, we must first address a fundamental concern in problem-posing: defining or delimiting the focus of our inquiry. Since this book is about language, learning, and teaching, let's see what happens when we try to "define" those three terms.

LANGUAGE

A definition of a concept or construct is a statement that captures its key features. Those features may vary, depending on your own (or the lexicographer's) understanding of the construct. And, most important, that understanding is essentially a "theory" that explicates the construct. So, a definition of a term may be thought of as a condensed version of a theory. Conversely, a theory is simply—or not so simply—an extended definition. Defining, therefore, is serious business: it requires choices about which facets of something are worthy of being included.

Suppose you were stopped by a reporter on the street, and, in the course of an interview about your field of study, you were asked: "Well, since you're interested in second language acquisition, please define *language* in a sentence or two." You would no doubt dig deep into your memory for a typical dictionary-type definition of language. Such definitions, if pursued seriously, could lead to a lexicographer's wild-goose chase, but they also can reflect a reasonably coherent synopsis of current understanding of just what it is that linguists are trying to study.

If you had had a chance to consult the *Concise Columbia Encyclopedia* (1994: 479), you might have responded to your questioner with an oversimplified "systematic communication by vocal symbols." Or, if you had recently read Pinker's *The Language Instinct* (1994), you might have come up with a sophisticated statement such as:

> Language is a complex, specialized skill, which develops in the child spontaneously, without conscious effort or formal instruction, is deployed without awareness of its underlying logic, is qualitatively the same in every individual, and is distinct from more general abilities to process information or behave intelligently. (p.18)

On the other hand, you might have offered a synthesis of standard definitions out of introductory textbooks: "Language is a system of arbitrary conventionalized vocal, written, or gestural symbols that enable members of a given community to communicate intelligibly with one another." Depending on how fussy you were in your response, you might also have included some mention of (a) the creativity of language, (b) the presumed primacy of speech over writing, and (c) the universality of language among human beings.

A consolidation of a number of possible definitions of language yields the following composite definition.

1. Language is systematic.
2. Language is a set of arbitrary symbols.
3. Those symbols are primarily vocal, but may also be visual.
4. The symbols have conventionalized meanings to which they refer.
5. Language is used for communication.
6. Language operates in a speech community or culture.
7. Language is essentially human, although possibly not limited to humans.
8. Language is acquired by all people in much the same way; language and language learning both have universal characteristics.

These eight statements provide a reasonably concise "twenty-five-word-or-less" definition of language. But the simplicity of the eightfold definition should not be allowed to mask the sophistication of linguistic research underlying each concept. Enormous fields and subfields, year-long university courses, are suggested in each of the eight categories. Consider some of these possible areas:

1. Explicit and formal accounts of the system of language on several possible levels (most commonly phonological, syntactic, and semantic).

2. The symbolic nature of language; the relationship between language and reality; the philosophy of language; the history of language.
3. Phonetics; phonology; writing systems; kinesics, proxemics, and other "paralinguistic" features of language.
4. Semantics; language and cognition; psycholinguistics.
5. Communication systems; speaker-hearer interaction; sentence processing.
6. Dialectology; sociolinguistics; language and culture; bilingualism and second language acquisition.
7. Human language and nonhuman communication; the physiology of language.
8. Language universals; first language acquisition.

Serious and extensive thinking about these eight topics involves a complex journey through a labyrinth of linguistic science—a maze that continues to be negotiated. Yet the language teacher needs to know something about this system of communication that we call language. Can foreign language teachers effectively teach a language if they do not know, even in general, something about the relationship between language and cognition, writing systems, nonverbal communication, sociolinguistics, and first language acquisition? And if the second language learner is being asked to be successful in acquiring a system of communication of such vast complexity, isn't it reasonable that the teacher have awareness of what the components of that system are?

Your understanding of the components of language determines to a large extent how you teach a language. If, for example, you believe that nonverbal communication is a key to successful second language learning, you will devote some attention to nonverbal systems and cues. If you perceive language as a phenomenon that can be dismantled into thousands of discrete pieces and those pieces programmatically taught one by one, you will attend carefully to an understanding of the separability of the forms of language. If you think language is essentially cultural and interactive, your classroom methodology will be imbued with sociolinguistic strategies and communicative tasks.

This book touches on some of the general aspects of language as defined above. More specific aspects will have to be understood in the context of an academic program in a particular language, in which specialized study of linguistics is obviously recommended along with a careful analysis of the foreign language itself.

LEARNING AND TEACHING

In similar fashion, we can ask questions about constructs like **learning** and **teaching**. Consider again some traditional definitions. A search in contemporary dictionaries reveals that learning is "acquiring or getting of knowledge of a subject or a skill by study, experience, or instruction." A more specialized definition might read as follows: "Learning is a relatively permanent change in a behavioral tendency and is the result of reinforced practice" (Kimble & Garmezy 1963: 133). Similarly, teaching, which is implied in the first definition of learning, may be defined as "showing or helping someone to learn how to do something, giving instructions, guiding in the study of something, providing with knowledge, causing to know or understand." How awkward these definitions are! Isn't it curious that professional lexicographers cannot devise more precise scientific definitions? More than perhaps anything else, such definitions reflect the difficulty of defining complex concepts like learning and teaching.

Breaking down the components of the definition of learning, we can extract, as we did with language, domains of research and inquiry.

1. Learning is acquisition or "getting."
2. Learning is retention of information or skill.
3. Retention implies storage systems, memory, cognitive organization.
4. Learning involves active, conscious focus on and acting upon events outside or inside the organism.
5. Learning is relatively permanent but subject to forgetting.
6. Learning involves some form of practice, perhaps reinforced practice.
7. Learning is a change in behavior.

These concepts can also give way to a number of subfields within the discipline of psychology: acquisition processes, perception, memory (storage) systems, recall, conscious and subconscious learning styles and strategies, theories of forgetting, reinforcement, the role of practice. Very quickly the concept of learning becomes every bit as complex as the concept of language. Yet the second language learner brings all these (and more) variables into play in the learning of a second language.

Teaching cannot be defined apart from learning. Teaching is guiding and facilitating learning, enabling the learner to learn, setting the conditions for learning. Your understanding of how the learner learns will determine your philosophy of education, your teaching style, your approach, methods, and classroom techniques. If, like B.F. Skinner, you look at learning as a process of operant conditioning through a carefully paced program of reinforcement, you will teach accordingly. If you view second language learning as a deductive rather than an inductive process, you will probably choose to present copious rules and paradigms to your students rather than let them "discover" those rules inductively.

An extended definition—or theory—of teaching will spell out governing principles for choosing certain methods and techniques. A theory of teaching, in harmony with your integrated understanding of the learner and of the subject matter to be learned, will point the way to successful procedures on a given day for given learners under the various constraints of the particular context of learning. In other words, your theory of teaching is your theory of learning "stood on its head."

SCHOOLS OF THOUGHT IN SECOND LANGUAGE ACQUISITION

While the general definitions of language, learning, and teaching offered above might meet with the approval of most linguists, psychologists, and educators, points of clear disagreement become apparent after a little probing of the components of each definition. For example, is language a "set of habits" or a "system of internalized rules"? Differing viewpoints emerge from equally knowledgeable scholars.

Yet with all the possible disagreements among applied linguists and SLA researchers, some historical patterns emerge that highlight trends and fashions in the study of second language acquisition. These trends will be described here in the form of three different schools of thought that follow somewhat historically, even though components of each school overlap chronologically to some extent. Bear in mind that such a sketch highlights contrastive ways of thinking, and such contrasts are seldom overtly evident in the study of any one issue in SLA.

Structuralism/Behaviorism

In the 1940s and 1950s, the **structural**, or **descriptive**, school of linguistics, with its advocates—Leonard Bloomfield, Edward Sapir, Charles Hockett, Charles Fries, and others—prided itself in a rigorous application of the scientific principle of observation of human languages. Only the "publicly observable responses" could be subject to investigation. The linguist's task, according to the structuralist, was to describe human languages and to identify the structural characteristics of those languages. An important axiom of structural linguistics was that "languages can differ from each other without limit," and that no preconceptions could apply to the field. Freeman Twaddell (1935: 57) stated this principle in perhaps its most extreme terms:

> Whatever our attitude toward mind, spirit, soul, etc., as realities,
> we must agree that the scientist proceeds as though there were

no such things, as though all his information were acquired through processes of his physiological nervous system. Insofar as he occupies himself with psychical, nonmaterial forces, the scientist is not a scientist. The scientific method is quite simply the convention that mind does not exist . . .

The structural linguist examined only the overtly observable data. Such attitudes prevail in B.F. Skinner's thought, particularly in *Verbal Behavior* (1957), in which he said that any notion of "idea" or "meaning" is explanatory fiction, and that the speaker is merely the locus of verbal behavior, not the cause. Charles Osgood (1957) reinstated meaning in verbal behavior, explaining it as a "representational mediation process," but still did not depart from a generally nonmentalistic view of language.

Of further importance to the structural or descriptive linguist was the notion that language could be dismantled into small pieces or units and that these units could be described scientifically, contrasted, and added up again to form the whole. From this principle emerged an unchecked rush of linguists, in the 1940s and 1950s, to the far reaches of the earth to write the grammars of exotic languages.

Among psychologists, a **behavioristic** paradigm also focused on publicly observable responses—those that can be objectively perceived, recorded, and measured. The "scientific method" was rigorously adhered to, and therefore such concepts as consciousness and intuition were regarded as "mentalistic," illegitimate domains of inquiry. The unreliability of observation of states of consciousness, thinking, concept formation, or the acquisition of knowledge made such topics impossible to examine in a behavioristic framework. Typical behavioristic models were classical and operant conditioning, rote verbal learning, instrumental learning, discrimination learning, and other **empirical** approaches to studying human behavior. You may be familiar with the classical experiments with Pavlov's dog and Skinner's boxes; these too typify the position that organisms can be conditioned to respond in desired ways, given the correct degree and scheduling of reinforcement.

Rationalism and Cognitive Psychology

In the decade of the 1960s, the **generative-transformational** school of linguistics emerged through the influence of Noam Chomsky. Chomsky was trying to show that human language cannot be scrutinized simply in terms of observable stimuli and responses or the volumes of raw data gathered by field linguists. The generative linguist was interested not only in describing language (achieving the level of **descriptive** adequacy) but also in arriving at an **explanatory** level of adequacy in the study of language, that is, a "principled basis, independent of any particular language, for the selection of the descriptively adequate grammar of each language" (Chomsky 1964: 63).

Early seeds of the generative-transformational revolution were planted near the beginning of the twentieth century. Ferdinand de Saussure (1916) claimed that there was a difference between *parole* (what Skinner "observes," and what Chomsky called **performance**) and *langue* (akin to the concept of **competence**, or our underlying and unobservable language ability). A few decades later, however, descriptive linguists chose largely to ignore *langue* and to study *parole*, as was noted above. The revolution brought about by generative linguistics broke with the descriptivists' preoccupation with performance—the outward manifestation of language—and capitalized on the important distinction between the overtly observable aspects of language and the hidden levels of meaning and thought that give birth to and generate observable linguistic performance.

Similarly, cognitive psychologists asserted that meaning, understanding, and knowing were significant data for psychological study. Instead of focusing rather mechanistically on stimulus–response connections, cognitivists tried to discover psychological principles of organization and functioning. David Ausubel (1965: 4) noted:

> From the standpoint of cognitive theorists, the attempt to ignore conscious states or to reduce cognition to mediational processes reflective of implicit behavior not only removes from the field of psychology what is most worth studying but also dangerously oversimplifies highly complex psychological phenomena.

Cognitive psychologists, like generative linguists, sought to discover underlying motivations and deeper structures of human behavior by using a **rational** approach. That is, they freed themselves from the strictly **empirical** study typical of behaviorists and employed the tools of logic, reason, extrapolation, and inference in order to derive explanations for human behavior. Going beyond descriptive to explanatory power took on utmost importance.

Both the structural linguist and the behavioral psychologist were interested in description, in answering *what* questions about human behavior: objective measurement of behavior in controlled circumstances. The generative linguist and cognitive psychologist were, to be sure, interested in the *what* question; but they were far more interested in a more ultimate question, *why*: What underlying reasons, genetic and environmental factors, and circumstances caused a particular event?

If you were to observe someone walk into your house, pick up a chair and fling it through your window, and then walk out, different kinds of questions could be asked. One set of questions would relate to what happened:

the physical description of the person, the time of day, the size of the chair, the impact of the chair, and so forth. Another set of questions would ask why the person did what he did: What were the person's motives and psychological state, what might have been the cause of the behavior, and so on. The first set of questions is very rigorous and exacting: it allows no flaw, no mistake in measurement; but does it give you ultimate answers? The second set of questions is richer, but obviously riskier. By daring to ask some difficult questions about the unobserved, we may lose some ground but gain more profound insight about human behavior.

Constructivism

Constructivism is hardly a new school of thought. Jean Piaget and Lev Vygotsky, names often associated with constructivism, are not by any means new to the scene of language studies. Yet constructivism emerged as a prevailing paradigm only in the last part of the twentieth century. What is constructivism, and how does it differ from the other two viewpoints described above?

Constructivists, not unlike some cognitive psychologists, argue that all human beings construct their own version of reality, and therefore multiple contrasting ways of knowing and describing are equally legitimate. This perspective might be described as

> an emphasis on active processes of construction [of meaning], attention to texts as a means of gaining insights into those processes, and an interest in the nature of knowledge and its variations, including the nature of knowledge associated with membership in a particular group. (Spivey 1997: 23-24)

Constructivist scholarship can focus on "individuals engaged in social practices, . . . on a collaborative group, [or] on a global community" (Spivey 1997: 24).

A constructivist perspective goes a little beyond the rationalist/innatist and the cognitive psychological perspective in its emphasis on the primacy of each individual's construction of reality. Piaget and Vygotsky, both commonly described as constructivists (in Nyikos & Hashimoto 1997), differ in the extent to which each emphasizes social context. Piaget (1972) stressed the importance of individual cognitive development as a relatively solitary act. Biological timetables and stages of development were basic; social interaction was claimed only to trigger development at the right moment in time. On the other hand, Vygotsky (1978), described as a "social" constructivist by some, maintained that social interaction was foundational in cognitive development and rejected the notion of predetermined stages.

Researchers studying first and second language acquisition have demonstrated constructivist perspectives through studies of conversational discourse, sociocultural factors in learning, and interactionist theories. In many ways, constructivist perspectives are a natural successor to cognitivist studies of universal grammar, information processing, memory, artificial intelligence, and interlanguage systematicity. (Note: These terms will be defined and explained in subsequent chapters of this book.)

All three positions must be seen as important in creating balanced descriptions of human linguistic behavior. Consider for a moment the analogy of a very high mountain, viewed from a distance. From one direction the mountain may have a sharp peak, easily identified glaciers, and distinctive rock formations. From another direction, however, the same mountain might now appear to have two peaks (the second formerly hidden from view) and different configurations of its slopes. From still another direction, yet further characteristics emerge, heretofore unobserved. The study of SLA is very much like the viewing of our mountain: we need multiple tools and vantage points in order to ascertain the whole picture.

Table 1.1 summarizes concepts and approaches described in the three perspectives above. The table may help to pinpoint certain broad ideas that are associated with the respective positions.

Table 1.1 Schools of thought in second language acquisition

Time Frame	Schools of Thought	Typical Themes
Early 1900s & 1940s & 1950s	Structuralism & Behaviorism	description observable performance scientific method empiricism surface structure conditioning, reinforcement
1960s & 1970s	Rationalism & Cognitive Psychology	generative linguistics acquisition, innateness interlanguage systematicity universal grammar competence deep structure
1980s, 1990s & early 2000	Constructivism	interactive discourse sociocultural variables cooperative group learning interlanguage variability interactionist hypotheses

The patterns that are illustrated in Table 1.1 are typical of what Kuhn (1970) described as the structure of scientific revolutions. A successful paradigm is followed by a period of anomaly (doubt, uncertainty, questioning of prevailing theory), then crisis (the fall of the existing paradigm) with all the professional insecurity that comes therewith; and then finally a new paradigm, a novel theory, is put together. This cycle is evident in both psychology and linguistics, although the limits and bounds are not always easily perceived—perhaps less easily perceived in psychology, in which all three paradigms currently operate somewhat simultaneously. The cyclical nature of theories underscores the fact that no single theory or paradigm is right or wrong. It is impossible to refute with any finality one theory with another. Some truth can be found in virtually every theory.

LANGUAGE TEACHING METHODOLOGY

One of the major foci of applied linguistic scholarship for the last half a century has been the foreign or second language classroom. A glance through the past century or so of language teaching gives us an interesting picture of varied interpretations of the best way to teach a foreign language. As schools of thought have come and gone, so have language teaching trends waxed and waned in popularity. Pedagogical innovation both contributes to and benefits from the kind of theory-building described in the previous section.

Albert Marckwardt (1972: 5) saw these "changing winds and shifting sands" as a cyclical pattern in which a new paradigm (to use Kuhn's term) of teaching methodology emerged about every quarter of a century, with each new method breaking from the old but at the same time taking with it some of the positive aspects of the previous paradigm. One of the best examples of the cyclical nature of methods is seen in the revolutionary Audiolingual Method (ALM) of the late 1940s and 1950s. The ALM borrowed tenets from its predecessor by almost half a century, the Direct Method, while breaking away entirely from the Grammar-Translation paradigm. (See "In the Classroom" vignettes to follow, for a definition of these methods.) Within a short time, however, ALM critics were advocating more attention to rules and to the "cognitive code" of language, which, to some, smacked of a return to Grammar Translation! Shifting sands indeed.

Since the early 1970s, the relationship of theoretical disciplines to teaching methodology has been especially evident. The field of psychology has witnessed a growing interest in interpersonal relationships, in the value of group work, and in the use of numerous self-help strategies for attaining desired goals. The same era has seen linguists searching ever more deeply for answers to the nature of communication and communicative competence and for explanations of the interactive process of language. The language teaching profession responded to these theoretical trends with approaches and techniques that have stressed the importance of self-esteem, of students cooperatively learning together, of developing individual strategies for success, and above all of focusing on the communicative process in language learning. Today the term "communicative language teaching" is a byword for language teachers. Indeed, the single greatest challenge in the profession is to move significantly beyond the teaching of rules, patterns, definitions, and other knowledge "about" language to the point that we are teaching our students to communicate genuinely, spontaneously, and meaningfully in the second language.

This book is intended to give you a comprehensive picture of the theoretical foundations of language learning and teaching. But that theory remains abstract and relatively powerless without its application to the practical concerns of pedagogy in the classroom. In an attempt to help to build bridges between theory and practice, I have provided at the end of each of the chapters of this book a brief "vignette" on classroom considerations. These vignettes are designed to acquaint you progressively with some of the major methodological trends and issues in the profession. The vignettes are obviously not intended to be exhaustive (refer to such books as Brown 2000; Richard-Amato 1996; Nunan 1991b; Richards and Rodgers 1986 for more specific treatments), but they should begin to give you a bit of history and a picture of the practical consequences of developing the theoretical principles of language learning and teaching.

Today, language teaching is not easily categorized into methods and trends. Instead, each teacher is called on to develop a sound overall **approach** to various language classrooms. This approach is a principled basis upon which the teacher can choose particular designs and techniques for teaching a foreign language in a particular context. Such a prospect may seem formidable. There are no instant recipes. No quick and easy method is guaranteed to provide success. Every learner is unique. Every teacher is unique. Every learner-teacher relationship is unique, and every context is unique. Your task as a teacher is to understand the properties of those relationships. Using a cautious, enlightened, eclectic approach, you can build a theory based on principles of second language learning and teaching. The chapters that follow are designed to help you formulate that approach.

In the Classroom: The Grammar Translation Method

We begin a series of end-of-chapter vignettes on classroom applications with a language teaching "tradition" that, in various manifestations and adaptations, has been practiced in language classrooms worldwide for centuries. A glance back in history reveals few if any research-based language teaching methods prior to the twentieth century. In the Western world, "foreign" language learning in schools was synonymous with the learning of Latin or Greek. Latin, thought to promote intellectuality through "mental gymnastics," was until relatively recently held to be indispensable to an adequate higher education. Latin was taught by means of what has been called the Classical Method: focus on grammatical rules, memorization of vocabulary and of various declensions and conjugations, translation of texts, doing written exercises. As other languages began to be taught in educational institutions in the eighteenth and nineteenth centuries, the Classical Method was adopted as the chief means for teaching foreign languages. Little thought was given at the time to teaching oral use of languages; after all, languages were not being taught primarily to learn oral/aural communication, but to learn for the sake of being "scholarly" or, in some instances, for gaining a reading proficiency in a foreign language. Since there was little if any theoretical research on second language acquisition in general, or on the acquisition of reading proficiency, foreign languages were taught as any other skill was taught.

Late in the nineteenth century, the Classical Method came to be known as the Grammar Translation Method. There was little to distinguish Grammar Translation from what had gone on in foreign language classrooms for centuries, beyond a focus on grammatical rules as the basis for translating from the second to the native language. But the Grammar Translation Method remarkably withstood attempts at the outset of the twentieth century to "reform" language teaching methodology, and to this day it remains a standard methodology for language teaching in educational institutions. Prator and Celce-Murcia (1979: 3) list the major characteristics of Grammar Translation:

1. Classes are taught in the mother tongue, with little active use of the target language.
2. Much vocabulary is taught in the form of lists of isolated words.
3. Long elaborate explanations of the intricacies of grammar are given.
4. Grammar provides the rules for putting words together, and instruction often focuses on the form and inflection of words.
5. Reading of difficult classical texts is begun early.
6. Little attention is paid to the content of texts, which are treated as exercises in grammatical analysis.

7. Often the only drills are exercises in translating discon-
   nected sentences from the target language into the mother
   tongue.
8. Little or no attention is given to pronunciation.

It is remarkable, in one sense, that this method has been so stal-
wart among many competing models. It does virtually nothing to
enhance a student's communicative ability in the language. It is
"remembered with distaste by thousands of school learners, for
whom foreign language learning meant a tedious experience of
memorizing endless lists of unusable grammar rules and vocabulary
and attempting to produce perfect translations of stilted or literary
prose" (Richards & Rodgers 1986: 4). In another sense, however,
one can understand why Grammar Translation is so popular. It
requires few specialized skills on the part of teachers. Tests of
grammar rules and of translations are easy to construct and can be
objectively scored. Many standardized tests of foreign languages still
do not attempt to tap into communicative abilities, so students have
little motivation to go beyond grammar analogies, translations, and
rote exercises. And it is sometimes successful in leading a student
toward a reading knowledge of a second language. But, as Richards
and Rodgers (1986: 5) pointed out, "it has no advocates. It is a
method for which there is no theory. There is no literature that offers
a rationale or justification for it or that attempts to relate it to issues
in linguistics, psychology, or educational theory." As we continue to
examine theoretical principles in this book, I think we will understand more fully the "theorylessness" of the Grammar Translation
Method.

TOPICS AND QUESTIONS FOR STUDY AND DISCUSSION

Note: Items listed below are coded for either individual (I) work, group/pair
(G) work, or whole-class (C) discussion, as suggestions to the instructor on
how to incorporate the topics and questions into a class session.

1. (G) In the first paragraph of this chapter, second language learning is
   described as a complex, long-term effort that requires much of the
   learner. In small groups of three to five, share your own experiences in
   learning, or attempting to learn, a foreign language. Describe your own
   (a) commitment, (b) involvement, and (c) effort to learn. This discussion
   should introduce you to a variety of patterns of learning.
2. (C) Look at the two definitions of language, one from an encyclopedia
   and the other from Pinker's book (page 5). Why are there differences
   between these two definitions? What assumptions or biases do they

reflect on the part of the lexicographer? How do those definitions represent "condensed theories"?

3. (I/G) Write your own "twenty-five-words-or-less" definitions of language, learning, and teaching. What would you add to or delete from the definitions given in this chapter? Share your definitions with another classmate or in a small group. Compare differences and similarities.

4. (G) Consider the eight subfields of linguistics listed on page 6, and, assigning one subfield to a pair or small group, discuss briefly the type of approach to second language teaching that might emerge from emphasizing the exclusive importance of your particular subfield. Report your thoughts to the whole class.

5. (C) What did Twaddell (1935: 57) mean when he said, "The scientific method is quite simply the convention that mind does not exist"? What are the advantages and disadvantages of attending only to "publicly observable responses" in studying human behavior? Don't limit yourself only to language teaching in considering the ramifications of behavioristic principles.

6. (C) Looking back at the three schools of thought described in this chapter, try to come up with some examples of activities in the language classroom that would match the three perspectives.

7. (C) Considering the productive relationship between theory and practice, think of some examples (from any field of study) that show that theory and practice are interactive. Next, think of some specific types of activities typical of a foreign language class you have been in (choral drills, translation, reading aloud, using a vocabulary word in a sentence, etc.). What kind of theoretical assumptions underlie these activities? How might the success of the activity possibly alter the theory behind it?

8. (G) Richards and Rodgers (1986: 5) said the Grammar Translation Method "is a method for which there is no theory." Why did they make that statement? Do you agree with them? Share in a group any experiences you have had with Grammar Translation in your foreign language classes.

SUGGESTED READINGS

Mitchell, Rosamond and Myles, Florence. 1998. *Second Language Learning Theories.* New York: Oxford University Press.

Skehan, Peter. 1998. *A Cognitive Approach to Language Learning.* New York: Oxford University Press.

Williams, Marion and Burden, Robert L. 1997. *Psychology for Language Teachers: A Social Constructivist Approach.* Cambridge: Cambridge University Press.

A number of references were made in this chapter to trends in research on applied linguistics and SLA. These three informative books offer further perspectives on the three major schools of thought described here, and are written in a user-friendly style.

Annual Review of Applied Linguistics, published by Cambridge University Press.

Comprehensive and current information on various subfields of interest within what is broadly termed "applied linguistics" is available through this annually published journal.

Thomas Kuhn. 1970. *The Structure of Scientific Revolutions.* Chicago: University of Chicago Press.

This classic work describes the waxing and waning of scientific trends through history. It helps one to understand SLA research trends in a context of other scientific disciplines.

Brown, H. Douglas. 2000. *Teaching by Principles: An Interactive Approach to Language Pedagogy.* Second Edition. White Plains, NY: Pearson Education.

Richard-Amato, Patricia A. 1996. Making It Happen: Interaction in the Second Language Classroom, From Theory to Practice. White Plains, NY: Pearson Education.

Richards, Jack and Rodgers, Theodore. 1986. *Approaches and Methods in Language Teaching.* Cambridge: Cambridge University Press.

These three books offer a historical overview and critical analysis of language teaching methods in a context of theoretical foundations that underlie pedagogical practices.

LANGUAGE LEARNING EXPERIENCE: JOURNAL ENTRY 1

In each of the ten chapters in this book, a brief set of journal-writing guidelines will be offered. Here, you are strongly encouraged to commit yourself to a process of weekly journal entries that chronicle a previous or concurrent foreign language learning experience. In so doing, you will be better able to connect the issues that you read about in this book with a real-life, personal experience.

Remember, a journal is meant to be "freely" written, without much concern for beautiful prose, rhetorical eloquence, or even grammaticality. It is your diary in which you can spontaneously record feelings, thoughts, reactions, and questions. The prompts that are offered here are not meant to be exhaustive, so feel free to expand on them considerably. The one rule of thumb to follow in writing your journal is: connect your own experiences learning a foreign language with issues and models and studies that are presented in the chapters of the book. Your experiences then become vivid examples of what might otherwise remain somewhat abstract theories.

If you decide to focus your writing on a previous experience learning a foreign language, you will need to "age regress" yourself to the time that you were learning the language. If at all possible, choose a language you learned (or tried to learn!) as an adult, that is, after the age of twelve or so. Then, describe what you were feeling and thinking and doing then.

If your journal centers on a concurrent experience, so much the better, because your memory of the ongoing events will be more vivid. The journal-writing process may even prompt you to adopt certain strategies for more successful learning.

Guidelines for Entry 1

- As you start(ed) your foreign language class, what is your overall emotional feeling? Are you overwhelmed? challenged? unmotivated? Is the course too easy?
- How do you feel about your classmates? the class spirit or mood? Is the class upbeat and motivating, or boring and tedious? Analyze why you have this perception. What is causing it? Is it your own attitude, or the teacher's style, or the makeup of the class?
- Describe activities that you did in the early days of the class that illustrate (a) a behavioristic perspective on second language acquisition, (b) a cognitive perspective, and (c) a constructivist perspective.
- Describe your teacher's teaching style. Is it effective? Why or why not? Does your teacher seem to have an approach to language teaching that is consistent with what you've read so far?

CHAPTER 2

FIRST LANGUAGE

ACQUISITION

T HE MARVELOUS capacity for acquiring competence in one's native language within the first few years of life has been a subject of interest for many centuries. "Modern" research on child language acquisition dates back to the latter part of the eighteenth century, when the German philosopher Dietrich Tiedemann recorded his observations of the psychological and linguistic development of his young son. For a century and a half, few if any significant advances were made in the study of child language; for the most part research was limited to diarylike recordings of observed speech with some attempts to classify word types. Not until the second half of the twentieth century did researchers begin to analyze child language systematically and to try to discover the nature of the psycholinguistic process that enables every human being to gain fluent control of an exceedingly complex system of communication. In a matter of a few decades, some giant strides were taken, especially in the generative and cognitive models of language, in describing the acquisition of particular languages, and in probing universal aspects of acquisition.

This wave of research in child language acquisition led language teachers and teacher trainers to study some of the general findings of such research with a view to drawing analogies between first and second language acquisition, and even to justifying certain teaching methods and techniques on the basis of first language learning principles. On the surface, it is entirely reasonable to make the analogy. After all, all children, given a normal developmental environment, acquire their native languages fluently and efficiently; moreover, they acquire them "naturally," without special instruction, although not without significant effort and attention to language. The direct comparisons must be treated with caution, however. There are dozens of salient differences between first and second language learning; the most obvious difference, in the case of adult second language learning, is the tremendous cognitive and affective contrast between adults and children. A detailed examination of these differences is made in Chapter 3.

This chapter is designed to outline issues in first language learning as a foundation on which you can build an understanding of principles of second language learning. A coherent grasp of the nature of first language learning is an invaluable aid, if not an essential component, in the construction of a theory of second language acquisition. This chapter provides an overview of various theoretical positions—positions that can be related to the paradigms discussed in Chapter 1—in first language acquisition, and a discussion of some key issues that are particularly significant for an understanding of second language learning.

THEORIES OF FIRST LANGUAGE ACQUISITION

Everyone at some time has witnessed the remarkable ability of children to communicate. As small babies, children babble and coo and cry and vocally or nonvocally send an extraordinary number of messages and receive even more messages. As they reach the end of their first year, children make specific attempts to imitate words and speech sounds they hear around them, and about this time they utter their first "words." By about 18 months of age, these words have multiplied considerably and are beginning to appear in two-word and three-word "sentences"—commonly referred to as "telegraphic" utterances—such as "allgone milk," "bye-bye Daddy," "gimme toy," and so forth. The production tempo now begins to increase as more and more words are spoken every day and more and more combinations of two- and three-word sentences are uttered. By about age three, children can comprehend an incredible quantity of linguistic input; their speech capacity mushrooms as they become the generators of nonstop chattering and incessant conversation, language thereby becoming a mixed blessing for those around them! This fluency continues into school age as children internalize increasingly complex structures, expand their vocabulary, and sharpen communicative skills. At school age, children not only learn what to say but what *not* to say as they learn the social functions of their language.

How can we explain this fantastic journey from that first anguished cry at birth to adult competence in a language? From the first word to tens of thousands? From telegraphese at eighteen months to the compound-complex, cognitively precise, socioculturally appropriate sentences just a few short years later? These are the sorts of questions that theories of language acquisition attempt to answer.

In principle, one could adopt one of two polarized positions in the study of first language acquisition. Using the schools of thought referred to in the previous chapter, an extreme behavioristic position would claim that children come into the world with a *tabula rasa*, a clean slate bearing no preconceived notions about the world or about language, and that these children are then shaped by their environment and slowly conditioned through various schedules of reinforcement. At the other constructivist extreme is the position that makes not only the rationalist/cognitivist claim that children come into this world with very specific innate knowledge, predispositions, and biological timetables, but that children learn to function in a language chiefly through interaction and discourse.

These positions represent opposites on a continuum, with many possible positions in between. Three such points are elucidated in this chapter. The first (behavioristic) position is set in contrast to the second (nativist) and third (functional) positions.

Behavioristic Approaches

Language is a fundamental part of total human behavior, and behaviorists examined it as such and sought to formulate consistent theories of first language acquisition. The behavioristic approach focused on the immediately perceptible aspects of linguistic behavior—the publicly observable responses—and the relationships or associations between those responses and events in the world surrounding them. A behaviorist might consider effective language behavior to be the production of correct responses to stimuli. If a particular response is reinforced, it then becomes habitual, or conditioned. Thus children produce linguistic responses that are reinforced. This is true of their comprehension as well as production responses, although to consider comprehension is to wander just a bit out of the publicly observable realm. One learns to comprehend an utterance by responding appropriately to it and by being reinforced for that response.

One of the best-known attempts to construct a behavioristic model of linguistic behavior was embodied in B.F. Skinner's classic, *Verbal Behavior* (1957). Skinner was commonly known for his experiments with animal behavior, but he also gained recognition for his contributions to education through teaching machines and programmed learning (Skinner 1968). Skinner's theory of verbal behavior was an extension of his general theory of learning by **operant conditioning**. Operant conditioning refers to conditioning in which the organism (in this case, a human being) emits a response, or **operant** (a sentence or utterance), without necessarily observable stimuli; that operant is maintained (learned) by reinforcement (for example, a positive verbal or nonverbal response from another person). If a child says "want milk" and a parent gives the child some milk, the operant is reinforced and, over repeated instances, is conditioned. According to Skinner, verbal behavior, like other behavior, is controlled by its consequences. When consequences are rewarding, behavior is maintained and is increased in strength and perhaps frequency. When consequences are punishing, or when there is a total lack of reinforcement, the behavior is weakened and eventually extinguished.

Skinner's theories attracted a number of critics, not the least among them Noam Chomsky (1959), who penned a highly critical review of *Verbal Behavior*. Some years later, however, Kenneth MacCorquodale (1970) published a reply to Chomsky's review in which he eloquently defended Skinner's points of view. And so the battle raged on. Today virtually no one would agree that Skinner's model of verbal behavior adequately accounts for the capacity to acquire language, for language development itself, for the abstract nature of language, or for a theory of meaning. A theory based on conditioning and reinforcement is hard-pressed to explain the fact that every sentence you speak or write—with a few trivial exceptions—is novel, never before uttered either by you or by anyone else! These novel utterances are nevertheless created by the speaker and processed by the hearer.

In an attempt to broaden the base of behavioristic theory, some psychologists proposed modified theoretical positions. One of these positions was **mediation** theory, in which meaning was accounted for by the claim that the linguistic stimulus (a word or sentence) elicits a "mediating" response that is self-stimulating. Charles Osgood (1953, 1957) called this self-stimulation a "representational mediation process," a process that is really covert and invisible, acting within the learner. It is interesting that mediation theory thus attempted to account for abstraction by a notion that reeked of "mentalism"—a cardinal sin for dyed-in-the-wool behaviorists! In fact, in some ways mediation theory was really a rational/cognitive theory masquerading as behavioristic.

Mediation theories still left many questions about language unanswered. The abstract nature of language and the relationship between meaning and utterance were unresolved. All sentences have deep structures—the level of underlying meaning that is only manifested overtly by surface structures. These deep structures are intricately interwoven in a person's total cognitive and affective experience. Such depths of language were scarcely plumbed by mediational theory.

Yet another attempt to account for first language acquisition within a behavioristic framework was made by Jenkins and Palermo (1964). While admitting (p. 143) that their conjectures were "speculative" and "premature," the authors attempted to synthesize notions of generative linguistics and mediational approaches to child language. They claimed that the child may acquire frames of a linear pattern of sentence elements and learn the stimulus-response equivalences that can be substituted within each frame; imitation was an important, if not essential, aspect of establishing stimulus–response associations. But this theory, too, failed to account for the abstract nature of language, for the child's creativity, and for the interactive nature of language acquisition.

It would appear that the rigor of behavioristic psychology, with its emphasis on empirical observation and the scientific method, only began to explain the miracle of language acquisition. It left untouched genetic and interactionist domains that could be explored only by approaches that probed more deeply.

The Nativist Approach

Nativist approaches to the study of child language asked some of those deeper questions. The term **nativist** is derived from the fundamental assertion that language acquisition is innately determined, that we are born with a genetic capacity that predisposes us to a systematic perception of language around us, resulting in the construction of an internalized system of language.

Innateness hypotheses gained support from several sides. Eric Lenneberg (1967) proposed that language is a "species-specific" behavior and that certain modes of perception, categorizing abilities, and other language-related mechanisms are biologically determined. Chomsky (1965) similarly claimed the existence of innate properties of language to explain the child's mastery of a native language in such a short time despite the highly abstract nature of the rules of language. This innate knowledge, according to Chomsky, is embodied in a "little black box" of sorts, a **language acquisition device** (LAD). McNeill (1966) described LAD as consisting of four innate linguistic properties:

1. the ability to distinguish speech sounds from other sounds in the environment,
2. the ability to organize linguistic data into various classes that can later be refined,
3. knowledge that only a certain kind of linguistic system is possible and that other kinds are not, and
4. the ability to engage in constant evaluation of the developing linguistic system so as to construct the simplest possible system out of the available linguistic input.

McNeill and other Chomskyan disciples composed eloquent arguments for the appropriateness of the LAD proposition, especially in contrast to behavioristic, stimulus–response (S-R) theory, which was so limited in accounting for the generativity of child language. Aspects of meaning, abstractness, and creativity were accounted for more adequately. Even though it was readily recognized that the LAD was not literally a cluster of brain cells that could be isolated and neurologically located, such inquiry on the rationalistic side of the linguistic–psychological continuum stimulated a great deal of fruitful research.

More recently, researchers in the nativist tradition have continued this line of inquiry through a genre of child language acquisition research that focuses on what has come to be known as **Universal Grammar** (see Cook 1993: 200-245; Mitchell & Myles 1998: 42-71, for an overview). Positing that all human beings are genetically equipped with abilities that enable them to acquire language, researchers expanded the LAD notion into a system of universal linguistic rules that went well beyond what was originally proposed for the LAD. Universal Grammar (UG) research is attempting to discover what it is that all children, regardless of their environmental stimuli (the language[s] they hear around them) bring to the language acquisition process. Such studies have looked at question formation, negation, word order, discontinuity of embedded clauses ("The ball that's on the table is blue"), subject deletion ("Es mi hermano"), and other grammatical phenomena.

One of the more practical contributions of nativist theories is evident if you look at the kinds of discoveries that have been made about how the system of child language works. Research has shown that the child's language, at any given point, is a legitimate system in its own right. The child's linguistic development is not a process of developing fewer and fewer "incorrect" structures, not a language in which earlier stages have more "mistakes" than later stages. Rather, the child's language at any stage is **systematic** in that the child is constantly forming hypotheses on the basis of the input received and then testing those hypotheses in speech (and comprehension). As the child's language develops, those hypotheses are continually revised, reshaped, or sometimes abandoned.

Before generative linguistics came into vogue, Jean Berko (1958) demonstrated that children learn language not as a series of separate discrete items, but as an integrated system. Using a simple nonsense-word test, Berko discovered that English-speaking children as young as four years of age applied rules for the formation of plural, present progressive, past tense, third singular, and possessives. She found, for example, that if a child saw one "wug" he could easily talk about two "wugs," or if he were presented with a person who knows how to "gling," the child could talk about a person who "glinged" yesterday, or sometimes who "glang."

Nativist studies of child language acquisition were free to construct hypothetical **grammars** (that is, descriptions of linguistic systems) of child language, although such grammars were still solidly based on empirical data. These grammars were largely formal representations of the deep structure—the abstract rules underlying surface output, the structure not overtly manifest in speech. Linguists began to examine child language from early one- and two-word forms of "telegraphese" to the complex language of five- to ten-year-olds. Borrowing one tenet of structural and behavioristic paradigms, they approached the data with few preconceived notions about what the child's language ought to be, and probed the data for internally consistent systems, in much the same way that a linguist describes a language in the "field." The use of a generative framework was, of course, a departure from structural methodology.

The generative model has enabled researchers to take some giant steps toward understanding the process of first language acquisition. The early grammars of child language were referred to as **pivot grammars**. It was commonly observed that the child's first two-word utterances seemed to manifest two separate word classes, and not simply two words thrown together at random. Consider the following utterances:

My cap	All gone milk
That horsie	Mommy sock

Linguists noted that the words on the left-hand side seemed to belong to a class that words on the right-hand side generally did not belong to. That is, *my* could co-occur with *cap, horsie, milk,* or *sock,* but not with *that* or *all gone. Mommy* is, in this case, a word that belongs in both classes. The first class of words was called "pivot," since they could pivot around a number of words in the second, "open" class. Thus the first rule of the generative grammar of the child was described as follows:

Sentence ➔ Pivot word + Open word

Research data gathered in the generative framework yielded a multitude of such rules. Some of these rules appear to be grounded in the UG of the child. As the child's language matures and finally becomes adult-like, the number and complexity of generative rules accounting for language competence of course boggles the mind.

In subsequent years the generative "rule-governed" model in the Chomskyan tradition has been challenged. The assumption underlying this tradition is that those generative rules, or "items" in a linguistic sense, are connected **serially**, with one connection between each pair of neurons in the brain. A new "messier but more fruitful picture" (Spolsky 1989: 149) was provided by what has come to be known as the **parallel distributed**

processing (PDP) model (also called **connectionism**) in which neurons in the brain are said to form multiple connections: each of the 100 billion nerve cells in the brain may be linked to as many as 10,000 of its counterparts. Thus, a child's (or adult's) linguistic performance may be the consequence of many levels of simultaneous neural interconnections rather than a serial process of one rule being applied, then another, then another, and so forth.

A simple analogy to music illustrates this complex notion. Think of an orchestra playing a symphony. The score for the symphony may have, let's say, twelve separate parts that are performed simultaneously. The "symphony" of the human brain enables us to process many segments and levels of language, cognition, affect, and perception all at once—in a parallel configuration. And so, according to the PDP model, a sentence—which has phonological, morphological, syntactic, lexical, semantic, discourse, sociolinguistic, and strategic properties—is not "generated" by a series of rules (Ney & Pearson 1990; Sokolik 1990). Rather, sentences are the result of the simultaneous interconnection of a multitude of brain cells.

All of these approaches within the nativist framework have made at least three important contributions to our understanding of the first language acquisition process:

1. freedom from the restrictions of the so-called "scientific method" to explore the unseen, unobservable, underlying, abstract linguistic structures being developed in the child;
2. systematic description of the child's linguistic repertoire as either rule-governed or operating out of parallel distributed processing capacities; and
3. the construction of a number of potential properties of Universal Grammar.

Functional Approaches

More recently, with an increase in constructivist approaches to the study of language, we have seen a shift in patterns of research. The shift has not been so much away from the generative/cognitive side of the continuum, but perhaps better described as a move even more deeply into the essence of language. Two emphases have emerged: (a) Researchers began to see that language was one manifestation of the cognitive and affective ability to deal with the world, with others, and with the self. (b) Moreover, the generative rules that were proposed under the nativistic framework were abstract, formal, explicit, and quite logical, yet they dealt specifically with the **forms** of language and not with the the deeper **functional** levels of meaning constructed from social interaction. Examples of forms of language are morphemes, words, sentences, and the rules that govern them. Functions are the meaningful, interactive purposes, within a social (pragmatic) context, that we accomplish with the forms.

Cognition and Language Development

Lois Bloom (1971) cogently illustrated the first issue in her criticism of pivot grammar when she pointed out that the relationships in which words occur in telegraphic utterances are only superficially similar. For example, in the utterance "Mommy sock," which nativists would describe as a sentence consisting of a pivot word and an open word, Bloom found at least three possible underlying relations: agent-action (Mommy is putting the sock on), agent-object (Mommy sees the sock), and possessor-possessed (Mommy's sock). By examining data in reference to contexts, Bloom concluded that children learn underlying structures, and not superficial word order. Thus, depending on the social context, "Mommy sock" could mean a number of different things to a child. Those varied meanings were inadequately captured in a pivot grammar approach.

Lewis Carroll aptly captured this characteristic of language in *Through the Looking Glass* (1872), where Alice argues with Humpty Dumpty about the meanings of words:

> "When I use a word," Humpty Dumpty said, in a rather scornful tone, "it means just what I choose it to mean—neither more nor less."
> "The question is," said Alice, "whether you can make words mean so many different things."
> "The question is," said Humpty Dumpty, "which is to be master—that's all."

Bloom's research, along with that of Jean Piaget, Dan Slobin, and others, paved the way for a new wave of child language study, this time centering on the relationship of cognitive development to first language acquisition. Piaget (Piaget & Inhelder 1969) described overall development as the result of children's interaction with their environment, with a complementary interaction between their developing perceptual cognitive capacities and their linguistic experience. What children learn about language is determined by what they already know about the world. As Gleitman and Wanner (1982: 13) noted in their review of the state of the art in child language research, "children appear to approach language learning equipped with conceptual interpretive abilities for categorizing the world. . . . Learners are biased to map each semantic idea on the linguistic unit *word*."

Dan Slobin (1971, 1986), among others, demonstrated that in all languages, semantic learning depends on cognitive development and that sequences of development are determined more by semantic complexity than by structural complexity. "There are two major pacesetters to language development, involved with the poles of function and of form: (1) on the functional level, development is paced by the growth of conceptual and communicative capacities, operating in conjunction with innate schemas of cognition; and (2) on the formal level, development is paced by the growth of perceptual and information-processing capacities, operating in conjunction with innate schemas of grammar" (Slobin 1986: 2). Bloom (1976: 37) noted that "an explanation of language development depends upon an explanation of the cognitive underpinnings of language: what children know will determine what they learn about the code for both speaking and understanding messages." So child language researchers began to tackle the formulation of the rules of the **functions** of language, and the relationships of the **forms** of language to those functions.

Social Interaction and Language Development

In recent years it has become quite clear that language functioning extends well beyond cognitive thought and memory structure. Here we see the second, social constructivist emphasis of the functional perspective. Holzman (1984: 119), in her "reciprocal model" of language development, proposed that "a reciprocal behavioral system operates between the language-developing infant-child and the competent [adult] language user in a socializing-teaching-nurturing role." Some research (Berko-Gleason 1988, Lock 1991) looked at the interaction between the child's language acquisition and the learning of how social systems operate in human behavior. Other investigations (for example, Budwig 1995, Kuczaj 1984) of child language centered on one of the thorniest areas of linguistic research: the function of language in **discourse**. Since language is used for interactive communication, it is only fitting that one study the communicative functions of language: What do children know and learn about talking with others? about connected pieces of discourse (relations between sentences)? the interaction between hearer and speaker? conversational cues? Within such a perspective, the very heart of language—its communicative and pragmatic function—is being tackled in all its variability.

Of interest in this genre of research is the renewed interest in the performance level of language. All those overt responses that were so carefully observed by structuralists and hastily weeded out as "performance variables" by generative linguists in their zeal to get at competence have now returned to the forefront. Hesitations, pauses, backtracking, and the like are indeed significant conversational cues. Even some of the contextual categories described by—of all people—Skinner, in *Verbal Behavior*, turn out to be relevant! The linguist can no longer deal with abstract, formal rules without dealing with all those minutiae of day-to-day performance that were previously set aside in a search for systematicity.

Several theoretical positions have been sketched out here. (See Figure 2.1 for a summary.) A complete, consistent, unified theory of first language acquisition cannot yet be claimed; however, child language research has

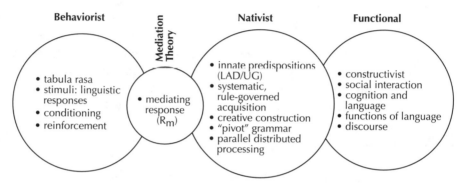

Figure 2.1. Theories of first language acquisition

manifested some enormous strides toward that ultimate goal. And even if all the answers are far from evident, maybe we are asking more of the right questions.

We turn now to a number of issues in first language acquisition—key questions and problems that have been and are being addressed by researchers in the field. A study of these issues will help you to round out your understanding of the nature of child language acquisition.

ISSUES IN FIRST LANGUAGE ACQUISITION

Competence and Performance

For centuries scientists and philosophers operated with the basic distinction between competence and performance. **Competence** refers to one's underlying knowledge of a system, event, or fact. It is the nonobservable ability to do something, to perform something. **Performance** is the overtly observable and concrete manifestation or realization of competence. It is the actual doing of something: walking, singing, dancing, speaking. In technological societies we have used the competence–performance distinction in all walks of life. In our schools, for example, we have assumed that children possess certain competence in given areas and that this competence can be measured and assessed by means of the observation of elicited samples of performance called "tests" and "examinations."

In reference to language, competence is one's underlying knowledge of the system of a language—its rules of grammar, its vocabulary, all the pieces of a language and how those pieces fit together. Performance is actual production (speaking, writing) or the comprehension (listening, reading) of linguistic events. Chomsky (1965) likened competence to an "idealized" speaker-hearer who does not display such performance variables as memory limitations, distractions, shifts of attention and interest, errors, and hesitation phenomena, such as repeats, false starts, pauses, omissions, and additions. Chomsky's point was that a theory of language had to be a theory of competence lest the linguist try in vain to categorize an infinite number of performance variables that are not reflective of the underlying linguistic ability of the speaker-hearer.

The distinction is one that linguists and psychologists in the generative/cognitive framework have operated under for some time, a mentalistic construct that structuralists and behaviorists obviously did not deal with: How could one scientifically assess this unobservable, underlying level?

Brown and Bellugi (1964) gave us a delightful example of the difficulty of attempting to extract underlying grammatical knowledge from children. Unlike adults, who can be asked, for example, whether it is better to say "two foots" or "two feet," children exhibit what is called the "pop-go-weasel" effect, as witnessed in the following dialogue between an adult and a two-year-old child:

Adult: Now Adam, listen to what I say. Tell me which is better to
      say: *some water* or *a water*?
Adam: Pop go weasel.

The child obviously had no interest in—or cognizance of—the adult's grammatical interrogation and therefore said whatever he wanted to! The researcher is thus forced to devise indirect methods of judging competence. Among those methods are the tape recording and transcription of countless hours of speech followed by studious analysis, or the direct administration of certain imitation, production, or comprehension tests, all with numerous disadvantages. How is one, for example, to infer some general competence about the linguistic system of a five-year-old, monolingual, English-speaking girl whose recounting of an incident viewed on television is transcribed below:

they heared 'em underground ca-cause they went through a hoyle—a hole—and they pulled a rock from underground and then they saw a wave going in—that the hole—and they brought a table and the wave brought 'em out the k—tunnel and then the—they went away and then—uh—m—ah—back on top and it was—uh—going under a bridge and they went—then the braves hit the—the bridge—they—all of it—th-then they looked there— then they—then they were safe.

On the surface it might appear that this child is severely impaired in her attempts to communicate. In fact, I once presented this same transcript, without identification of the speaker, to a group of speech therapists and asked them to analyze the various possible "disorders" manifested in the data. After they cited quite a number of technical manifestations of aphasia, I gleefully informed them of the real source! The point is that every day in our processing of linguistic data, we comprehend such strings of speech and comprehend them rather well because we know something about story-telling, about hesitation phenomena, and about the context of the narrative.

If we were to record many more samples of the five-year-old's speech, we would still be faced with the problem of inferring her competence. What is her knowledge of the verb system? of the concept of a "sentence"? Even if we administer rather carefully designed tests of comprehension or production to a child, we are still left with the problem of inferring, as accurately as possible, the child's underlying competence. Continued research helps us to confirm those inferences through multiple observations.

Adult talk, incidentally, is often no less fraught with monstrosities, as we can see in the following verbatim transcription of comments made on a talk show by a professional golfer discussing tips on how to improve a golf game.

Concentration is important. But uh—I also—to go with this of course if you're playing well—if you're playing well then you get up tight about your game. You get keyed up and it's easy to concentrate. You know you're playing well and you know . . . in with a chance than it's easier, much easier to—to you know get in there and—and start to . . . you don't have to think about it. I mean it's got to be automatic.

Perhaps the guest would have been better off if he had simply uttered the very last sentence and omitted all the previous verbiage!

The competence–performance model has not met with universal acceptance. Major criticisms of the model focus on the notion that competence, as defined by Chomsky, consists of the abilities of an "idealized" hearer-speaker, devoid of any so-called performance variables. Stubbs (1996), reviewing the issue, reminded us of the position of British linguists Firth and Halliday: dualisms are unnecessary, and the only option for linguists is to study language in use. Tarone (1988) pointed out that idealizing the language user disclaims responsibility for a number of linguistic goofs and slips of the tongue that may well arise from the context within which a person is communicating. In other words, all of a child's (or adult's) slips and hesitations and self-corrections are potentially connected to what Tarone calls **heterogeneous competence**—abilities that are in the process of being formed. So, while we may be tempted to claim that the five-year-old quoted above knows the difference, say, between a "hole" and a "hoyle," we must not too quickly pass off the latter as an irrelevant slip of the tongue.

What can we conclude about language acquisition theory based on a competence–performance model? A cautious approach to inferring someone's competence will allow you to draw some conclusions about overall ability while still leaving the door open for some significance to be attributed to those linguistic tidbits that you might initially be tempted to discount.

Comprehension and Production

Not to be confused with the competence/performance distinction, **comprehension** and **production** can be aspects of both performance and competence. One of the myths that has crept into some foreign language teaching materials is that comprehension (listening, reading) can be equated with competence, while production (speaking, writing) is performance. It is important to recognize that this is not the case: production is of course more directly observable, but comprehension is as much performance—a "willful act," to use Saussure's term—as production is.

In child language, most observational and research evidence points to the general superiority of comprehension over production: children seem to understand "more" than they actually produce. For instance, a child may understand a sentence with an embedded relative in it (e.g., "The ball that's in the sandbox is red") but not be able to produce one. W.R. Miller (1963: 863) gave us a good example of this phenomenon in phonological development: "Recently a three-year-old child told me her name was Litha. I answered 'Litha?' 'No, Litha.' 'Oh, Lisa.' 'Yes, Litha.'" The child clearly perceived the contrast between English *s* and *th*, even though she could not produce the contrast herself.

How are we to explain this difference, this apparent "lag" between comprehension and production? We know that even adults understand more vocabulary than they ever use in speech, and also perceive more syntactic variation than they actually produce. Could it be that the same competence accounts for both modes of performance? Or can we speak of comprehension competence as something that is identified as separate from production competence? Because comprehension for the most part runs ahead of production, is it more completely indicative of our overall competence? Is production indicative of a smaller portion of competence? Surely not. It is therefore necessary to make a distinction between production competence and comprehension competence. A theory of language must include some accounting of the separation of the two types of competence. In fact, linguistic competence no doubt has several modes or levels, at least as many as four, since speaking, listening, reading, and writing are all separate modes of performance.

Perhaps an even more compelling argument for the separation of competencies comes from research that appears to support the superiority of production over comprehension. Gathercole (1988) reported on a number of studies in which children were able to produce certain aspects of language they could not comprehend. For example, Rice (1980) found that children who did not previously know terms for color were able to respond verbally to such questions as "What color is this?" But they were not able to respond correctly (by giving the correct colored object) to "Give me the [color] one." While lexical and grammatical instances of production-before-comprehension seem to be few in number, it still behooves us to be wary in concluding that *all* aspects of linguistic comprehension precede, or facilitate, linguistic production.

Nature or Nurture?

Nativists contend that a child is born with an innate knowledge of or predisposition toward language, and that this innate property (the LAD or UG) is universal in all human beings. The innateness hypothesis was a possible resolution of the contradiction between the behavioristic notion that language is a set of habits that can be acquired by a process of conditioning and the fact that such conditioning is much too slow and inefficient a process to account for the acquisition of a phenomenon as complex as language.

But the innateness hypothesis presented a number of problems itself. One of the difficulties has already been discussed in this chapter: the LAD proposition simply postpones facing the central issue of the nature of the human being's capacity for language acquisition. Having thus "explained" language acquisition, one must now scientifically explain the genetic transmission of linguistic ability—which we cannot yet do with certainty. On the other hand, while the LAD remains a rationalistic hypothesis, I think we can take heart in slowly mounting genetic (scientific) evidence of the transmission of certain abilities, and assume that among those abilities we will one day find hard evidence of "language genes."

We must not put all our eggs in the innateness basket. Environmental factors cannot by any means be ignored. For years psychologists and educators have been embroiled in the "nature–nurture" controversy: What are those behaviors that "nature" provides innately, in some sort of predetermined biological timetable, and what are those behaviors that are, by environmental exposure—by "nurture," by teaching—learned and internalized? We do observe that language acquisition is universal, that every child acquires language. But how are the efficiency and success of that learning determined by the environment the child is in? or by the child's individual construction of linguistic reality in interaction with others? The waters of the innateness hypothesis are considerably muddied by such questions.

An interesting line of research on innateness was pursued by Derek Bickerton (1981), who found evidence, across a number of languages, of common patterns of linguistic and cognitive development. He proposed that human beings are "bio-programmed" to proceed from stage to stage. Like flowering plants, people are innately programmed to "release" certain properties of language at certain developmental ages. Just as we cannot make a geranium bloom before its "time," so human beings will "bloom" in predetermined, preprogrammed steps.

Universals

Closely related to the innateness controversy is the claim that language is universally acquired in the same manner, and moreover, that the deep structure of language at its deepest level may be common to all languages. Decades ago Werner Leopold (1949), who was far ahead of his time, made an eloquent case for certain phonological and grammatical universals in language. Leopold inspired later work by Greenberg (1963, 1966), Bickerton (1981), and Slobin (1986, 1992).

Currently, as noted earlier in this chapter, research on Universal Grammar continues this quest. One of the keys to such inquiry lies in research on child language acquisition across many different languages in order to determine the commonalities. Slobin (1986, 1992) and his colleagues gathered data on language acquisition in, among others, Japanese, French, Spanish, German, Polish, Hebrew, and Turkish. Interesting universals of pivot grammar and other telegraphese emerged. Maratsos (1988) enumerated some of the universal linguistic categories under investigation by a number of different researchers. These categories are still the subject of current inquiry:

  word order
  morphological marking tone

agreement (e.g., of subject and verb)
reduced reference (e.g., pronouns, ellipsis) nouns and noun classes
verbs and verb classes
predication
negation
question formation

Much of current UG research is centered around what have come to be known as **principles** and **parameters**. The child's "initial state is supposed to consist of a set of universal principles which specify some limited possibilities of variation, expressible in terms of parameters which need to be fixed in one of a few possible ways" (Saleemi 1992: 58). In simpler terms, this means that the child's task of language learning is manageable because of certain naturally occurring constraints. For example, the principle of **structure dependency** "states that language is organized in such a way that it crucially depends on the structural relationships between elements in a sentence (such as words, morphemes, etc.)" (Holzman 1998: 49). Take, for example, the following sentences:

1. The boy kicked the ball.
2. The boy that's wearing a red shirt and standing next to my brother kicked the ball.
3. She's a great teacher.
4. Is she a great teacher?

The first two sentences rely on a structural grouping, characteristic of all languages, called "phrase," or more specifically, "noun phrase." Without awareness of such a principle, someone would get all tangled up in sentence (2). Likewise, the principle of word order permutation allows one to perceive the difference between (3) and (4). Children, of course, are not born with such sophisticated perceptions of language; in fact, sentences like (2) are incomprehensible to most native English speaking children until about the age of four or five. Nevertheless, the principle of structure dependency eventually appears in both the comprehension and production of the child.

According to UG, languages cannot vary in an infinite number of ways. Parameters determine ways in which languages can vary. Just one example should suffice to illustrate. One parameter, known as "head parameter," specifies the position of the "head" of a phrase in relation to its complements in the phrase. While these positions vary across languages, their importance is primary in all languages. Languages are either "head first" or "head last." English is a typical head-first language, with phrases like "the boy that's wearing a red shirt" and "kicked the ball." Japanese is a head-last language, with sentences like "E wa kabe ni kakkatte imasu" (picture wall on is hanging) (from Cook & Newson 1996:14).

Systematicity and Variability

One of the assumptions of a good deal of current research on child language is the **systematicity** of the process of acquisition. From pivot grammar to three- and four-word utterances, and to full sentences of almost indeterminate length, children exhibit a remarkable ability to infer the phonological, structural, lexical, and semantic system of language. Ever since Berko's (1958) groundbreaking "wug" study, we have been discovering more and more about the systematicity of the acquisition process.

But in the midst of all this systematicity, there is an equally remarkable amount of **variability** in the process of learning! Researchers do not agree on how to define various "stages" of language acquisition, even in English. Certain "typical" patterns appear in child language. For example, it has been found that young children who have not yet mastered the past-tense morpheme tend first to learn past tenses as separate items ("walked," "broke," "drank") without knowledge of the difference between regular and irregular verbs. Then, around the age of four or five, they begin to perceive a system in which the *-ed* morpheme is added to a verb, and at this point all verbs become regularized ("breaked," "drinked," "goed"). Finally, after school age, children perceive that there are two classes of verbs, regular and irregular, and begin to sort out verbs into the two classes, a process that goes on for many years and in some cases persists into young adulthood.

In both first and second language acquisition, the problem of variability is being carefully addressed by researchers (see Bayley & Preston 1996 and Tarone 1988, for example). One of the major current research problems is to account for all this variability: to determine if what is now variable in our present point of view can some day be deemed systematic through such careful accounting.

Language and Thought

For years researchers have probed the relationship between language and cognition. The behavioristic view that cognition is too mentalistic to be studied by the scientific method is diametrically opposed to such positions as that of Piaget (1972), who claimed that cognitive development is at the very center of the human organism and that language is dependent upon and springs from cognitive development.

Others emphasized the influence of language on cognitive development. Jerome Bruner (Bruner, Olver, & Greenfield 1966), for example, singled out sources of language-influenced intellectual development: words shaping concepts, dialogues between parent and child or teacher and child serving to orient and educate, and other sources. Vygotsky (1962, 1978) also differed from Piaget in claiming that social interaction, through language, is a prerequisite to cognitive development. Thought and language were seen as two distinct cognitive operations that grow together (Schinke-Llano 1993). Moreover, every child reaches his or her potential development, in part, through social interaction with adults and peers. Vygotsky's **zone of proximal development** is the distance between a child's actual cognitive capacity and the level of potential development (Vygotsky 1978: 86).

One of the champions of the position that language affects thought was Benjamin Whorf, who with Edward Sapir formed the well-known Sapir-Whorf hypothesis of linguistic relativity—namely, that each language imposes on its speaker a particular "world view." (See Chapter 7 for more discussion of the Sapir-Whorf hypothesis.)

The issue at stake in child language acquisition is to determine how thought affects language, how language affects thought, and how linguists can best describe and account for the interaction of the two. While we do not have complete answers, it is clear that research has pointed to the fact that cognitive and linguistic development are inextricably intertwined with dependencies in both directions. And we do know that language is a way of life, is at the foundation of our being, and interacts simultaneously with thoughts and feelings.

Imitation

It is a common informal observation that children are good imitators. We think of children typically as imitators and mimics, and then conclude that imitation is one of the important strategies a child uses in the acquisition of language. That conclusion is not inaccurate on a global level. Indeed, research has shown that **echoing** is a particularly salient strategy in early language learning and an important aspect of early phonological acquisition. Moreover, imitation is consonant with behavioristic principles of language acquisition—principles relevant, at least, to the earliest stages.

But it is important to ask what type of imitation is implied. Behaviorists assume one type of imitation, but a deeper level of imitation is far more important in the process of language acquisition. The first type is surface-structure imitation, where a person repeats or mimics the surface strings, attending to a phonological code rather than a semantic code. It is this level of imitation that enables an adult to repeat random numbers or nonsense syllables, or even to mimic nonsense syllables. The semantic data, if any, underlying the surface output are perhaps only peripherally attended to. In foreign language classes, rote pattern drills often evoke surface imitation: a repetition of sounds by the student without the vaguest understanding of what the sounds might possibly mean.

The earliest stages of child language acquisition may manifest a good deal of surface imitation since the baby may not possess the necessary semantic categories to assign "meaning" to utterances. But as children perceive the importance of the semantic level of language, they attend to a greater extent to that meaningful semantic level—the deep structure of language. They engage in deep-structure imitation. In fact, the imitation of the deep structure of language can literally block their attention to the surface structure so that they become, on the face of it, poor imitators. Consider the following conversation as recorded by McNeill (1966: 69).

Child: Nobody don't like me.
Mother: No, say "nobody likes me."
Child: Nobody don't like me.
            (eight repetitions of this dialogue)
Mother: No, now listen carefully; say "nobody likes me."
Child: Oh! Nobody don't likes me.

You can imagine the frustration of both mother and child, for the mother was attending to a rather technical, surface grammatical distinction, and yet the child sought to derive some meaning value. The child was expressing a deep feeling, while the mother was concerned about grammar!

A similar case in point occurred one day when the teacher of an elementary-school class asked her pupils to write a few sentences on a piece of paper, to which one rather shy pupil responded, "Ain't got no pencil." Disturbed at this nonstandard response, the teacher embarked on a barrage of corrective models for the child: "I don't have any pencils, you don't have a pencil, they don't have pencils, . . ." When the teacher finally ended her monologue of patterns, the intimidated and bewildered child said, "Ain't nobody got no pencils?" The teacher's purpose was lost on this child because he too was attending to language as a meaningful and communicative tool, and not to the question of whether certain forms were "correct" and others were not. The child, like all children, was attending to the **truth value** of the utterance.

Research has also shown that children, when explicitly asked to repeat a sentence in a test situation, will often repeat the correct underlying deep structure with a change in the surface rendition. For example, sentences such as "The ball that is rolling down the hill is black" and "The boy who's in the sandbox is wearing a red shirt" tend to be repeated back by preschool children as "The black ball is rolling down the hill" and "The red boy is in the sandbox" (Brown 1970). Children are excellent imitators. It is simply a matter of understanding exactly what it is that they are imitating.

Practice

Closely related to the notion of imitation is a somewhat broader question, the nature of **practice** in child language. Do children practice their language? If so, how? What is the role of the **frequency** of hearing and producing items in the acquisition of those items? It is common to observe children and conclude that they "practice" language constantly, especially in the early stages of single-word and two-word utterances. A behavioristic model of first language acquisition would claim that practice—repetition and association—is the key to the formation of habits by operant conditioning.

One unique form of practice by a child was recorded by Ruth Weir (1962). She found that her children produced rather long monologues in bed at night before going to sleep. Here is one example: "What color . . . What color blanket . . . What color mop . . . What color glass . . . Mommy's home sick . . . Mommy's home sick . . . Where's Mommy home sick . . . Where's Mikey sick . . . Mikey sick." Such monologues are not uncommon among children, whose inclination it is to "play" with language just as they do with all objects and events around them. Weir's data show far more structural patterning than has commonly been found in other data. Nevertheless, children's practice seems to be a key to language acquisition.

Practice is usually thought of as referring to speaking only. But one can also think in terms of comprehension practice, which is often considered under the rubric of the frequency of linguistic input to the child. Is the acquisition of particular words or structures directly attributable to their frequency in the child's linguistic environment? There is evidence that certain very frequent forms are acquired first: *what* questions, irregular past tense forms, certain common household items and persons. Brown and Hanlon (1970), for example, found that the frequency of occurrence of a linguistic item in the speech of mothers was an overwhelmingly strong predictor of the order of emergence of those items in their children's speech.

There are some conflicting data, however. Telegraphic speech is one case in point. Some of the most frequently occurring words in the language are omitted in such two- and three-word utterances. And McNeill (1968: 416) found that a Japanese child produced the Japanese postposition *ga* far more frequently and more correctly than another contrasting postposition *wa*, even though her mother was recorded as using *wa* twice as often as *ga*. McNeill attributed this finding to the fact that *ga* as a subject marker is of more importance, grammatically, to the child, and she therefore acquired the use of that item since it was more meaningful on a deep-structure level. Another feasible explanation for that finding might lie in the easier pronunciation of *ga*.

The frequency issue may be summed up by noting that nativists who claim that "the relative frequency of stimuli is of little importance in language acquisition" (Wardhaugh 1971: 12) might, in the face of evidence now available, be more cautious in their claims. It would appear that frequency of *meaningful* occurrence may well be a more precise refinement of the notion of frequency.

Input

The role of input in the child's acquisition of language is undeniably crucial. Whatever one's position is on the innateness of language, the speech that young children hear is primarily the speech heard in the home, and much of that speech is parental speech or the speech of older siblings. Linguists once claimed that most adult speech is basically semigrammatical (full of performance variables), that children are exposed to a chaotic sample of language, and only their innate capacities can account for their successful acquisition of language. McNeill, for example, wrote: "The speech of adults from which a child discovers the locally appropriate manifestation of the linguistic universals is a completely random, haphazard sample, in no way contrived to instruct the child on grammar" (1966: 73). However, Labov's (1970) studies showed that the presumed ungrammaticality of everyday speech appears to be a myth. Bellugi and Brown (1964) and Drach (1969) found that the speech addressed to children was carefully grammatical and lacked the usual hesitations and false starts common in adult-to-adult speech. Landes's (1975) summary of a wide range of research on parental input supported their conclusions. Later studies of parents' speech in the home (Hladik & Edwards 1984; Moerk 1985) confirmed earlier evidence demonstrating the selectivity of parental linguistic input to their children.

At the same time, it will be remembered that children react very consistently to the deep structure and the communicative function of language, and they do not react overtly to expansions and grammatical corrections as in the "nobody likes me" dialogue quoted above. Such input is largely ignored unless there is some truth or falsity that the child can attend to. Thus, if a child says "Dat Harry" and the parent says "No, that's *John*," the child might readily self-correct and say "Oh, dat *John*." But what Landes and others showed is that in the long run, children will, after consistent, repeated models in meaningful contexts, eventually transfer correct forms to their own speech and thus correct "dat" to "that's."

The importance of the issue lies in the fact that it is clear from more recent research that adult and peer input to the child is far more important than nativists earlier believed. Adult input seems to shape the child's acquisition, and the interaction patterns between child and parent change according to the increasing language skill of the child. Nurture and environment in this case are tremendously important, although it remains to be seen just how important parental input is as a proportion of total input.

Discourse

A subfield of research that is occupying the attention of an increasing number of child language researchers, especially in an era of social constructivist research, is the area of **conversational** or **discourse** analysis. While parental input is a significant part of the child's development of conversational rules, it is only one aspect, as the child also interacts with peers and, of course, with other adults. Berko-Gleason (1982: 20) described the perspective:

> While it used to be generally held that mere *exposure* to language is sufficient to set the child's language generating machinery in motion, it is now clear that, in order for successful first language acquisition to take place, *interaction*, rather than exposure, is required; children do not learn language from overhearing the conversations of others or from listening to the radio, and must, instead, acquire it in the context of being spoken to.

While conversation is a universal human activity performed routinely in the course of daily living, the means by which children learn to take part in conversation appear to be very complex. Sinclair and Coulthard (1975) proposed that conversations be examined in terms of **initiations** and **responses**. What might in a grammatical sentence-based model of language be described as sentences, clauses, words, and morphemes, are viewed as transactions, exchanges, moves, and acts. The child learns not only how to initiate a conversation but how to respond to another's initiating utterance. Questions are not simply questions, but are recognized functionally as requests for information, for action, or for help. At a relatively young age, children learn subtle differences between, say, assertions and challenges. They learn that utterances have both a literal and an intended or functional meaning. Thus, in the case of the question "Can you go to the movies tonight?," the response "I'm busy" is understood correctly as a negative response ("I can't go to the movies"). How do children learn discourse rules? What are the key features children attend to? How do they detect pragmatic or intended meaning? How are gender roles acquired? These and other questions about the acquisition of discourse ability are slowly being answered in the research (see Holmes 1995 and Tannen 1996).

Much remains to be studied in the area of the child's development of conversational knowledge (see Shatz & McCloskey 1984, and McTear 1984 for a good summary). Nevertheless, such development is perhaps the next frontier to be mastered in the quest for answers to the mystery of language acquisition. Clearly there are important implications here, as we shall see in the next chapter, for second language learners. The barrier of discourse is one of the most difficult for second language learners to break through.

A number of theories and issues in child language have been explored in this chapter with the purpose of both briefly characterizing the current state of child language research and of highlighting a few of the key concepts that emerge in the formation of an understanding of how babies learn to talk and eventually become sophisticated linguistic beings. There is much to be learned in such an understanding. Every human being who attempts to learn a second language has already learned a first language. It is said that the second time around on something is always easier. In the case of language, this is not necessarily true. But in order to understand why it is not, you need to understand the nature of that initial acquisition process, for it may be that some of the keys to the mystery are found therein. That search is continued in the next chapter as we compare and contrast first and second language acquisition.

In the Classroom:
Gouin and Berlitz—The First Reformers

In the second of our series of vignettes on classroom applications of theory, we turn the clock back about a hundred years to look in on the first two reformers in the history of "modern" language teaching, François Gouin and Charles Berlitz. Their perceptive observations about language teaching helped set the stage for the development of language teaching methodologies for the century following.

In his *The Art of Learning and Studying Foreign Languages* (1880), François Gouin described a painful set of experiences that finally led to his insights about language teaching. Having decided in midlife to learn German, he took up residency in Hamburg for one year. But rather than attempting to converse with the natives, he engaged in a rather bizarre sequence of attempts to "master" the language. Upon arrival in Hamburg he felt he should memorize a German grammar book and a table of the 248 irregular German verbs! He did this in a matter of only ten days and then hurried to "the academy" (the university) to test his new knowledge. "But alas!" he wrote, "I could not understand a single word, not a single word!" Gouin was undaunted. He returned to the isolation of his room, this time to memorize the German roots and to rememorize the grammar book and irregular verbs. Again he emerged with expectations of success. "But alas!"—the result was the same as before. In the course of the year in Germany, Gouin memorized books, translated Goethe and Schiller, and even memorized 30,000 words in a German dictionary, all in the isolation of his room, only to be crushed by his failure to understand German afterward. Only once did he try to "make conversation" as a method, but because this caused people to laugh at him, he was too embarrassed to continue. At the end of the year, having reduced the Classical Method to absurdity, Gouin was forced to return home, a failure.

But there was a happy ending. Upon returning home Gouin discovered that his three-year-old nephew had, during that year, gone through that wonderful stage of child language acquisition in which he went from saying virtually nothing to becoming a veritable chatterbox of French. How was it that this little child succeeded so easily in a task, mastering a first language, that Gouin, in a second language, had found impossible? The child must hold the secret to learning a language! So Gouin spent a great deal of time observing his nephew and other children and came to the following conclusions: Language learning is primarily a matter of transforming perceptions into conceptions. Children use language to represent their conceptions. Language is a means of thinking, of representing the world to oneself. (These insights, remember, were formed by a language teacher more than a century ago!)

So Gouin set about devising a teaching method that would follow from these insights. And thus the Series Method was created, a method that taught learners directly (without translation) and conceptually (without grammatical rules and explanations) a "series" of connected sentences that are easy to perceive. The first lesson of a foreign language would thus teach the following series of fifteen sentences:

I walk toward the door. I draw near to the door. I draw nearer to the door. I get to the door. I stop at the door.

I stretch out my arm. I take hold of the handle. I turn the handle. I open the door. I pull the door.

The door moves. The door turns on its hinges. The door turns and turns. I open the door wide. I let go of the handle.

The fifteen sentences have an unconventionally large number of grammatical properties, vocabulary items, word orders, and complexity. This is no simple *Voici la table* lesson! Yet Gouin was successful with such lessons because the language was so easily understood, stored, recalled, and related to reality.

The "naturalistic"—simulating the "natural" way in which children learn first languages—approaches of Gouin and a few of his contemporaries did not take hold immediately. A generation later, largely through the efforts of Charles Berlitz, applied linguists finally established the credibility of such approaches in what became known as the Direct Method.

The basic premise of Berlitz's method was that second language learning should be more like first language learning: lots of active oral interaction, spontaneous use of the language, no translation between first and second languages, and little or no analysis of grammatical rules. Richards and Rodgers (1986: 9–10) summarized the principles of the Direct Method:

1. Classroom instruction was conducted exclusively in the target language.
2. Only everyday vocabulary and sentences were taught.
3. Oral communication skills were built up in a carefully graded progression organized around question-and-answer exchanges between teachers and students in small, intensive classes.
4. Grammar was taught inductively.
5. New teaching points were introduced orally.
6. Concrete vocabulary was taught through demonstration, objects, and pictures; abstract vocabulary was taught by association of ideas.
7. Both speech and listening comprehension were taught.
8. Correct pronunciation and grammar were emphasized.

The Direct Method enjoyed considerable popularity through the end of the nineteenth century and well into the twentieth. It was most widely accepted in private language schools where students were highly motivated and where native-speaking teachers could be employed. To this day, "Berlitz" is a household word; Berlitz language schools are thriving in every country of the world. But almost any "method" can succeed when clients are willing to pay high prices for small classes, individual attention, and intensive study. The Direct Method did not take well in public education, where the constraints of budget, classroom size, time, and teacher background made the method difficult to use. Moreover, the Direct Method was criticized for its weak theoretical foundations. The methodology was not so much to be credited for its success as the general skill and personality of the teacher.

By the end of the first quarter of the twentieth century, the use of the Direct Method had declined both in Europe and in the United States. Most language curricula returned to the Grammar Translation Method or to a "reading approach" that emphasized reading skills in foreign languages. But it is interesting that in the middle of the twentieth century, the Direct Method was revived and redirected into what was probably the most visible of all language teaching "revolutions" in the modern era, the Audiolingual Method (see Chapter 3). So even this somewhat short-lived movement in language teaching would reappear in the changing winds and shifting sands of history.

TOPICS AND QUESTIONS FOR
STUDY AND DISCUSSION

[Note: (I) individual work; (G) group or pair work; (C) whole-class discussion.]

1. (G) In a small group, discuss why it is that behavioristic theories can account sufficiently well for the earliest utterances of the child, but not for utterances at the sentence and discourse level. Do nativistic and functional approaches provide the necessary tools for accounting for those later, more complex utterances?

2. (G/C) If you can, with a partner, try to record on tape samples of a young child's speech. A child of about three is an ideal subject to observe in the study of growing competence in a language. Transcribe a segment of your recording and see if, inductively, you can determine some of the rules the child is using. Present your findings to the rest of the class for discussion.

3. (I) Review the sections that dealt with Universal Grammar. Is it something different from the nativists' concept of LAD?

4. (G) In a group, look at the two samples of speech on pages 31 and 32 (one by a five-year-old, and the other by a professional golfer). Identify what you would consider to be "performance variables" in those transcripts. Then, try to reconstruct an "idealized" form of the two monologues, and share with other groups.

5. (C) Competence and performance are difficult to define. In what sense are they interdependent? How does competence increase? Can it decrease? Try to illustrate with non-language examples of learning certain skills, such as musical or athletic skills.

6. (G) In a group, recall experiences learning a foreign language at some point in your past. Share with others any examples of your comprehension exceeding your production abilities. How about the reverse? Share your findings with the rest of the class.

7. (I) Name some **forms** of language and some **functions** of language. In your own experience learning a previous foreign language, did you experience any difficulty with the latter?

8. (C) In what way do you think Gouin reflected some ideas about language and about language acquisition that are now current more than a hundred years later? Would the Series Method or the Direct Method work for you as a teacher? Discuss pros and cons.

SUGGESTED READINGS

Carroll, David W. 1994. *Psychology of Language.* Pacific Grove, CA: Brooks/Cole Publishing Company.

Holzman, Mathilda. 1998.   *The Language of Children.* Second Edition. Cambridge, MA: Blackwell Publishers.

Most of the topics covered in this chapter are given full treatment in these two textbooks, which survey issues in first language acquisition.

Pinker, Steven. 1994. *The Language Instinct.* New York: William Morrow and Company.

Steven Pinker's book hit the best seller list a few years ago. It offers a wealth of information for the lay reader on such topics as child language acquisition, innateness, thought and language, and linguistics in general.

Cook, V. and Newson, M. 1996. *Chomsky's Universal Grammar: An Introduction.* Oxford: Blackwell.

Saleemi, A. 1992. *Universal Grammar and Language Learnability.* Cambridge: Cambridge University Press.

These two books provide introductory surveys of research on Universal Grammar. They are more readable than the technical research studies themselves, which are often difficult to comprehend without a substantive background in linguistic theory.

Bickerton, Derek. 1981. *Roots of Language.* Ann Arbor, MI: Karoma Publishers.

Derek Bickerton's book, which focuses principally on the topic of creolization, also outlines his theory of bioprogramming mentioned in this chapter.

Diller, Karl C. 1978. *The Language Teaching Controversy.* Rowley, MA: Newbury House Publishers.

A summary of François Gouin's language learning experiences and his Series Method can be found in this survey of language methodology.

LANGUAGE LEARNING EXPERIENCE:
JOURNAL ENTRY 2

[Note: See pages 18 and 19 of Chapter 1 for general guidelines for writing a journal on a previous or concurrent language learning experience.]

- As you learn(ed) a foreign language, did you feel any of the learning was due to a "knack" you had for it? Think of some examples to illustrate either the presence or the absence of some ability to pick up the language.
- Is your class focused more on the forms of language than the functions? Illustrate with examples.
- Go through the issues discussed in this chapter and ask yourself if, in your foreign language class, you have had opportunities to understand and to speak, to imitate the teacher, to practice discourse and conversation?
- Consider how children learn their first language and figure out inductively (before you go on to Chapter 3) what some of the child's "secrets" are that enable them to acquire a language seemingly efficiently.

AGE AND

ACQUISITION

THE INCREASED pace of research on first language acquisition in the last half of the twentieth century attracted the attention not only of linguists of all kinds but also of educators in various language-related fields. Today the applications of research findings in first language acquisition are widespread. In language arts education, for example, teacher trainees are required to study first language acquisition, particularly acquisition after age five, in order to improve their understanding of the task of teaching language skills to native speakers. In foreign language education, most standard texts and curricula now include some introductory material in first language acquisition. The reasons for this are clear. We have all observed children acquiring their first language easily and well, yet individuals learning a second language, particularly in an educational setting, can meet with great difficulty and sometimes failure. We should therefore be able to learn something from a systematic study of that first language learning experience.

What may not be quite as obvious, though, is how the second language teacher should interpret the many facets and sometimes conflicting findings of first language research. First language acquisition starts in very early childhood, but second language acquisition can happen in childhood, early or late, as well as in adulthood. Do childhood and adulthood, and differences between them, hold some keys to language acquisition models and theories? The purpose of this chapter is to address some of those questions and to set forth explicitly some of the parameters for looking at the effects of age and acquisition.

DISPELLING MYTHS

The first step in investigating age and acquisition might be to dispel some myths about the relationship between first and second language acquisition. H.H. Stern (1970: 57–58) summarized some common arguments that cropped up from time to time to recommend a second language teaching method or procedure on the basis of first language acquisition:

1. In language teaching, we must practice and practice, again and again. Just watch a small child learning his mother tongue. He repeats things over and over again. During the language learning stage he practices all the time. This is what we must also do when we learn a foreign language.

2. Language learning is mainly a matter of imitation. You must be a mimic. Just like a small child. He imitates everything.

3. First, we practice the separate sounds, then words, then sentences. That is the natural order and is therefore right for learning a foreign language.

4. Watch a small child's speech development. First he listens, then he speaks. Understanding always precedes speaking. Therefore, this must be the right order of presenting the skills in a foreign language.

5. A small child listens and speaks and no one would dream of making him read or write. Reading and writing are advanced stages of language development. The natural order for first and second language learning is listening, speaking, reading, writing.

6. You did not have to translate when you were small. If you were able to learn your own language without translation, you should be able to learn a foreign language in the same way.

7. A small child simply uses language. He does not learn formal grammar. You don't tell him about verbs and nouns. Yet he learns the language perfectly. It is equally unnecessary to use grammatical conceptualization in teaching a foreign language.

These statements represent the views of those who felt that "the first language learner was looked upon as the foreign language teacher's dream: a pupil who mysteriously laps up his vocabulary, whose pronunciation, in spite of occasional lapses, is impeccable, while morphology and syntax, instead of being a constant headache, come to him like a dream" (Stern 1970: 58). The statements also tend to represent the views of those who were dominated by a behavioristic theory of language in which the first language acquisition process was viewed as consisting of rote practice, habit formation, shaping, overlearning, reinforcement, conditioning, association, stimulus and response, and who therefore assumed that the second language learning process involves the same constructs.

There are flaws in each view. Sometimes the flaw is in the assumption behind the statement about first language learning, and sometimes it is in the analogy or implication that is drawn; sometimes it is in both. The flaws represent some of the misunderstandings that need to be demythologized for the second language teacher. Through a careful examination of those shortcomings in this chapter, you should be able, on the one hand, to avoid certain pitfalls, and on the other hand, to draw enlightened, plausible analogies wherever possible, thereby enriching your understanding of the second language learning process itself.

As cognitive and constructivist research on first language acquisition gathered momentum, second language researchers and foreign language teachers began to recognize the mistakes in drawing direct global analogies between first and second language acquisition. Some of the first warning signals were raised early in the process by the cognitive psychologist David Ausubel (1964). In foreboding terms, Ausubel outlined a number of glaring problems with the then-popular Audiolingual Method, some of whose procedures were ostensibly derived from notions of "natural" (first) language learning. He issued the following warnings and statements:

- The rote learning practice of audiolingual drills lacked the meaningfulness necessary for successful first and second language acquisition.
- Adults learning a foreign language could, with their full cognitive capacities, benefit from deductive presentations of grammar.
- The native language of the learner is not just an interfering factor—it can facilitate learning a second language.
- The written form of the language could be beneficial.
- Students could be overwhelmed by language spoken at its "natural speed," and they, like children, could benefit from more deliberative speech from the teacher.

These conclusions were derived from Ausubel's cognitive perspective, which ran counter to prevailing behavioristic paradigms on which the Audiolingual Method was based. But Ausubel's criticism may have been ahead of its time, for in 1964 few teachers were ready to entertain doubts about the widely accepted method. (See the vignette at the end of this chapter for a further discussion of the Audiolingual Method.)

By the 1970s and 1980s, criticism of earlier direct analogies between first and second language acquisition had reached full steam. Stern (1970), Cook (1973, 1995), and Schachter (1988), among others, addressed the inconsistencies of such analogies, but at the same time recognized the legitimate similarities that, if viewed cautiously, allowed one to draw some constructive conclusions about second language learning.

TYPES OF COMPARISON AND CONTRAST

The comparison of first and second language acquisition can easily be oversimplified. At the very least, one needs to approach the comparison by first considering the differences between children and adults. It is, in one sense, illogical to compare the first language acquisition of a child with the second language acquisition of an adult (see Schachter 1988; Scovel 1999). This involves trying to draw analogies not only between first and second language learning situations but also between children and adults. It is much more logical to compare first and second language learning in children or to compare second language learning in children and adults. Nevertheless, child first language acquisition and adult second language acquisition are common and important categories of acquisition to compare. It is reasonable, therefore, to view the latter type of comparison within a matrix of possible comparisons. Figure 3.1 represents four possible categories to compare, defined by age and type of acquisition. Note that the vertical shaded area between the child and the adult is purposely broad to account for varying definitions of adulthood. In general, however, an adult is considered to be one who has reached the age of puberty.

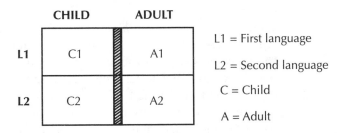

Figure 3.1. First and second language acquisition in adults and children

Cell A1 is clearly representative of an abnormal situation. There have been few recorded instances of an adult acquiring a first language. In one widely publicized instance, Curtiss (1977) wrote about Genie, a thirteen-year-old girl who had been socially isolated and abused all her life until she was discovered, and who was then faced with the task of acquiring a first language. Accounts of "wolf children" and instances of severe disability fall into this category. Since we need not deal with abnormal or pathological cases of language acquisition, we can ignore category A1. That leaves three possible comparisons:

1. first and second language acquisition in children (C1–C2), holding age constant
2. second language acquisition in children and adults (C2–A2), holding second language constant
3. first language acquisition in children and second language acquisition in adults (C1–A2).

In the C1–C2 comparison (holding age constant), one is manipulating the language variable. However, it is important to remember that a two-year-old and an eleven-year-old exhibit vast cognitive, affective, and physical differences, and that comparisons of all three types must be treated with caution when varying ages of children are being considered. In the C2–A2 comparison, one is holding language constant and manipulating the differences between children and adults. Such comparisons are, for obvious reasons, the most fruitful in yielding analogies for adult second language classroom instruction. The third comparison, C1–A2, unfortunately manipulates both variables. Many of the traditional comparisons were of this type; however, such comparisons must be made only with extreme caution because of the enormous cognitive, affective, and physical differences between children and adults.

Much of the focus of the rest of this chapter will be made on C2–A2 and C1–C2 comparisons. In both cases, comparisons will be embedded within a number of issues, controversies, and other topics that have attracted the attention of researchers interested in the relationship of age to acquisition.

THE CRITICAL PERIOD HYPOTHESIS

Most discussions about age and acquisition center on the question of whether there is a **critical period** for language acquisition: a biologically determined period of life when language can be acquired more easily and beyond which time language is increasingly difficult to acquire. The Critical Period Hypothesis (CPH) claims that there is such a biological timetable. Initially the notion of a critical period was connected only to first language acquisition. Pathological studies of children who failed to acquire their first language, or aspects thereof, became fuel for arguments of biologically determined predispositions, timed for release, which would wane if the correct environmental stimuli were not present at the crucial stage. We have already seen, in the last chapter, that researchers like Lenneberg (1967) and Bickerton (1981) made strong statements in favor of a critical period before which and after which certain abilities do not develop.

Second language researchers have outlined the possibilities of extrapolating the CPH to second language contexts (see Bialystok 1997; Singleton & Lengyel 1995; Scovel 1988, 1999 for useful summaries). The "classic" argument is that a critical point for second language acquisition occurs around puberty, beyond which people seem to be relatively incapable of acquiring a second language. This has led some to assume, incorrectly, that by the age of twelve or thirteen you are "over the hill" when it comes to the possibility of successful second language learning. Such an assumption must be viewed in the light of what it really means to be "successful" in learning a second language, and particularly the role of *accent* as a component of success. To examine these issues, we will first look at neurological and phonological considerations, then examine cognitive, affective, and linguistic considerations.

NEUROLOGICAL CONSIDERATIONS

One of the most promising areas of inquiry in age and acquisition research has been the study of the function of the brain in the process of acquisition (see Schumann 1998, Jacobs & Schumann 1992, and Scovel 1988 for synopses). How might neurological development affect second language success? Does the maturation of the brain at some stage spell the doom of language acquisition ability?

Hemispheric Lateralization

Some scholars have singled out the **lateralization** of the brain as the key to answering such a question. There is evidence in neurological research that as the human brain matures, certain functions are assigned, or "lateralized," to the left hemisphere of the brain, and certain other functions to the right hemisphere. Intellectual, logical, and analytic functions appear to be largely located in the left hemisphere, while the right hemisphere controls functions related to emotional and social needs. (See Chapter 5 for more discussion of left- and right-brain functioning.) Language functions appear to be controlled mainly in the left hemisphere, although there is a good deal of conflicting evidence. For example, patients who have had left hemispherectomies have been capable of comprehending and producing an amazing amount of language (see Zangwill 1971: 220). But in general, a stroke or accident victim who suffers a lesion in the left hemisphere will manifest some language impairment, which is less often the case with right hemisphere lesions.

While questions about how language is lateralized in the brain are interesting indeed, a more crucial question for second language researchers has centered on when lateralization takes place, and how that lateralization process affects language acquisition. Eric Lenneberg (1967) and others suggested that lateralization is a slow process that begins around the age of two and is completed around puberty. During this time the child is neurologically assigning functions little by little to one side of the brain or the other; included in these functions, of course, is language. And it has been found that children up to the age of puberty who suffer injury to the left hemisphere are able to relocalize linguistic functions to the right hemisphere, to "relearn" their first language with relatively little impairment. Thomas Scovel (1969) extended these findings to propose a relationship between lateralization and second language acquisition. He suggested that the plasticity of the brain prior to puberty enables children to acquire not only their first language but also a second language, and that possibly it is the very accomplishment of lateralization that makes it difficult for people to be able ever again to easily acquire fluent control of a second language, or at least to acquire it with what Alexander Guiora et al. (1972a) called "authentic" (nativelike) pronunciation.

While Scovel's (1969) suggestion had only marginal experimental basis, it prompted him (Scovel 1988) and other researchers (e.g., Singleton & Lengyel 1995) to take a careful look at neurological factors in first and second language acquisition. This research considered the possibility that there is a critical period not only for first language acquisition but also, by extension, for second language acquisition. Much of the neurological argument centers on the *time* of lateralization. While Lenneberg (1967) contended that lateralization is complete around puberty, Norman Geschwind (1970), among others, suggested a much earlier age. Stephen Krashen (1973) cited research to support the completion of lateralization around age five. Krashen's suggestion does not grossly conflict with research on first language acquisition if one considers "fluency" in the first language to be achieved by age five. Scovel (1984: 1) cautioned against assuming, with Krashen, that lateralization is *complete* by age five. "One must be careful to distinguish between 'emergence' of lateralization (at birth, but quite evident at five) and 'completion' (only evident at about puberty)." If lateralization is not completed until puberty, then one can still construct arguments for a critical period based on lateralization.

Biological Timetables

One of the most compelling arguments for an accent-related critical period came from Thomas Scovel's (1988) fascinating multidisciplinary review of the evidence that has been amassed. Scovel cited evidence for a **sociobiological** critical period in various species of mammals and birds. (Others, such as Neapolitan et al. 1988, had drawn analogies between the acquisition of birdsong and human language acquisition.) Scovel's evidence pointed toward the development of a socially bonding accent at puberty, enabling species (a) to form an identity with their own community as they anticipate roles of parenting and leadership, and (b) to attract mates of "their own kind" in an instinctive drive to maintain their own species.

If the stabilization of an accepted, authentic accent is biologically pre-programmed for baboons and birds, why not for human beings? The socio-biological evidence that Scovel cited persuades us to conclude that native accents, and therefore "foreign" accents after puberty, may be a genetic left-over that, in our widespread human practice of mating across dialectal, linguistic, and racial barriers, is no longer necessary for the preservation of the human species. "In other words," explained Scovel (1988: 80), "an accent emerging after puberty is the price we pay for our preordained ability to be articulate apes."

Following another line of research, Walsh and Diller (1981: 18) concluded that different aspects of a second language are learned optimally at different ages:

> Lower-order processes such as pronunciation are dependent on early maturing and less adaptive macroneural circuits, which makes foreign accents difficult to overcome after childhood. Higher-order language functions, such as semantic relations, are more dependent on late maturing neural circuits, which may explain why college students can learn many times the amount of grammar and vocabulary that elementary school students can learn in a given period of time.

This conclusion lends support for a neurologically based critical period, but principally for the acquisition of an authentic (nativelike) accent, and not very strongly for the acquisition of communicative fluency and other "higher-order" processes. We return to the latter issue in the next section.

Right-Hemispheric Participation

Yet another branch of neurolinguistic research focused on the role of the right hemisphere in the acquisition of a second language. Obler (1981: 58) noted that in second language learning, there is significant right hemisphere participation and that "this participation is particularly active during the early stages of learning the second language." But this "participation" to some extent consists of what we will later (Chapter 5) define as "strategies" of acquisition. Obler cited the strategy of guessing at meanings, and of using formulaic utterances, as examples of right hemisphere activity. Others

(Genesee 1982; Seliger 1982) also found support for right hemisphere involvement in the form of complex language processing as opposed to early language acquisition.

Genesee (1982: 321) concluded that "there may be greater right hemisphere involvement in language processing in bilinguals who acquire their second language late relative to their first language and in bilinguals who learn it in informal contexts." While this conclusion may appear to contradict Obler's statement above, it does not. Obler found support for more right hemisphere activity during the early stages of second language acquisition, but her conclusions were drawn from a study of seventh-, ninth-, and eleventh-grade subjects—all postpubescent. Such studies seem to suggest that second language learners, particularly adult learners, might benefit from more encouragement of right-brain activity in the classroom context. But, as Scovel (1982: 324–325) noted, that sort of conclusion needs to be cautious, since the research provides a good deal of conflicting evidence, some of which has been grossly misinterpreted in "an unhappy marriage of single-minded neuropsychologists and double-minded educationalists. . . . Brain research . . . will not provide a quick fix to our teaching problems."

Anthropological Evidence

Some adults have been known to acquire an authentic accent in a second language after the age of puberty, but such individuals are few and far between. Anthropologist Jane Hill (1970) provided an intriguing response to Scovel's (1969) study by citing anthropological research on non-Western societies that yielded evidence that adults can, in the normal course of their lives, acquire second languages perfectly. One unique instance of second language acquisition in adulthood was reported by Sorenson (1967), who studied the Tukano culture of South America. At least two dozen languages were spoken among these communities, and each tribal group, identified by the language it speaks, is an exogamous unit; that is, people must marry outside their group, and hence almost always marry someone who speaks another language. Sorenson reported that during adolescence, individuals actively and almost suddenly began to speak two or three other languages to which they had been exposed at some point. Moreover, "in adulthood [a person] may acquire more languages; as he approaches old age, field observation indicates, he will go on to perfect his knowledge of all the languages at his disposal" (Sorenson 1967: 678). In conclusion, Hill (1970: 247–248) suggested that

> the language acquisition situation seen in adult language learners
> in the largely monolingual American English middle class speech
> communities . . . may have been inappropriately taken to be a uni-

versal situation in proposing an innatist explanation for adult foreign accents. Multilingual speech communities of various types deserve careful study. . . . We will have to explore the influence of social and cultural roles which language and phonation play, and the role which attitudes about language play, as an alternative or a supplement to the cerebral dominance theory as an explanation of adult foreign accents.

Hill's challenge was taken up in subsequent decades. Flege (1987) and Morris and Gerstman (1986), for example, cited motivation, affective variables, social factors, and the quality of input as important in explaining the apparent advantage of the child. However, both Long (1990b) and Patkowski (1990) disputed such conclusions and sided with Scovel in their relatively strong interpretation of an age-related critical period for first and second language acquisition.

THE SIGNIFICANCE OF ACCENT

Implicit in the comments of the preceding section is the assumption that the emergence of what we commonly call "foreign accent" is of some importance in our arguments about age and acquisition. We can appreciate the fact that given the existence of several hundred muscles (throat, larynx, mouth, lips, tongue, and others) that are used in the articulation of human speech, a tremendous degree of muscular control is required to achieve the fluency of a native speaker of a language. At birth the speech muscles are developed only to the extent that the larynx can control sustained cries. These speech muscles gradually develop, and control of some complex sounds in certain languages (in English the *r* and *l* are typical) is sometimes not achieved until after age five, although complete phonemic control is present in virtually all children before puberty.

Research on the acquisition of authentic control of the **phonology** of a foreign language supports the notion of a critical period. Most of the evidence indicates that persons beyond the age of puberty do not acquire what has come to be called **authentic** (native-speaker) pronunciation of the second language. Possible causes of such an age-based factor have already been discussed: neuromuscular plasticity, cerebral development, sociobiological programs, and the environment of sociocultural influences.

It is tempting immediately to cite exceptions to the rule ("My Aunt Mary learned French at twenty-five, and everyone in France said she sounded just like a native"). These exceptions, however, appear to be (a) isolated instances or (b) only anecdotally supported. True, there are special people who possess somewhere within their competence the ability to override neurobiological critical period effects and to achieve a virtually perfect nativelike pronunciation of a foreign language. But in terms of statistical probability (see Scovel 1988), it is clear that the chances of any one individual commencing a second language after puberty and achieving a scientifically verifiable authentic native accent are infinitesimal.

So, where do we go from here? First, some sample studies, spanning two decades, will serve as examples of the kind of research on adult phonological acquisition that appears to contradict Scovel's "strong" CPH.

Gerald Neufeld (1977, 1979, 1980) undertook a set of studies to determine to what extent adults could approximate native-speaker accents in a second language never before encountered. In his earliest experiment, twenty adult native English speakers were taught to imitate ten utterances, each from one to sixteen syllables in length, in Japanese and in Chinese. Native-speaking Japanese and Chinese judges listened to the taped imitations. The results indicated that eleven of the Japanese and nine of the Chinese imitations were judged to have been produced by "native speakers." While Neufeld recognized the limitations of his own studies, he suggested that "older students have neither lost their sensitivity to subtle differences in sounds, rhythm, and pitch nor the ability to reproduce these sounds and contours" (1979: 234). Nevertheless, Scovel (1988: 154–159) and Long (1990b: 266–268) later pointed out glaring experimental flaws in Neufeld's experiments, stemming from the methodology used to judge "native speaker" and from the information initially given to the judges.

In more recent years, Moyer (1999) and Bongaerts, Planken, and Schils (1995) have also challenged the strong version of the CPH. Moyer's study with native English-speaking graduate students of German upheld the strong CPH: subjects' performance was not judged to be comparable to native speakers of German. The Bongaerts et al. study reported on a group of adult Dutch speakers of English, all late learners, who recorded a monologue, a reading of a short text, and readings of isolated sentences and isolated words. Some of the non-native performances, for some of the trials, were judged to have come from native speakers. However, in a later review of this study, Scovel (1997: 213) carefully noted that it was also the case that many native speakers of English in their study were judged to be nonnative! The earlier Neufeld experiments and these more recent studies have thus essentially left the strong CPH unchallenged.

Upon reviewing the research on age and accent acquisition, as Scovel (1999) did, we are left with powerful evidence of a critical period for accent, but for accent only! It is important to remember in all these considerations that pronunciation of a language is not by any means the sole criterion for acquisition, nor is it really the most important one. We all know people who have less than perfect pronunciation but who also have magnificent and fluent control of a second language, control that can even exceed that of many native speakers. I like to call this the "Henry Kissinger effect" in honor of the former U.S. Secretary of State whose German accent is so noticeable yet who is clearly more eloquent than the large majority of native speakers of American English. The acquisition of the communicative and functional purposes of language is, in most circumstances, far more important than a perfect native accent. Scovel (1988: 186) captured the spirit of this way of looking at second language acquisition:

> For me, the acquisition of a new language will remain a phenomenon of natural fascination and mystery, not simply because it is a special skill of such incredible complexity that it remains one of the greatest achievements of the human mind, but because it also is a testimony of how much we can accomplish within the limitations that nature has placed upon us.

Perhaps, in our everyday encounters with second language users, we are too quick to criticize the "failure" of adult second language learners by nitpicking at minor pronunciation points or nonintrusive grammatical errors. Cook (1995: 55) warned against "using native accent as the yardstick" in our penchant for holding up monolingualism as the standard. And so, maybe instead, we can turn those perspectives into a more positive focus on the "multi-competence" (Cook 1995: 52) of second language learners. Instead of being so perplexed and concerned about how bad people are at learning second languages, we should be fascinated with how much those same learners have accomplished.

Today researchers are continuing the quest for answers to child–adult differences by looking beyond simple phonological factors. Bongaerts et al. (1995) found results that suggested that certain learner characteristics and contexts may work together to override the disadvantages of a late start. Slavoff and Johnson (1995) found that younger children (ages seven to nine) did not have a particular advantage in rate of learning over older (ten- to twelve-year-old) children. Longitudinal studies such as Ioup et al.'s (1994) study of a highly nativelike adult learner of Egyptian Arabic are useful in their focus on the factors beyond phonology that might be relevant in helping us to be more successful in teaching second languages to adults. Studies on the effect of input, on lexical acquisition, on Universal Grammar (see Singleton & Lengyel 1995), and on discourse acquisition are highly promising domains of research on age and acquisition.

COGNITIVE CONSIDERATIONS

Human cognition develops rapidly throughout the first sixteen years of life and less rapidly thereafter. Some cognitive changes are critical; others are more gradual and difficult to detect. Jean Piaget (1972; Piaget & Inhelder 1969) outlined the course of intellectual development in a child through various stages:

- Sensorimotor stage (birth to two)
- Preoperational stage (ages two to seven)
- Operational stage (ages seven to sixteen)
  - Concrete operational stage (ages seven to eleven)
  - Formal operational stage (ages eleven to sixteen).

A critical stage for a consideration of the effects of age on second language acquisition appears to occur, in Piaget's outline, at puberty (age eleven in his model). It is here that a person becomes capable of abstraction, of formal thinking which transcends concrete experience and direct perception. Cognitively, then, a strong argument can be made for a critical period of language acquisition by connecting language acquisition and the concrete/formal stage transition.

Ausubel (1964) hinted at the relevance of such a connection when he noted that adults learning a second language could profit from certain grammatical explanations and deductive thinking that obviously would be pointless for a child. Whether adults do in fact profit from such explanations depends, of course, on the suitability and efficiency of the explanation, the teacher, the context, and other pedagogical variables. We have observed, though, that children do learn second languages well without the benefit—or hindrance—of formal operational thought. Does this capacity of formal, abstract thought have a facilitating or inhibiting effect on language acquisition in adults? Ellen Rosansky (1975: 96) offered an explanation noting that initial language acquisition takes place when the child is highly "centered": "He is not only egocentric at this time, but when faced with a problem he can focus (and then only fleetingly) on one dimension at a time. This lack of flexibility and lack of decentration may well be a necessity for language acquisition."

Young children are generally not "aware" that they are acquiring a language, nor are they aware of societal values and attitudes placed on one language or another. It is said that "a watched pot never boils"; is it possible that a language learner who is too consciously aware of what he or she is doing will have difficulty in learning the second language?

You may be tempted to answer that question affirmatively, but there is both logical and anecdotal counterevidence. Logically, a superior intellect should facilitate what is in one sense a highly complex intellectual activity. Anecdotal evidence shows that some adults who have been successful language learners have been very much aware of the process they were going through, even to the point of utilizing self-made paradigms and other fabricated linguistic devices to facilitate the learning process. So, if mature cognition is a liability to successful second language acquisition, clearly some intervening variables allow some persons to be very successful second language learners after puberty. These variables may in most cases lie outside the cognitive domain entirely, perhaps more centrally in the affective—or emotional—domain.

The lateralization hypothesis may provide another key to cognitive differences between child and adult language acquisition. As the child matures into adulthood, the left hemisphere (which controls the analytical and intellectual functions) becomes more dominant than the right hemisphere (which controls the emotional functions). It is possible that the dominance of the left hemisphere contributes to a tendency to overanalyze and to be too intellectually centered on the task of second language learning.

Another construct that should be considered in examining the cognitive domain is the Piagetian notion of **equilibration**. Equilibration is defined as "progressive interior organization of knowledge in a stepwise fashion" (Sullivan 1967: 12), and is related to the concept of equilibrium. That is, cognition develops as a process of moving from states of doubt and uncertainty (disequilibrium) to stages of resolution and certainty (equilibrium) and then back to further doubt that is, in time, also resolved. And so the cycle continues. Piaget (1970) claimed that conceptual development is a process of progressively moving from states of disequilibrium to equilibrium and that periods of disequilibrium mark virtually all cognitive development up through age fourteen or fifteen, when formal operations finally are firmly organized and equilibrium is reached.

It is conceivable that disequilibrium may provide significant motivation for language acquisition: language interacts with cognition to achieve equilibrium. Perhaps until that state of final equilibrium is reached, the child is cognitively ready and eager to acquire the language necessary for achieving the cognitive equilibrium of adulthood. That same child was, until that time, decreasingly tolerant of cognitive ambiguities. Children are amazingly indifferent to contradictions, but intellectual growth produces an awareness of ambiguities about them and heightens the need for resolution. Perhaps a general intolerance of contradictions produces an acute awareness of the enormous complexities of acquiring an additional language, and so perhaps around the age of fourteen or fifteen, the prospect of learning a second language becomes overwhelming, thus discouraging the learner from proceeding a step at a time as a younger child would do.

The final consideration in the cognitive domain is the distinction that Ausubel made between *rote* and *meaningful* learning. Ausubel noted that people of all ages have little need for rote, mechanistic learning that is not related to existing knowledge and experience. Rather, most items are acquired by meaningful learning, by anchoring and relating new items and experiences to knowledge that exists in the cognitive framework. It is a myth to contend that children are good rote learners, that they make good use of meaningless repetition and mimicking. We have already seen in Chapter 2 that children's practice and imitation is a very meaningful activity that is contextualized and purposeful. Adults have developed even greater concentration and so have greater ability for rote learning, but they usually use rote learning only for short-term memory or for somewhat artificial purposes. By inference, we may conclude that the foreign language classroom should not become the locus of excessive rote activity: rote drills, pattern practice without context, rule recitation, and other activities that are not in the context of meaningful communication.

It is interesting to note that C2–A2 comparisons almost always refer, in the case of children, to natural untutored learning, and for adults, to the classroom learning of a second language. Even so, many foreign language classrooms around the world still utilize an excessive number of rote-learning procedures. So, if adults learning a foreign language by rote methods are compared with children learning a second language in a natural, meaningful context, the child's learning will seem to be superior. The cause of such superiority may not be in the age of the person, but in the context of learning. The child happens to be learning language meaningfully, and the adult is not.

The cognitive domain holds yet other areas of interest for comparing first and second language acquisition. These areas will be treated more fully in Chapters 4 and 5. We turn now to what may be the most complex, yet the most illuminating, perspective on age and acquisition: the affective domain.

AFFECTIVE CONSIDERATIONS

Human beings are emotional creatures. At the heart of all thought and meaning and action is emotion. As "intellectual" as we would like to think we are, we are influenced by our emotions. It is only logical, then, to look at the affective (emotional) domain for some of the most significant answers to the problems of contrasting the differences between first and second language acquisition.

Research on the affective domain in second language acquisition has been mounting steadily for a number of decades. This research has been inspired by a number of factors. Not the least of these is the fact that linguistic theory is now asking the deepest possible questions about human language, with some applied linguists examining the inner being of the person to discover if, in the affective side of human behavior, there lies an explanation to the mysteries of language acquisition. A full treatment of affective variables in second language acquisition is provided in Chapters 6 and 7; in this chapter it is important to take a brief look at selected affective factors as they relate to the age and acquisition issue.

The affective domain includes many factors: empathy, self-esteem, extroversion, inhibition, imitation, anxiety, attitudes—the list could go on. Some of these may seem at first rather far removed from language learning, but when we consider the pervasive nature of language, any affective factor can conceivably be relevant to second language learning.

A case in point is the role of egocentricity in human development. Very young children are highly egocentric. The world revolves about them, and they see all events as focusing on themselves. Small babies at first do not even distinguish a separation between themselves and the world around them. A rattle held in a baby's hand, for example, is simply an inseparable extension of the baby as long as it is grasped; when the baby drops it or loses sight of it, the rattle ceases to exist. As children grow older they become more aware of themselves, more self-conscious as they seek both to define and to understand their self-identity. In preadolescence children develop an acute consciousness of themselves as separate and identifiable entities but ones which, in their still-wavering insecurity, need protecting. They therefore develop **inhibitions** about this self-identity, fearing to expose too much self-doubt. At puberty these inhibitions are heightened in the trauma of undergoing critical physical, cognitive, and emotional changes. Adolescents must acquire a totally new physical, cognitive, and emotional identity. Their egos are affected not only in how they understand themselves but also in how they reach out beyond themselves, how they relate to others socially, and how they use the communicative process to bring on affective equilibrium.

Several decades ago, Alexander Guiora, a researcher in the study of personality variables in second language learning, proposed what he called the **language ego** (Guiora et al. 1972b; see also Ehrman 1993) to account for the identity a person develops in reference to the language he or she speaks. For any monolingual person, the language ego involves the interaction of the native language and ego development. One's self-identity is inextricably bound up with one's language, for it is in the communicative process—the process of sending out messages and having them "bounced" back—that such identities are confirmed, shaped, and reshaped. Guiora suggested that the language ego may account for the difficulties that adults have in learning a second language. The child's ego is dynamic and growing and flexible through the age of puberty. Thus a new language at this stage does not pose a substantial "threat" or inhibition to the ego, and adaptation is made relatively easily as long as there are no undue confounding socio-cultural factors such as, for example, a damaging attitude toward a language or language group at a young age. Then the simultaneous physical, emotional, and cognitive changes of puberty give rise to a defensive mechanism in which the language ego becomes protective and defensive. The language ego clings to the security of the native language to protect the fragile ego of the young adult. The language ego, which has now become part and parcel of self-identity, is threatened, and thus a context develops in which you must be willing to make a fool of yourself in the trial-and-error struggle of speaking and understanding a foreign language. Younger children are less frightened because they are less aware of language *forms*, and the possibility of making mistakes in those forms—mistakes that one really must make in an attempt to communicate spontaneously—does not concern them greatly.

It is no wonder, then, that the acquisition of a new language ego is an enormous undertaking not only for young adolescents but also for an adult who has grown comfortable and secure in his or her own identity and who possesses inhibitions that serve as a wall of defensive protection around the ego. Making the leap to a new or second identity is no simple matter; it can be successful only when one musters the necessary ego strength to overcome inhibitions. It is possible that the successful adult language learner is someone who can bridge this affective gap. Some of the seeds of success might have been sown early in life. In a bilingual setting, for example, if a child has already learned one second language in childhood, then affectively, learning a third language as an adult might represent much less of a threat. Or such seeds may be independent of a bilingual setting; they may simply have arisen out of whatever combination of nature and nurture makes for the development of a strong ego.

In looking at SLA in children, it is important to distinguish younger and older children. Preadolescent children of nine or ten, for example, are beginning to develop inhibitions, and it is conceivable that children of this age have a good deal of affective dissonance to overcome as they attempt to learn a second language. This could account for difficulties that older pre-pubescent children encounter in acquiring a second language. Adult vs. child comparisons are of course highly relevant. We know from both observational and research evidence that mature adults manifest a number of inhibitions. These inhibitions surface in modern language classes where the learner's attempts to speak in the foreign language are often fraught with embarrassment. We have also observed the same inhibition in the "natural" setting (a nonclassroom setting, such as a learner living in a foreign culture), although in such instances there is the likelihood that the necessity to communicate overrides the inhibitions.

Other affective factors seem to hinge on the basic notion of ego identification. It would appear that the study of second language learning as the acquisition of a **second identity** might pose a fruitful and important issue in understanding not only some differences between child and adult first and second language learning but second language learning in general (see Chapter 7).

Another affectively related variable deserves mention here even though it will be given fuller consideration in Chapter 6: the role of **attitudes** in language learning. From the growing body of literature on attitudes, it seems clear that negative attitudes can affect success in learning a language. Very young children, who are not developed enough cognitively to possess "attitudes" toward races, cultures, ethnic groups, classes of people, and languages, may be less affected than adults. Macnamara (1975: 79) noted that "a child suddenly transported from Montreal to Berlin will rapidly learn German no matter what he thinks of the Germans." But as children reach school age, they also begin to acquire certain attitudes toward types and stereotypes of people. Most of these attitudes are "taught," consciously or unconsciously, by parents, other adults, and peers. The learning of negative attitudes toward the people who speak the second language or toward the second language itself has been shown to affect the success of language learning in persons from school age on up.

Finally, **peer pressure** is a particularly important variable in considering child–adult comparisons. The peer pressure children encounter in language learning is quite unlike what the adult experiences. Children usually have strong constraints upon them to conform. They are told in words, thoughts, and actions that they had better "be like the rest of the kids." Such peer pressure extends to language. Adults experience some peer pressure, but of a different kind. Adults tend to tolerate linguistic differences more than children, and therefore errors in speech are more easily excused. If adults can understand a second language speaker, for example, they will usually provide positive cognitive and affective feedback, a level of tolerance that might encourage some adult learners to "get by." Children are harsher critics of one another's actions and words and may thus provide a necessary and sufficient degree of mutual pressure to learn the second language.

LINGUISTIC CONSIDERATIONS

We have so far looked at learners themselves and considered a number of different issues in age and acquisition. Now we turn to some issues that center on the subject matter itself: language. What are some of the **linguistic** considerations in age-related questions about SLA? A growing number of research studies are now available to shed some light on the linguistic processes of second language learning and how those processes differ between children and adults. A good deal of this research will be treated in Chapters 8 through 10, but here we will look briefly at some specific issues that arise in examining the child's acquisition of a second language.

Bilingualism

It is clear that children learning two languages simultaneously acquire them by the use of similar strategies. They are, in essence, learning two first languages, and the key to success is in distinguishing separate contexts for the two languages. People who learn a second language in such separate contexts can often be described as **coordinate bilinguals**; they have two meaning systems, as opposed to **compound bilinguals** who have one meaning system from which both languages operate. Children generally do not have problems with "mixing up languages," regardless of the separateness of contexts for use of the languages. Moreover, "bilinguals are not two monolinguals in the same head" (Cook 1995: 58). Most bilinguals, however, engage in **code-switching** (the act of inserting words, phrases, or even longer stretches of one language into the other), especially when communicating with another bilingual.

In some cases the acquisition of both languages in bilingual children is slightly slower than the normal schedule for first language acquisition. However, a respectable stockpile of research (see Reynolds 1991; Schinke-Llano 1989) shows a considerable cognitive benefit of early childhood bilingualism, supporting Lambert's (1972) contention that bilingual children are more facile at concept formation and have a greater mental flexibility.

Interference Between First and Second Languages

A good deal of the research on nonsimultaneous second language acquisition, in both children and adults, has focused on the interfering effects of the first and second languages. For the most part, research confirms that the linguistic and cognitive processes of second language learning in young children are in general similar to first language processes. Ravem (1968), Natalicio and Natalicio (1971), Dulay and Burt (1974a), Ervin-Tripp (1974), Milon (1974), and Hansen-Bede (1975), among others, concluded that similar strategies and linguistic features are present in both first and second language learning in children. Dulay and Burt (1974a) found, for example, that 86 percent of more than 500 errors made by Spanish-speaking children learning English reflected normal developmental characteristics—

that is, expected intralingual strategies, not interference errors from the first language. Hansen-Bede (1975) examined such linguistic structures as possession, gender, word order, verb forms, questions, and negation in an English-speaking three-year-old child who learned Urdu upon moving to Pakistan. In spite of some marked linguistic contrasts between English and Urdu, the child's acquisition did not appear to show first language interference and, except for negation, showed similar strategies and rules for both the first and the second language.

Interference in Adults

Adult second language linguistic processes are more vulnerable to the effect of the first language on the second, especially the farther apart the two events are. Whether adults learn a foreign language in a classroom or out in the "arena," they approach the second language—either focally or peripherally—systematically, and they attempt to formulate linguistic rules on the basis of whatever linguistic information is available to them: information from the native language, the second language, teachers, classmates, and peers. The nature and sequencing of these systems has been the subject of a good deal of second language research in the last half of the twentieth century. What we have learned above all else from this research is that the saliency of interference from the first language does not imply that interference is the most relevant or most crucial factor in adult second language acquisition. Adults learning a second language manifest some of the same types of errors found in children learning their first language (see Chapter 8).

Adults, more cognitively secure, appear to operate from the solid foundation of the first language and thus manifest more interference. But it was pointed out earlier that adults, too, manifest errors not unlike some of the errors children make, the result of creative perception of the second language and an attempt to discover its rules apart from the rules of the first language. The first language, however, may be more readily used to bridge gaps that the adult learner cannot fill by generalization within the second language. In this case we do well to remember that the first language can be a facilitating factor, and not just an interfering factor.

Order of Acquisition

One of the first steps toward demonstrating the importance of factors other than first language interference was taken in a series of research studies by Heidi Dulay and Marina Burt (1972, 1974a, 1974b, 1976). They even went so far at one point as to claim that "transfer of L1 syntactic patterns rarely occurs" in child second language acquisition (1976: 72). They claimed that children learning a second language use a **creative construction** process, just as they do in their first language. This conclusion was supported by some massive research data collected on the acquisition order of eleven English morphemes in children learning English as a second language. Dulay and Burt found a common order of acquisition among children of several native language backgrounds, an order very similar to that found by Roger Brown (1973) using the same morphemes but for children acquiring English as their first language.

There were logical and methodological arguments about the validity of morpheme-order findings. Rosansky (1976) argued that the statistical procedures used were suspect, and others (Larsen-Freeman 1976; Roger Andersen 1978) noted that eleven English morphemes constitute only a minute portion of English syntax, and therefore lack generalizability. More recently, Zobl and Liceras (1994: 161), in a "search for a unified theoretical account for the L1 and L2 morpheme orders," reexamined the morpheme-order studies and concluded the generalizability of morpheme acquisition order.

We have touched on several significant perspectives on questions about age and acquisition. In all this, it is important to maintain the distinction among the three types (C1–C2; C2–A2; C1–A2) of age and language comparisons mentioned at the beginning of the chapter. By considering three logically possible comparisons, unnecessary loopholes in reasoning should be minimized. While some answers to our questions are less than conclusive, in many cases research has been historically revealing. By operating on our collective understanding of the effects of age on acquisition, one can construct one's own personal integrated understanding of that relationship, and how that relationship might hold fruitful implications for second language teaching.

Above all else, I call attention the balanced perspective recently offered by Thomas Scovel (1999: 1). "The younger, the better" is a myth that has been fueled by media hype and, sometimes, "junk science." We are led to believe that children are better at learning foreign languages without fully considering all the evidence and without looking at all aspects of acquisition. On at least several planes—literacy, vocabulary, pragmatics, schematic knowledge, and even syntax—adults have been shown to be superior learners (Scovel 1999). Perpetuating a younger-the-better myth in arguments about bilingual education and other forms of early language, intervention does a disservice to our children and to our educational enterprise. We have seen in this chapter that there certainly appear to be some potential advantages to an early age for SLA, but there is absolutely no evidence that an adult cannot overcome all of those disadvantages save one, accent, and the latter is hardly the quintessential criterion for effective interpersonal communication.

ISSUES IN FIRST LANGUAGE ACQUISITION REVISITED

Having examined the comparison of first and second language acquisition across a number of domains of human behavior, we turn in this final section to a brief consideration of the eight issues in first language acquisition that were presented in Chapter 2. In most cases the implications of these issues are already clear, from the comments in the previous chapter, from the reader's logical thinking, or from comments in this chapter. Therefore what follows is a way of highlighting the implications of the issues for second language learning.

Competence and Performance

It is as difficult to "get at" linguistic competence in a second language as it is in a first. For children, judgments of grammaticality may elicit a second language "pop-go-weasel" effect. You can be a little more direct in inferring competence in adults; adults can make choices between two alternative forms, and sometimes they manifest an awareness of grammaticality in a second language. But you must remember that adults are not in general able to verbalize "rules" and paradigms consciously even in their native language. Furthermore, in judging utterances in the modern language classroom and responses on various tests, teachers need to be cautiously attentive to the discrepancy between performance on a given day or in a given context and competence in a second language in general. Remember that one isolated sample of second language speech may on the surface appear to be rather malformed until you consider that sample in comparison with the everyday mistakes and errors of native speakers.

Comprehension and Production

Whether or not comprehension is derived from a separate level of competence, there is a universal distinction between comprehension and production. Learning a second language usually means learning to speak it *and* to comprehend it! When we say "Do you speak English?" or "Parlez-vous français?" we usually mean "and do you *understand* it too?" Learning involves both modes (unless you are interested only in, say, learning to read in the second language). So teaching involves attending to both compre-

hension and production and the full consideration of the gaps and differences between the two. Adult second language learners will, like children,
often *hear* a distinction but not be able to produce it. The inability to produce an item, therefore, should not be taken to mean that the learner
cannot comprehend the item.

Nature or Nurture?

What happens after puberty to the magic "little black box" called LAD?
Does the adult suffer from linguistic "hardening of the arteries"? Does LAD
"grow up" somehow? Does lateralization signal the death of LAD? We do
not have complete answers to these questions, but there have been some
hints in the discussion of physical, cognitive, and affective factors. What we
do know is that adults and children alike appear to have the capacity to
acquire a second language at any age. The only trick that nature might play
on adults is to virtually rule out the acquisition of authentic accent. As you
have seen above, this still leaves a wide swath of language properties that
may actually be more efficiently acquired in an adult. If an adult does not
acquire a second language successfully, it is probably because of intervening cognitive or affective variables and not the absence of innate capacities. Defining those intervening variables appears to be more relevant than
probing the properties of innateness.

Universals

In recent years Universal Grammar has come to the attention of a growing
number of researchers. The conclusions from this research are mixed (Van
Buren 1996). Research on child SLA suggests that children's developing
second language grammars are indeed constrained by UG (Lakshmanan
1995). But it is not immediately clear whether this knowledge is available
directly from a truly universal "source," or through the mediation of the first
language. Yet even in the first language, UG seems to predict certain syntactic domains but not others. This has led some to conclude that second
language learners have only "partial access" to UG (O'Grady 1996). But Bley-
Vroman (1988) went a step further in claiming a "no access" position for
adults learning a second language: adults acquire second language systems
without any reference to UG.

Others disagree strongly with the partial- and no-access claim. Cook
(1993: 244) provocatively asks, "Why should second language users be
treated as failed monolinguals? . . . A proper account of second language
learning would treat multi-competence on its own terms, not in L1 related
terms." In other words, why look to monolingualism as a standard by which
UG or any other means of inquiry should be modeled? If UG models do

not fit second language learning processes, then it may be "the description of UG that is at fault, and not the L2 learner" (Cook 1993: 245). Where does this leave us? Perhaps in a position of keeping an open mind as teachers and an inquisitive spirit as researchers.

Systematicity and Variability

It is clear that second language acquisition, both child and adult, is characterized by both systematicity and variability. Second language linguistic development appears in many instances to mirror the first language acquisition process: learners induce rules, generalize across a category, overgeneralize, and proceed in stages of development (more on this in Chapter 9). The variability of second language data poses thorny problems that have been addressed by people like Tarone (1988), Ellis (1987, 1989), and Preston (1996). The variability of second language acquisition is exacerbated by a host of cognitive, affective, cultural, and contextual variables that are sometimes not applicable to a first language learning situation.

Language and Thought

Another intricately complex issue in both first and second language acquisition is the precise relationship between language and thought. We can see that language helps to shape thinking and that thinking helps to shape language. What happens to this interdependence when a second language is acquired? Does the bilingual person's memory consist of one storage system (compound bilingualism) or two (coordinate bilingualism)? The second language learner is clearly presented with a tremendous task in sorting out new meanings from old, distinguishing thoughts and concepts in one language that are similar but not quite parallel to the second language, perhaps really acquiring a whole new system of conceptualization. The second language teacher needs to be acutely aware of cultural thought patterns that may be as interfering as the linguistic patterns themselves.

Imitation

While children are good deep-structure imitators (centering on meaning, not surface features), adults can fare much better in imitating surface structure (by rote mechanisms) if they are explicitly directed to do so. Sometimes their ability to center on surface distinctions is a distracting factor; at other times it is helpful. Adults learning a second language might do well to attend consciously to truth value and to be less aware of surface structure as they communicate. The implication is that meaningful contexts for language learning are necessary; second language learners ought not to become too preoccupied with form lest they lose sight of the function and purpose of language.

Practice

Too many language classes are filled with rote practice that centers on surface forms. Most cognitive psychologists agree that the frequency of stimuli and the number of times spent practicing a form are not highly important in learning an item. What is important is meaningfulness. Contextualized, appropriate, meaningful communication in the second language seems to be the best possible practice the second language learner could engage in.

Input

In the case of classroom second language learning, parental input is replaced by teacher input. Teachers might do well to be as deliberate, but meaningful, in their communications with students as the parent is to the child since input is as important to the second language learner as it is to the first language learner. And that input should foster meaningful communicative use of the language in appropriate contexts.

Discourse

We have only begun to scratch the surface of possibilities of second language discourse analysis. As we search for better ways of teaching communicative competence to second language learners, research on the acquisition of discourse becomes more and more important. Perhaps a study of children's amazing dexterity in acquiring rules of conversation and in perceiving intended meaning will help us to find ways of teaching such capacities to second language learners. We will look more at these issues in Chapter 9.

In the Classroom: The Audiolingual Method

In the first part of the twentieth century, the Direct Method did not take hold in the United States the way it did in Europe. While one could easily procure native-speaking teachers of modern foreign languages in Europe, such was not the case in the United States. Also, European high school and university students did not have to travel far to find opportunities to put the oral skills of another language to actual, practical use. Moreover, U.S. educational institutions had become firmly convinced that a reading approach to foreign languages was more useful than an oral approach, given the perceived linguistic isolation of the United States at the time. The highly influential Coleman Report of 1929 (Coleman 1929) had persuaded foreign language teachers that it was impractical to teach oral skills, and that reading should become the focus. Thus schools returned in the 1930s and 1940s to Grammar Translation, "the handmaiden of reading" (Bowen et al. 1985).

The outbreak of World War II thrust the United States into a worldwide conflict, heightening the need for Americans to become orally proficient in the languages of both their allies and their enemies. The time was ripe for a language-teaching revolution. The U.S. military provided the impetus with funding for special, intensive language courses that focused on the aural/oral skills; these courses came to be known as the Army Specialized Training Program (ASTP), or, more colloquially, the "Army Method." Characteristic of these courses was a great deal of oral activity—pronunciation and pattern drills and conversation practice—with virtually none of the grammar and translation found in traditional classes. It was ironic that numerous foundation stones of the discarded Direct Method were borrowed and injected into this new approach. Soon, the success of the Army Method and the revived national interest in foreign languages spurred educational institutions to adopt the new methodology. In all its variations and adaptations, the Army Method came to be known in the 1950s as the Audiolingual Method.

The Audiolingual Method (ALM) was firmly grounded in linguistic and psychological theory. Structural linguists of the 1940s and 1950s were engaged in what they claimed was a "scientific descriptive analysis" of various languages; teaching methodologists saw a direct application of such analysis to teaching linguistic patterns (Fries 1945). (We will return to this particular theory-practice issue in Chapter 8.) At the same time, behavioristic psychologists advocated conditioning and habit-formation models of learning, which were perfectly married with the mimicry drills and pattern practices of audiolingual methodology.

The characteristics of the ALM may be summed up in the following list (adapted from Prator and Celce-Murcia 1979):

1. New material is presented in dialog form.
2. There is dependence on mimicry, memorization of set phrases, and overlearning.
3. Structures are sequenced by means of contrastive analysis and taught one at a time.
4. Structural patterns are taught using repetitive drills.
5. There is little or no grammatical explanation: grammar is taught by inductive analogy rather than deductive explanation.
6. Vocabulary is strictly limited and learned in context.
7. There is much use of tapes, language labs, and visual aids.
8. Great importance is attached to pronunciation.
9. Very little use of the mother tongue by teachers is permitted.

10. Successful responses are immediately reinforced.

11. There is a great effort to get students to produce error-free utterances.

12. There is a tendency to manipulate language and disregard content.

For a number of reasons the ALM enjoyed many years of popularity, and even to this day, adaptations of the ALM are found in contemporary methodologies. The ALM was firmly rooted in respectable theoretical perspectives at the time. Materials were carefully prepared, tested, and disseminated to educational institutions. "Success" could be more overtly experienced by students as they practiced their dialogs in off-hours.

But the popularity did not last forever. Due in part to Wilga Rivers's (1964) eloquent exposure of the shortcomings of the ALM, and its ultimate failure to teach long-term communicative proficiency, its popularity waned. We discovered that language was not really acquired through a process of habit formation and overlearning, that errors were not necessarily to be avoided at all costs, and that structural linguistics did not tell us everything about language that we needed to know. While the ALM was a valiant attempt to reap the fruits of language teaching methodologies that had preceded it, in the end it still fell short, as all methods do. But we learned something from the very failure of the ALM to do everything it had promised, and we moved forward.

TOPICS AND QUESTIONS FOR STUDY AND DISCUSSION

[Note: (I) individual work; (G) group or pair work; (C) whole-class discussion.]

1. (G/C) Each group or pair should be assigned one of the seven common arguments (page 50) cited by Stern (1970) that were used to justify analogies between first language learning and second language teaching. In the group, determine what is assumed or presupposed in the statement. Then reiterate the flaw in each analogy. Report conclusions back to the whole class for further discussion.

2. (C) Are there students in the class who were exposed to, or learned, second languages before puberty? What were the circumstances, and what difficulties, if any, were encountered? Has authentic pronunciation in the language remained to this day?

3. (C) Is there anyone in the class, or anyone who knows someone else, who started learning a second language after puberty and who nevertheless has an almost "perfect" accent? How did you assess whether

the accent was perfect? Why do you suppose such a person was able to be so successful?

4. (I) In your words, write down the essence of Scovel's claim that the acquisition of a native accent around the age of puberty is an evolutionary left-over of sociobiological critical periods evident in many species of animals and birds. In view of widely accepted cross-cultural, cross-linguistic, and interracial marriages today, how relevant is the biological claim for mating within the gene pool?

5. (G/C) In groups, try to determine the criteria for deciding whether or not someone is an authentic native speaker of your native language. In the process, consider the wide variety of "World Englishes" commonly spoken today. How clearly definitive can your criteria be? Talk about occupations, if any, in which a native accent is indispensable. Share with the rest of the class, and try to come to a consensus.

6. (G) In groups, talk about any cognitive or affective blocks you have experienced in your own attempts to learn a second language. What could you do (or what could you have done) to overcome those barriers?

7. (I) Summarize the ten "revisited" issues in your own words. How does your understanding of those issues, as they apply to second language learning, help you to formulate a better understanding of the total process of second language acquisition? Cite what you think might be some practical classroom implications of the ten issues.

8. (C) Do you think it is worthwhile to teach children a second language in the classroom? If so, how might approaches and methods differ between a class of children and a class of adults?

SUGGESTED READINGS

Scovel, Thomas. 1988. *A Time to Speak: A Psycholinguistic Inquiry into the Critical Period for Human Speech.* New York: Newbury House Publishers.

Scovel, Thomas. 1999. "'The Younger the Better' Myth and Bilingual Education." In Gonzalez, Roseann & Melis, Ildiko (Eds.), *Language Ideologies: Critical Perspectives on the English Only Movement.* Urbana, IL: National Council of Teachers of English.

For two entertaining and informative reads, I highly recommend Thomas Scovel's book and article. The former is well-researched and written in a user-friendly style, and the latter is a down-to-earth, practical exposé of common myths about age and acquisition.

Singleton, David and Lengyel, Zsolt (Eds.). 1995. *The Age Factor in Second Language Acquisition.* Clevedon, U.K.: Multilingual Matters.

For some original research data, and for a good current set of examples of research on the age acquisition issue, consult Singleton and Lengyel's anthology. A warning: some of the articles may be difficult for beginning graduate students in the field.

Cook, Vivian. 1993. *Linguistics and Second Language Acquisition.* New York: St. Martin's Press: 200–245.

This is a very reader-friendly survey of the field of second language acquisition. Especially useful are the chapters on morpheme acquisition, pidgins and creoles, and Universal Grammar.

LANGUAGE LEARNING EXPERIENCE: JOURNAL ENTRY 3

[Note: See pages 18 and 19 of Chapter 1 for general guidelines for writing a journal on a previous or concurrent language learning experience.]

• How good do you think your pronunciation of your foreign language is? Assuming you would not expect to be "perfect," what steps can you take (or could you have taken) to improve your pronunciation to a point of maximum clarity of articulation?

• Children might have some secrets of success: not monitoring themselves too much, not analyzing grammar, not being too worried about their egos, shedding inhibitions, not letting the native language interfere much. In what way did you, or could you, put those secrets to use in your own learning?

• In learning a foreign language, were any aspects (such as listening discrimination exercises, pronunciation drills, learning grammar rules, small group conversations, reading, or writing) easier than others for you? Analyze.

• Do you think you might have some advantages over children in learning a foreign language? Speculate on what those advantages might be. Then, if possible, resolve to capitalize on them.

CHAPTER 4

HUMAN

LEARNING

S O FAR, in outlining a theory of second language acquisition, we have discovered that the cognitive domain of human behavior is of key importance in the acquisition of both a first and a second language. The processes of perceiving, attending, storing, and recalling are central to the task of internalizing a language. In this chapter we focus specifically on cognitive processes by examining the general nature of human learning. In the first part of the chapter, different learning theories are outlined. Then, we deal with some other universal learning principles. Finally, some current thoughts about aptitude and intelligence are presented.

LEARNING AND TRAINING

How do human beings learn? Are there certain basic principles of learning that apply to all learning acts? Is one theory of learning "better" than another? If so, how can you evaluate the usefulness of a theory? These and other important questions need to be answered in order to achieve an integrated understanding of second language acquisition.

Before tackling theories of human learning directly, consider the following situation as an illustration of sorting out cognitive considerations in any task in which you are trying to determine what it means to conclude that an organism has learned something. Suppose you have decided to train your somewhat untalented pet dog to catch frisbees in midair at a distance of thirty or more yards. What would you need to know about your dog and how would you go about the training program?

First, you will need to specify *entry behavior:* what your dog already "knows." What abilities does it possess upon which you, the trainer, can build? What are its drives, needs, motivations, limitations? Next, you need to formulate explicitly the *goals* of the task. You have a general directive; what are your specific objectives? How successfully and with what sort of "style points" must this dog perform? In what differing environments? You would also need to devise some *methods of training*. Based on what you know about entry behavior and goals of the task, how would you go about the training process? Where would you begin? Would you start at three feet? Place the frisbee in the dog's mouth? Would you use rewards? Punishment? What alternatives would you have ready if the dog failed to learn? Finally, you would need some sort of *evaluation procedure*. How would you determine whether or not the dog had indeed learned what you set out to teach? You would need to determine short-term and long-term evaluation measures. If the dog performs correctly after one day of training, what will happen one month later? That is, will the dog *maintain* what it has learned?

Already a somewhat simple task has become quite complex with questions that require considerable forethought and expertise. But we are talking only about a dog performing a simple trick. If we talk about human beings learning a second language, the task is of course much, much more complex. Nevertheless, the questions and procedures that apply to you, the language teacher, are akin to those that applied to you, the dog trainer. You must have a comprehensive knowledge of the entry behavior of a person, of objectives you wish to reach, of possible methods that follow from your understanding of the first two factors, and of an evaluation procedure. These steps derive from your conception of how human beings learn, and that is what this chapter is all about.

In turning now to varied theories of how human beings learn, consider once again the definition of learning given in Chapter 1: "acquiring or getting of knowledge of a subject or a skill by study, experience, or instruction," or "a relatively permanent change in a behavioral tendency, . . . the result of reinforced practice." When we consider such definitions, it is clear that one can understand learning in many different ways, which is why there are so many different theories, extended definitions, and schools of thought on the topic of learning.

We now focus on how psychologists have defined **learning**, and we will look at these theories through the eyes of four psychologists, two representing a behavioristic viewpoint (Pavlov and Skinner), one representing a rational/cognitive stance (Ausubel), and one that stretches into what could be loosely defined as a constructivist school of thought (Rogers). The four positions should illustrate not only some of the history of learning theory, but also the diverse perspectives that form the foundations of varying language teaching approaches and methods.

PAVLOV'S CLASSICAL BEHAVIORISM

Certainly the best-known classical behaviorist is the Russian psychologist Ivan Pavlov, who at the turn of the century conducted a series of experiments in which he trained a dog to salivate to the tone of a tuning fork through a procedure that has come to be labeled **classical conditioning**. For Pavlov the learning process consisted of the formation of associations between stimuli and reflexive responses. All of us are aware that certain stimuli automatically produce or elicit rather specific responses or reflexes, and we have also observed that sometimes that reflex occurs in response to stimuli that appear to be indirectly related to the reflex. Pavlov used the salivation response to the sight or smell of food (an unconditioned response) in many of his pioneering experiments. In the classical experiment he trained a dog, by repeated occurrences, to associate the sound of a tuning fork with salivation until the dog acquired a **conditioned response**: salivation at the sound of the tuning fork. A previously neutral stimulus (the sound of the tuning fork) had acquired the power to elicit a response (salivation) that was originally elicited by another stimulus (the smell of meat).

Drawing on Pavlov's findings, John B. Watson (1913) coined the term **behaviorism**. In the empirical tradition of John Locke, Watson contended that human behavior should be studied objectively, rejecting mentalistic notions of innateness and instinct. He adopted classical conditioning theory as the explanation for all learning: by the process of conditioning, we build an array of stimulus–response connections, and more complex behaviors are learned by building up series or chains of responses. Pavlov's and Watson's emphasis on the study of overt behavior and rigorous adherence to the scientific method had a tremendous influence on learning theories for decades. Language teaching practices likewise for many years were influenced by a behavioristic tradition.

SKINNER'S OPERANT CONDITIONING

In 1938 B.F. Skinner published his *Behavior of Organisms* and in so doing established himself as one of the leading behaviorists in the United States. He followed the tradition of Watson, but other psychologists (see Anderson and Ausubel 1965: 5) have called Skinner a neobehaviorist because he added a unique dimension to behavioristic psychology. The classical conditioning of Pavlov was, according to Skinner, a highly specialized form of learning utilized mainly by animals and playing little part in human conditioning. Skinner called Pavlovian conditioning **respondent conditioning** since it was concerned with respondent behavior—that is, behavior that is *elicited* by a preceding stimulus.

Skinner's **operant conditioning** attempted to account for most of human learning and behavior. Operant behavior is behavior in which one "operates" on the environment; within this model the importance of stimuli is de-emphasized. For example, we cannot identify a specific stimulus leading a baby to rise to a standing position or to take a first step; we therefore need not be concerned about that stimulus, but we should be concerned about the consequences—the stimuli that follow the response. Stressing Thorndike's Law of Effect, Skinner demonstrated the importance of those events that follow a response. Suppose that another baby accidentally touches a nearby object and a tinkling bell-sound occurs. The infant may look in the direction from which the sound came, become curious about it, and after several such "accidental" responses discover exactly which toy it is that makes the sound and how to produce that sound. The baby operated on her environment. Her responses were reinforced until finally a particular concept or behavior was learned.

According to Skinner, the events or stimuli—the reinforcers—that follow a response and that tend to strengthen behavior or increase the probability of a recurrence of that response constitute a powerful force in the control of human behavior. Reinforcers are far stronger aspects of learning than is mere association of a prior stimulus with a following response, as in the classical conditioning model. We are governed by the consequences of our behavior, and therefore Skinner felt we ought, in studying human behavior, to study the effect of those consequences. And if we wish to control behavior, say, to teach someone something, we ought to attend carefully to reinforcers.

Operants are classes of responses. Crying, sitting down, walking, and batting a baseball are operants. They are sets of responses that are **emitted** and governed by the consequences they produce. In contrast, **respondents** are sets of responses that are **elicited** by identifiable stimuli. Certain physical reflex actions are respondents. Crying can be respondent or operant behavior. Sometimes crying is elicited in direct reaction to a hurt. Often, however, it is an *emitted* response that produces the consequences of getting fed, cuddled, played with, comforted, and so forth. Such operant crying can be controlled. If parents wait until a child's crying reaches a certain intensity before responding, loud crying is more likely to appear in the future. If parents ignore crying (when they are certain that it is operant crying), eventually the absence of reinforcers will extinguish the behavior.

Operant crying depends on its effect on the parents and is maintained or changed according to their response to it.

Skinner believed that, in keeping with the above principle, punishment "works to the disadvantage of both the punished organism and the punishing agency" (1953: 183). Punishment can be either the withdrawal of a positive reinforcer or the presentation of an aversive stimulus. More commonly we think of punishment as the latter—a spanking, a harsh reprimand—but the removal of certain positive reinforcers, such as a privilege, can also be considered a form of punishment. Skinner felt that in the long run, punishment does not actually eliminate behavior, but that mild punishment may be necessary for temporary suppression of an undesired response, although no punishment of such a kind should be meted out without positively reinforcing *alternate* responses.

The best method of extinction, said Skinner, is the absence of any reinforcement; however, the active reinforcement of alternative responses hastens that extinction. So if a parent wishes the children would not kick a football in the living room, Skinner would maintain that instead of punishing them adversely for such behavior when it occurs, the parent should refrain from any negative reaction and should instead provide positive reinforcement for kicking footballs outside; in this way the undesired behavior will be effectively extinguished. Such a procedure is, of course, easier said than done, especially if the children break your best table lamp in the absence of any punishment!

Skinner was extremely methodical and empirical in his theory of learning, to the point of being preoccupied with scientific controls. While many of his experiments were performed on lower animals, his theories had an impact on our understanding of human learning and on education. His book *The Technology of Teaching* (1968) was a classic in the field of programmed instruction. Following Skinner's model, one is led to believe that virtually any subject matter can be taught effectively and successfully by a carefully designed program of step-by-step reinforcement. Programmed instruction had its impact on foreign language teaching, though language is such complex behavior, penetrating so deeply into both cognitive and affective domains, that programmed instruction in languages was limited to very specialized subsets of language.

The impact of Skinnerian psychology on foreign language teaching extended well beyond programmed instruction. Skinner's *Verbal Behavior* (1957) described language as a system of verbal operants, and his understanding of the role of conditioning led to a whole new era in language teaching around the middle of the twentieth century. A Skinnerian view of both language and language learning dominated foreign language teaching methodology for several decades, leading to a heavy reliance in the classroom on the controlled practice of verbal operants under carefully designed schedules of reinforcement. The popular Audiolingual Method, discussed in the end-of-chapter vignette in Chapter 3, was a prime example of Skinner's impact on American language teaching practices in the decades of the 1950s, 1960s, and early 1970s.

There is no doubt that behavioristic learning theories have had a lasting impact on our understanding of the process of human learning. There is much in the theory that is true and valuable. There is another side to the coin, however. We have looked at the side that claims that human behavior can be predicted and controlled and scientifically studied and validated. We have not looked at the side that views human behavior as essentially abstract in nature, as being composed of such a complex of variables that behavior, except in its extreme abnormality, simply cannot be predicted or easily controlled. We turn next to two representatives of this side of the coin—David Ausubel's meaningful learning theory and Carl Rogers's humanistic psychology.

AUSUBEL'S MEANINGFUL LEARNING THEORY

David Ausubel contended that learning takes place in the human organism through a meaningful process of relating new events or items to already existing cognitive concepts or propositions—hanging new items on existing cognitive pegs. Meaning is not an implicit response, but a "clearly articulated and precisely differentiated conscious experience that emerges when potentially meaningful signs, symbols, concepts, or propositions are related to and incorporated within a given individual's cognitive structure on a nonarbitrary and substantive basis" (Anderson & Ausubel 1965: 8). It is this relatability that, according to Ausubel, accounts for a number of phenomena: the acquisition of new meanings (knowledge), retention, the psychological organization of knowledge as a hierarchical structure, and the eventual occurrence of forgetting.

The cognitive theory of learning as put forth by Ausubel is perhaps best understood by contrasting **rote** learning and **meaningful** learning. In the perspective of rote learning, the concept of meaningful learning takes on new significance. Ausubel described rote learning as the process of acquiring material as "discrete and relatively isolated entities that are relatable to cognitive structure only in an arbitrary and verbatim fashion, not permitting the establishment of [meaningful] relationships" (1968: 108). That is, rote learning involves the mental storage of items having little or no association with existing cognitive structure. Most of us, for example, can learn a few necessary phone numbers and ZIP codes by rote without reference to cognitive hierarchical organization.

Meaningful learning, on the other hand, may be described as a process of relating and anchoring new material to relevant established entities in cognitive structure. As new material enters the cognitive field, it interacts with, and is appropriately **subsumed** under, a more inclusive conceptual system. The very fact that material is subsumable, that is, relatable to stable elements in cognitive structure, accounts for its meaningfulness. If we think of cognitive structure as a system of building blocks, then rote learning is the process of acquiring isolated blocks with no particular function in the building of a structure and no relationship to other blocks. Meaningful learning is the process whereby blocks become an integral part of already established categories or systematic clusters of blocks. For the sake of a visual picture of the distinction, consider the graphic representation in Figures 4.1 and 4.2.

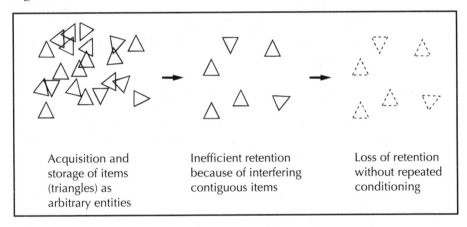

Acquisition and storage of items (triangles) as arbitrary entities

Inefficient retention because of interfering contiguous items

Loss of retention without repeated conditioning

Figure 4.1. Schematic representation of rote learning and retention

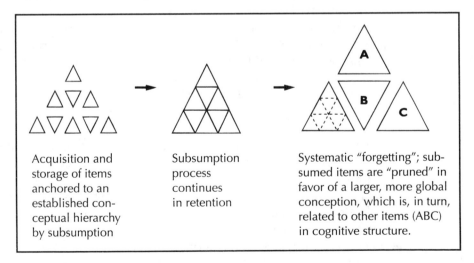

Acquisition and storage of items anchored to an established conceptual hierarchy by subsumption

Subsumption process continues in retention

Systematic "forgetting"; subsumed items are "pruned" in favor of a larger, more global conception, which is, in turn, related to other items (ABC) in cognitive structure.

Figure 4.2. Schematic representation of meaningful learning and retention (subsumption)

Any learning situation can be meaningful if (a) learners have a meaningful learning set—that is, a disposition to relate the new learning task to what they already know, and (b) the learning task itself is potentially meaningful to the learners—that is, relatable to the learners' structure of knowledge. The second method of establishing meaningfulness—one that Frank Smith (1975: 162) called "manufacturing meaningfulness"—is a potentially powerful factor in human learning. We can make things meaningful if necessary and if we are strongly motivated to do so. Students cramming for an examination often invent a mnemonic device for remembering a list of items; the meaningful retention of the device successfully retrieves the whole list of items.

Frank Smith (1975) also noted that similar strategies can be used in parlor games in which, for example, you are called upon to remember for a few moments several items presented to you. By associating items either in groups or with some external stimuli, retention is enhanced. Imagine "putting" each object in a different location on your person: a safety pin in your pocket, a toothpick in your mouth, a marble in your shoe. By later "taking a tour around your person," you can "feel" the objects there in your imagination. More than a century ago William James (1890: 662) described meaningful learning:

> In mental terms, the more other facts a fact is associated with in the mind, the better possession of it our memory retains. Each of its associates becomes a hook to which it hangs, a means to fish it up by when sunk beneath the surface. Together, they form a network of attachments by which it is woven into the entire issue of our thought. The "secret of good memory" is thus the secret of forming diverse and multiple associations with every fact we care to retain.... Briefly, then, of two men [sic] with the same outward experiences and the same amount of mere native tenacity, the one who thinks over his experiences most, and weaves them into systematic relation with each other, will be the one with the best memory.

The distinction between rote and meaningful learning may not at first appear to be important since in either case material can be learned. But the significance of the distinction becomes clear when we consider the relative efficiency of the two kinds of learning in terms of retention, or long-term memory. We are often tempted to examine learning from the perspective of input alone, failing to consider the uselessness of a learned item that is not retained. Human beings are capable of learning almost any given item within the so-called "magic seven, plus or minus two" (Miller 1956) units for perhaps a few seconds, but long-term memory is a different matter. We can remember an unfamiliar phone number, for example, long enough to dial the number, after which point it is usually extinguished by interfering factors. But a meaningfully learned, subsumed item has far greater potential for retention. Try, for example, to recall all your previous phone numbers (assuming you have moved a number of times in your life). It is doubtful you will be very successful; a phone number is quite arbitrary, bearing little meaningful relationship to reality (other than perhaps area codes and other such numerical systematization). But previous street addresses, for example, are sometimes more efficiently retained since they bear some meaningful relationship to the reality of physical images, directions, streets, houses, and the rest of the town, and are therefore more suitable for long-term retention without concerted reinforcement.

Systematic Forgetting

Ausubel provided a plausible explanation for the universal nature of forgetting. Since rotely learned materials do not interact with cognitive structure in a substantive fashion, they are learned in conformity with the laws of association, and their retention is influenced primarily by the interfering effects of similar rote materials learned immediately before or after the learning task (commonly referred to as **proactive** and **retroactive inhibition**). In the case of meaningfully learned material, retention is influenced primarily by the properties of "relevant and cumulatively established ideational systems in cognitive structure with which the learning task interacts" (Ausubel 1968: 108). Compared to this kind of extended interaction, concurrent interfering effects have relatively little influence on meaningful learning, and retention is highly efficient. Hence, addresses are retained as part of a meaningful set, while phone numbers, being self-contained, isolated entities, are easily forgotten.

We cannot say, of course, that meaningfully learned material is never forgotten. But in the case of such learning, forgetting takes place in a much more intentional and purposeful manner because it is a continuation of the very process of subsumption by which one learns; forgetting is really a second or "obliterative" stage of subsumption, characterized as "memorial reduction to the least common denominator" (Ausubel 1963: 218). Because it is more economical and less burdensome to retain a single inclusive concept than to remember a large number of more specific items, the importance of a specific item tends to be incorporated into the generalized meaning of the larger item. In this obliterative stage of subsumption, the specific items become progressively less identifiable as entities in their own right until they are finally no longer available and are said to be forgotten (see Figure 4.2).

It is this second stage of subsumption that operates through what I have called "cognitive pruning" procedures (Brown 1972). Pruning is the elimination of unnecessary clutter and a clearing of the way for more material to enter the cognitive field, in the same way that pruning a tree ultimately allows greater and fuller growth. Using the building-block analogy, one might say that, at the outset, a structure made of blocks is seen as a few individual blocks, but as "nucleation" begins to give the structure a perceived shape, some of the single blocks achieve less and less identity in their own right and become subsumed into the larger structure. Finally, the single blocks are lost to perception, or pruned out, to use the metaphor, and the total structure is perceived as a single whole without clearly defined parts.

An example of such pruning may be found in a child's learning of the concept of "hot"—that is, excessive heat capable of burning. A small child's first exposure to such heat may be either direct contact with or verbally mediated exposure to hot coffee, a pan of boiling water, a stove, an iron, a candle. That first exposure may be readily recalled for some time as the child maintains a meaningful association between a parent's hot coffee and hurting. After a number of exposures to things that are very hot, the child begins to form a concept of "hotness" by clustering experiences together and forming a generalization. In so doing the bits and pieces of experience that actually built the concept are slowly forgotten—pruned—in favor of the general concept that, in the years that follow, enables the child to extrapolate to future experiences and to avoid burning fingers on hot objects.

An important aspect of the pruning stage of learning is that subsumptive forgetting, or pruning, is not haphazard or chance—it is systematic. Thus by promoting optimal pruning procedures, we have a potential learning situation that will produce retention beyond that normally expected under more traditional theories of forgetting.

Research on language **attrition** has focused on a variety of possible causes for the loss of second language skills (see Weltens & Cohen 1989; Weltens 1987; Lambert & Freed 1982). Some of the more common reasons center on the strength and conditions of initial learning, on the kind of use that a second language has been put to, and on the motivational factors contributing to forgetting. Robert Gardner (1982) contended that in some contexts a lack of an "integrative" orientation (but see caveats in Chapter 6) toward the target culture could contribute to forgetting.

Native language forgetting occurs in some cases of **subtractive bilingualism** (members of a minority group learn the language of the majority group, and the latter group downgrades speakers of the minority language). Some researchers have suggested that "neurolinguistic blocking" and left-/right-brain functioning could contribute to forgetting (Obler 1982). And it appears that long-term forgetting can apply to certain linguistic features (lexical, phonological, syntactic, and so on) and not to others (Andersen 1982). Finally, Olshtain (1989) suggested that some aspects of attrition can be explained as a reversal of the acquisition process.

Research on language attrition usually focuses on long-term loss and not on those minute-by-minute or day-by-day losses of material that learners experience as they cope with large quantities of new material in the course of a semester or year of classroom language learning. It is this classroom context that poses the more immediate problem for the language teacher. Ausubel's solution to that problem would lie in the initial learning process: systematic, meaningful subsumption of material at the outset in order to enhance the retention process.

Ausubel's theory of learning has important implications for second language learning and teaching. The importance of meaning in language and of meaningful contexts for linguistic communication has been discussed in the first three chapters. Too much rote activity, at the expense of meaningful communication in language classes, could stifle the learning process.

Subsumption theory provides a strong theoretical basis for the rejection of conditioning models of practice and repetition in language teaching. In a meaningful process like second language learning, mindless repetition, imitation, and other rote practices in the language classroom have no place. The Audiolingual Method, which emerged as a widely used and accepted method of foreign language teaching, was based almost exclusively on a behavioristic theory of conditioning that relied heavily on rote learning. The mechanical "stamping in" of the language through saturation with little reference to meaning is seriously challenged by subsumption theory. Rote learning can be effective on a short-term basis, but for any long-term retention it fails because of the tremendous buildup of interference. In those cases in which efficient long-term retention *is* attained in rote-learning situations like those often found in the Audiolingual Method, maybe by sheer dogged determination, the learner has somehow subsumed the material meaningfully *in spite* of the method!

The notion that forgetting is systematic also has important implications for language learning and teaching. In the early stages of language learning, certain devices (definitions, paradigms, illustrations, or rules) are often used to facilitate subsumption. These devices can be made initially meaningful by assigning or "manufacturing" meaningfulness. But in the process of making language automatic, the devices serve only as interim entities, meaningful at a low level of subsumption, and then they are systematically pruned out at later stages of language learning. We might thus better achieve the goal of communicative competence by removing unnecessary barriers to automaticity. A definition or a paraphrase, for example, might be initially facilitative, but as its need is minimized by larger and more global conceptualizations, it is pruned.

While we are all fully aware of the decreasing dependence upon such devices in language learning, Ausubel's theory of learning may help to give explanatory adequacy to the notion. Language teachers might consider urging students to "forget" these interim, mechanical items as they make progress in a language and instead to focus more on the communicative use (comprehension or production) of language.

ROGERS'S HUMANISTIC PSYCHOLOGY

Carl Rogers is not traditionally thought of as a "learning" psychologist, yet he and his colleagues and followers have had a significant impact on our present understanding of learning, particularly learning in an educational or pedagogical context. Rogers's humanistic psychology has more of an affective focus than a cognitive one, and so it may be said to fall into the perspective of a constructivist view of learning. Certainly, Rogers and Vygotsky (1978) share some views in common in their highlighting of the social and interactive nature of learning.

Rogers devoted most of his professional life to clinical work in an attempt to be of therapeutic help to individuals. In his classic work *Client-Centered Therapy* (1951), Rogers carefully analyzed human behavior in general, including the learning process, by means of the presentation of nineteen formal principles of human behavior. All nineteen principles were concerned with learning from a "phenomenological" perspective, a perspective that is in sharp contrast to that of Skinner. Rogers studied the "whole person" as a physical and cognitive, but primarily emotional, being. His formal principles focused on the development of an individual's self-concept and of his or her personal sense of reality, those internal forces that cause a person to act. Rogers felt that inherent in principles of behavior is the ability of human beings to adapt and to grow in the direction that enhances their existence. Given a nonthreatening environment, a person will form a picture of reality that is indeed congruent with reality and will grow and learn. "Fully functioning persons," according to Rogers, live at peace with all of their feelings and reactions; they are able to reach their full potential.

Rogers's position has important implications for education (see Curran 1972; Rogers 1983). The focus is away from "teaching" and toward "learning." The goal of education is the facilitation of change and learning. Learning how to learn is more important than being taught something from the "superior" vantage point of a teacher who unilaterally decides what shall be taught. Many of our present systems of education, in prescribing curricular goals and dictating what shall be learned, deny persons both freedom and dignity. What is needed, according to Rogers, is for teachers to become facilitators of learning through the establishment of interpersonal relationships with learners. Teachers, to be facilitators, must first be real and genuine, discarding masks of superiority and omniscience. Second, teachers need to have genuine trust, acceptance, and a prizing of the other person—the student—as a worthy, valuable individual. And third, teachers need to communicate openly and empathetically with their students and vice versa. Teachers with these characteristics will not only understand themselves better but will also be effective teachers, who, having set the optimal stage and context for learning, will succeed in the goals of education.

We can see in Carl Rogers's humanism quite a departure from the scientific analysis of Skinnerian psychology and even from Ausubel's rationalistic theory. Rogers is not as concerned about the actual cognitive process of learning because, he feels, if the context for learning is properly created, then human beings will, in fact, learn everything they need to.

Rogers's theory is not without its flaws. The educator may be tempted to take the nondirective approach too far, to the point that valuable time is lost in the process of allowing students to "discover" facts and principles for themselves. Also, a nonthreatening environment might become so nonthreatening that the facilitative tension needed for learning is absent. There is ample research documenting the positive effects of competitiveness in a classroom, as long as that competitiveness does not damage self-esteem and hinder motivation to learn (see Bailey 1983).

One much talked-about educational theorist in the Rogersian tradition is the well-known Brazilian educator Paolo Freire, whose seminal work, *Pedagogy of the Oppressed* (1970), has inspired many a teacher to consider the importance of the *empowerment* of students in classrooms. Freire vigorously objected to traditional "banking" concepts of education in which teachers think of their task as one of "filling" students "by making deposits of information which [they] consider to constitute true knowledge—deposits which are detached from reality" (1970: 62). Instead, Freire has continued to argue, students should be allowed to negotiate learning outcomes, to cooperate with teachers and other learners in a process of discovery, to engage in critical thinking, and to relate everything they do in school to their reality outside the classroom. While such "liberationist" views of education must be approached with some caution (Clarke 1990), learners may nevertheless be empowered to achieve solutions to real problems in the real world.

The work of Rogers (1983), Freire (1970), and other educators of a similar frame of mind has contributed significantly in recent years to a redefinition of the educational process. In adapting Rogers's ideas to language teaching and learning, we need to see to it that learners understand themselves and communicate this self to others freely and nondefensively. Teachers as facilitators must therefore provide the nurturing context for learners to construct their meanings in interaction with others. When teachers rather programmatically feed students quantities of knowledge, which they subsequently devour, they may foster a climate of **defensive learning** in which learners try to protect themselves from failure, from criticism, from competition with fellow students, and possibly from punishment. Classroom activities and materials in language learning should therefore utilize meaningful contexts of genuine communication with students engaged together in the process of becoming "persons."

The various perspectives on learning that have been outlined in this section are schematically represented in Table 4.1.

Table 4.1 Theories of learning

BEHAVIORISTIC		COGNITIVE	CONSTRUCTIVIST
Classical	**Operant**		
[Pavlov] • respondent conditioning • elicited response • S → R	[Skinner] • governed by consequences • emitted response • R → S (reward) • no punishment • programmed instruction	[Ausubel] • meaningful = powerful • rote = weak • subsumption • association • systematic forgetting • cognitive "pruning"	[Rogers] • fully functioning person • learn how to learn • community of learners • empowerment

Note: S = stimulus, R = response-reward

TYPES OF LEARNING

Theories of learning of course do not capture all of the possible elements of general principles of human learning. In addition to the four learning theories just considered are various taxonomies of types of human learning and other mental processes universal to all. The educational psychologist Robert Gagné (1965), for example, ably demonstrated the importance of identifying a number of *types* of learning that all human beings use. Types of learning vary according to the context and subject matter to be learned, but a complex task such as language learning involves every one of Gagné's types of learning—from simple signal learning to problem solving. Gagné (1965: 58–59) identified eight types of learning:

1. **Signal learning.** The individual learns to make a general diffuse response to a signal. This is the classical conditioned response of Pavlov.

2. **Stimulus–response learning.** The learner acquires a precise response to a discriminated stimulus. What is learned is a connection or, in Skinnerian terms, a discriminated operant, sometimes called an instrumental response.

3. **Chaining.** What is acquired is a chain of two or more stimulus–response connections. The conditions for such learning have also been described by Skinner.

4. **Verbal association.** Verbal association is the learning of chains that are verbal. Basically, the conditions resemble those for other (motor) chains. However, the presence of language in the human being makes this a special type of chaining because internal links may be selected from the individual's previously learned repertoire of language.

5. **Multiple discrimination.** The individual learns to make a number of different identifying responses to many different stimuli, which may resemble each other in physical appearance to a greater or lesser degree. Although the learning of each stimulus–response connection is a simple occurrence, the connections tend to interfere with one another.

6. **Concept learning.** The learner acquires the ability to make a common response to a class of stimuli even though the individual members of that class may differ widely from each other. The learner is able to make a response that identifies an entire class of objects or events.

7. **Principle learning.** In simplest terms, a principle is a chain of two or more concepts. It functions to organize behavior and experience. In Ausubel's terminology, a principle is a "subsumer"—a cluster of related concepts.

8. **Problem solving.** Problem solving is a kind of learning that requires the internal events usually referred to as "thinking." Previously acquired concepts and principles are combined in a conscious focus on an unresolved or ambiguous set of events.

It is apparent from just a cursory definition of these eight types of learning that some types are better explained by certain theories than others. For example, the first five types seem to fit easily into a behavioristic framework, while the last three are better explained by Ausubel's or

Rogers's theories of learning. Since all eight types of learning are relevant to second language learning, the implication is that certain "lower"-level aspects of second language learning may be more adequately treated by behavioristic approaches and methods, while certain "higher"-order types of learning are more effectively taught by methods derived from a cognitive approach to learning.

The second language learning process can be further efficiently categorized and sequenced in cognitive terms by means of the eight types of learning.

1. Signal learning in general occurs in the total language process: human beings make a general response of some kind (emotional, cognitive, verbal, or nonverbal) to language.

2. Stimulus-response learning is evident in the acquisition of the sound system of a foreign language in which, through a process of conditioning and trial and error, the learner makes closer and closer approximations to nativelike pronunciation. Simple lexical items are, in one sense, acquired by stimulus-response connections; in another sense they are related to higher-order types of learning.

3. Chaining is evident in the acquisition of phonological sequences and syntactic patterns—the stringing together of several responses—although we should not be misled into believing that verbal chains are necessarily linear. Generative linguists (like McNeill, as we saw in Chapter 2) have wisely shown that sentence structure is hierarchical.

4. The fourth type of learning involves Gagné's distinction between verbal and nonverbal chains, and is not really therefore a separate type of language learning.

5. Multiple discriminations are necessary particularly in second language learning where, for example, a word has to take on several meanings, or a rule in the native language is reshaped to fit a second language context.

6. Concept learning includes the notion that language and cognition are inextricably interrelated, also that rules themselves—rules of syntax, rules of conversation—are linguistic concepts that have to be acquired.

7. Principle learning is the extension of concept learning to the formation of a linguistic system, in which rules are not isolated in rote memory, but conjoined and subsumed in a total system.

8. Finally, problem solving is clearly evident in second language learning as the learner is continually faced with sets of events that are truly problems to be solved—problems every bit as difficult as

algebra problems or other "intellectual" problems. Solutions to the problems involve the creative interaction of all eight types of learning as the learner sifts and weighs previous information and knowledge in order to correctly deter-mine the meaning of a word, the interpretation of an utterance, the rule that governs a common class of linguistic items, or a conversationally appropriate response.

It is not difficult, upon some reflection, to discern the importance of varied types of learning in the second language acquisition process (see Larsen-Freeman 1991). Teachers and researchers have all too often dismissed certain theories of learning as irrelevant or useless because of the misperception that language learning consists of only one type of learning. "Language is concept learning," say some; "Language is a conditioning process," say others. Both are correct in that part of language learning consists of each of the above. But both are incorrect to assume that all of language learning can be so simply classified. Methods of teaching, in recognizing different levels of learning, need to be consonant with whichever aspect of language is being taught at a particular time while also recognizing the interrelatedness of all levels of language learning.

TRANSFER, INTERFERENCE, AND OVERGENERALIZATION

Human beings approach any new problem with an existing set of cognitive structures and, through insight, logical thinking, and various forms of hypothesis testing, call upon whatever prior experiences they have had and whatever cognitive structures they possess to attempt a solution. In the literature on language learning processes, three terms have commonly been singled out for explication: transfer, interference, and overgeneralization. The three terms are sometimes mistakenly considered to represent separate processes; they are more correctly understood as several manifestations of one principle of learning—the interaction of previously learned material with a present learning event. From the beginning of life the human organism, or any organism for that matter, builds a structure of knowledge by the accumulation of experiences and by the storage of aspects of those experiences in memory. Let us consider these common terms in two associated pairs.

Transfer is a general term describing the carryover of previous performance or knowledge to subsequent learning. Positive transfer occurs when the prior knowledge benefits the learning task—that is, when a previous item is correctly applied to present subject matter. Negative transfer occurs when previous performance disrupts the performance of a second task. The latter can be referred to as **interference**, in that previously learned material interferes with subsequent material—a previous item is incorrectly transferred or incorrectly associated with an item to be learned.

It has been common in second language teaching to stress the role of interference—that is, the interfering effects of the native language on the target (the second) language. It is of course not surprising that this process has been so singled out, for native language interference is surely the most immediately noticeable source of error among second language learners. The saliency of interference has been so strong that some have viewed second language learning as exclusively involving the overcoming of the effects of the native language. It is clear from learning theory that a person will use whatever previous experience he or she has had with language to facilitate the second language learning process. The native language is an obvious set of prior experiences. Sometimes the native language is negatively transferred, and we say then that interference has occurred. For example, a French native speaker might say in English, "I am in New York since January," a perfectly logical transfer of the comparable French sentence "Je suis à New York depuis janvier." Because of the negative transfer of the French verb form to English, the French system has, in this case, interfered with the person's production of a correct English form.

It is exceedingly important to remember, however, that the native language of a second language learner is often positively transferred, in which case the learner benefits from the facilitating effects of the first language. In the above sentence, for example, the correct one-to-one word order correspondence, the personal pronoun, and the preposition have been positively transferred from French to English. We often mistakenly overlook the facilitating effects of the native language in our penchant for analyzing errors in the second language and for overstressing the interfering effects of the first language. A more detailed discussion of the syndrome is provided in Chapter 8.

In the literature on second language acquisition, interference is almost as frequent a term as **overgeneralization**, which is, of course, a particular subset of generalization. Generalization is a crucially important and pervading strategy in human learning. To generalize means to infer or derive a law, rule, or conclusion, usually from the observation of particular instances. The principle of generalization can be explained by Ausubel's concept of meaningful learning. Meaningful learning is, in fact, generalization: items are subsumed (generalized) under higher-order categories for meaningful retention. Much of human learning involves generalization. The learning of concepts in early childhood is a process of generalizing. A child who has been exposed to various kinds of animals gradually acquires a generalized concept of "animal." That same child, however, at an early stage of generalization, might in his or her familiarity with dogs see a horse for the first time and overgeneralize the concept of "dog" and call the horse a dog. Similarly, a number of animals might be placed into a category of "dog" until the general attributes of a larger category, "animal," have been learned.

In second language acquisition it has been common to refer to over-generalization as a process that occurs as the second language learner acts within the target language, generalizing a particular rule or item in the second language—irrespective of the native language—beyond legitimate bounds. We have already observed that children, at a particular stage of learning English as a native language, overgeneralize regular past-tense endings (walked, opened) as applicable to all past-tense forms (goed, flied) until they recognize a subset of verbs that belong in an "irregular" category. After gaining some exposure and familiarity with the second language, second language learners similarly will overgeneralize within the target language. Typical examples in learning English as a second language are past-tense regularization and utterances like "John doesn't can study" (negativization requires insertion of the *do* auxiliary before verbs) or "He told me when should I get off the train" (indirect discourse requires normal word order, not question word order, after the *wh-* word). Unaware that these rules have special constraints, the learner overgeneralizes. Such over-generalization is committed by learners of English from almost any native language background. (Chapter 8 gives a more detailed discussion of linguistic overgeneralization.)

Many have been led to believe that there are only two processes of second language acquisition: interference and overgeneralization. This is obviously a misconception. First, interference and overgeneralization are the negative counterparts of the facilitating processes of transfer and generalization. (See Figure 4.3.) Second, while they are indeed aspects of

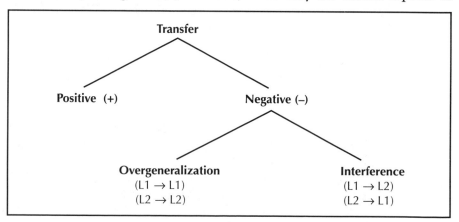

Figure 4.3. Transfer, overgeneralization, and interference

somewhat different processes, they represent fundamental and interrelated components of all human learning, and when applied to second language acquisition, are simply extensions of general psychological principles. Interference of the first language in the second is simply a form of generalizing that takes prior first language experiences and applies them incorrectly. Overgeneralization is the incorrect application—negative transfer—of previously learned second language material to a present second language context. All generalizing involves transfer, and all transfer involves generalizing.

INDUCTIVE AND DEDUCTIVE REASONING

Inductive and deductive reasoning are two polar aspects of the generalization process. In the case of **inductive** reasoning, one stores a number of specific instances and induces a general law or rule or conclusion that governs or subsumes the specific instances. **Deductive** reasoning is a movement from a generalization to specific instances: specific subsumed facts are inferred or deduced from a general principle. Second language learning in the "field" (natural, untutored language learning), as well as first language learning, involves a largely inductive process, in which learners must infer certain rules and meanings from all the data around them.

Classroom learning tends to rely more than it should on deductive reasoning. Traditional—especially Grammar Translation—methods have overemphasized the use of deductive reasoning in language teaching. While it may be appropriate at times to articulate a rule and then proceed to its instances, most of the evidence in communicative second language learning points to the superiority of an inductive approach to rules and generalizations. However, both inductively and deductively oriented teaching methods can be effective, depending on the goals and contexts of a particular language teaching situation.

An interesting extension of the inductive/deductive dichotomy was reported in Peters's (1981) case study of a child learning a first language. Peters pointed out that we are inclined, too often, to assume that a child's linguistic development proceeds from the parts to the whole, that is, children first learn sounds, then words, then sentences, and so forth. However, Peters's subject manifested a number of "Gestalt" characteristics, perceiving the whole before the parts. The subject demonstrated the perception of these wholes in the form of intonation patterns that appeared in his speech well before the particular words that would make up sentences. Peters cited other evidence of Gestalt learning in children and concluded that such "sentence learners" (versus "word learners") may be more common than researchers had previously assumed.

The implications of Peters's study for second language teaching are rather tantalizing. We should perhaps pay close attention to learners' production of overall, meaning-bearing intonation patterns. Wong (1986) capitalizes on just such a concept in a discussion of teaching communicative oral production.

APTITUDE AND INTELLIGENCE

The learning theories, types of learning, and other processes that have so far been explained in this chapter deal with mental perception, storage, and recall. Little has been said about two related and somewhat controversial issues in learning psychology: aptitude and intelligence. In brief, the questions are:

1. Is there such a thing as foreign language aptitude? If so, what are its properties? Can they be reliably measured? Are aptitudinal factors predictive of success in learning a foreign language?
2. What is intelligence? How is intelligence defined in terms of the foreign language learning process? What kinds of intelligence are related to foreign language learning?

Aptitude

Do certain people have a "knack" for learning foreign languages? Anecdotal evidence would suggest that, for a variety of causal factors, some people are indeed able to learn languages faster and more efficiently than others. One perspective of looking at such aptitude is the identification of a number of characteristics of successful language learners. Risk-taking behavior, memory efficiency, intelligent guessing, and ambiguity tolerance are but a few of the many variables that have been cited (see Brown 1991 and Rubin & Thompson 1982, among others). Such factors will be the focus of the next chapter.

A more traditional way of examining what we mean by aptitude is through a historical progression of research that began around the middle of the twentieth century with John Carroll's (Carroll & Sapon 1958) construction of the Modern Language Aptitude Test (MLAT). The MLAT required prospective language learners (before they began to learn a foreign language) to perform such tasks as learning numbers, listening, detecting spelling clues and grammatical patterns, and memorizing, all either in the native language, English, or utilizing words and morphemes from a constructed, hypothetical language. The MLAT was considered to be independent of a specific foreign language, and therefore predictive of success in the learning of any language. This test, along with another similar one, the Pimsleur Language Aptitude Battery (PLAB) (Pimsleur 1966), was used for some time in such contexts as Peace Corps volunteer training programs to help predict successful language learners.

In the decade or so following their publication, these two aptitude tests were quite well received by foreign language teachers and administrators. Since then, their popularity has steadily waned, with few attempts to experiment with alternative measures of language aptitude (Skehan 1998; Parry & Child 1990). Two factors account for this decline. First, even though the MLAT and the PLAB claimed to measure language aptitude, it soon became apparent that they simply reflected the general intelligence or academic ability of a student (see Skehan 1989a). At best, they measured ability to perform focused, analytical, *context-reduced* activities that occupy a student in a traditional language classroom. They hardly even began to tap into the kinds of learning strategies and styles that recent research (Cohen 1998; Reid 1995; Ehrman 1990; Oxford 1990b, 1996, for example) has shown to be crucial in the acquisition of communicative competence in *context-embedded* situations. As we will see in the next chapter, learners can be successful for a multitude of reasons, many of which are much more related to motivation and determination than to so-called "native" abilities (Lett & O'Mara 1990).

Second, how is one to interpret a language aptitude test? Rarely does an institution have the luxury or capability to test people before they take a foreign language in order to counsel certain people out of their decision to do so. And in cases where an aptitude test might be administered, such a test clearly biases both student and teacher. Both are led to believe that they will be successful or unsuccessful, depending on the aptitude test score, and a self-fulfilling prophecy is likely to occur. It is better for teachers to be optimistic for students, and in the early stages of a student's process of language learning, to monitor styles and strategies carefully, leading the student toward strategies that will aid in the process of learning and away from those blocking factors that will hinder the process.

Only a few isolated recent efforts have continued to address foreign language aptitude and success (Harley & Hart 1997; Sasaki 1993a, 1993b, for example). Skehan's (1998) bold attempts to pursue the construct of aptitude have exposed some of the weaknesses of aptitude constructs, but unfortunately have not yielded a coherent theory of language aptitude. So today the search for verifiable factors that make up aptitude, or "knack," is headed in the direction of a broader spectrum of learner characteristics. Some of those characteristics fall into the question of intelligence and foreign language learning. How does general cognitive ability intersect with successful language learning?

Intelligence

Intelligence has traditionally been defined and measured in terms of linguistic and logical-mathematical abilities. Our notion of **IQ** (intelligence quotient) is based on several generations of testing of these two domains, stemming from the research of Alfred Binet early in the twentieth century. Success in educational institutions and in life in general seems to be a correlate of high IQ. In terms of Ausubel's meaningful learning model, high intelligence would no doubt imply a very efficient process of storing items that are particularly useful in building conceptual hierarchies and systematically pruning those that are not useful. Other cognitive psychologists have dealt in a much more sophisticated way with memory processing and recall systems.

In relating intelligence to second language learning, can we say simply that a "smart" person will be capable of learning a second language more successfully because of greater intelligence? After all, the greatest barrier to second language learning seems to boil down to a matter of memory, in the sense that if you could just remember everything you were ever taught, or you ever heard, you would be a very successful language learner. Or would you? It appears that our "language learning IQs" are much more complicated than that.

Howard Gardner (1983) advanced a controversial theory of intelligence that blew apart our traditional thoughts about IQ. Gardner described seven different forms of knowing which, in his view, provide a much more comprehensive picture of intelligence. Beyond the usual two forms of intelligence (listed as 1 and 2 below), he added five more:

1. linguistic
2. logical-mathematical
3. spatial (the ability to find one's way around an environment, to form mental images of reality, and to transform them readily)
4. musical (the ability to perceive and create pitch and rhythmic patterns)
5. bodily-kinesthetic (fine motor movement, athletic prowess)
6. interpersonal (the ability to understand others, how they feel, what motivates them, how they interact with one another)
7. intrapersonal intelligence (the ability to see oneself, to develop a sense of self-identity)

Gardner maintained that by looking only at the first two categories we rule out a great number of the human being's mental abilities; we see only a portion of the total capacity of the human mind. Moreover, he showed that our traditional definitions of intelligence are culture-bound. The "sixth-sense" of a hunter in New Guinea or the navigational abilities of a sailor in Micronesia are not accounted for in our Westernized definitions of IQ.

In a likewise revolutionary style, Robert Sternberg (1985, 1988) has also been shaking up the world of traditional intelligence measurement. In his "triarchic" view of intelligence, Sternberg proposed three types of "smartness":

- componential ability for analytical thinking
- experiential ability to engage in creative thinking, combining disparate experiences in insightful ways
- contextual ability: "street smartness" that enables people to "play the game" of manipulating their environment (others, situations, institutions, contexts).

Sternberg contended that too much of psychometric theory is obsessed with mental speed, and therefore dedicated his research to tests that measure insight, real-life problem solving, "common sense," getting a wider picture of things, and other practical tasks that are closely related to success in the real world.

Finally, in another effort to remind us of the bias of traditional definitions and tests of intelligence, Daniel Goleman's *Emotional Intelligence* (1995) is persuasive in placing emotion at the seat of intellectual functioning. The management of even a handful of core emotions—anger, fear, enjoyment, love, disgust, shame, and others—drives and controls efficient mental or cognitive processing. Even more to the point, Goleman argued that "the emotional mind is far quicker than the rational mind, springing into action without even pausing to consider what it is doing. Its quickness precludes the deliberate, analytic reflection that is the hallmark of the thinking mind" (Goleman 1995: 291). Gardner's sixth and seventh types of intelligence (inter- and intrapersonal) are of course laden with emotional processing, but Goleman would place emotion at the highest level of a hierarchy of human abilities.

By expanding constructs of intelligence as Gardner, Sternberg, and Goleman have done, we can more easily discern a relationship between intelligence and second language learning. In its traditional definition, intelligence may have little to do with one's success as a second language learner: people within a wide range of IQs have proven to be successful in acquiring a second language. But Gardner attaches other important attributes to the notion of intelligence, attributes that could be crucial to second language success. Musical intelligence could explain the relative ease that some learners have in perceiving and producing the intonation patterns of a language. Bodily-kinesthetic modes have already been discussed in connection with the learning of the phonology of a language.

Interpersonal intelligence is of obvious importance in the communicative process. Intrapersonal factors will be discussed in detail in Chapter 6 of this book. One might even be able to speculate on the extent to which spatial intelligence, especially a "sense of direction," may assist the second culture learner in growing comfortable in a new environment. Sternberg's experiential and contextual abilities cast further light on the components of the "knack" that some people have for quick, efficient, unabashed language acquisition. Finally, the EQ (emotional quotient) suggested by Goleman may be far more important than any other factor in accounting for second language success both in classrooms and in untutored contexts.

Educational institutions have recently been applying Gardner's seven intelligences to a multitude of school-oriented learning. Thomas Armstrong (1993, 1994), for example, has focused teachers and learners on "seven ways of being smart," and helped educators to see that linguistics and logical-mathematical intelligences are not the only pathways to success in the real world. A high IQ in the traditional sense may garner high scholastic test scores, but may not indicate success in business, marketing, art, communications, counseling, or teaching.

Quite some time ago, Oller suggested, in an eloquent essay, that intelligence may after all be language-based. "Language may not be merely a vital link in the social side of intellectual development, it may be the very foundation of intelligence itself" (1981a: 466). According to Oller, arguments from genetics and neurology suggest "a deep relationship, perhaps even an identity, between intelligence and language ability" (p. 487). The implications of Oller's hypothesis for second language learning are enticing. Both first and second languages must be closely tied to meaning in its deepest sense. Effective second language learning thus links surface forms of a language with meaningful experiences, as we have already noted in Ausubel's learning theory. The strength of that link may indeed be a factor of intelligence in a multiple number of ways.

We have much to gain from the understanding of learning principles that have been presented here, and of the various ways of understanding what intelligence is. Some aspects of language learning may call upon a conditioning process; other aspects require a meaningful cognitive process; others depend upon the security of supportive co-learners interacting freely and willingly with one another; still others are related to one's total intellectual structure. Each aspect is important, but there is no consistent amalgamation of theory that works for every context of second language learning. Each teacher has to adopt a somewhat intuitive process of discerning the best synthesis of theory for an enlightened analysis of the particular context at hand. That intuition will be nurtured by an integrated understanding of the appropriateness and of the strengths and weaknesses of each theory of learning.

In the Classroom:
The "Designer" Methods of the 1970s

The age of audiolingualism, with its emphasis on surface forms and on the rote practice of scientifically produced patterns, began to wane when the Chomskyan revolution in linguistics turned linguists and language teachers toward the "deep structure" of language and when psychologists began to recognize the fundamentally affective and interpersonal nature of all learning. The decade of the 1970s was a chaotic but exceedingly fruitful era during which second language research not only came into its own but also began to inspire innovative methods for language teaching. As we increasingly recognized the importance of both cognitive and affective factors in second language learning, certain teaching methods came into vogue.

These methods attempted to capitalize on the perceived importance of psychological factors in language learners' success. At the same time they were touted as "innovative" and "revolutionary," especially when compared to Audiolingual or Grammar Translation methodology. Claims for their success, originating from their proprietary founders and proponents, were often overstated in the interest of attracting teachers to weekend workshops and seminars, to new books and tapes and videos, and, of course, to getting their learners to reach the zenith of their potential. These claims, often overstated and overgeneralized, led David Nunan (1989: 97) to refer to the methods of the day as "designer" methods: promises of success, one size fits all!

Despite the overly strong claims that were made for such methods, they were an important part of our language teaching history, and they gave us some insights about language learning that still enlighten our teaching practices. What follows is a brief summary of five of the most popular of the "designer" methods.

Community Language Learning

In his "Counseling-Learning" model of education, Charles Curran (1972) was inspired by Carl Rogers's view of education in which students and teacher join together to facilitate learning in a context of valuing and prizing each individual in the group. In such a surrounding, each person lowers the defenses that prevent open, interpersonal communication. The anxiety caused by the educational context is lessened by means of the supportive community. The teacher's presence is not perceived as a threat, nor is it the teacher's purpose to impose limits and boundaries; rather, as a "counselor," the teacher's role is to center his or her attention on the clients (the students) and their needs.

Curran's model of education was extended to language learning contexts in the form of Community Language Learning (CLL) (LaForge 1971). While particular adaptations of CLL are numerous, the basic methodology was explicit. The group of clients (learners), having first established in their native language an interpersonal relationship and trust, are seated in a circle with the counselor (teacher) on the outside of the circle. The students may be complete beginners in the foreign language. When one of them wishes to say something to the group or to an individual, he or she says it in the native language (say, English) and the counselor translates the utterance back to the learner in the second language (say, Japanese). The learner then repeats that Japanese sentence as accurately as possible. Another client responds, in English; the utterance is translated by the counselor; the client repeats it; and the conversation continues. If possible the conversation is taped for later listening, and at the end of each session the learners together inductively attempt to glean information about the new language. If desirable, the counselor may take a more directive role and provide some explanation of certain linguistic rules or items.

As the learners gain more and more familiarity with the foreign language, more and more direct communication can take place, with the counselor providing less and less direct translation and information, until after many sessions, even months or years later, the learner achieves fluency in the spoken language. The learner has at that point become independent.

There are advantages and disadvantages to a method like CLL. CLL is an attempt to put Carl Rogers's philosophy into action and to overcome some of the threatening affective factors in second language learning. But there are some practical and theoretical problems with CLL. The counselor-teacher can become too nondirective. While some intense inductive struggle is a necessary component of second language learning, the initial grueling days and weeks of floundering in ignorance in CLL could be alleviated by more directed, deductive learning: by being told. Perhaps only later, when the learner has moved to more independence, is an inductive strategy really successful. And, of course, the success of CLL depends largely on the translation expertise of the counselor. Translation is an intricate and complex process that is often easier said than done; if subtle aspects of language are mistranslated, there could be a less than effective understanding of the target language.

Despite its weaknesses, CLL offers certain insights to teachers. We are reminded to lower learners' anxiety, to create as much of a supportive group in our classrooms as possible, to allow students to initiate language, and to point learners toward autonomous learning in preparation for the day when they no longer have the teacher to guide them.

Suggestopedia

Suggestopedia was another educational innovation that promised great results if we would simply use our brain power. According to Lozanov (1979), people are capable of learning much more than they give themselves credit for. Drawing on insights from Soviet psychological research on extrasensory perception and from yoga, Lozanov created a method for learning that capitalized on relaxed states of mind for maximum retention of material. Music was central to his method. Baroque music, with its 60 beats per minute and its specific rhythm, created the kind of "relaxed concentration" that led to "superlearning" (Ostrander & Schroeder 1979: 65). According to Lozanov, during the soft playing of Baroque music, one can take in tremendous quantities of material due to an increase in alpha brain waves and a decrease in blood pressure and pulse rate.

In applications of Suggestopedia to foreign language learning, Lozanov and his followers experimented with the presentation of vocabulary, readings, dialogs, role-plays, drama, and a variety of other typical classroom activities. Some of the classroom methodology did not have any particular uniqueness. The difference was that a significant proportion of activity was carried on with classical music in the background, and with students sitting in soft, comfortable seats in relaxed states of consciousness. Students were encouraged to be as "childlike" as possible, yielding all authority to the teacher and sometimes assuming the roles (and names) of native speakers of the foreign language. Students thus became "suggestible."

Suggestopedia was criticized on a number of fronts. Scovel (1979) showed quite eloquently that Lozanov's experimental data, in which he reported astounding results with Suggestopedia, were highly questionable. Moreover, the practicality of using Suggestopedia was an issue that teachers faced where music and comfortable chairs were not available. More serious was the issue of the place of memorization in language learning. On a more positive note, we can adapt certain aspects of Suggestopedia in our communicative classrooms without "buying into" the whole method. A relaxed and unanxious mind, achieved through music and/or any other means, will often help a learner to build confidence. Role playing, drama, and other activities may be very helpful techniques to stimulate meaningful interaction in the classroom. And perhaps we should never underestimate the "superlearning" powers of the human brain.

The Silent Way

Like Suggestopedia, the Silent Way rested on more cognitive than affective arguments for its theoretical sustenance. While Caleb Gattegno, its founder, was said to be interested in a "humanistic" approach (Chamot & McKeon 1984: 2) to education, much of the Silent Way was characterized by a problem-solving approach to learning. Richards and Rodgers (1986: 99) summarized the theory of learning behind the Silent Way:

1. Learning is facilitated if the learner discovers or creates rather than remembers and repeats what is to be learned.
2. Learning is facilitated by accompanying (mediating) physical objects.
3. Learning is facilitated by problem solving involving the material to be learned.

The Silent Way capitalized on discovery-learning procedures. Gattegno (1972) believed that learners should develop independence, autonomy, and responsibility. At the same time, learners in a classroom must cooperate with each other in the process of solving language problems. The teacher—a stimulator but not a hand-holder—is silent much of the time, thus the name of the method. Teachers must resist their instinct to spell everything out in black and white—to come to the aid of students at the slightest downfall—and must "get out of the way" while students work out solutions.

In a language classroom the Silent Way typically utilized as materials a set of Cuisinere rods—small colored rods of varying lengths—and a series of colorful wall charts. The rods were used to introduce vocabulary (colors, numbers, adjectives [*long, short,* and so on], verbs [*give, take, pick up, drop*]), and syntax (tense, comparatives, pluralization, word order, and the like). The teacher provided single-word stimuli, or short phrases and sentences once or twice, and then the students refined their understanding and pronunciation among themselves, with minimal corrective feedback from the teacher. The charts introduced pronunciation models and grammatical paradigms.

Like Suggestopedia, the Silent Way had its share of criticism. In one sense, the Silent Way was too harsh a method, and the teacher too distant, to encourage a communicative atmosphere. A number of aspects of language can indeed be "told" to students to their benefit; they need not, as in CLL as well, struggle for hours or days with a concept that could be easily clarified by the teacher's direct guidance. The rods and charts wore thin after a few lessons, and other materials had to be introduced, at which point the Silent Way resembled any other language classroom.

There are, of course, insights to be derived. All too often we are tempted as teachers to provide everything for our students, served up on a silver platter. We could benefit from injecting healthy doses of discovery learning into our classroom activities and from providing less teacher talk so that the students can work things out on their own. These are some of the contributions of innovation. They expose us to new thoughts that we can—through our developing theoretical rationale for language teaching—sift through, weigh, and adapt to multiple contexts.

Total Physical Response

The founder of the Total Physical Response (TPR), James Asher (1977), noted that children, in learning their first language, appear to do a lot of listening before they speak, and that their listening is accompanied by physical responses (reaching, grabbing, moving, looking, and so forth). He also gave some attention to right-brain learning. According to Asher, motor activity is a right-brain function that should precede left-brain language processing. Asher was also convinced that language classes were often the locus of too much anxiety and wished to devise a method that was as stress-free as possible, where learners would not feel overly self-conscious and defensive. The TPR classroom, then, was one in which students did a great deal of listening and acting. The teacher was very directive in orchestrating a performance: "The instructor is the director of a stage play in which the students are the actors" (Asher 1977: 43).

A typical TPR class utilized the imperative mood, even at more advanced proficiency levels. Commands were an easy way to get learners to move about and to loosen up: "Open the window," "Close the door," "Stand up," "Sit down," "Pick up the book," "Give it to John," and so on. No verbal response was necessary. More complex syntax was incorporated into the imperative: "Draw a rectangle on the chalkboard." "Walk quickly to the door and hit it." Humor was easy to introduce: "Walk slowly to the window and jump." "Put your toothbrush in your book" (Asher 1977: 55). Interrogatives were also easily dealt with: "Where is the book?" "Who is John?" (students point to the book or to John). Eventually students, one by one, presumably felt comfortable enough to venture verbal responses to questions, then to ask questions themselves, and the process continued.

Like other methods discussed here, TPR—as a method—had its limitations. It was especially effective in the beginning levels of language proficiency, but lost its distinctiveness as learners advanced in their competence. But today TPR is used more as a type of classroom activity, which is a more useful way to view it. Many successful communicative, interactive classrooms utilize TPR activities to provide both auditory input and physical activity.

The Natural Approach

Stephen Krashen's (1982) theories of second language acquisition have been widely discussed and hotly debated since the 1970s. (Chapter 10 will offer further details on Krashen's influence on second language acquisition theory.) The major methodological off-shoot of Krashen's work was manifested in the Natural Approach, developed by one of Krashen's colleagues, Tracy Terrell (Krashen & Terrell 1983). Acting on many of the claims that Asher made for TPR, Krashen and Terrell felt that learners would benefit from delaying production until speech "emerges," that learners should be as relaxed as possible in the classroom, and that a great deal of communication and "acquisition" should take place, as opposed to analysis. In fact, the Natural Approach advocated the use of TPR activities at the beginning level of language learning, when "comprehensible input" is essential for triggering the acquisition of language.

The Natural Approach was aimed at the goal of basic interpersonal communication skills, that is, everyday language situations—conversations, shopping, listening to the radio, and the like. The initial task of the teacher was to provide comprehensible input—spoken language that is understandable to the learner—or just a little beyond the learner's level. Learners did not need to say anything during this "silent period" until they felt ready to do so. The teacher was the source of the learners' input and the creator of an interesting and stimulating variety of classroom activities—commands, games, skits, and small-group work.

The most controversial aspects of the Natural Approach were its "silent period" and its reliance on the notion of "comprehensible input." One could argue, with Gibbons (1985), that the delay of oral production can be pushed too far and that at an early stage it is important for the teacher to step in and encourage students to talk. And determining just what we mean by "comprehensible" is exceedingly difficult (see Chapter 10 for further comments). Language learning is an interactive process, and therefore an over-reliance on the role of input at the expense of the stimulation of output could thwart the second language acquisition process.

But, of course, we also can look at the Natural Approach and be reminded that sometimes we insist that students speak much too soon, thereby raising anxiety and lessening the possibility of further risk-taking as the learner tries to progress. And so, once again, your responsibility as a teacher is to choose the best of what others have experimented with, and to adapt those insights to your own situation. There is a good deal of insight to be gained, and intuition to be developed, from examining the merits of all of these five "designer" methods. Those insights and intuitions can become a part of your own cautious, enlightened eclecticism.

TOPICS AND QUESTIONS FOR
STUDY AND DISCUSSION

[Note: (I) individual work; (G) group or pair work; (C) whole-class discussion.]

1. (G) The class should be divided into four groups, with one of the four learning theorists discussed in the chapter assigned to each group. Tasks for the groups are to "defend" their particular theory as the most insightful or complete. To do so, each group will need to summarize strengths and to anticipate arguments from other groups.

2. (C) The results of the four groups' findings can be presented to the rest of the class in a "debate" about which learning theory has the most to contribute to understanding the SLA process.

3. (C) Tease apart the distinction between elicited and emitted responses. Can you specify some operants that are emitted by the learner in a foreign language class? And some responses that are elicited? Specify some of the reinforcers that are present in language classes. How effective are certain reinforcers?

4. (I) Skinner felt that punishment, or negative reinforcement, was just another way of calling attention to undesired behavior and therefore should be avoided. Do you think correction of student errors in a classroom is negative reinforcement? How can error treatment be given a positive spin, in Skinnerian terms?

5. (G) List some activities you consider to be rote and others that are meaningful in foreign language classes you have taken (or are teaching). Do some activities fall into a gray area between the two? Evaluate the effectiveness of all the activities your group has listed. Share your conclusions with the rest of the class.

6. (G) In pairs, quickly brainstorm some examples of "cognitive pruning" or systematic forgetting that occur in a foreign language classroom. For example, do definitions fall into this category? Or grammatical rules? Cite some ways that a teacher might foster such pruning.

7. (C) In one sense Skinner, Ausubel, and Rogers represent quite different points of view—at least they focus on different facets of human learning. Do you think it is possible to synthesize the three points of view? In what way are all three psychologists expressing the "truth"? In what way do they differ substantially? Try to formulate an integrated understanding of human learning by taking the best of all three points of view. Does your integrated theory tell you something about how people learn a second language? about how you should teach a second language?

8. (G) Look back at the section on foreign language aptitude. From what you have learned, what factors do you think should be represented in a comprehensive test of aptitude? Compare your group's suggestions with those of other groups.

9. (G/C) The class should be divided into at least seven groups or pairs. To each group/pair, assign one of Gardner's seven multiple intelligences. In your group, brainstorm typical language classroom activities or techniques that foster your type of intelligence. Make a list of your activities and compare it with the other lists.

SUGGESTED READINGS

Lightbown, Patsy and Spada, Nina. 1993. *How Languages Are Learned.* Oxford: Oxford University Press.

Mitchell, Rosamond and Myers, Florence. 1998. *Second Language Learning Theories.* New York: Oxford University Press.

These two introductory SLA textbooks, written in language that is comprehensible to first-level graduate students, provide useful summaries of theories of learning.

Skehan, Peter. 1998. *A Cognitive Approach to Language Learning.* Oxford: Oxford University Press.

Peter Skehan is one of the current champions of continued research on foreign language aptitude. Chapters 8 and 9 of his book capsulize the state of the art on this topic.

Armstrong, Thomas. 1994. *Multiple Intelligences in the Classroom.* Philadelphia: Association for Curriculum Development.

The author provides a practical summary of Howard Gardner's theory of multiple intelligences combined with a remarkably comprehensive set of pedagogical applications.

LANGUAGE LEARNING EXPERIENCE: JOURNAL ENTRY 4

[Note: See pages 18 and 19 of Chapter 1 for general guidelines for writing a journal on a previous or concurrent language learning experience.]

- If you had to classify your approach to learning a foreign language, would it be more Skinnerian, Ausubelian, or Rogersian? Or a combination of them?
- Sometimes teachers don't give students opportunities to *emit* language in the classroom, and just keep *eliciting* too much. Sometimes it's the other way around. What is your experience? If you feel (or have felt) that you don't have enough chances to volunteer to speak, what can (could) you do to change that pattern?
- Rogers recommended "non-defensive" learning. Do you feel that you are learning to defend yourself against the teacher's disapproval, or against your classmates, or against bad grades? Are your classmates your allies or competitors?
- Do any of Gardner's seven types of intelligence strike you as being crucial to your success in your foreign language? Are there any that you under-utilize? What can you do about that?
- Have you been taught with any of the methods summarized at the end of the chapter? If so, what is (was) your assessment of its effectiveness?

CHAPTER 5

STYLES AND

STRATEGIES

Theories of learning, Gagné's "types" of learning, transfer processes, and aptitude and intelligence models are all attempts to describe universal human traits in learning. They seek to explain globally how people perceive, filter, store, and recall information. Such **processes**, the unifying theme of the previous chapter, do not account for the plethora of differences across individuals in the way they learn, or for differences within any one individual. While we all exhibit inherently human traits of learning, every individual approaches a problem or learns a set of facts or organizes a combination of feelings from a unique perspective. This chapter deals with cognitive variations in learning a second language: variations in learning **styles** that differ across individuals, and in **strategies** employed by individuals to attack particular problems in particular contexts.

PROCESS, STYLE, AND STRATEGY

Before we look specifically at some styles and strategies of second language learning, a few words are in order to explain the differences among process, style, and strategy as the terms are used in the literature on second language acquisition. Historically, there has been some confusion in the use of these three terms, and so it is important to carefully define them at the outset.

Process is the most general of the three concepts. All human beings engage in certain universal processes. Just as we all need air, water, and food for our survival, so do all humans of normal intelligence engage in certain levels or types of learning. Human beings universally engage in association, transfer, generalization, and attrition. We all make stimulus–response connections and are driven by reinforcement. We all possess, in varying proportions, abilities in the seven intelligences. Process is characteristic of every human being.

Style is a term that refers to consistent and rather enduring tendencies or preferences *within* an individual. Styles are those general characteristics of intellectual functioning (and personality type, as well) that pertain to you as an individual, and that differentiate you from someone else. For example, you might be more visually oriented, more tolerant of ambiguity, or more reflective than someone else—these would be styles that characterize a general pattern in your thinking or feeling.

Strategies are specific methods of approaching a problem or task, modes of operation for achieving a particular end, planned designs for controlling and manipulating certain information. They are contextualized "battle plans" that might vary from moment to moment, or day to day, or year to year. Strategies vary intraindividually; each of us has a number of possible ways to solve a particular problem, and we choose one—or several in sequence—for a given problem.

As we turn to a study of styles and strategies in second language learning, we can benefit by understanding these "layers of an onion," or points on a continuum, ranging from universal properties of learning to specific intraindividual variations in learning.

LEARNING STYLES

Suppose you are visiting a foreign country whose language you don't speak or read. You have landed at the airport and your contact person, whose name you don't know, is not there to meet you. To top it off, your luggage is missing. It's 3:00 A.M. and no one in the sparsely staffed airport speaks English. What should you do? There is obviously no single solution to this multifaceted problem. Your solution will be based to a great extent on the *styles* you happen to bring to bear. For example, if you are *tolerant of ambiguity,* you will not easily get flustered by your unfortunate circumstances. If you are *reflective,* you will exercise patience and not jump quickly to a conclusion about how to approach the situation. If you are *field independent,* you will focus on the necessary and relevant details and not be distracted by surrounding but irrelevant details.

The way we learn things in general and the way we attack a problem seem to hinge on a rather amorphous link between personality and cognition; this link is referred to as **cognitive style**. When cognitive styles are specifically related to an educational context, where affective and physiological factors are intermingled, they are usually more generally referred to as **learning styles**.

Learning styles might be thought of as "cognitive, affective, and physiological traits that are relatively stable indicators of how learners perceive, interact with, and respond to the learning environment" (Keefe 1979: 4). Or, more simply, as "a general predisposition, voluntary or not, toward processing information in a particular way" (Skehan 1991: 288). In the enormous task of learning a second language, one that so deeply involves affective factors, a study of learning style brings important variables to the forefront. Such styles can contribute significantly to the construction of a unified theory of second language acquisition.

Learning styles mediate between emotion and cognition, as you will soon discover. For example, a reflective style invariably grows out of a reflective personality or a reflective mood. An impulsive style, on the other hand, usually arises out of an impulsive emotional state. People's styles are determined by the way they internalize their total environment, and since that internalization process is not strictly cognitive, we find that physical, affective, and cognitive domains merge in learning styles. Some would claim that styles are stable traits in adults. This is a questionable view. It would appear that individuals show general tendencies toward one style or another, but that differing contexts will evoke differing styles in the same individual. Perhaps an "intelligent" and "successful" person is one who is "bicognitive"—one who can manipulate both ends of a style continuum.

If I were to try to enumerate all the learning styles that educators and psychologists have identified, a very long list would emerge. From early research by Ausubel (1968: 171) and Hill (1972), to recent research by Reid (1995), Ehrman (1996), and Cohen (1998), literally dozens of different styles have been identified. These include just about every imaginable sensory, communicative, cultural, affective, cognitive, and intellectual factor. A select few of those styles have emerged in second language research as potentially significant contributors to successful acquisition. These will be discussed in the next sections.

Field Independence

Do you remember, in those coloring books you pored over as a child, a picture of a forest scene with exotic trees and flowers, and a caption saying, "Find the hidden monkeys in the trees." If you looked carefully, you soon began to spot them, some upside-down, some sideways, some high and some low, a dozen or so monkeys camouflaged by the lines of what at first sight looked like just leaves and trees. The ability to find those hidden monkeys hinged upon your **field independent** style: your ability to perceive a particular, relevant item or factor in a "field" of distracting items. In general psychological terms, that "field" may be perceptual, or it may be more abstract and refer to a set of thoughts, ideas, or feelings from which your task is to perceive specific relevant subsets. **Field dependence** is, conversely, the tendency to be "dependent" on the total field so that the parts embedded within the field are not easily perceived, although that total field is perceived more clearly as a unified whole. Field dependence is synonymous with **field sensitivity**, a term that may carry a more positive connotation.

A field independent (FI) style enables you to distinguish parts from a whole, to concentrate on something (like reading a book in a noisy train station), to analyze separate variables without the contamination of neighboring variables. On the other hand, *too much* FI may result in cognitive "tunnel vision": you see only the parts and not their relationship to the whole. "You can't see the forest for the trees," as the saying goes. Seen in this light, development of a field dependent (FD) style has positive effects: you perceive the whole picture, the larger view, the general configuration of a problem or idea or event. It is clear, then, that *both* FI and FD are necessary for most of the cognitive and effective problems we face.

The literature on FI/D has shown that FI increases as a child matures to adulthood, that a person tends to be dominant in one mode or the other, and that FI/D is a relatively stable trait in adulthood. It has been found in Western culture that males tend to be more FI, and that FI is related to one of the three main factors traditionally used to define intelligence (the analytical factor), but not to the other two factors (verbal-comprehension and attention-concentration). Cross-culturally, the extent of the development of a FI/D style as children mature is a factor of the type of society and home in which the child is reared. Authoritarian or agrarian societies, which are usually highly socialized and utilize strict rearing practices, tend to produce more FD. A democratic, industrialized, competitive society with freer rearing norms tends to produce more FI persons.

Affectively, persons who are more predominantly FI tend to be generally more independent, competitive, and self-confident. FD persons tend to be more socialized, to derive their self-identity from persons around them, and are usually more empathic and perceptive of the feelings and thoughts of others.

How does all this relate to second language learning? Two conflicting hypotheses have emerged. First, we could conclude that FI is closely related to classroom learning that involves analysis, attention to details, and mastering of exercises, drills, and other focused activities. Indeed, recent research supports such a hypothesis. Naiman et al. (1978) found in a study of English-speaking eighth, tenth, and twelfth graders who were learning French in Toronto that FI correlated positively and significantly with language success in the classroom. Other studies (L. Hansen 1984, Hansen &

Stansfield 1983, Stansfield & Hansen 1981) found relatively strong evidence in groups of adult second language learners of a relationship between FI and cloze test performance, which in some respects requires analytical abilities.

Chapelle and Roberts (1986) found support for the correlation of a FI style with language success as measured both by traditional, analytic, paper-and-pencil tests and by an oral interview. (The latter finding—the correlation with the oral interview—was a bit surprising in light of the second of our two hypotheses, to be taken up below.) Abraham (1985) found that second language learners who were FI performed better in deductive lessons, while those with FD styles were more successful with inductive lesson designs. Still other studies (Chapelle & Green 1992, Alptekin & Atakan 1990, Chapelle & Abraham 1990) provide further evidence of superiority of a FI style for second language success. More recently, Elliott (1995a, 1995b) found a moderate correlation between FI and pronunciation accuracy. And in a review of several decades of research on FI/D, Hoffman (1997: 225) concluded that "further research . . . should be pursued before the hypothesis that there is a relationship between FD/I and SLA is abandoned."

The second of the conflicting hypotheses proposes that primarily FD persons will, by virtue of their empathy, social outreach, and perception of other people, be successful in learning the communicative aspects of a second language. While no one denies the plausibility of this second hypothesis, little empirical evidence has been gathered to support it. The principal reason for the dearth of such evidence is the absence of a true test of FD. The standard test of FI requires subjects to discern small geometric shapes embedded in larger geometric designs. A high score on such embedded-figures tests indicates FI, but a low score does *not* necessarily imply relatively high FD. (This latter fact has unfortunately not been recognized by all who have interpreted results of embedded-figures tests.) So we are left with no standardized means of measuring FD, and thus the second hypothesis has been confirmed largely through anecdotal or observational evidence.

The two hypotheses could be seen as paradoxical: How could FD be most important on the one hand and FI equally important? The answer to the paradox would appear to be that clearly *both* styles are important. The two hypotheses deal with two different kinds of language learning. One kind of learning implies natural, face-to-face communication, the kind of communication that occurs too rarely in the average language classroom. The second kind of learning involves the familiar classroom activities: drills, exercises, tests, and so forth. It is most likely that "natural" language learning in the "field," beyond the constraints of the classroom, requires a FD style, and the classroom type of learning requires, conversely, a FI style.

There is some research to support such a conclusion. Guiora et al. (1972b) showed that empathy is related to language acquisition, and though one could argue with some of their experimental design factors (see H.D. Brown 1973), the conclusion seems reasonable and also supportable by observational evidence and intuition. Some pilot studies of FI/D (Brown 1977a) indicated that FI correlated *negatively* with informal oral interviews of adult English learners in the United States. And so it would appear that FI/D might provide one construct that differentiates "classroom" (tutored) second language learning from "natural" (untutored) second language learning.

FI/D may also prove to be a valuable tool for differentiating child and adult language acquisition. The child, more predominantly FD, may have a cognitive style advantage over the more FI adult. Stephen Krashen (1977) has suggested that adults use more "monitoring," or "learning," strategies (conscious attention to forms) for language acquisition, while children utilize strategies of "acquisition" (subconscious attention to functions). This distinction between acquisition and learning could well be explicated by the FI/D dichotomy. (See Chapter 10 for further discussion of Krashen's Monitor model.)

FI/D has been conceived by psychological researchers as a construct in which a person is relatively stable. Unfortunately, there seems to be little room in such research for considering the possibility that FI/D is contextualized and variable. Logically and observationally, FI/D is quite variable within one person. Depending upon the context of learning, individual learners can vary their utilization of FI or FD. If a task requires FI, individuals may invoke their FI style; if it requires FD, they may invoke a FD style. Such ambiguities fueled Griffiths and Sheen's (1992: 133) passionate attempt to discredit the whole FI construct, where they concluded that this "theoretically flawed" notion "does not have, and has never had, any relevance for second language learning."

Carol Chapelle (1992; see also Chapelle & Green 1992), in a more balanced and optimistic viewpoint on the relevance of FI to communicative language ability, exposed flaws in Griffiths and Sheen's remarks and suggested, as did Hoffman (1997), avenues of future research. I surmise from Chapelle's comments that her optimism springs from—among other things—our acceptance of the view that FI and FD are not in complementary distribution within an individual. Some persons might be both highly FI and highly FD as contexts vary. Such variability is not without its parallels in almost every other psychological construct. A generally extroverted person might, for example, be relatively introverted at certain times. In second language learning, then, it may be incorrect to assume that learners should be either FI or FD; it is more likely that persons have general inclinations, but, given certain contexts, can exercise a sufficient degree of an appropriate style. The burden on the learner is to invoke the appropriate style for the context. The burden on the teacher is to understand the preferred styles of each learner and to sow the seeds for flexibility.

Left- and Right-Brain Functioning

We have already observed in Chapter 3 that left- and right-brain dominance is a potentially significant issue in developing a theory of second language acquisition. As the child's brain matures, various functions become *lateralized* to the left or right hemisphere. The left hemisphere is associated with logical, analytical thought, with mathematical and linear processing of information. The right hemisphere perceives and remembers visual, tactile, and auditory images; it is more efficient in processing holistic, integrative, and emotional information. Torrance (1980) lists several characteristics of left- and right-brain dominance. (See Table 5.1.)

While we can cite many differences between left- and right-brain characteristics, it is important to remember that the left and right hemispheres operate together as a "team." Through the *corpus collosum*, messages are sent back and forth so that both hemispheres are involved in most of the neurological activity of the human brain. Most problem solving involves the capacities of both hemispheres, and often the best solutions to problems are those in which each hemisphere has participated optimally (see Danesi 1988). We must also remember Scovel's (1982) warning that left- and right-brain differences tend to draw more attention than the research warrants at the present time.

Nevertheless, the left-/right-brain construct helps to define another useful learning style continuum, with implications for second language learning and teaching. Danesi (1988), for example, used "neurological bimodality" to analyze the way in which various language teaching methods have failed: by appealing too strongly to left-brain processes, past methods were inadequately stimulating important right-brain processes in the language classroom. Krashen, Seliger, and Hartnett (1974) found support for the hypothesis that left-brain-dominant second language learners preferred a deductive style of teaching, while right-brain-dominant learners appeared to be more successful in an inductive classroom environment. Stevick (1982) concluded that left-brain-dominant second language learners are better at producing separate words, gathering the specifics of language, carrying out sequences of operations, and dealing with abstraction, classification, labeling, and reorganization. Right-brain-dominant learners, on the other hand, appear to deal better with whole images (not with reshuffling parts), with generalizations, with metaphors, and with emotional reactions and artistic expressions. In Chapter 3 I noted the role of the right hemisphere in second language learning. This may suggest a greater need to perceive whole meanings in those early stages, and to analyze and monitor oneself more in the later stages.

Table 5.1. Left- and right-brain characteristics

Left-Brain Dominance	Right-Brain Dominance
Intellectual	Intuitive
Remembers names	Remembers faces
Responds to verbal instructions and explanations	Responds to demonstrated, illustrated, or symbolic instructions
Experiments systematically and with control	Experiments randomly and with less restraint
Makes objective judgments	Makes subjective judgments
Planned and structured	Fluid and spontaneous
Prefers established, certain information	Prefers elusive, uncertain information
Analytic reader	Synthesizing reader
Reliance on language in thinking and remembering	Reliance on images in thinking and remembering
Prefers talking and writing	Prefers drawing and manipulating objects
Prefers multiple-choice tests	Prefers open-ended questions
Controls feelings	More free with feelings
Not good at interpreting body language	Good at interpreting body language
Rarely uses metaphors	Frequently uses metaphors
Favors logical problem solving	Favors intuitive problem solving

You may be asking yourself how left- and right-brain functioning differs from FI and FD. While few studies have set out explicitly to correlate the two factors, intuitive observation of learners and conclusions from studies of both hemispheric preference and FI show a strong relationship. Thus, in dealing with either type of cognitive style, we are dealing with two styles that are highly parallel. Conclusions that were drawn above for FI and FD generally apply well for left- and right-brain functioning, respectively.

Ambiguity Tolerance

A third style concerns the degree to which you are cognitively willing to tolerate ideas and propositions that run counter to your own belief system or structure of knowledge. Some people are, for example, relatively open-minded in accepting ideologies and events and facts that contradict their own views; they are more content than others to entertain and even internalize contradictory propositions. Others, more closed-minded and dogmatic, tend to reject items that are contradictory or slightly incongruent with their existing system; they wish to see every proposition fit into an acceptable place in their cognitive organization, and if it does not fit, it is rejected.

Again, advantages and disadvantages are present in each style. The person who is tolerant of ambiguity is free to entertain a number of innovative and creative possibilities and not be cognitively or affectively disturbed by ambiguity and uncertainty. In second language learning a great amount of apparently contradictory information is encountered: words that differ from the native language, rules that not only differ but that are internally inconsistent because of certain "exceptions," and sometimes a whole cultural system that is distant from that of the native culture. Successful language learning necessitates tolerance of such ambiguities, at least for interim periods or stages, during which time ambiguous items are given a chance to become resolved. On the other hand, too much tolerance of ambiguity can have a detrimental effect. People can become "wishy-washy," accepting virtually every proposition before them, not efficiently subsuming necessary facts into their cognitive organizational structure. Such excess tolerance has the effect of hampering or preventing meaningful subsumption of ideas. Linguistic rules, for example, might not be effectively integrated into a whole system; rather, they may be gulped down in meaningless chunks learned by rote.

Intolerance of ambiguity also has its advantages and disadvantages. A certain intolerance at an optimal level enables one to guard against the wishy-washiness referred to above, to close off avenues of hopeless possibilities, to reject entirely contradictory material, and to deal with the reality of the system that one has built. But intolerance can close the mind too soon, especially if ambiguity is perceived as a threat; the result is a rigid, dogmatic, brittle mind that is too narrow to be creative. This may be particularly harmful in second language learning.

A few research findings are available on this style in second language learning. Naiman et al. (1978) found that ambiguity tolerance was one of only two significant factors in predicting the success of their high school learners of French in Toronto. Chapelle and Roberts (1986) measured tolerance of ambiguity in learners of English as a second language in Illinois. They found that learners with a high tolerance for ambiguity were slightly more successful in certain language tasks. These findings suggest—though not strongly so—that ambiguity tolerance may be an important factor in second language learning. The findings have intuitive appeal. It is hard to imagine a compartmentalizer—a person who sees everything in black and white with no shades of gray—ever being successful in the overwhelmingly ambiguous process of learning a second language.

Reflectivity and Impulsivity

It is common for us to show in our personalities certain tendencies toward **reflectivity** sometimes and **impulsivity** at other times. Psychological studies have been conducted to determine the degree to which, in the cognitive domain, a person tends to make either a quick or gambling (impulsive) guess at an answer to a problem or a slower, more calculated (reflective) decision. David Ewing (1977) refers to two styles that are closely related to the reflectivity/impulsivity (R/I) dimension: systematic and intuitive styles. An intuitive style implies an approach in which a person makes a number of different gambles on the basis of "hunches," with possibly several successive gambles before a solution is achieved. Systematic thinkers tend to weigh all the considerations in a problem, work out all the loopholes, and then, after extensive reflection, venture a solution.

The implications for language acquisition are numerous. It has been found that children who are conceptually reflective tend to make fewer errors in reading than impulsive children (Kagan 1965); however, impulsive persons are usually faster readers, and eventually master the "psycholinguistic guessing game" (Goodman 1970) of reading so that their impulsive style of reading may not necessarily deter comprehension. In another study (Kagan, Pearson & Welch 1966), inductive reasoning was found to be more effective with reflective persons, suggesting that generally reflective persons could benefit more from inductive learning situations. Virtually all research on R/I has used the Matching Familiar Figures Test (Kagan 1965; revised by Cairns & Cammock 1989), in which subjects are required to find, among numerous slightly different drawings of figures (people, ships, buildings, etc.), the drawing that matches the criterion figure. And most of the research to date on this cognitive style has looked at American, monolingual, English-speaking children.

A few studies have related R/I to second language learning. Doron (1973) found that among her sample of adult learners of ESL in the USA, reflective students were slower but more accurate than impulsive students in reading. In another study of adult ESL students, Abraham (1981) concluded that reflection was weakly related to performance on a proofreading task. Jamieson (1992) reported on yet another study of adult ESL learners. She found that "fast-accurate" learners, or good guessers, were better language learners as measured by the standardized Test of English as a Foreign Language, but warned against assuming that impulsivity always implies accuracy. Some of her subjects were fast and inaccurate.

R/I has some important considerations for classroom second language learning and teaching. Teachers tend to judge mistakes too harshly, especially in the case of a learner with an impulsive style who may be more willing than a reflective person to gamble at an answer. On the other hand, a reflective person may require patience from the teacher, who must allow more time for the student to struggle with responses. It is also conceivable that those with impulsive styles may go through a number of rapid transitions of semigrammatical stages of SLA, with reflective persons tending to remain longer at a particular stage with "larger" leaps from stage to stage.

Visual and Auditory Styles

Yet another dimension of learning style—one that is salient in a formal classroom setting—is the preference that learners show toward either **visual** or **auditory** input. Visual learners tend to prefer reading and studying charts, drawings, and other graphic information, while auditory learners prefer listening to lectures and audiotapes. Of course, most successful learners utilize both visual and auditory input, but slight preferences one way or the other may distinguish one learner from another, an important factor for classroom instruction.

In one study of adult learners of ESL, Joy Reid (1987) found some significant cross-cultural differences in visual and auditory styles. By means of a self-reporting questionnaire, the subjects rated their own preferences. The students rated statements like "When I read instructions, I learn them better" and "I learn more when I make drawings as I study" on a five-point scale ranging from "strongly agree" to "strongly disagree." Among Reid's results: Korean students were significantly more visually oriented than native English-speaking Americans; Japanese students were the least auditory students, significantly less auditorily inclined than Chinese and Arabic students. Reid also found that some of the preferences of her subjects were a factor of gender, length of time in the US, academic field of study, and level of education. Such findings underscore the importance of recognizing learners' varying style preferences, but also of not assuming that they are easily predicted by cultural/linguistic backgrounds alone.

STRATEGIES

We now turn to the second of our principal categories in this chapter, the level at which activity varies considerably within individuals as well as across individuals. Styles are general characteristics that differentiate one individual from another; strategies are those specific "attacks" that we make on a given problem. They are the moment-by-moment techniques that we employ to solve "problems" posed by second language input and output. The field of second language acquisition has distinguished between two types of strategy: **learning** strategies and **communication** strategies. The former relate to input—to processing, storage, and retrieval, that is, to taking in messages from others. The latter pertain to output, how we productively express meaning, how we deliver messages to others. We will examine both types of strategy here.

First, a brief historical note on the study of second language learners' strategies. As our knowledge of second language acquisition increased markedly during the 1970s, teachers and researchers came to realize that no single research finding and no single method of language teaching would usher in an era of universal success in teaching a second language. We saw that certain learners seemed to be successful regardless of methods or techniques of teaching. We began to see the importance of individual variation in language learning. Certain people appeared to be endowed with abilities to succeed; others lacked those abilities. This observation led Rubin (1975) and Stern (1975) to describe "good" language learners in terms of personal characteristics, styles, and strategies. Rubin (Rubin & Thompson 1982) later summarized fourteen such characteristics. Good language learners

1. find their own way, taking charge of their learning.
2. organize information about language.
3. are creative, developing a "feel" for the language by experimenting with its grammar and words.
4. make their own opportunities for practice in using the language inside and outside the classroom.
5. learn to live with uncertainty by not getting flustered and by continuing to talk or listen without understanding every word.
6. use mnemonics and other memory strategies to recall what has been learned.
7. make errors work for them and not against them.
8. use linguistic knowledge, including knowledge of their first language, in learning a second language.
9. use contextual cues to help them in comprehension.
10. learn to make intelligent guesses.
11. learn chunks of language as wholes and formalized routines to help them perform "beyond their competence."
12. learn certain tricks that help to keep conversations going.
13. learn certain production strategies to fill in gaps in their own competence.
14. learn different styles of speech and writing and learn to vary their language according to the formality of the situation.

Such lists, speculative as they were in the mid-1970s, inspired a group of collaborators in Toronto to undertake a study of good language learning traits (Naiman et al. 1978, reprinted 1996). While the empirical results of the Toronto study were somewhat disappointing, they nevertheless spurred many other researchers to try to identify characteristics of "successful" language learners (see Stevick 1989, for example). Such research led others (Rubin & Thompson 1982; Brown 1989, 1991; Marshall 1989) to offer advice to would-be students of foreign language on how to become better learners.

Learning Strategies

The research of the mid-1970s led to some very careful defining of specific learning strategies. In some of the most comprehensive research of this kind, Michael O'Malley and Anna Chamot and colleagues (O'Malley et al. 1983, 1985a, 1985b, 1987, 1989; Chamot & O'Malley 1986, 1987; O'Malley and Chamot 1990; Chamot et al. 1999) studied the use of strategies by learners of English as a second language in the United States. Typically, strategies were divided into three main categories, as noted in Table 5.2. **Metacognitive** is a term used in information-processing theory to indicate an "executive" function, strategies that involve planning for learning, thinking about the learning process as it is taking place, monitoring of one's production or comprehension, and evaluating learning after an activity is completed (Purpura 1997). **Cognitive** strategies are more limited to specific learning tasks and involve more direct manipulation of the learning material itself. **Socioaffective** strategies have to do with social-mediating activity and interacting with others. Note that the latter strategy, along with some of the other strategies listed in Table 5.2, are actually **communication** strategies.

In subsequent years numerous studies were carried out on the effectiveness of learners' using a variety of strategies in their quest for language competence. O'Malley, Chamot, and Kupper (1989) found that second language learners developed effective listening skills through the use of monitoring, elaboration, and inferencing. Forty-seven different reading strategies were identified by Anderson (1991). Men and women appeared to use listening comprehension strategies differentially (Bacon 1992). And even studies of unsuccessful learners (Vann & Abraham 1990, for example) yielded important information.

In more recent years, we have seen mounting evidence of the usefulness of learners' incorporating strategies into their acquisition process. Two major forms of strategy use have been documented: classroom-based or textbook-embedded training, now called **strategies-based instruction** (SBI), and autonomous self-help training (see later in this chapter for more on these two forms). Both have been demonstrated to be effective for various learners in various contexts (McDonough 1999; Cohen 1998; Hill 1994; Wenden 1992).

Table 5.2. Learning strategies (O'Malley et al. 1985b: 582–584)

LEARNING STRATEGY	DESCRIPTION
Metacognitive Strategies	
Advance Organizers	Making a general but comprehensive preview of the organizing concept or principle in an anticipated learning activity
Directed Attention	Deciding in advance to attend in general to a learning task and to ignore irrelevent distractors
Selective Attention	Deciding in advance to attend to specific aspects of language input or situational details that will cue the retention of language input
Self-Management	Understanding the conditions that help one learn and arranging for the presence of those conditions
Functional Planning	Planning for and rehearsing linguistic components necessary to carry out an upcoming language task
Self-Monitoring	Correcting one's speech for accuracy in pronunciation, grammar, vocabulary, or for appropriateness related to the setting or to the people who are present
Delayed Production	Consciously deciding to postpone speaking in order to learn initially through listening comprehension
Self-Evaluation	Checking the outcomes of one's own language learning against an internal measure of completeness and accuracy
Cognitive Strategies	
Repetition	Imitating a language model, including overt practice and silent rehearsal
Resourcing	Using target language reference materials
Translation	Using the first language as a base for understanding and/or producing the second language
Grouping	Reordering or reclassifying, and perhaps labeling, the material to be learned based on common attributes
Note Taking	Writing down the main idea, important points, outline, or summary of information presented orally or in writing

(Continued on next page)

Table 5.2. Learning strategies (continued)

LEARNING STRATEGY	DESCRIPTION
Cognitive Strategies	
Deduction	Consciously applying rules to produce or understand the second language
Recombination	Constructing a meaningful sentence or larger language sequence by combining known elements in a new way
Imagery	Relating new information to visual concepts in memory via familiar, easily retrievable visualizations, phrases, or locations
Auditory Representation	Retention of the sound or a similar sound for a word, phrase, or longer language sequence
Keyword	Remembering a new word in the second language by (1) identifying a familiar word in the first language that sounds like or otherwise resembles the new word and (2) generating easily recalled images of some relationship between the new word and the familiar word
Contextualization	Placing a word or phrase in a meaningful language sequence
Elaboration	Relating new information to other concepts in memory
Transfer	Using previously acquired linguistic and/or conceptual knowledge to facilitate a new language learning task
Inferencing	Using available information to guess meanings of new items, predict outcomes, or fill in missing information
Socioaffective Strategies	
Cooperation	Working with one or more peers to obtain feedback, pool information, or model a language activity
Question for Clarification	Asking a teacher or other native speaker for repetition, paraphrasing, explanation, and/or examples

Of particular interest in both prongs of research and practice is the extent to which cross-cultural variables may facilitate or interfere with strategy use among learners (Oxford 1996, Oxford & Anderson 1995). General conclusions from studies conducted in China, Japan, Israel, Egypt, and Russia, among others, promise more than a glimmer of hope that SBI and autonomous learning are viable avenues to success (McDonough 1999, Oxford 1996, Pemberton 1996), cultural differences notwithstanding.

Communication Strategies

While learning strategies deal with the receptive domain of intake, memory, storage, and recall, communication strategies pertain to the employment of verbal or nonverbal mechanisms for the productive communication of information. In the arena of linguistic interaction, it is sometimes difficult, of course, to distinguish between the two, as Tarone (1983) aptly noted, since comprehension and production can occur almost simultaneously. Nevertheless, as long as one can appreciate the slipperiness of such a dichotomy, it remains a useful distinction in understanding the nature of strategies, especially for pedagogical purposes.

The speculative early research of the 1970s (Varadi 1973 and others) has now led to a great deal of recent attention to communication strategies (see, for example, McDonough 1999; Dornyei 1995; Rost & Ross 1991; Bialystok 1990a; Bongaerts & Poulisse 1989; Oxford & Crookall 1989). Some time ago, Faerch and Kasper (1983a: 36) defined communication strategies as "potentially conscious plans for solving what to an individual presents itself as a problem in reaching a particular communicative goal." While the research of the last decade does indeed focus largely on the *compensatory* nature of communication strategies, more recent approaches seem to take a more positive view of communication strategies as elements of an overall *strategic* competence (see Chapter 9) in which learners bring to bear all the possible facets of their growing competence in order to send clear messages in the second language. Moreover, such strategies may or may not be "potentially conscious"; support for such a conclusion comes from observations of first language acquisition strategies that are similar to those used by adults in second language learning contexts (Bongaerts & Poulisse 1989).

Perhaps the best way to understand what is meant by communication strategy is to look at a typical list of such strategies. Table 5.3 offers a taxonomy that reflects accepted categories over several decades of research (adapted from Dörnyei 1995: 58).

Dörnyei's classification is a good basis for some further comments on communication strategies. We will elaborate here on a few of the categories.

Table 5.3. Communication strategies (adapted from Dörnyei 1995:58)

Avoidance Strategies

1. Message abandonment: Leaving a message unfinished because of language difficulties.

2. Topic avoidance: Avoiding topic areas or concepts that pose language difficulties.

Compensatory Strategies

3. Circumlocution: Describing or exemplifying the target object of action (e.g., *the thing you open bottles with* for *corkscrew*).

4. Approximation: Using an alternative term which expresses the meaning of the target lexical item as closely as possible (e.g., *ship* for *sailboat*).

5. Use of all-purpose words: Extending a general, empty lexical item to contexts where specific words are lacking (e.g., the overuse of *thing, stuff, what-do-you-call -it, thingie*).

6. Word coinage: Creating a nonexisting L2 word based on a supposed rule (e.g., *vegetarianist* for *vegetarian*).

7. Prefabricated patterns: Using memorized stock phrases, usually for "survival" purposes (e.g., *Where is the ___* or *Comment allez -vous?*, where the morphological components are not known to the learner).

8. Nonlinguistic signals: Mime, gesture, facial expression, or sound imitation.

9. Literal translation: Translating literally a lexical item, idiom, compound word, or structure from L1 to L2.

10. Foreignizing: Using a L1 word by adjusting it to L2 phonology (i.e., with a L2 pronunciation) and/or morphology (e.g., adding to it a L2 suffix).

11. Code-switching: Using a L1 word with L1 pronunciation or a L3 word with L3 pronunciation while speaking in L2.

12. Appeal for help: Asking for aid from the interlocutor either directly (e.g., *What do you call . . . ?*) or indirectly (e.g., rising intonation, pause, eye contact, puzzled expression).

13. Stalling or time-gaining strategies: Using fillers or hesitation devices to fill pauses and to gain time to think (e.g., *well, now let's see, uh, as a matter of fact*).

Avoidance Strategies

Avoidance is a common communication strategy that can be broken down into several subcategories. The most common type of avoidance strategy is **syntactic** or **lexical** avoidance within a semantic category. Consider the following conversation between a learner and a native speaker:

L: I lost my road.
NS: You lost your *road?*
L: Uh, . . . I lost. I lost. I got lost.

The learner avoided the lexical item *road* entirely, not being able to come up with the word *way* at that point. A French learner who wishes to avoid the use of the subjunctive in the sentence *Il faut que nous partions* may, for example, use instead the sentence *Il nous faut partir*. Or, not being sure of the use of *en* in the sentence *J'en ai trois*, the learner might simply say *J'ai trois pommes*. **Phonological** avoidance is also common, as in the case of a Japanese tennis partner of mine who avoided using the word *rally* (because of its phonological difficulty) and instead opted to say, simply, "hit the ball."

A more direct type of avoidance is **topic** avoidance, in which a whole topic of conversation (say, talking about what happened yesterday if the past tense is unfamiliar) might be avoided entirely. Learners manage to devise ingenious methods of topic avoidance: changing the subject, pretending not to understand (a classical means for avoiding answering a question), simply not responding at all, or noticeably abandoning a message when a thought becomes too difficult to express.

Compensatory Strategies

Another common set of communication devices involves compensation for missing knowledge. We will elaborate here on just three of the eleven strategy types in Table 5.3.

Typical of rock-bottom beginning-level learners, for example, is the memorization of certain stock phrases or sentences without internalized knowledge of their components. These memorized chunks of language, known as **prefabricated patterns**, are often found in pocket bilingual phrase books, which list hundreds of sentences for various occasions: "How much does this cost?" "Where is the toilet?" "I don't speak English." "I don't understand you." Such phrases are memorized by rote to fit their appropriate context. Prefabricated patterns are sometimes the source of some merriment. In my first few days of Kikongo learning in Africa, I tried to say, in Kikongo, "I don't know Kikongo" to those who attempted to converse with me. I was later embarrassed to discover that, in the first few attempts at producing this prefabricated avoidance device, instead of saying *Kizeyi Kikongo ko*, I had said *Kizolele Kikongo ko* (I don't *like* Kikongo), which brought on reactions ranging from amusement to hostility.

Code-switching is the use of a first or third language within a stream of speech in the second language. Often code-switching subconsciously occurs between two advanced learners with a common first language, but in such a case, usually not as a compensatory strategy. Learners in the early stages of acquisition, however, might code-switch—use their native language to fill in missing knowledge—whether the hearer knows that native language or not. Sometimes the learner slips in just a word or two, in the hope that the hearer will get the gist of what is being communicated. It is surprising that context of communication coupled with some of the universals of nonverbal expression sometimes enables learners to communicate an idea in their own language to someone unfamiliar with that language. Such marvels of communication are a tribute to the universality of human experience and a balm for those who feel the utter despair of attempting to communicate in a foreign tongue.

Yet another common compensatory strategy is a direct appeal for help. Learners may, if stuck for a particular word or phrase, directly ask a native speaker or the teacher for the form ("How do you say ___?"). Or they might venture a possible guess and then ask for verification from the native speaker of the correctness of the attempt. Also within this category are those instances where the learner might appeal to a bilingual dictionary for help. The latter case can also produce some rather amusing situations. Once a student of English as a second language, when asked to introduce himself to the class and the teacher, said, "Allow me to introduce myself and tell you some of the . . ." At this point he quickly got out his pocket dictionary and, finding the word he wanted, continued, "some of the *head-lights* of my past."

The list of potentially useful communication strategies is not limited to the thirteen listed in Table 5.3. Cohen and Aphek (1981) found that successful learners in their study made use of word association and generating their own rules. Chesterfield and Chesterfield (1985) reported instances of self talk as learners practiced their second language. Rost and Ross (1991) discovered that learners benefited from asking for repetition and seeking various forms of clarification. Huang and Van Naerssen (1987) attributed the oral production success of Chinese learners of English to functional practice (using language for communication) and, even more interesting, to reading practice. And the research continues.

STRATEGIES-BASED INSTRUCTION

Much of the work of researchers and teachers on the application of both learning and communication strategies to classroom learning has come to be known generically as **strategies-based instruction** (SBI) (McDonough 1999, Cohen 1998), or as learner strategy training. As we seek to make the language classroom an effective milieu for learning, it has become increasingly apparent that "teaching learners how to learn" is crucial. Wenden (1985) was among the first to assert that learner strategies are the key to learner autonomy, and that one of the most important goals of language teaching should be the facilitation of that autonomy.

Teachers can benefit from an understanding of what makes learners successful and unsuccessful, and establish in the classroom a milieu for the realization of successful strategies. Teachers cannot always expect instant success in that effort since students often bring with them certain preconceived notions of what "ought" to go on in the classroom (Bialystok 1985). However, it has been found that students will benefit from SBI if they (a) understand the strategy itself, (b) perceive it to be effective, and (c) do not consider its implementation to be overly difficult (MacIntyre & Noels 1996). Therefore our efforts to teach students some technical know-how about how to tackle a language are well advised.

Several different models of SBI are now being practiced in language classes around the world.

1. As part of a standard communicative methodology, teachers help students to become aware of their own style preferences and the strategies that are derived from those styles (Thompson & Rubin 1996, Oxford 1990a). (See also the "In the Classroom" vignette at the end of this chapter for some details.) Through checklists, tests, and interviews, teachers can become aware of students' tendencies and then offer advice on beneficial in-class and extra-class strategies.

2. Teachers can embed strategy awareness and practice into their pedagogy (Rubin & Thompson 1994; Brown 1989, 1990; Ellis & Sinclair 1989). As they utilize such techniques as communicative games, rapid reading, fluency exercises, and error analysis, teachers can help students both consciously and subconsciously to practice successful strategies.

3. Certain compensatory techniques are sometimes practiced to help students overcome certain weaknesses. Omaggio (1981) provided diagnostic instruments and procedures for determining students' preferences, then outlined exercises that help students to overcome certain blocks or to develop successful strategies here they are weak.

4. Finally, textbooks (Brown 1998, Chamot, O'Malley & Küpper 1992) include strategy instruction as part of a content-centered approach.

One of the most useful manuals of SBI available is Rebecca Oxford's (1990a) practical guide for teachers. She outlined a host of learning and communication strategies that have been successful among learners. Her taxonomy (see Figure 5.1) is both comprehensive and practical. Also, for younger learners, Chamot et al. (1999) produced a strategies handbook for teachers in elementary and secondary schools.

Figure 5.1. Oxford's strategy classification system

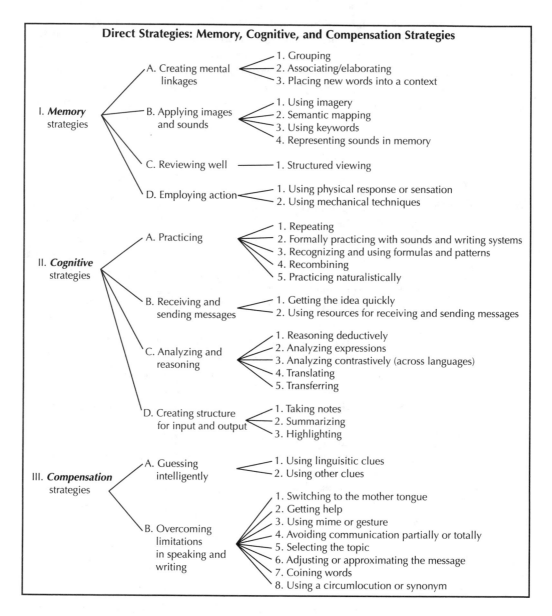

Figure 5.1. Oxford's strategy classification system (continued)

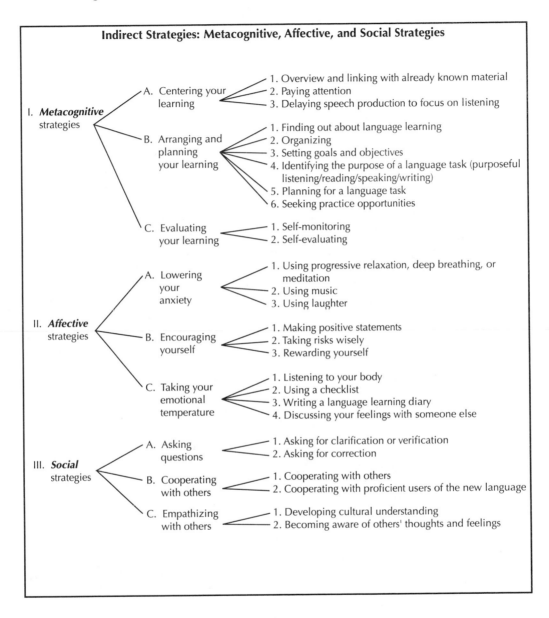

Indirect Strategies: Metacognitive, Affective, and Social Strategies

I. **Metacognitive** strategies

A. Centering your learning
1. Overview and linking with already known material
2. Paying attention
3. Delaying speech production to focus on listening

B. Arranging and planning your learning
1. Finding out about language learning
2. Organizing
3. Setting goals and objectives
4. Identifying the purpose of a language task (purposeful listening/reading/speaking/writing)
5. Planning for a language task
6. Seeking practice opportunities

C. Evaluating your learning
1. Self-monitoring
2. Self-evaluating

II. **Affective** strategies

A. Lowering your anxiety
1. Using progressive relaxation, deep breathing, or meditation
2. Using music
3. Using laughter

B. Encouraging yourself
1. Making positive statements
2. Taking risks wisely
3. Rewarding yourself

C. Taking your emotional temperature
1. Listening to your body
2. Using a checklist
3. Writing a language learning diary
4. Discussing your feelings with someone else

III. **Social** strategies

A. Asking questions
1. Asking for clarification or verification
2. Asking for correction

B. Cooperating with others
1. Cooperating with others
2. Cooperating with proficient users of the new language

C. Empathizing with others
1. Developing cultural understanding
2. Becoming aware of others' thoughts and feelings

We have much to learn in the creation of practical techniques for teaching learners how to use strategies effectively, but this remains a very exciting and promising area of pedagogical research at the present time.

★   ★   ★   ★   ★

In this chapter we have looked at a number of relevant and salient cognitive variables in the learning of a foreign language. It should by now be apparent that cognitive variables alone represent a complex system of factors that must be channeled into an understanding of the total second language acquisition process. An awareness of these factors will help you, the teacher, to perceive in your learners some wide-ranging individual differences. Not all learners are alike. No one can be neatly pigeon-holed into a cognitive type. With many styles and strategies operating within a person, hundreds of cognitive "profiles" might be identified! If we could discover some overriding and all-pervading variable that classifies learners neatly into categories of "successful" and "unsuccessful," then of course we could make a case for "typing" language learners. But, as Earl Stevick (1989) showed in his profile of seven successful language learners, such is not the case. Instead, teachers need to recognize and understand a multiplicity of cognitive variables active in the second language learning process and to make appropriate judgments about individual learners, meeting them where they are and providing them with the best possible opportunities for learning.

In the Classroom: Styles and Strategies in Practice

Strategies-based instruction, discussed at the end of the chapter, has a number of possible manifestations in the classroom. Sometimes textbooks themselves include exercises in style awareness and strategy development (Brown 1998). Or teachers might consult a manual of techniques (such as Chamot et al. 1999, Oxford 1990a) that offers guidelines on constructing their own strategy-building activities. Yet another option gives students an opportunity to fill out inventories to determine which of many possible strategies they use or fail to use. Or teachers might simply provide impromptu advice to learners as the occasions arise. To give you just a few examples of how learner strategy training works, three suggestions are offered here.

1. Administer a learning styles checklist. More often than not, language students enter a classroom with little or no conception of what good language learning strategies are. They dutifully sit at their desks waiting for the teacher to tell them "Open your books" or "Repeat after me." One thing that teachers can do to begin to open up students' minds to the possibility that they may *not* be engaging in strategies that could make them successful is to administer a very simple checklist on which students rate themselves. Figure 5.2 is an example of such a checklist. Once students have had a chance, with no advance "coaching," to fill out the checklist, you can engage them in any or all of the following: (a) a discussion of why they responded as they did, (b) small-group sharing of feelings underlying their responses, (c) an informal tabulation of how people responded to each item, (d) some advice, from your own experience, on why certain practices may be successful or unsuccessful, or (e) reaching the general consensus that responses in the A and B categories are usually indicative of successful approaches to language learning.

2. Engage in frequent spontaneous hints about successful learning and communication strategies. In spite of the fact that a good deal of what we know about second language acquisition is not unequivocally proven, we nevertheless know quite a lot about what generally applies to most learners most of the time. Most learners, for example, come to language classes with raised inhibitions and fears that prevent them taking the necessary risks that learners must take in order to try out language and receive constructive feedback. Such principles may be stated for learners in the form of ten "commandments" (or, you might want to simply call them "suggestions") for learners. A teacher's version (in somewhat more technical jargon) and

Figure 5.2. Check one box in each item that best describes you. Boxes A and E would indicate that the sentence is very much like you. Boxes B and D would indicate that the sentence is somewhat descriptive of you. Box C would indicate that you have no inclination one way or another.

A   B   C   D   E

1. I don't mind if people laugh at me when I speak. ☐ ☐ ☐ ☐ ☐ I get embarassed if people laugh at me when I speak.

2. I like to try out new words and structures that I'm not completely sure of. ☐ ☐ ☐ ☐ ☐ I like to use only language that I am certain is correct.

3. I feel very confident in my ability to succeed in learning this language. ☐ ☐ ☐ ☐ ☐ I feel quite uncertain about my ability to succeed in learning this language.

4. I want to learn this language because of what I can personally gain from it. ☐ ☐ ☐ ☐ ☐ I am learning this language only because someone else is requiring it.

5. I really enjoy working with other people in groups. ☐ ☐ ☐ ☐ ☐ I would much rather work alone than with other people.

6. I like to "absorb" language and get the general "gist" of what is said or written. ☐ ☐ ☐ ☐ ☐ I like to analyze the many details of language and understand exactly what is said or written.

7. If there is an abundance of language to master, I just try to take things one step at a time. ☐ ☐ ☐ ☐ ☐ I am very annoyed by an abundance of language material presented all at once.

8. I am not overly conscious of myself when I speak. ☐ ☐ ☐ ☐ ☐ I "monitor" myself very closely and consciously when I speak.

9. When I make mistakes, I try to use them to learn something about the language. ☐ ☐ ☐ ☐ ☐ When I make a mistake, it annoys me because that's a symbol of how poor my performance is.

10. I find ways to continue learning language outside of the classroom. ☐ ☐ ☐ ☐ ☐ I look to the teacher and the classroom activities for everything I need to be successful.

a learner's version of these ten rules for successful class-room learning are given in Table 5.4. These rules might simply take on the form of little reminders sprinkled into your classroom routines. You will note that each rule corresponds to the numbered items in the checklist above. Caution should be taken in both cases, of course, in assuming that *all* learners will benefit from the direction-ality of the advice in these suggestions; a few learners, for example, may be too confident or too right-brain oriented.

Table 5.4. "Ten Commandments" for good language learning

Teacher's Version	Learner's Version
1. Lower inhibitions	Fear not!
2. Encourage risk-taking	Dive in.
3. Build self-confidence	Believe in yourself.
4. Develop intrinsic motivation	Seize the day.
5. Engage in cooperative learning	Love thy neighbor.
6. Use right-brain processes	Get the BIG picture.
7. Promote ambiguity tolerance	Cope with the chaos.
8. Practice intuition	Go with your hunches.
9. Process error feedback	Make mistakes work FOR you.
10. Set personal goals	Set your own goals.

3.   Build strategic techniques. Perhaps a more subtle but no less effective way to manifest learner strategy training in a classroom is to make sure that techniques are directed as much as possible toward good language learning behaviors. Overt admonition or calling students' conscious attention to principles need not be the major approach; instead, teachers can encourage successful subconscious strategy employment through their choice of classroom techniques that enhance strategy building. By extending the "ten commandments" into classroom activities, suggestions for building strategic competence emerge, as shown in Table 5.5.

Table 5.5. Building strategic techniques

1. To lower inhibitions: play guessing games and communication games; do role-plays and skits; sing songs; use plenty of group work; laugh **with** your students; have them share their fears in small groups.

2. To encourage risk taking: praise students for making sincere efforts to try out language; use fluency exercises where errors are not corrected at that time; give outside-of-class assignments to speak or write or otherwise try out the language.

3. To build students' self-confidence: tell students explicity (verbally and nonverbally) that you do indeed believe in them; have them make lists of their strengths, of what they know or have accomplished so far in the course.

4. To help them to develop intrinsic motivation: remind them explicitly about the rewards for learning English; describe (or have students look up) jobs that require English; play down the final examination in favor of helping students to see rewards for themselves beyond the final exam.

5. To promote cooperative learning: direct students to share their knowledge; play down competition among students; get your class to think of themselves as a team; do a considerable amount of small-group work.

6. To encourage them to use right-brain processing: use movies and tapes in class; have them read passages rapidly; do skimming exercises; do rapid "free writes"; do oral fluency exercises where the object is to get students to talk (or write) a lot without being corrected.

7. To promote ambiguity tolerance: encourage students to ask you, and each other, questions when they don't understand something; keep your theoretical explanations very simple and brief; deal with just a few rules at a time; occasionally resort to translation into a native language to clarify a word or meaning.

8. To help them use their intuition: praise students for good guesses; do not always give explanations of errors—let a correction suffice; correct only selected errors, preferably just those that interfere with learning.

9. To get students to make their mistakes work FOR them: tape record students' oral production and get them to identify errors; let students catch and correct each other's errors—do not always give them the correct form; encourage students to make lists of their common errors and to work on them on their own.

10. To get students to set their own goals: explicitly encourage or direct students to go beyond the classroom goals; have them make lists of what they will accomplish on their own in a particular week; get students to make specific time commitments at home to study the language; give "extra credit" work.

These three suggestions for bringing strategies-based instruction into the classroom of course only begin to provide an idea of what can be done to sensitize learners to the importance of taking charge of their own learning—of taking some responsibility for their eventual success and not just leaving it all up to the teacher to "deliver" everything to them. If teachers everywhere would do no more than simply follow the above suggestions, significant steps could be made toward encouraging students to make a strategic investment in their own language learning success.

TOPICS AND QUESTIONS FOR STUDY AND DISCUSSION

[Note: (I) individual work; (G) group or pair work; (C) whole-class discussion.]

1. (I) In order to make sure you understand the continuum of process, style, and strategy, make a list of some of the universal processes you have read in previous chapters, then a list of styles and strategies from this chapter. How do they differ?
2. (G) In a small group, share what each of you perceives to be your more dominant cognitive style along the continua presented here: FI/D, right/left brain, ambiguity tolerance, reflective/impulsive, and visual/auditory. Talk about examples of how you manifest those styles both in your approach in general to problems and in your approach to SLA.
3. (I) Look at the list of differences between right- and left-brain processing in Table 5.1 on page 119. Check or circle the side that corresponds to your own preference, and total the items on each side. Are you right- or left-brain dominant? Does this result match your general perception of yourself?
4. (G) Form five groups, with one of the five cognitive styles assigned to each group. Each group will list the types of activities or techniques in foreign language classes that illustrate its style. Then, decide which list of activities is better for what kinds of purposes. Share the results with the rest of the class.
5. (I) Someone once claimed that FD is related to farsightedness. That is, farsighted people tend to be more FD, and vice versa. If that is true, how would you theoretically justify such a finding?
6. (C) Look at the list of "good language learner" characteristics on page 123 as enumerated by Rubin and Thompson. Which ones seem the most important? Which the least? Would you be able to add some items to this list, from your own or others' experiences?

7. (C) Discuss any instances in which you have used any of the thirteen communication strategies listed in Table 5.3 on page 128. Are there some other strategies that you could add?

8. (I/G/C) First, individually take the Learning Styles Checklist on page 136. Then, in pairs look at a partner's responses and find one item on which you differ greatly (e.g., A vs. E, A vs. D, or B vs. E). Next, talk about experiences in your own language learning that illustrate your choice. Finally, decide which side of the continuum (the "A-B" side or the "D-E" side) gives you more of an advantage. Share the results with the rest of the class.

9. (C) When you were learning a foreign language, what advice would you like to have had that you did not have at the time? Which of the suggestions at the end of the chapter for SBI appeal to you, and why?

SUGGESTED READINGS

Gardner, Robert C. and MacIntyre, Peter D. 1992. "A student's contributions to second language learning. Part I: Cognitive variables." *Language Teaching* 25: 211–220.

A summary of issues and research on cognitive variables in second language acquisition is included in this state-of-the-art article.

Oxford, Rebecca (Ed.). 1996. *Learning Strategies Around the World: Cross-Cultural Perspectives.* Honolulu: University of Hawaii Press.

Oxford, Rebecca and Anderson, Neil J. 1995. "A crosscultural view of learning styles." *Language Teaching* 28: 201–215.

These two publications offer a comprehensive summary of cross-cultural research on learning styles, and more than a dozen specific cross-cultural studies of style awareness and strategy use.

Cohen, Andrew. 1998. *Strategies in Learning and Using a Second Language.* New York: Addison Wesley Longman.

A state-of-the-art summary of concepts and research, and some practical thoughts about strategies-based instruction.

Oxford, Rebecca. 1990a. Language *Learning Strategies: What Every Teacher Should Know.* Boston: Heinle & Heinle.

A must-read for a wealth of practical information on strategies-based instruction along with explanations of dozens of types of strategies.

Brown, H. Douglas. 2000a. *Strategies for Success: A Practical Guide.* In press.

This little strategies guide for students, accompanied by a teacher's guide, gives an idea of how to get learners strategically involved in their acquisition process. It also contains a number of self-check tests.

LANGUAGE LEARNING EXPERIENCE: JOURNAL ENTRY 5

[Note: See pages 18 and 19 of Chapter 1 for general guidelines for writing a journal on a previous or concurrent language learning experience.]

- List each of the five learning styles discussed in the chapter (FI/D, right/left brain, ambiguity tolerance, reflectivity/impulsivity, visual/auditory). Write a few sentences about which side you think is dominant for you, and list some examples to illustrate.
- Which of your tendencies, if any, do you think might be working against you? Make a short list of specific things you could do to help push yourself to a more favorable position.
- Take the Learning Styles Checklist on page 136. Do you think you should try to change some of your styles, as they are described on the checklist? How would you do that?
- Using the list of learning strategies (Table 5.2), describe examples of two or three of them that you have already used. Pick one or two that you don't use very much and list them as your challenge for the near future.
- Write about communication strategies that you have used. Does the list of communication strategies in Table 5.3 give you some ideas about what you could be doing to advance your communicative success? Try to write down one or two specific things you will try out in the near future in a foreign language.
- How does your teacher (either now or in the past) measure up as a strategies-based instructor? What does this tell you about how your own teaching might help students to be more successful learners?

CHAPTER **6**

PERSONALITY

FACTORS

THE PREVIOUS two chapters dealt with two facets of the cognitive domain of language learning: human learning processes in general, and cognitive variations in learning—styles and strategies. Similarly, this chapter and Chapter 7 deal with two facets of the affective domain of second language acquisition. The first of these is the intrinsic side of affectivity: personality factors within a person that contribute in some way to the success of language learning. The second facet, treated in Chapter 7, encompasses extrinsic factors—sociocultural variables that emerge as the second language learner brings not just two languages into contact but two cultures, and in some sense must learn a second culture along with a second language.

If we were to devise theories of second language acquisition or teaching methodologies that were based only on cognitive considerations, we would be omitting the most fundamental side of human behavior. Ernest Hilgard, well known for his study of human learning and cognition, once noted that "purely cognitive theories of learning will be rejected unless a role is assigned to affectivity" (1963: 267). In recent thinking (Arnold 1999), there is no doubt at all about the importance of examining personality factors in building a theory of second language acquisition.

The affective domain is difficult to describe scientifically. A large number of variables are implied in considering the emotional side of human behavior in the second language learning process. One problem in striving for affective explanations of language success is presented by the task of subdividing and categorizing the factors of the affective domain. We are often tempted to use rather sweeping terms as if they were carefully defined.

For example, it is easy enough to say that "culture conflict" accounts for many language learning problems, or that "motivation" is the key to success in a foreign language; but it is quite another matter to define such terms with precision. Psychologists also experience a difficulty in defining terms. Abstract concepts such as empathy, aggression, extroversion, and other common labels are difficult to define empirically. Standardized psychological tests often form an operational definition of such concepts, but constant revisions are evidence of an ongoing struggle for validity. Nevertheless, the elusive nature of affective and cognitive concepts need not deter us from seeking answers to questions. Careful, systematic study of the role of personality in second language acquisition has already led to a greater understanding of the language learning process and to improved language teaching designs.

THE AFFECTIVE DOMAIN

Affect refers to emotion or feeling. The affective domain is the emotional side of human behavior, and it may be juxtaposed to the cognitive side. The development of affective states or feelings involves a variety of personality factors, feelings both about ourselves and about others with whom we come into contact.

Benjamin Bloom and his colleagues (Krathwohl, Bloom, & Masia 1964) provided a useful extended definition of the affective domain that is still widely used today.

1. At the first and fundamental level, the development of affectivity begins with *receiving*. Persons must be aware of the environment surrounding them and be conscious of situations, phenomena, people, objects; be willing to receive—to tolerate a stimulus, not avoid it—and give a stimulus their controlled or selected attention.
2. Next, persons must go beyond receiving to *responding*, committing themselves in at least some small measure to a phenomenon or a person. Such responding in one dimension may be in acquiescence, but in another, higher, dimension the person is willing to respond voluntarily without coercion, and then to receive satisfaction from that response.
3. The third level of affectivity involves *valuing*: placing worth on a thing, a behavior, or a person. Valuing takes on the characteristics of beliefs or attitudes as values are internalized. Individuals do not

merely accept a value to the point of being willing to be identified with it, but commit themselves to the value to pursue it, seek it out, and want it, finally, to the point of conviction.

4. The fourth level of the affective domain is the *organization* of values into a system of beliefs, determining interrelationships among them, and establishing a hierarchy of values within the system.

5. Finally, individuals become characterized by and understand themselves in terms of their *value system*. Individuals act consistently in accordance with the values they have internalized and integrate beliefs, ideas, and attitudes into a total philosophy or world view. It is at this level that problem solving, for example, is approached on the basis of a total, self-consistent system.

Bloom's taxonomy was devised for educational purposes, but it has been used for a general understanding of the affective domain in human behavior. The fundamental notions of receiving, responding, and valuing are universal. Second language learners need to be receptive both to those with whom they are communicating and to the language itself, responsive to persons and to the context of communication, and willing and able to place a certain value on the communicative act of interpersonal exchange.

Lest you feel at this point that the affective domain as described by Bloom is a bit too far removed from the essence of language, it is appropriate to recall that language is inextricably woven into the fabric of virtually every aspect of human behavior. Language is so pervasive a phenomenon in our humanity that it cannot be separated from the larger whole—from the whole persons that live and breathe and think and feel. Kenneth Pike (1967: 26) said that

language is behavior, that is, a phase of human activity which must not be treated in essence as structurally divorced from the structure of nonverbal human activity. The activity of man constitutes a structural whole in such a way that it cannot be subdivided into neat "parts" or "levels" or "compartments" with language in a behavioral compartment insulated in character, content, and organization from other behavior.

Understanding how human beings feel and respond and believe and value is an exceedingly important aspect of a theory of second language acquisition.

We turn now to a consideration of specific personality factors in human behavior and how they relate to second language acquisition.

Self-Esteem

Self-esteem is probably the most pervasive aspect of any human behavior. It could easily be claimed that no successful cognitive or affective activity can be carried out without some degree of self-esteem, self-confidence, knowledge of yourself, and belief in your own capabilities for that activity. Malinowski (1923) noted that all human beings have a need for *phatic communion*—defining oneself and finding acceptance in expressing that self in relation to valued others. Personality development universally involves the growth of a person's concept of self, acceptance of self, and reflection of self as seen in the interaction between self and others.

The following is a well-accepted definition of self-esteem (Coopersmith 1967: 4–5):

> By self-esteem, we refer to the evaluation which individuals make and customarily maintain with regard to themselves; it expresses an attitude of approval or disapproval, and indicates the extent to which individuals believe themselves to be capable, significant, successful and worthy. In short, self-esteem is a personal judgment of worthiness that is expressed in the attitudes that individuals hold towards themselves. It is a subjective experience which the individual conveys to others by verbal reports and other overt expressive behavior.

People derive their sense of self-esteem from the accumulation of experiences with themselves and with others and from assessments of the external world around them. Three general levels of self-esteem have been described in the literature to capture its multidimensionality:

1. General, or **global**, self-esteem is said to be relatively stable in a mature adult, and is resistant to change except by active and extended therapy. It is the general or prevailing assessment one makes of one's own worth over time and across a number of situations. In a sense, it might be analogized to a statistical mean or median level of overall self-appraisal.
2. **Situational** or **specific** self-esteem refers to one's self-appraisals in particular life situations, such as social interaction, work, education, home, or on certain relatively discretely defined traits, such as intelligence, communicative ability, athletic ability, or personality traits like gregariousness, empathy, and flexibility. The degree of specific self-esteem a person has may vary depending upon the situation or the trait in question.

3. **Task** self-esteem relates to particular tasks within specific situations. For example, within the educational domain, task self-esteem might refer to one subject-matter area. In an athletic context, skill in a sport—or even a facet of a sport such as net play in tennis or pitching in baseball—would be evaluated on the level of task self-esteem. Specific self-esteem might encompass second language acquisition in general, and task self-esteem might appropriately refer to one's self-evaluation of a particular aspect of the process: speaking, writing, a particular class in a second language, or even a special kind of classroom exercise.

Adelaide Heyde (1979) studied the effects of the three levels of self-esteem on performance of an oral production task by American college students learning French as a foreign language. She found that all three levels of self-esteem correlated positively with performance on the oral production measure, with the highest correlation occurring between task self-esteem and performance on oral production measures. Watkins, Biggs, and Regmi (1991), Brodkey and Shore (1976), and Gardner and Lambert (1972) all included measures of self-esteem in their studies of success in language learning. The results revealed that self-esteem appears to be an important variable in second language acquisition, particularly in view of cross-cultural factors of second language learning that will be discussed in the next chapter.

MacIntyre, Dörnyei, Clément, and Noels (1998) saw the significance of self-confidence in their model of "willingness to communicate" in a foreign language. A number of factors appear to contribute to predisposing one learner to seek, and another learner to avoid, second language communication. Noting that a high level of communicative ability does not necessarily correspond with a high willingness to communicate, MacIntyre et al. proposed a number of cognitive and affective factors that underlie the latter: motivation, personality, intergroup climate, and two levels of self-confidence. The first level resembles what has already been described as situational self-esteem, or "state communicative self-confidence" (MacIntyre et al. 1998: 547), and the second, an overall global level simply labeled "L2 self-confidence." Both self-confidence factors assume important roles in determining one's willingness to communicate.

What we do not know at this time is the answer to the classic chicken-or-egg question: Does high self-esteem cause language success, or does language success cause high self-esteem? Clearly, both are interacting factors. It is difficult to say whether teachers should try to "improve" global self-esteem or simply improve a learner's proficiency and let self-esteem take care of itself. Heyde (1979) found that certain sections of a beginning college French course had better oral production and self-esteem scores than other sections after only eight weeks of instruction. This finding suggests that teachers really can have a positive and influential effect on both the linguistic performance and the emotional well-being of the student. Andrés (1999: 91) concurred and suggested classroom techniques that can help learners to "unfold their wings." Perhaps these teachers succeeded because they gave optimal attention both to linguistic goals and to the personhood of their students.

Inhibition

Closely related to and in some cases subsumed under the notion of self-esteem is the concept of inhibition. All human beings, in their under-standing of themselves, build sets of defenses to protect the ego. The newborn baby has no concept of its own self; gradually it learns to identify a self that is distinct from others. In childhood, the growing degrees of awareness, responding, and valuing begin to create a system of affective traits that individuals identify with themselves. In adolescence, the phys-ical, emotional, and cognitive changes of the pre-teenager and teenager bring on mounting defensive inhibitions to protect a fragile ego, to ward off ideas, experiences, and feelings that threaten to dismantle the organization of values and beliefs on which appraisals of self-esteem have been founded. The process of building defenses continues into adulthood. Some per-sons—those with higher self-esteem and ego strength—are more able to withstand threats to their existence, and thus their defenses are lower. Those with weaker self-esteem maintain walls of inhibition to protect what is self-perceived to be a weak or fragile ego, or a lack of self-confidence in a situation or task.

The human ego encompasses what Guiora (1972a) and Ehrman (1996) refer to as **language ego** or the very personal, egoistic nature of second language acquisition. Meaningful language acquisition involves some degree of identity conflict as language learners take on a new iden-tity with their newly acquired competence. An adaptive language ego enables learners to lower the inhibitions that may impede success.

In a classic study of inhibition in relation to second language learning, Guiora, Beit-Hallami, Brannon, Dull, and Scovel (1972a) designed an experi-ment using small quantities of alcohol to induce temporary states of less-than-normal inhibition in an experimental group of subjects. The perform-ance on a pronunciation test in Thai of subjects given the alcohol was sig-nificantly better than the performance of a control group. Guiora and colleagues concluded that a direct relationship existed between inhibition (a component of language ego) and pronunciation ability in a second language.

But there were some serious problems in the researchers' conclusion. Alcohol may lower inhibitions, but alcohol also tends to affect muscular tension, and while "mind" and "body" in this instance may not be clearly separable, the physical effect of the alcohol may have been a more important factor than the mental effect in accounting for the superior pronunciation performance of the subjects given alcohol. Furthermore, pronunciation may be a rather poor indicator of overall language competence. Nevertheless, the Guiora research team provided an important hypothesis that has tremendous intuitive—if not experimental—support.

In another experiment (Guiora et al. 1980), Guiora and his associates studied the effect of Valium on pronunciation of a second language. Inspired by a study (Schumann et al. 1978) that showed that hypnotized subjects performed well on pronunciation tests, Guiora and colleagues hypothesized that various dosages of a chemical relaxant would have a similar effect on subjects' pronunciation performance. It is unfortunate that the results were nonsignificant, but it is interesting that the tester made a significant difference. In other words, the person doing the testing made a bigger difference on scores than did the dosage of Valium. I wonder if this result says something about the importance of teachers!

Some have facetiously suggested that the moral to Guiora's experiments is that we should provide cocktails—or prescribe tranquilizers—for foreign language classes! While students might be delighted by such a proposal, the experiments have highlighted a most interesting possibility: that the inhibitions, the defenses, that we place between ourselves and others are important factors contributing to second language success. Ehrman (1999, 1993) has provided further support for the importance of language ego in studies of learners with "thin" (permeable) and "thick" (not as permeable) ego boundaries. While neither extreme has been found to have necessarily beneficial or deleterious effects on success, Ehrman has suggested that the openness, vulnerability, and ambiguity tolerance of those with "thin" ego boundaries create different pathways to success from those with hard-driving, systematic, perfectionistic, "thick" ego boundaries.

Such findings, coupled with Guiora's earlier work, have given rise to a number of steps that have been taken in practices to create techniques that reduce inhibition in the foreign language classroom. Language teaching approaches in the last three decades have been characterized by the creation of contexts in which students are made to feel free to take risks, to orally try out hypotheses, and in so doing to break down some of the barriers that often make learners reluctant to try out their new language.

Anyone who has learned a foreign language is acutely aware that second language learning actually necessitates the making of mistakes. We test out hypotheses about language by trial and many errors; children learning their first language and adults learning a second can really make progress only by learning from their mistakes. If we never ventured to speak a sentence until we were absolutely certain of its total correctness, we would likely never communicate productively at all. But mistakes can be viewed as threats to one's ego. They pose both internal and external threats. Internally, one's critical self and one's performing self can be in conflict: the learner performs something "wrong" and becomes critical of his or her own mistake. Externally, learners perceive others to be critical, even judging their very person when they blunder in a second language.

Earl Stevick (1976b) spoke of language learning as involving a number of forms of "alienation": alienation between the critical me and the performing me, between my native culture and my target culture, between me and my teacher, and between me and my fellow students. This alienation arises from the defenses that we build around ourselves. These defenses inhibit learning, and their removal can therefore promote language learning, which involves self-exposure to a degree manifested in few other endeavors.

Risk-Taking

In the last chapter we saw that one of the prominent characteristics of good language learners, according to Rubin and Thompson (1982), was the ability to make intelligent guesses. Impulsivity was also described as a style that could have positive effects on language success. And we have just seen that inhibitions, or building defenses around our egos, can be a detriment. These factors suggest that risk-taking is an important characteristic of successful learning of a second language. Learners have to be able to gamble a bit, to be willing to try out hunches about the language and take the risk of being wrong.

Beebe (1983: 40) described some of the negative ramifications that foster fear of risk-taking both in the classroom and in natural settings.

> In the classroom, these ramifications might include a bad grade in the course, a fail on the exam, a reproach from the teacher, a smirk from a classmate, punishment or embarrassment imposed by oneself. Outside the classroom, individuals learning a second language face other negative consequences if they make mistakes. They fear looking ridiculous; they fear the frustration coming from a listener's blank look, showing that they have failed to communicate; they fear the danger of not being able to take care of themselves; they fear the alienation of not being able to communicate and thereby get close to other human beings. Perhaps worst of all, they fear a loss of identity.

The classroom antidote to such fears, according to Dufeu (1994: 89–90), is to establish an adequate affective framework so that learners "feel comfortable as they take their first public steps in the strange world of a foreign language. To achieve this, one has to create a climate of acceptance that will stimulate self-confidence, and encourage participants to experiment and to discover the target language, allowing themselves to take risks without feeling embarrassed."

On a continuum ranging from high to low risk-taking, we may be tempted to assume with Ely (1986) that high risk-taking will yield positive results in second language learning; however, such is not usually the case. Beebe (1983: 41) cited a study which claimed that "persons with a high motivation to achieve are . . . . moderate, not high, risk-takers. These individuals like to be in control and like to depend on skill. They do not take wild, frivolous risks or enter into no-win situations." Successful second language learners appear to fit the same paradigm. A learner might be too bold in blurting out meaningless verbal garbage that no one can quite understand, while success lies in an optimum point where calculated guesses are ventured. As Rubin (1994) noted, successful language learners make willing and *accurate* guesses.

Risk-taking variation seems to be a factor in a number of issues in second language acquisition and pedagogy. The silent student in the classroom is one who is unwilling to appear foolish when mistakes are made. Self-esteem seems to be closely connected to a risk-taking factor: when those foolish mistakes are made, a person with high global self-esteem is not daunted by the possible consequences of being laughed at. Beebe (1983) noted that fossilization, or the relatively permanent incorporation of certain patterns of error, may be due to a lack of willingness to take risks. It is "safe" to stay within patterns that accomplish the desired function even though there may be some errors in those patterns. (See Chapter 8 for further discussion of fossilization.) The implications for teaching are important. In a few uncommon cases, overly high risk-takers, as they dominate the classroom with wild gambles, may need to be "tamed" a bit by the teacher. But most of the time our problem as teachers will be to encourage students to guess somewhat more willingly than the usual student is prone to do, and to value them as persons for those risks that they take.

Anxiety

Intricately intertwined with self-esteem and inhibition and risk-taking, the construct of anxiety plays an important affective role in second language acquisition. Even though we all know what anxiety is and we all have experienced feelings of anxiousness, anxiety is still not easy to define in a simple sentence. It is associated with feelings of uneasiness, frustration, self-doubt, apprehension, or worry (Scovel 1978: 134).

The research on anxiety suggests that, like self-esteem, anxiety can be experienced at various levels (Oxford 1999). At the deepest, or global, level, **trait** anxiety is a more permanent predisposition to be anxious. Some people are predictably and generally anxious about many things. At a more momentary, or situational level, **state** anxiety is experienced in relation to some particular event or act. As we learned in the case of self-esteem, then, it is important in a classroom for a teacher to try to determine whether a student's anxiety stems from a more global trait or whether it comes from a particular situation at the moment.

Trait anxiety, because of its global and somewhat ambiguously defined nature, has not proved to be useful in predicting second language achievement (MacIntyre & Gardner 1991c). However, recent research on *language anxiety*, as it has come to be known, focuses more specifically on the situational nature of state anxiety. Three components of foreign language anxiety have been identified (Horwitz et al. 1986; MacIntyre & Gardner 1989, 1991c) in order to break down the construct into researchable issues:

1. communication apprehension, arising from learners' inability to adequately express mature thoughts and ideas;
2. fear of negative social evaluation, arising from a learner's need to make a positive social impression on others; and
3. test anxiety, or apprehension over academic evaluation.

A decade of research (MacIntyre & Gardner 1988, 1989, 1991a, 1991b, 1991c, 1994; Gardner & MacIntyre 1993b; MacIntyre, Noels, & Clément 1997; Horwitz & Young 1991; Young 1991; Phillips 1992; Ganschow et al. 1994; Ganschow & Sparks 1996; Vogely 1998; Oxford 1999) has now given us useful information on foreign language anxiety. Most of these studies conclude that "foreign language anxiety can be distinguished from other types of anxiety and that it can have a negative effect on the language learning process" (MacIntyre & Gardner 1991c: 112).

Yet another important insight to be applied to our understanding of anxiety lies in the distinction between **debilitative** and **facilitative** anxiety (Alpert and Haber 1960, Scovel 1978), or what Oxford (1999) called "harmful" and "helpful" anxiety. We may be inclined to view anxiety as a negative factor, something to be avoided at all costs. But the notion of facilitative anxiety is that some concern—some apprehension—over a task to be accomplished is a positive factor. Otherwise, a learner might be inclined to be "wishy-washy," lacking that facilitative tension that keeps one poised, alert, and just slightly unbalanced to the point that one cannot relax entirely. The feeling of nervousness before giving a public speech is, in experienced speakers, often a sign of facilitative anxiety, a symptom of just enough tension to get the job done.

Several studies have suggested the benefit of facilitative anxiety in learning foreign languages (Ehrman & Oxford 1995, Young 1992, Horwitz 1990). In Bailey's (1983) study of competitiveness and anxiety in second language learning, facilitative anxiety was one of the keys to success, closely related to competitiveness. I noted in Chapter 4 that Rogers's humanistic theory of learning promotes low anxiety among learners and a nondefensive posture where learners do not feel they are in competition with one another. Bailey found in her self-analysis, however, that while competitiveness sometimes hindered her progress (for example, the pressure to outdo her peers sometimes caused her to retreat even to the point of skipping class), at other times it motivated her to study harder (as in the case of carrying out an intensive review of material in order to feel more at ease in oral work in the classroom). She explained the positive effects of competitiveness by means of the construct of facilitative anxiety.

So the next time your language students are anxious, you would do well to ask yourself if that anxiety is truly debilitative. It could well be that a little nervous tension in the process is a good thing. Once again, we find that a construct has an optimal point along its continuum: both too much and too little anxiety may hinder the process of successful second language learning.

Empathy

The human being is a social animal, and the chief mechanism for maintaining the bonds of society is language. Some approaches to language teaching fail to accomplish the goal of communicativity in the learner by overlooking the social nature of language. While we tend to recognize the importance of the social aspect of language, we also tend to oversimplify that aspect by not recognizing the complexity of the relation between language and society, or by considering socially oriented problems in language learning as a simple matter of "acculturation." Chapter 7 demonstrates that acculturation is no simple process, and it will become clear in this chapter that the social **transactions** that the second language learner is called upon to make constitute complex endeavors.

Transaction is the process of reaching out beyond the self to others, and language is a major tool used to accomplish that process. A variety of transactional variables may apply to second language learning: imitation, modeling, identification, empathy, extroversion, aggression, styles of communication, and others. Two of these variables, chosen for their relevance to a global understanding of second language acquisition, will be treated here: empathy and extroversion.

In common terminology, **empathy** is the process of "putting yourself into someone else's shoes," of reaching beyond the self to understand what another person is feeling. It is probably the major factor in the harmonious coexistence of individuals in society. Language is one of the primary means of empathizing, but nonverbal communication facilitates the process of empathizing and must not be overlooked.

In more sophisticated terms, empathy is usually described as the projection of one's own personality into the personality of another in order to understand him or her better. Empathy is not synonymous with **sympathy**. Empathy implies more possibility of detachment; sympathy connotes an agreement or harmony between individuals. Guiora (1972b: 142) defined empathy as "a process of comprehending in which a temporary fusion of self-object boundaries permits an immediate emotional apprehension of the affective experience of another." Psychologists generally agree with Guiora's definition and add that there are two necessary aspects to the development and exercising of empathy: first, an awareness and knowledge of one's own feelings, and second, identification with another person (Hogan 1969). In other words, you cannot fully empathize—or know someone else—until you adequately know yourself.

Communication requires a sophisticated degree of empathy. In order to communicate effectively you need to be able to understand the other person's affective and cognitive states; communication breaks down when false presuppositions or assumptions are made about the other person's state. From the very mechanical, syntactic level of language to the most abstract, meaningful level, we assume certain structures of knowledge and certain emotional states in any communicative act. In order to make those assumptions correctly, we need to transcend our own ego boundaries, or, using Guiora's term, to "permeate" our ego boundaries so that we can send and receive messages clearly.

Oral communication is a case in which, cognitively at least, it is easy to achieve empathetic communication because there is immediate feedback from the hearer. A misunderstood word, phrase, or idea can be questioned by the hearer and then rephrased by the speaker until a clear message is interpreted. Written communication requires a special kind of empathy— a "cognitive" empathy in which the writer, without the benefit of immediate feedback from the reader, must communicate ideas by means of a very clear empathetic intuition and judgment of the reader's state of mind and structure of knowledge.

So in a second language learning situation, the problem of empathy becomes acute. Not only must learner-speakers correctly identify cognitive and affective sets in the hearer, but they must do so in a language in which they are insecure. Then, learner-hearers, attempting to comprehend a second language, often discover that their own states of thought are misinterpreted by a native speaker, and the result is that linguistic, cognitive, and affective information easily passes in one ear and out the other.

Guiora and his colleagues (1972a, 1972b) found that a modified version of the Micro-Momentary Expression (MME) test, a test claiming to measure degrees of empathy, successfully predicted authenticity of pronunciation of a foreign language. Naiman, Fröhlich, Stern, and Tedesco (1978, 1996) included an empathy measure (Hogan's Empathy Scale—see Hogan 1969) in their battery of tests used to try to discover characteristics of the "good language learner," but found no significant correlation between empathy and language success as measured by an imitation test and a listening test. Their finding was not unexpected, however, since they found field independence to be positively correlated with language success; the presumed antithesis of field independence—field dependence—has been shown to correlate highly with empathy (Witkin et al. 1971). But a great deal of the problem of the study of most personality variables lies in the accuracy of the tests used to measure traits. Serious methodological problems surround such measurement; the MME and Hogan's Empathy Scale are cases in point. It has been shown that such tests accurately identify personality extremes (schizophrenic, paranoid, or psychotic behavior, for example) but fail to differentiate among the vast "normal" population.

Certainly one of the more interesting implications of the study of empathy is the need to define empathy cross-culturally—to understand how different cultures express empathy. Most of the empathy tests devised in the United States are culture-bound to Western, North American, middle-class society. Chapter 7 will deal more specifically with empathy in cross-cultural settings, particularly with the role of empathy in defining the concept of acculturation.

Extroversion

Extroversion and its counterpart, introversion, are also potentially important factors in the acquisition of a second language. The terms are often misunderstood because of a tendency to stereotype extroversion. We are prone to think of an extroverted person as a gregarious, "life of the party" person. Introverts, conversely, are thought of as quiet and reserved, with tendencies toward reclusiveness. Western society values the stereotypical extrovert. Nowhere is this more evident than in the classroom where teachers admire the talkative, outgoing student who participates freely in class discussions. On the other hand, introverts are sometimes thought of as not being as bright as extroverts.

Such a view of extroversion is misleading. **Extroversion** is the extent to which a person has a deep-seated need to receive ego enhancement, self-esteem, and a sense of wholeness *from other people* as opposed to receiving that affirmation within oneself. Extroverts actually need other people in order to feel "good." But extroverts are not necessarily loud-mouthed and talkative. They may be relatively shy but still need the affirmation of others. **Introversion**, on the other hand, is the extent to which a person derives a sense of wholeness and fulfillment apart from a reflection of this self from other people. Contrary to our stereotypes, introverts can have an inner strength of character that extroverts do not have.

It is unfortunate that these stereotypes have influenced teachers' perceptions of students. Ausubel (1968: 413) noted that introversion and extroversion are a "grossly misleading index of social adjustment," and other educators have warned against prejudging students on the basis of perceived extroversion. In language classes, where oral participation is highly valued, it is easy to view active participants with favor and to assume that their visibility in the classroom is due to an extroversion factor (which may not be so). Culturally, American society differs considerably from a number of other societies where it is improper to speak out in the classroom. Teachers need to consider cultural norms in their assessment of a student's presumed "passivity" in the classroom.

Extroversion is commonly thought to be related to empathy, but such may not be the case. The extroverted person may actually behave in an extroverted manner in order to protect his or her own ego, with extroverted behavior being symptomatic of defensive barriers and high ego boundaries. At the same time the introverted, quieter, more reserved person may show high empathy—an intuitive understanding and apprehension of others—and simply be more reserved in the outward and overt expression of empathy.

It is not clear then, that extroversion or introversion helps or hinders the process of second language acquisition. The Toronto study (Naiman et al. 1978, 1996) found no significant effect for extroversion in characterizing the good language learner. Busch (1982), in a comprehensive study on extroversion, explored the relationship of introversion and extroversion to English proficiency in adult Japanese learners of English in Japan. She hypothesized that extroverted students (as measured by a standard personality inventory) would be more proficient than introverts. Her hypothesis was not supported by her findings. In fact, introverts were significantly *better* than extroverts in their pronunciation (one of four factors which were measured in an oral interview)! This latter result clouded our stereotype of the extroverted language learner as a frequent and willing participant in class activities. But more appropriately, it suggested that introverts may have the patience and focus to attend to clear articulation in a foreign language.

Even in the light of an appropriate definition of extroversion, it is nevertheless conceivable that extroversion may be a factor in the development of general oral communicative competence (see Dewaele & Furnham 1998), which requires face-to-face interaction, but not in listening, reading, and writing. It is also readily apparent that cross-cultural norms of nonverbal and verbal interaction vary widely, and what in one culture (say, the United States) may appear as introversion is, in another culture (say, Japan), respect and politeness. Nevertheless, on a practical level, the facilitating or interfering effects of certain language teaching practices that invoke extroversion need to be carefully considered. How effective are techniques that incorporate drama, pantomime, humor, role-plays, and overt personality exposure? A teacher needs to beware of trying to "create" in a student more so-called extroversion than is really necessary. We need to be sensitive to cultural norms, to a student's willingness to speak out in class, and to optimal points between extreme extroversion and introversion that may vary from student to student.

MYERS-BRIGGS CHARACTER TYPES

In the last several decades there has been a tremendous wave of interest, in Western society, in the relationship between personality "type" and one's success in a job, in management of time, in academic pursuits, in marriage, in child rearing, and in other contexts. We have become hypersensitized to the "different strokes for different folks" syndrome that alerts us all to how unique every individual is and how each person can act on that uniqueness to succeed in business, school, sex life, and interpersonal relationships. The champions of this syndrome are Isabel Myers and Katheryn Briggs, whose research in the 1950s and 1960s has come to fruition in the form of the widespread use, today, of the Myers-Briggs Type Indicator (Myers 1962), commonly referred to as the "Myers-Briggs test."

The Myers-Briggs test revived the work of Carl Jung of a half-century earlier. Jung (1923) said that people are different in fundamental ways, and that an individual has preferences for "functioning" in ways that are characteristic, or "typical," of that particular individual. Jung's work was all but forgotten with the boom of behavioristic psychology in the middle part of the century, but we have now returned to a recognition of the acute importance of individual variation, especially in the realm of education.

Borrowing from some of Jung's "types," the Myers-Briggs team tested four dichotomous styles of functioning in the Myers-Briggs test: (1) introversion versus extroversion, (2) sensing versus intuition, (3) thinking versus feeling, and (4) judging versus perceiving. Table 6.1 on page 158 defines the four categories (Keirsey & Bates 1984: 25–26) in simple words and phrases.

The Extroversion–Introversion (E/I) category relates to an aspect of personality already discussed in this chapter, the way we either "turn inward" or "turn outward" for our sense of wholeness and self-esteem. The Sensing–Intuition (S/N) category has to do with the way we perceive and "take in" the world around us. Sensing types are data-oriented and empirically inclined to stick to observable, measurable facts, while intuitive types are more willing to rely on hunches, inspiration, and imagination for perceiving reality. The Thinking–Feeling (T/F) category describes ways of arriving at conclusions and of storing reality in memory. Thinking types are generally cognitive, objective, impartial, and logical. Feeling involves more affectivity, a desire for harmony, a capacity for warmth, empathy, and compassion. Myers and Briggs extended beyond Jung's types to add the Judging–Perceiving (J/P) dichotomy, which has to do with one's attitude toward the "outer world." "Js" want closure, planning, organization, while "Ps" are spontaneous, flexible, and comfortable with open-ended contexts.

With four two-dimensional categories, sixteen personality profiles, or combinations, are possible. Disciples of the Myers-Briggs research (Keirsey & Bates 1984, for example) describe the implications of being an "ENFJ" or an "ISTP," and all the fourteen other combinations of types. Managers are aided in their understanding of employees by understanding their character type. ISTJs, for example, make better behind-the-scenes workers on jobs that require meticulous precision, while ENFPs might be better at dealing with the public. Young people seeking a career can understand better how certain occupations might be more or less suited to them by knowing their own character type. Lawrence (1984) stressed the importance of a teacher's understanding the individual differences of learners in a classroom: Es will excel in group work; Is will prefer individual work; SJs are "linear learners with a strong need for structure" (p. 52); NTs are good at paper-and-pencil tests. The generalizations are many.

What might all this have to do with the second language learner? A few studies (Carrell, Prince, & Astika 1996; Ehrman 1989, 1990; Ehrman & Oxford 1989, 1990, 1995; Moody 1988; Oxford & Ehrman 1988) have sought to discover a link between Myers-Briggs types and second language learning. Notable among these is Ehrman and Oxford's (1990) study of seventy-nine foreign language learners at the Foreign Service Institute. They found that their subjects exhibited some differences in *strategy* use, depending on their Myers-Briggs type. For example, extroverts (E) used social strategies consistently and easily, while introverts (I) rejected them.

Table 6.1. Myers-Briggs character types

Extroversion (E)	Introversion (I)
Sociability	Territoriality
Interaction	Concentration
External	Internal
Breadth	Depth
Extensive	Intensive
Multiplicity of relationships	Limited relationships
Expenditure of energies	Conservation of energies
Interest in external events	Interest in internal reaction

Sensing (S)	Intuition (N)
Experience	Hunches
Past	Future
Realistic	Speculative
Perspiration	Inspiration
Actual	Possible
Down-to-earth	Head-in-clouds
Utility	Fantasy
Fact	Fiction
Practicality	Ingenuity
Sensible	Imaginative

Thinking (T)	Feeling (F)
Objective	Subjective
Principles	Values
Policy	Social values
Laws	Extenuating circumstances
Criterion	Intimacy
Firmness	Persuasion
Impersonal	Personal
Justice	Humane
Categories	Harmony
Standards	Good or bad
Critique	Appreciative
Analysis	Sympathy
Allocation	Devotion

Judging (J)	Perceiving (P)
Settled	Pending
Decided	Gather more data
Fixed	Flexible
Plan ahead	Adapt as you go
Run one's life	Let life happen
Closure	Open options
Decision-making	Treasure hunting
Planned	Open ended
Completed	Emergent
Decisive	Tentative
Wrap it up	Something will turn up
Urgency	There's plenty of time
Deadline!	What deadline?
Get the show on the road	Let's wait and see . . .

Sensing (S) students displayed a strong liking for memory strategies; intuitives (N) were better at compensation strategies. The T/F distinction yielded the most dramatic contrast: thinkers (T) commonly used metacognitive strategies and analysis, while feelers (F) rejected such strategies; and feelers used social strategies while thinkers did not. And judgers (J) rarely used the affective strategies that the perceivers (P) found so useful. These findings notwithstanding, we should not be too quick to conclude that psychological type can predict successful and unsuccessful learning, as the authors readily admit. In another study, Ehrman (1989) outlined both the assets *and* the liabilities of each side of the Myers-Briggs continuum (see Table 6.2).

Table 6.2. Assets and liabilities of Myers-Briggs Types (Ehrman 1989)

Major Assets Associated with Each Preference

Extraversion	Willing to take conversational risks
Introversion	Concentration, self-sufficiency
Sensing	Hard, systematic work; attention to detail, close observation
Intuition	Inferencing and guessing from context, structuring own training, conceptualizing and model-building
Thinking	Analysis, self-discipline; instrumental motivation
Feeling	Integrative motivation, bonding with teachers, good relations lead to good self-esteem
Judging	Systematic work, get the job (whatever it is) done
Perceiving	Open, flexible, adaptable to change and new experiences

Major Liabilities Associated with Each Preference
(Note: Not all students showed these liabilities.)

Extraversion	Dependent on outside stimulation and interaction
Introversion	Need to process ideas before speaking sometimes led to avoidance of linguistic risks in conversation
Sensing	Hindered by lack of clear sequence, goals, syllabus, structure in language or course
Intuition	Inaccuracy and missing important details, sought excessive complexity of discourse
Thinking	Performance anxiety because self-esteem was attached to achievement, excessive need for control (language, process)
Feeling	Discouraged if not appreciated, disrupted by lack of interpersonal harmony
Judging	Rigidity, intolerance of ambiguous stimuli
Perceiving	Laziness, inconsistent pacing over the long haul

It would appear that success in a second language depends on the "mobilization of (a) the strategies associated with one's native learning style preferences (indicated by the four MBTI letters) and (b) the strategies associated with the less preferred functions that are the opposites of the four letters of a person's type" (Ehrman & Oxford 1990: 323). In other words, successful learners know their preferences, their strengths, and their weaknesses, and effectively utilize strengths and compensate for weaknesses regardless of their "natural" preferences.

MOTIVATION

Motivation is probably the most frequently used catch-all term for explaining the success or failure of virtually any complex task. It is easy to assume that success in any task is due simply to the fact that someone is "motivated." It is easy in second language learning to claim that a learner will be successful with the proper motivation. Such claims are of course not erroneous, for countless studies and experiments in human learning have shown that motivation is a key to learning (see Dörnyei 1998). But these claims gloss over a detailed understanding of exactly what motivation is and what the subcomponents of motivation are. What does it mean to say that someone is motivated? How do you create, foster, and maintain motivation?

Various definitions of motivation have been proposed over the course of decades of research. Following the historical schools of thought described in Chapter 1, three different perspectives emerge:

1. From a *behavioristic* perspective, motivation is seen in very matter of fact terms. It is quite simply the anticipation of reward. Driven to acquire positive reinforcement, and driven by previous experiences of reward for behavior, we act accordingly to achieve further reinforcement. In this view, our acts are likely to be at the mercy of external forces.

2. In *cognitive* terms, motivation places much more emphasis on the individual's decisions, "the choices people make as to what experiences or goals they will approach or avoid, and the degree of effort they will exert in that respect" (Keller 1983: 389). Some cognitive psychologists see underlying needs or drives as the compelling force behind our decisions. Ausubel (1968: 368–379), for example, identified six needs undergirding the construct of motivation:

    a. the need for *exploration*, for seeing "the other side of the mountain," for probing the unknown;

    b. the need for *manipulation*, for operating—to

use Skinner's term—on the environment and causing change;

   c. the need for *activity*, for movement and exercise, both physical and mental;

   d. the need for *stimulation*, the need to be stimulated by the environment, by other people, or by ideas, thoughts, and feelings;

   e. the need for *knowledge*, the need to process and internalize the results of exploration, manipulation, activity, and stimulation, to resolve contradictions, to quest for solutions to problems and for self-consistent systems of knowledge;

   f. finally, the need for *ego enhancement*, for the self to be known and to be accepted and approved of by others.

3. A *constructivist* view of motivation places even further emphasis on social context as well as individual personal choices (Williams & Burden 1997: 120). Each person is motivated differently, and will therefore act on his or her environment in ways that are unique. But these unique acts are always carried out within a cultural and social milieu and cannot be completely separated from that context. Several decades ago, Abraham Maslow (1970) viewed motivation as a construct in which ultimate attainment of goals was possible only by passing through a hierarchy of needs, three of which were solidly grounded in community, belonging, and social status. Maslow saw motivation as dependent on the satisfaction first of fundamental physical necessities (air, water, food), then of community, security, identity, and self-esteem, the fulfillment of which finally leads to *self-actualization*.

The "needs" concept of motivation in some ways belongs to all three schools of thought: the fulfillment of needs is rewarding, requires choices, and in many cases must be interpreted in a social context. Consider children who are motivated to learn to read. They are motivated because they perceive the value (reward) of reading, they meet the needs of exploration, stimulation, knowledge, self-esteem, and autonomy, and they do so in widely varying ways and schedules and in the context of a society that values literacy. On the other hand, you may be unmotivated to learn a foreign language because you fail to see the rewards, connect the learning only to superficial needs (e.g., fulfilling a requirement), and see no possibility of a social context in which this skill is useful. (See Table 6.3 for a schematic representation of views of motivation.)

Table 6.3. Three views of motivation

Behavioristic	Cognitive	Constructivist
• anticipation of reward • desire to receive positive reinforcement • external, individual forces in control	• driven by basic human needs (exploration, manipulation, etc.) • degree of effort expended • internal, individual forces in control	• social context • community • social status and • security of group • internal, interactive forces in control

Motivation is something that can, like self-esteem, be global, situational, or task-oriented. Learning a foreign language requires some of all three levels of motivation. For example, a learner may possess high "global" motivation but low "task" motivation to perform well on, say, the written mode of the language. Motivation is also typically examined in terms of the **intrinsic** and **extrinsic** motives of the learner. Those who learn for their own self-perceived needs and goals are intrinsically motivated, and those who pursue a goal only to receive an external reward from someone else are extrinsically motivated.(We will return to this extremely important concept.) Finally, studies of motivation in second language acquisition often refer to the distinction between integrative and instrumental orientations of the learner, which we now consider in the next section.

Instrumental and Integrative Orientations

One of the best-known and historically significant studies of motivation in second language learning was carried out by Robert Gardner and Wallace Lambert (1972). Over a period of twelve years they extensively studied foreign language learners in Canada, several parts of the United States, and the Philippines in an effort to determine how attitudinal and motivational factors affected language learning success. Motivation was examined as a factor of a number of different kinds of attitudes. Two different clusters of attitudes divided two basic types of what Gardner and Lambert at that time identified as "instrumental" and "integrative" motivation. The **instrumental** side of the dichotomy referred to acquiring a language as a means for attaining instrumental goals: furthering a career, reading technical material, translation, and so forth. The **integrative** side described learners who wished to integrate themselves into the culture of the second language group and become involved in social interchange in that group.

It is important to digress here for a moment to note that in 1972, instrumentality and integrativeness were referred to as types of *motivation*. A number of years later, Gardner and MacIntyre (1991) more appropriately referred to the dichotomy as a case of *orientation*. That is, depending on whether a learner's context or orientation was (a) academic or career-related (instrumental), or (b) socially or culturally oriented (integrative), different needs might be fulfilled in learning a foreign language. The importance of distinguishing orientation from motivation is that within either orientation, one can have either high or low motivation. One learner may be only mildly motivated to learn within, say, a career context, while another learner with the same orientation may be highly driven to succeed.

Gardner and Lambert (1972) and Spolsky (1969) found that integrativeness generally accompanied higher scores on proficiency tests in a foreign language. The conclusion from these studies was that integrativeness was indeed an important requirement for successful language learning. But evidence quickly began to accumulate that challenged such a claim. Yasmeen Lukmani (1972) demonstrated that among Marathi-speaking Indian students learning English in India, those with instrumental orientations scored higher in tests of English proficiency. Braj Kachru (1977, 1992) noted that Indian English is but one example of a variety of Englishes, which, especially in countries where English has become an international language, can be acquired very successfully for instrumental purposes alone.

In the face of claims and counter-claims about integrative and instrumental orientations, Au (1988) reviewed twenty-seven different studies of the integrative–instrumental construct and concluded that both its theoretical underpinnings and the instruments used to measure motivation were suspect. Because the dichotomy was based on notions about cultural beliefs, numerous ambiguities had crept into the construct, making it difficult to attribute foreign language success to certain presumably integrative or instrumental causes. Gardner and MacIntyre (1993) disputed Au's claims with strong empirical support for the validity of their measures. Nevertheless, to further muddy the waters, even Gardner found that certain contexts point toward instrumental orientation as an effective context for language success (Gardner & MacIntyre 1991), and that others favor an integrative orientation (Gardner, Day, & MacIntyre 1992).

Such variable findings in empirical investigations do not necessarily invalidate the integrative–instrumental construct. They point out once again that there is no single means of learning a second language: some learners in some contexts are more successful in learning a language if they are integratively oriented, and others in different contexts benefit from an instrumental orientation. The findings also suggest that the two orientations are not necessarily mutually exclusive. Second language learning is rarely taken up in contexts that are exclusively instrumental or exclusively integrative. Most situations involve a mixture of each orientation. For example, international students learning English in the United States for academic purposes may be relatively balanced in their desire to learn

English both for academic (instrumental) purposes and to understand and become somewhat integrated with the culture and people of the United States.

A further perspective on the integrative–instrumental construct may be gained by regarding the two orientations simply as two out of a number of possible orientations. Graham (1984) claimed that integrativeness was too broadly defined and suggested that some integrative orientations may be simply a moderate desire to socialize with or find out about speakers of the target language, while deeper, **assimilative** orientations may describe a more profound need to identify almost exclusively with the target language culture, possibly over a long-term period. Likewise, instrumentality might describe an academic orientation, on the one hand, and a career or business orientation, on the other. Motivational intensity, then, can have varying degrees within any one of these four orientations or contexts, and possibly more.

Intrinsic and Extrinsic Motivation

Yet another, but arguably the most powerful, dimension of the whole motivation construct in general is the degree to which learners are **intrinsically** or **extrinsically** motivated to succeed in a task. Edward Deci (1975: 23) defined intrinsic motivation:

> Intrinsically motivated activities are ones for which there is no apparent reward except the activity itself. People seem to engage in the activities for their own sake and not because they lead to an extrinsic reward. . . . Intrinsically motivated behaviors are aimed at bringing about certain internally rewarding consequences, namely, feelings of *competence* and *self-determination*.

Extrinsically motivated behaviors, on the other hand, are carried out in anticipation of a reward from outside and beyond the self. Typical extrinsic rewards are money, prizes, grades, and even certain types of positive feedback. Behaviors initiated solely to avoid punishment are also extrinsically motivated, even though numerous intrinsic benefits can ultimately accrue to those who, instead, view punishment avoidance as a challenge that can build their sense of competence and self-determination.

Which form of motivation is more powerful? Our growing stockpile of research on motivation (see Dörnyei 1998; Dörnyei & Csizér 1998; Crookes & Schmidt 1991; Brown 1990) strongly favors intrinsic orientations, especially for long-term retention. Jean Piaget (1972) and others pointed out that human beings universally view incongruity, uncertainty, and "disequilibrium" as motivating. In other words, we seek out a reasonable challenge.

Then we initiate behaviors intended to conquer the challenging situation. Incongruity is not itself motivating, but optimal incongruity—or what Krashen (1985) called "i+1" (see Chapter 10)—presents enough of a possibility of being resolved that we will pursue that resolution.

Maslow (1970) claimed that intrinsic motivation is clearly superior to extrinsic. According to his hierarchy of needs discussed above, we are ultimately motivated to achieve "self-actualization" once our basic physical, safety, and community needs are met. Regardless of the presence or absence of extrinsic rewards, we will strive for self-esteem and fulfillment.

Jerome Bruner (1966b), praising the "autonomy of self-reward," claimed that one of the most effective ways to help both children and adults think and learn is to free them from the control of rewards and punishments. One of the principal weaknesses of extrinsically driven behavior is its addictive nature. Once captivated, as it were, by the lure of an immediate prize or praise, our dependency on those tangible rewards increases, even to the point that their withdrawal can then extinguish the desire to learn. Ramage (1990), for example, found that foreign language high school students who were interested in continuing their study beyond the college entrance requirement were positively and intrinsically motivated to succeed. In contrast, those who were in the classes only to fulfill entrance requirements exhibited low motivation and weaker performance.

It is important to distinguish the intrinsic–extrinsic construct from Gardner's integrative–instrumental orientation. While many instances of intrinsic motivation may indeed turn out to be integrative, some may not. For example, one could, for highly developed intrinsic purposes, wish to learn a second language in order to advance in a career or to succeed in an academic program. Likewise, one could develop a positive affect toward the speakers of a second language for extrinsic reasons, such as parental reinforcement or a teacher's encouragement. Kathleen Bailey (1986) illustrated the relationship between the two dichotomies with the diagram in Table 6.4.

The intrinsic–extrinsic continuum in motivation is applicable to foreign language classrooms around the world. Regardless of the cultural beliefs and attitudes of learners and teachers, intrinsic and extrinsic factors can be easily identified. Dörnyei and Csizér (1998), for example, in a survey of Hungarian teachers of English, proposed a taxonomy of factors by which teachers could motivate their learners. They cited factors such as developing a relationship with learners, building learners' self-confidence and autonomy, personalizing the learning process, and increasing learners' goal-orientation. These all fall into the intrinsic side of motivation. Our ultimate quest in this language teaching business is, of course, to see to it that our pedagogical tools can harness the power of intrinsically motivated learners who are striving for excellence, autonomy, and self-actualization.

Table 6.4. Motivational dichotomies

	Intrinsic	Extrinsic
Integrative	L2 learner wishes to integrate with the L2 culture (e.g., for immigration or marriage)	Someone else wishes the L2 learner to know the L2 for integrative reasons (e.g., Japanese parents send kids to Japanese-language school)
Instrumental	L2 learner wishes to achieve goals utilizing L2 (e.g., for a career)	External power wants L2 learner to learn L2 (e.g., corporation sends Japanese businessman to U.S. for language training)

THE NEUROBIOLOGY OF AFFECT

It would not be appropriate to engage in a discussion of personality and language learning without touching on the neurological bases of affect. The last part of the twentieth century saw significant advances in the empirical study of the brain through such techniques as positron emission tomography (PET) and magnetic resonance imaging (MRI). Using such techniques, some connections have been made between affectivity and mental/emotional processing in general (Schumann 1998), as well as second language acquisition in particular. "Neurobiology, including neuroanatomy, neurochemistry and neurophysiology, . . . informs several areas of interest for language acquisition studies, for example, plasticity, affect, memory and learning" (Schumann 1999: 28).

John Schumann's (1997, 1998, 1999) work in this area has singled out one section of the temporal lobes of the human brain, the *amygdala*, as a major player in the relationship of affect to language learning. The amygdala is instrumental in our ability to make an appraisal of a stimulus. In other words, if you see or hear or taste something, the amygdala helps you decide whether or not your perception is novel, pleasant, relevant to your needs or goals, manageable (you can potentially cope with it), and compatible with your own social norms and self-concept. So, when a teacher in a foreign language class suddenly asks you to perform something that is, let's say, too complex, your reaction of fear and anxiety means that the amygdala has sent neural signals to the rest of the brain indicating that the stimulus is too novel, unpleasant, unmanageable at the moment, and a potential threat to self-esteem.

Schumann (1999) examined a number of foreign language motivation scales in terms of their neurobiological properties. He noted how certain questions about motivation refer to pleasantness ("I enjoy learning English very much"), goal relevance ("Studying French can be important to me because it will allow me to . . . "), coping potential ("I never feel quite sure of myself when . . . "), and norm/self compatibility ("Being able to speak English will add to my social status"). His conclusion: "positive appraisals of the language learning situation . . . enhance language learning and negative appraisals inhibit second language learning"(p. 32).

Research in the near future on the neurobiology of affect is likely to enlighten our current understanding of the physiology of the brain and its effect on human behavior. Even more specifically, we can look forward to verifying what we now hypothesize to be important connections between affect and second language acquisition.

MEASURING AFFECTIVE FACTORS

The measurement of affective factors has for many decades posed a perplexing problem. Most tests of personality are paper-and-pencil tests that ask for a self-rating of some kind. In typical tests, for example, "My friends have no confidence in me" and "I am generally very patient with people" are items on which a subject agrees or disagrees in order to measure self-esteem and empathy, respectively. Such tests present three problems.

1. The most important issue in measuring affectivity is the problem of validity. Because most tests use a self-rating method, one can justifiably ask whether or not self-perceptions are accurate. True, external assessments that involve interview, observation, indirect measures, and multiple methods (Campbell & Fiske 1959) have been shown to be more accurate, but often only at great expense. In Gardner and MacIntyre's (1993b) study of a large battery of self-check tests of affective variables, the validity of such tests was upheld. We can conclude, cautiously, that paper-and-pencil self-ratings may be valid if (a) the tests have been widely validated previously, and (b) we do not rely on only one instrument or method to identify a level of affectivity.

2. A second related problem in the measurement of affective variables lies in what has been called the "self-flattery" syndrome (Oller 1981b, 1982). In general, test takers will try to discern "right" answers to questions (that is, answers that make them look

"good" or that do not "damage" them), even though test directions say there are no right or wrong answers. In so doing, perceptions of self are likely to be considerably biased toward what the test taker perceives as a highly desirable personality type.

3. Finally, tests of self-esteem, empathy, motivation, and other factors can be quite culturally ethnocentric, using concepts and references that are difficult to interpret cross-culturally. One item testing empathy, for example, requires the subject to agree or disagree with the following statement: "Disobedience to the government is sometimes justified." In societies where one never under any circumstances criticizes the government, such an item is absurd. An extroversion test asks whether you like to "stay late" at parties or "go home early." Even the concept of "party" carries cultural connotations that may not be understood by all test takers.

★   ★   ★   ★   ★

A plausible conclusion to the study of affective factors in second language acquisition contains both a word of caution and a challenge to further research. Caution is in order lest we assume that current methods of measurement are highly reliable and valid instruments. But the challenge for teachers and researchers is to maintain the quest for identifying those personality factors that are significant for the acquisition of a second language, and to continue to find effective means for infusing those findings into our classroom pedagogy.

In the Classroom:
Putting Methods into Perspective

Throughout the twentieth century, the language teaching profession was involved in a search. That search was for what has popularly been called "methods," or ideally, a single method, generalizable across widely varying audiences, that would successfully teach students a foreign language in the classroom. Historical accounts of the profession tend therefore to describe a succession of methods, each of which is more or less discarded in due course as a new method takes its place.

The first four of these end-of-chapter vignettes on classroom practice provided a brief sketch of that hundred-year "methodical" history. From the revolutionary turn-of-the-century methods espoused by François Gouin and Charles Berlitz, through yet another revolution—the Audiolingual Method—in the middle of the twentieth century, and through the spirited "designer" methods of the seventies, we are now embarking on a new century. But now *methods*, as distinct, theoretically unified clusters of teaching practices presumably appropriate for a wide variety of audiences, are no longer the object of our search. Instead, the last few years of the twentieth century were characterized by an enlightened, dynamic *approach* to language teaching in which teachers and curriculum developers were searching for valid communicative, interactive techniques suitable for specified learners pursuing specific goals in specific contexts.

In order to understand the current paradigm shift in language teaching, it will be useful to examine what is meant by some commonly used terms—words like *method, approach, technique, procedure,* etc. What is a method? Four decades ago Edward Anthony (1963) gave us a definition that has withstood the test of time. His concept of method was the second of three hierarchical elements, namely, approach, method, and technique. An *approach*, according to Anthony, is a set of assumptions dealing with the nature of language, learning, and teaching. *Method* is an overall plan for systematic presentation of language based upon a selected approach. *Techniques* are the specific activities manifested in the classroom, which are consistent with a method and therefore in harmony with an approach as well.

To this day, Anthony's terms are still in common use among language teachers. A teacher may, for example, at the approach level, affirm the ultimate importance of learning in a relaxed state of mental awareness just above the threshold of consciousness. The method that follows might resemble, say, Suggestopedia. Techniques could include playing Baroque music while reading a passage in the foreign language, getting students to sit in the yoga position while listening to a list of words, learners adopting a new name in the classroom, or role-playing that new person.

A couple of decades later, Jack Richards and Theodore Rodgers

(1982, 1986) proposed a reformulation of the concept of method. Anthony's approach, method, and technique were renamed, respectively, *approach, design,* and *procedure,* with a superordinate term to describe this three-step process now called *method.* A method, according to Richards and Rodgers, "is an umbrella term for the specification and interrelation of theory and practice" (1982: 154). An approach defines assumptions, beliefs, and theories about the nature of language and language learning. Designs specify the relationship of those theories to classroom materials and activities. Procedures are the techniques and practices that are derived from one's approach and design.

Through their reformulation, Richards and Rodgers made two principal contributions to our understanding of the concept of method:

1. They specified the necessary elements of language teaching "designs" that had heretofore been left somewhat vague. They named six important features of "designs": objectives, syllabus (criteria for selection and organization of linguistic and subject-matter content), activities, learner roles, teacher roles, and the role of instructional materials.
2. Richards and Rodgers nudged us into at last relinquishing the notion that separate, definable, discrete methods are the essential building blocks of *methodology.* By helping us think in terms of an approach that undergirds our language designs (or, we could say, curricula), which are realized by various procedures (or techniques), we could see that methods, as we still use and understand the term, are too restrictive, too pre-programmed, and too "pre-packaged." Virtually all language teaching methods make the oversimplified assumption that what teachers "do" in the classroom can be conventionalized into a set of procedures that fits all contexts. We are now well aware that such is clearly not the case.

Richards and Rodgers's reformulation of the concept of method was soundly conceived; however, their attempt to give new meaning to an old term did not catch on in the pedagogical literature. What they would like us to call "method" is more comfortably referred to, I think, as "methodology," in order to avoid confusion with what we will no doubt always think of as those separate entities (like Audiolingual or Suggestopedia) that are no longer at the center of our teaching philosophy.

Another terminological problem lies in the use of the term "designs"; instead, we now more comfortably refer to "curricula" or "syllabuses" when we discuss design features of a language program.

What are we left with in this lexicographic confusion? It is interesting that the terminology of the pedagogical literature in the field appears to be more in line with Anthony's original terms, but with some important additions and refinements. Following is a set of definitions that reflect the current usage.

>   ***Methodology:*** The study of pedagogical practices in general (including theoretical underpinnings and related research). Whatever considerations are involved in "how to teach" are methodological.
>
>   ***Approach:*** Theoretical positions and beliefs about the nature of language, the nature of language learning, and the applicability of both to pedagogical settings.
>
>   ***Method:*** A generalized, prescribed set of classroom specifications for accomplishing linguistic objectives. Methods tend to be primarily concerned with teacher and student roles and behaviors, and secondarily with such features as linguistic and subject-matter objectives, sequencing, and materials. They are almost always thought of as being broadly applicable to a variety of audiences in a variety of contexts.
>
>   ***Curriculum/syllabus:*** Designs for carrying out a particular language program. Features include a primary concern with the specification of linguistic and subject-matter objectives, sequencing, and materials to meet the needs of a designated group of learners in a defined context. (The term "syllabus" is used more customarily in the United Kingdom to refer to what is referred to as a "curriculum" in the United States.)
>
>   ***Technique*** (also commonly referred to by other terms)[1]: Any of a wide variety of exercises, activities, or devices used in the language classroom for realizing lesson objectives.

And so, ironically, the methods that were such strong signposts of a century of language teaching are no longer of great consequence in marking our progress. How did that happen?

In the 1970s and early 1980s, there was a good deal of hoopla about the "designer" methods described in the earlier vignettes. Even though they weren't widely adopted as standard methods, they were symbolic of a profession at least partially caught up in a mad scramble to invent a new method when the very concept of "method" was eroding under our feet. We didn't need a new method. We needed, instead, to get on with the business of unifying our approach to language teaching and of designing effective tasks and techniques that are informed by that approach.

Today, those clearly identifiable and enterprising methods are an interesting, if not insightful, contribution to our professional reper-

---

1. There is currently quite an intermingling of such terms as *technique, task, procedure, activity,* and *exercise,* often used in somewhat careless free variation across the profession. Of these terms, *task* has received the most concerted attention recently, viewed by such scholars as Peter Skehan (1998) as incorporating specific communicative and pedagogical principles. Tasks, according to Skehan and others, should be thought of as a special kind of technique, and in fact, may actually include more than one technique.

toire, but few practitioners look to any one of them, or their predecessors, for a final answer on how to teach a foreign language. Method, as a unified, cohesive, finite set of design features, is now given only minor attention.[2] The profession has at last reached the point of maturity where we recognize that the complexity of language learners in multiple worldwide contexts demands an eclectic blend of tasks, each tailored for a particular group of learners studying for particular purposes in a given amount of time. David Nunan (1991b: 228) summed it up nicely: "It has been realized that there never was and probably never will be a method for all, and the focus in recent years has been on the development of classroom tasks and activities which are consonant with what we know about second language acquisition, and which are also in keeping with the dynamics of the classroom itself."

2 While we may have outgrown our need to search for such definable methods, the term "methodology" continues to be used, as it would in any other behavioral science, to refer to the systematic application of validated principles to practical contexts. It follows that you need not subscribe to a particular Method (with a capital M) in order to engage in a "methodology."

TOPICS AND QUESTIONS FOR STUDY AND DISCUSSION

[Note: (I) individual work; (G) group or pair work; (C) whole-class discussion.]

1. (C) Look at Bloom's five levels of affectivity, described at the beginning of the chapter. Try to put language into each level and give examples of how language is inextricably bound up in our affective processes of receiving, responding, valuing, organizing values, and creating value systems. How do such examples help to highlight the fact that second language acquisition is more than just the acquisition of language forms (nouns, verbs, rules, etc.)?

2. (G) Divide into six different groups (or multiples of six) for the following discussion. Each group should take one of the following factors: self-esteem, inhibition, risk-taking, anxiety, empathy, and extroversion. In your group, (a) define each factor and (b) agree on a generalized conclusion about the relevance of each factor for successful second language acquisition. In your conclusion, be sure to consider how your generalization needs to be qualified by some sort of "it depends" statement. For example, one might be tempted to conclude that low anxiety is necessary for successful learning, but depending on certain contextual and personal factors, facilitative anxiety may be helpful. Each group should report back to the rest of the class.

3. (I) Review the personality characteristics listed in Table 6.1 on page 158. Make a checkmark by either the left-or right-column descriptor; total up your checks for each of the four categories and see if you can come up with a four-letter "type" that describes you. For example, you might be an "ENFJ" or an "INTJ" or any of sixteen possible types. If you have a tie in any of the categories, allow your own intuition to determine which side of the fence you are on most of the time.

4. (G) Make sure you do item 3 above, then, in groups, share your personality type. Is your own four-letter combination a good description of who you are? Share this with the group and give others in the group examples of how your type manifests itself in problem solving, interpersonal relations, the workplace, etc. Offer examples of how your type explains how you might typically behave in a foreign language class.

5. (C) What are some examples of learning a foreign language in an *integrative* orientation and in an *instrumental* orientation? Offer further examples of how within both orientations one's motivation might be either high or low. Is one orientation necessarily better than another? Think of situations where either orientation could contain powerful motives.

6. (G) In pairs, make a quick list of activities or other things that happen in a foreign language class. Then decide whether each activity fosters *extrinsic* motivation or *intrinsic* motivation, or degrees of each type. Through class discussion, make a large composite list. Which activities seem to offer deeper, more long term success?

7. (I) One person in the class might want to consult Schumann's (1997, 1998) work on the neurobiology of affect and give a report to the rest of the class that spells out the theory in some detail. Of special interest is the importance of the amygdala in determining our affective response to a stimulus.

8. (I) Several students could be assigned to find tests of self-esteem, empathy, anxiety, extroversion, and the Myers-Briggs test, and bring copies of these self-rating tests to class for others to examine or take themselves. Follow-up discussion should include an intuitive evaluation of the validity of such tests.

SUGGESTED READINGS

Arnold, Jane (Ed.). 1999. *Affect in Language Learning*. Cambridge: Cambridge University Press.

Arnold's anthology gives some background on a variety of different perspectives on the affective domain. It includes chapters on anxiety (Oxford), ego boundaries (Ehrman), neurobiology (Schumann), self-esteem (Andrés), plus many other reader-friendly essays.

Dörnyei, Zoltán. 1998. Motivation in second and foreign language learning. *Language Teaching* 31:117–135.

Dörnyei's excellent recent summary of research on motivation also provides over 150 references.

Gardner, Robert C. and MacIntyre, Peter D. 1993a. A student's contributions to second language learning: Part II: affective variables. *Language Teaching* 26:1-11.

Gardner and MacIntyre's state-of-the-art article on affective variables focuses on attitudes, motivation, and anxiety, and contains a comprehensive bibliography of work up to that time.

Keirsey, David and Bates, Marilyn. 1984. *Please Understand Me: Character and Temperament Types*. Del Mar, CA: Prometheus Nemesis Book Company.

Lawrence, Gordon. 1984. *People Types and Tiger Stripes: A Practical Guide to Learning Styles*. Gainesville, FL: Center for Applications of Psychological Type.

These two little books written for the layperson, although about two decades old, still offer practical primers on applications of the Myers-Briggs personality types.

Schumann, John H. 1997. *The Neurobiology of Affect in Language*. Boston: Blackwell.

Schumann, John H. 1998. "The Neurobiology of Affect in Language." *Language Learning 48*, Supplement 1, Special Issue.

Either of the above references presents a comprehensive treatment of Schumann's work on the neurobiology of affect as it relates to language acquisition.

LANGUAGE LEARNING EXPERIENCE: JOURNAL ENTRY 6

[Note: See pages 18 and 19 of Chapter 1 for general guidelines for writing a journal on a previous or concurrent language learning experience.]

- Consider each of the following six affective factors: self-esteem, inhibition, risk-taking, anxiety, empathy, and extroversion. Intuitively assess your own level (from high to low on the first five; either extroversion or introversion on the last) on each factor. Then, in your journal, write your conclusions in a chart, and follow up with comments about how each factor manifests itself in you in your foreign language class (past or present).
- Look at the section on "language ego" and write about the extent to which you have felt or might feel a sense of a second ego developing within you as you use a foreign language. What are the negative and positive effects of that new language ego?
- Should any of your tendencies change? That is, if you have low task self-esteem, for example, when doing certain kinds of exercises, how might you change your general affective style so that you could be more successful? Or do you see strengths in your tendencies that you should maintain? Explain.
- Check your own Myers-Briggs type by doing item 3 on pages 172–173. In your journal, discuss the relevance of your personality type to typical language classroom activities. Evaluate the extent to which your characteristics are in your favor or not.
- Think about any present or past foreign language learning experiences. Pick one of them and assess the extent to which you feel (felt) intrinsically motivated or extrinsically motivated to learn. What specific factors make (made) you feel that way? Is there anything you could do (have done) to change that motivational intensity?

CHAPTER 7

SOCIOCULTURAL

FACTORS

T HE PREVIOUS chapter, with its focus on the affective domain of second language acquisition, looked at how the personal variables within oneself and the reflection of that self to other people affect our communicative interaction. This chapter touches on another affective aspect of the communicative process: the intersection of culture and affect. How do learners overcome the personal and transactional barriers presented by two cultures in contact? What is the relationship of culture learning to second language learning?

Culture is a way of life. It is the context within which we exist, think, feel, and relate to others. It is the "glue" that binds a group of people together. Several centuries ago, John Donne (1624) had this to say about culture:

> No man is an island, entire of itself; every man is a piece of the continent, a part of the main; . . . any man's death diminishes me, because I am involved in mankind; and therefore never send to know for whom the bell tolls; it tolls for thee.

Culture is our continent, our collective identity. Larson and Smalley (1972: 39) described culture as a "blueprint" that

> guides the behavior of people in a community and is incubated in family life. It governs our behavior in groups, makes us sensitive to matters of status, and helps us know what others expect of us

and what will happen if we do not live up to their expectations. Culture helps us to know how far we can go as individuals and what our responsibility is to the group.

Culture might also be defined as the ideas, customs, skills, arts, and tools that characterize a given group of people in a given period of time. But culture is more than the sum of its parts. "It is a system of integrated patterns, most of which remain below the threshold of consciousness, yet all of which govern human behavior just as surely as the manipulated strings of a puppet control its motions" (Condon 1973: 4). The fact that no society exists without a culture reflects the need for culture to fulfill certain biological and psychological needs in human beings. Consider the bewildering host of confusing and contradictory facts and propositions and ideas that present themselves every day to any human being; some organization of these facts is necessary to provide some order to potential chaos, and therefore conceptual networks of reality evolve within a group of people for such organization. The mental constructs that enable us thus to survive are a way of life that we call "culture."

Culture establishes for each person a context of cognitive and affective behavior, a template for personal and social existence. But we tend to perceive reality within the context of our own culture, a reality that we have "created," and therefore not necessarily a reality that is empirically defined. "The meaningful universe in which each human being exists is not a universal reality, but 'a category of reality' consisting of selectively organized features considered significant by the society in which he lives" (Condon 1973: 17). Although the opportunities for world travel in the last several decades have increased markedly, there is still a tendency for us to believe that our own reality is the "correct" perception.

Perception, though, is always subjective. Perception involves the filtering of information even before it is stored in memory, resulting in a selective form of consciousness. What appears to you to be an accurate and objective perception of an individual, a custom, an idea, might be "jaded" or "stilted" in the view of someone from another culture. Misunderstandings are therefore likely to occur between members of different cultures. People from other cultures may appear, in your eyes, to be "loud" or "quiet," "conservative" or "liberal" in reference to your own point of view.

It is apparent that culture, as an ingrained set of behaviors and modes of perception, becomes highly important in the learning of a second language. A language is a part of a culture, and a culture is a part of a language; the two are intricately interwoven so that one cannot separate the two without losing the significance of either language or culture. The acquisition of a second language, except for specialized, instrumental acquisition (as may be the case, say, in acquiring a reading knowledge of a language for examining scientific texts), is also the acquisition of a second culture. Both linguists and anthropologists bear ample testimony to this observation (Robinson-Stuart & Nocon 1996; Scollon & Scollon 1995).

This chapter attempts to highlight some of the important aspects of the relationship between learning a second language and learning the cultural context of the second language. Among topics to be covered are the problem of cultural stereotypes, attitudes, learning a second culture, sociopolitical considerations, and the relationship among language, thought, and culture.

FROM STEREOTYPES TO GENERALIZATIONS

Mark Twain gave us a delightfully biased view of other cultures and other languages in *The Innocents Abroad*. In reference to the French language, Twain commented that the French "always tangle up everything to that degree that when you start into a sentence you never know whether you are going to come out alive or not." In *A Tramp Abroad*, Twain noted that German is a most difficult language: "A gifted person ought to learn English (barring spelling and pronouncing) in 30 hours, French in 30 days, and German in 30 years." So he proposed to reform the German language, for "if it is to remain as it is, it ought to be gently and reverently set aside among the dead languages, for only the dead have time to learn it."

Twain, like all of us at times, expressed caricatures of linguistic and cultural stereotypes. In the bias of our own culture-bound world view, we too often picture other cultures in an oversimplified manner, lumping cultural differences into exaggerated categories, and then view every person in a culture as possessing stereotypical traits. Thus Americans are all rich, informal, materialistic, overly friendly, and drink coffee. Italians are passionate, demonstrative, great lovers, and drink red wine. Germans are stubborn, industrious, methodical, and drink beer. The British are stuffy, polite, thrifty, and drink tea. And Japanese are reserved, unemotional, take a lot of pictures, and also drink tea.

François Lierres, writing in the Paris newsmagazine *Le Point*, gave some tongue-in-cheek advice to French people on how to get along with Americans. "They are the Vikings of the world economy, descending upon it in their jets as the Vikings once did in their *drakars*. They have money, technology, and nerve.... We would be wise to get acquainted with them." And he offered some *do's* and *don't's*. Among the *do's:* Greet them, but after you have been introduced once, don't shake hands, merely emit a brief cluck of joy—"Hi." Speak without emotion and with self-assurance, giving the impression you have a command of the subject even if you haven't. Check the collar of your jacket—nothing is uglier in the eyes of an

American than dandruff. Radiate congeniality and show a good disposition—a big smile and a warm expression are essential. Learn how to play golf. Among the *don't's*: Don't tamper with your accent—Americans find French accents very romantic. And don't allow the slightest smell of perspiration to reach the offended nostrils of your American friends.

How do **stereotypes** form? Our cultural milieu shapes our world view—our *Weltanschauung*—in such a way that reality is thought to be objectively perceived through our own cultural pattern, and a differing perception is seen as either false or "strange" and is thus oversimplified. If people recognize and understand differing world views, they will usually adopt a positive and open-minded attitude toward cross-cultural differences. A closed-minded view of such differences often results in the maintenance of a stereotype—an oversimplification and blanket assumption. A stereotype assigns group characteristics to individuals purely on the basis of their cultural membership.

The stereotype may be accurate in depicting the "typical" member of a culture, but it is inaccurate for describing a particular individual, simply because every person is unique and all of a person's behavioral characteristics cannot be accurately predicted on the basis of an overgeneralized median point along a continuum of cultural norms. To judge a single member of a culture by overall traits of the culture is both to prejudge and to misjudge that person. Worse, stereotypes have a way of potentially devaluing people from other cultures. Mark Twain's comments about the French and German languages, while written in a humorous vein and without malice, could be interpreted by some to be insulting.

Sometimes our oversimplified concepts of members of another culture are downright false. Americans sometimes think of Japanese as being unfriendly because of their cultural norms of respect and politeness. The false view that members of another culture are "dirty" or "smelly"—with verbal and nonverbal messages conveying that view—in fact usually stems from different customs of bathing or olfactory norms. Muriel Saville-Troike noted that

> Middle-class whites may objectively note that the lower socioeconomic classes frequently lack proper bathing facilities or changes of clothing, but may be surprised to discover that a common stereotype blacks hold of whites is that they "smell like dogs coming in out of the rain." Asians have a similar stereotype of Caucasians. (1976: 51)

While stereotyping, or overgeneralizing, people from other cultures should be avoided, cross-cultural research has shown that there are indeed characteristics of culture that make one culture different from another.

Condon (1973) concluded from cross-cultural research that American, French, and Hispanic world views are quite different in their concepts of time and space. Americans tend to be dominated by a "psychomotor" view of time and space that is dynamic, diffuse, and nominalistic. French orientation is more "cognitive" with a static, centralized, and universalistic view. The Hispanic orientation is more "affectively" centered with a passive, relational, and intuitive world view. We will see later in this chapter that cultures can also differ according to degrees of collectivism, power distance, uncertainty avoidance, and gender role prescriptions.

Both learners and teachers of a second language need to understand cultural differences, to recognize openly that people are not all the same beneath the skin. There are real differences between groups and cultures. We can learn to perceive those differences, appreciate them, and above all to respect and value the personhood of every human being.

ATTITUDES

Stereotyping usually implies some type of **attitude** toward the culture or language in question. The following passage, an excerpt from an item on "Chinese literature" in the *New Standard Encyclopedia* published in 1940, is an incredible example of a negative attitude stemming from a stereotype:

> The Chinese Language is monosyllabic and uninflectional. . . . With a language so incapable of variation, a literature cannot be produced which possesses the qualities we look for and admire in literary works. Elegance, variety, beauty of imagery—these must all be lacking. A monotonous and wearisome language must give rise to a forced and formal literature lacking in originality and interesting in its subject matter only. Moreover, a conservative people . . . profoundly reverencing all that is old and formal, and hating innovation, must leave the impress of its own character upon its literature. (Volume VI)

Fortunately such views would probably not be expressed in encyclopedias today. Such biased attitudes are based on insufficient knowledge, misinformed stereotyping, and extreme ethnocentric thinking.

Attitudes, like all aspects of the development of cognition and affect in human beings, develop early in childhood and are the result of parents' and peers' attitudes, of contact with people who are "different" in any number of ways, and of interacting affective factors in the human experience. These attitudes form a part of one's perception of self, of others, and of the culture in which one is living.

Gardner and Lambert's (1972) extensive studies were systematic attempts to examine the effect of attitudes on language learning. After studying the interrelationships of a number of different types of attitudes, they defined motivation as a construct made up of certain attitudes. The most important of these is group-specific, the attitude learners have toward the members of the cultural group whose language they are learning. Thus, in Gardner and Lambert's model, an English-speaking Canadian's positive attitude toward French-Canadians—a desire to understand them and to empathize with them—will lead to an integrative orientation to learn French, which in the 1972 study was found to be a significant correlate of success.

John Oller and his colleagues (see Oller, Hudson, & Liu 1977; Chihara & Oller 1978; Oller, Baca, & Vigil 1978) conducted several large-scale studies of the relationship between attitudes and language success. They looked at the relationship between Chinese, Japanese, and Mexican students' achievement in English and their attitudes toward self, the native language group, the target language group, their reasons for learning English, and their reasons for traveling to the United States. The researchers were able to identify a few meaningful clusters of attitudinal variables that correlated positively with attained proficiency. Each of the three studies yielded slightly different conclusions, but for the most part, positive attitudes toward self, the native language group, and the target language group enhanced proficiency. There were mixed results on the relative advantages and disadvantages of integrative and instrumental orientations. For example, in one study they found that better proficiency was attained by students who did not want to stay in the United States permanently.

It seems clear that second language learners benefit from positive attitudes and that negative attitudes may lead to decreased motivation and, in all likelihood, because of decreased input and interaction, to unsuccessful attainment of proficiency. Yet the teacher needs to be aware that everyone has both positive and negative attitudes. The negative attitudes *can* be changed, often by exposure to reality—for example, by encounters with actual persons from other cultures. Negative attitudes usually emerge from one's indirect exposure to a culture or group through television, movies, news media, books, and other sources that may be less than reliable. Teachers can aid in dispelling what are often myths about other cultures, and replace those myths with an accurate understanding of the other culture as one that is different from one's own, yet to be respected and valued. Learners can thus move through the hierarchy of affectivity as described by Bloom in the preceding chapter, through awareness and responding, to valuing, and finally to an organized and systematic understanding and appreciation of the foreign culture.

SECOND CULTURE ACQUISITION

Because learning a second language implies some degree of learning a second culture, it is important to understand what we mean by the process of culture learning. Robinson-Stuart and Nocon (1996) synthesized some of the perspectives on culture learning that we have seen in recent decades. They observed that the notion that culture learning is a "magic carpet ride to another culture," achieved as an automatic byproduct of language instruction, is a misconception. Many students in foreign language classrooms learn the language with little or no sense of the depth of cultural norms and patterns of the people who speak the language. Another perspective was the notion that a foreign language curriculum could present culture as "a list of facts to be cognitively consumed" (p. 434) by the student, devoid of any significant interaction with the culture. Casting those perspectives aside as ineffective and misconceived, Robinson-Stuart and Nocon suggested that language learners undergo culture learning as a "process, that is, as a way of perceiving, interpreting, feeling, being in the world, . . . and relating to where one is and who one meets" (p. 432). Culture learning is a process of creating shared meaning between cultural representatives. It is experiential, a process that continues over years of language learning, and penetrates deeply into one's patterns of thinking, feeling, and acting.

Second language learning, as we saw in the previous chapter in the discussion of language ego, involves the acquisition of a second identity. This creation of a new identity is at the heart of culture learning, or what some might call **acculturation**. If a French person is primarily cognitive-oriented and an American is psychomotor-oriented and a Spanish speaker is affective-oriented, as claimed by Condon (1973: 22), it is not difficult on this plane alone to understand the complexity of the process of becoming oriented to a new culture. A reorientation of thinking and feeling, not to mention communication, is necessary. Consider the implications:

> To a European or a South American, the overall impression created by American culture is that of a frantic, perpetual round of actions which leave practically no time for personal feeling and reflection. But, to an American, the reasonable and orderly tempo of French life conveys a sense of hopeless backwardness and ineffectuality; and the leisurely timelessness of Spanish activities represents an appalling waste of time and human potential. And, to a Spanish speaker, the methodical essence of planned change in France may seem cold-blooded, just as much as his own proclivity toward spur-of-the-moment decisions may strike his French counterpart as recklessly irresponsible. (Condon 1973: 25)

The process of acculturation runs even deeper when language is brought into the picture. To be sure, culture is a deeply ingrained part of the very fiber of our being, but language—the means for communication among members of a culture—is the most visible and available expression of that culture. And so a person's world view, self-identity, and systems of thinking, acting, feeling, and communicating can be disrupted by a contact with another culture.

Sometimes that disruption is severe, in which case a person may experience **culture shock**. Culture shock refers to phenomena ranging from mild irritability to deep psychological panic and crisis. Culture shock is associated with feelings of estrangement, anger, hostility, indecision, frustration, unhappiness, sadness, loneliness, homesickness, and even physical illness. Persons undergoing culture shock view their new world out of resentment and alternate between self-pity and anger at others for not understanding them. Edward Hall (1959: 59) described a hypothetical example of an American living abroad for the first time.

> At first, things in the cities look pretty much alike. There are taxis, hotels with hot and cold running water, theaters, neon lights, even tall buildings with elevators and a few people who can speak English. But pretty soon the American discovers that underneath the familiar exterior there are vast differences. When someone says "yes" it often doesn't mean yes at all, and when people smile it doesn't always mean they are pleased. When the American visitor makes a helpful gesture he may be rebuffed; when he tries to be friendly nothing happens. People tell him that they will do things and don't. The longer he stays, the more enigmatic the new country looks.

This case of an American in Japan illustrates the point that persons in a second culture may initially be comfortable and delighted with the "exotic" surroundings. As long as they can perceptually filter their surroundings and internalize the environment in their *own* world view, they feel at ease. As soon as this newness wears off and the cognitive and affective contradictions of the foreign culture mount up, they become disoriented.

It is common to describe culture shock as the second of four successive stages of culture acquisition:

1. Stage 1 is a period of excitement and euphoria over the newness of the surroundings.
2. Stage 2—culture shock—emerges as individuals feel the intrusion of more and more cultural differences into their own images of

self and security. In this stage individuals rely on and seek out the support of their fellow countrymen in the second culture, taking solace in complaining about local customs and conditions, seeking escape from their predicament.

3. Stage 3 is one of gradual, and at first tentative and vacillating, recovery. This stage is typified by what Larson and Smalley (1972) called "culture stress": some problems of acculturation are solved while other problems continue for some time. But general progress is made, slowly but surely, as individuals begin to accept the differences in thinking and feeling that surround them, slowly becoming more empathic with other persons in the second culture.

4. Stage 4 represents near or full recovery, either assimilation or adaptation, acceptance of the new culture and self-confidence in the "new" person that has developed in this culture.

Wallace Lambert's (1967) work on attitudes in second language learning referred often to Durkheim's (1897) concept of *anomie*—feelings of social uncertainty or dissatisfaction—as a significant aspect of the relationship between language learning and attitude toward the foreign culture. As individuals begin to lose some of the ties of their native culture and to adapt to the second culture, they experience feelings of chagrin or regret, mixed with the fearful anticipation of entering a new group. Anomie might be described as the first symptom of the third stage of acculturation, a feeling of homelessness, where one feels neither bound firmly to one's native culture nor fully adapted to the second culture.

Lambert's research supported the view that the strongest dose of anomie is experienced when linguistically a person begins to "master" the foreign language. In Lambert's (1967) study, for example, when English-speaking Canadians became so skilled in French that they began to "think" in French and even dream in French, feelings of anomie were markedly high. For Lambert's subjects the interaction of anomie and increased skill in the language sometimes led persons to revert or to "regress" back to English—to seek out situations in which they could speak English. Such an urge corresponds to the tentativeness of the third stage of acculturation—periodic reversion to the escape mechanisms acquired in the earlier stage of culture shock. Not until a person is well into the third stage do feelings of anomie decrease because the learner is "over the hump" in the transition to adaptation.

The culture shock stage of acculturation need not be depicted as a point when learners are unwitting and helpless victims of circumstance. Peter Adler (1972: 14) noted that culture shock, while surely possessing manifestations of crisis, can also be viewed more positively as a profound cross-cultural learning experience, a set of situations or circumstances involving intercultural communication in which the individual, as a result of the experiences, becomes aware of his own growth, learning and change. As a result of the culture shock process, the individual has gained a new perspective on himself, and has come to understand his own identity in terms significant to himself. The cross-cultural learning experience, additionally, takes place when the individual encounters a different culture and as a result (a) examines the degree to which he is influenced by his own culture, and (b) understands the culturally derived values, attitudes and outlooks of other people.

SOCIAL DISTANCE

The concept of **social distance** emerged as an affective construct to give explanatory power to the place of culture learning in second language learning. Social distance refers to the cognitive and affective proximity of two cultures that come into contact within an individual. "Distance" is obviously used in a metaphorical sense to depict dissimilarity between two cultures. On a very superficial level one might observe, for example, that people from the United States are culturally similar to Canadians, while U.S. natives and Chinese are, by comparison, relatively dissimilar. We could say that the social distance of the latter case exceeds the former.

John Schumann (1976c: 136) described social distance as consisting of the following parameters:

1. *Dominance.* In relation to the TL [target language] group, is the L2 [second language learning] group politically, culturally, technically or economically dominant, non-dominant, or subordinate?
2. *Integration.* Is the integration pattern of the L2 group assimilation, acculturation, or preservation? What is the L2 group's degree of *enclosure*—its identity separate from other contiguous groups?
3. *Cohesiveness.* Is the L2 group cohesive? What is the size of the L2 group?
4. *Congruence.* Are the cultures of the two groups congruent—similar in their value and belief systems? What are the attitudes of the two groups toward each other?
5. *Permanence.* What is the L2 group's intended length of residence in the target language area?

Schumann used the above factors to describe hypothetically "good" and "bad" language learning situations, and illustrated each situation with two actual cross-cultural contexts. His two hypothetical "bad" language learning situations:

1. The TL group views the L2 group as dominant and the L2 group views itself in the same way. Both groups desire preservation and high enclosure for the L2 group, the L2 group is both cohesive and large, the two cultures are not congruent, the two groups hold negative attitudes toward each other, and the L2 group intends to remain in the TL area only for a short time.
2. The second bad situation has all the characteristics of the first except that in this case, the L2 group considers itself subordinate and is considered subordinate by the TL group.

The first situation is typical, according to Schumann, of Americans living in Riyadh, Saudi Arabia. The second situation is descriptive of Navajo Indians living in the southwestern part of the United States.

A "good" language learning situation, according to Schumann's model (p. 141), is one in which the L2 group is non-dominant in relation to the TL group, both groups desire assimilation (or at least acculturation) for the L2 group, low enclosure is the goal of both groups, the two cultures are congruent, the L2 group is small and non-cohesive, both groups have positive attitudes toward each other, and the L2 group intends to remain in the target language area for a long time. Under such conditions social distance would be minimal and acquisition of the target language would be enhanced. Schumann cites as a specific example of a "good" language learning situation the case of American Jewish immigrants living in Israel.

Schumann's hypothesis was that the greater the social distance between two cultures, the greater the difficulty the learner will have in learning the second language, and conversely, the smaller the social distance (the greater the social solidarity between two cultures), the better will be the language learning situation.

One of the difficulties in Schumann's hypothesis of social distance is the measurement of actual social distance. How can one determine degrees of social distance? By what means? And how would those means be quantifiable for comparison of relative distances? To this day the construct has remained a rather subjectively defined phenomenon that, like empathy, self-esteem, and so many other psychological constructs, defies definition even though one can intuitively grasp the sense of what is meant.

William Acton (1979) proposed a solution to the dilemma. Instead of trying to measure *actual* social distance, he devised a measure of *perceived* social distance. His contention was that the actual distance between cultures is not particularly relevant since it is what learners perceive that forms their own reality. We have already noted that human beings perceive the cultural environment through the filters and screens of their own world view and then act upon that perception, however biased it may be. According to Acton, when learners encounter a new culture, their acculturation process is a factor of how they perceive their own culture in relation to the culture of the target language, and vice versa. For example, objectively there may be a relatively large distance between Americans and Saudi Arabians, but an American learning Arabic in Saudi Arabia might for a number of reasons perceive little distance and in turn act on that perception.

By asking learners to respond to three dimensions of distance, Acton devised a measure of perceived social distance—the Professed Difference in Attitude Questionnaire (PDAQ)—which characterized the "good" or successful language learner (as measured by standard proficiency tests) with remarkable accuracy. Basically the PDAQ asked learners to quantify what they perceived to be the differences in attitude toward various concepts ("the automobile," "divorce," "socialism," "policemen," for example) on three dimensions: (a) distance (or difference) between themselves and their countrymen in general; (b) distance between themselves and members of the target culture in general; and (c) distance between their countrymen and members of the target culture. By using a semantic differential technique, three distance scores were computed for each dimension.

Acton found that in the case of learners of English who had been in the United States for four months, there is an *optimal* perceived social distance ratio (among the three scores) that typifies the "good" language learner. If learners perceived themselves as either too close to or too distant from either the target culture or the native culture, they fell into the category of "bad" language learners as measured by standard proficiency tests. The implication is that successful language learners see themselves as maintaining some distance between themselves and both cultures. That Acton's PDAQ did not predict success in language is no surprise since we know of no adequate instrument to predict language success or to assess language aptitude. But the PDAQ did describe empirically, in quantifiable terms, a relationship between social distance and second language acquisition.

Acton's theory of optimal perceived social distance supported Lambert's (1967) contention that mastery of the foreign language takes place hand-in-hand with feelings of anomie or homelessness, where learners have moved away from their native culture but are still not completely assimilated into or adjusted to the target culture. More important, Acton's model led us closer to an understanding of culture shock and the relationship of acculturation to language learning by supplying an important piece of a puzzle. If we combine Acton's research with Lambert's, an interesting hypothesis emerges—namely, that mastery or skillful fluency in a second language (within the second culture) occurs somewhere at the beginning of the third—recovery—stage of acculturation. The implication of such a hypothesis is that mastery might not effectively occur before that stage or, even more likely, that learners might never be successful in their mastery of the language if they have proceeded beyond early Stage 3 without accomplishing that linguistic mastery. Stage 3 may provide not only the optimal distance but the optimal cognitive and affective tension to produce the necessary pressure to acquire the language, pressure that is neither too overwhelming (such as the culture shock typical of Stage 2) nor too weak (which would be found in Stage 4, adaptation/assimilation). Language mastery at Stage 3, in turn, would appear to be an instrument for progressing psychologically through Stage 3 and finally into Stage 4.

According to this **optimal distance model** (Brown 1980) of second language acquisition, an adult who fails to master a second language in a second culture may for a host of reasons have failed to synchronize linguistic and cultural development. Adults who have achieved nonlinguistic means of coping in the foreign culture will pass through Stage 3 and into Stage 4 with an undue number of *fossilized* forms of language (see Chapter 8 for a discussion of fossilization), never achieving mastery. They have no reason to achieve mastery since they have learned to cope without sophisticated knowledge of the language. They may have acquired a sufficient number of functions of a second language without acquiring the correct forms. What is suggested in this optimal distance model might well be seen as a culturally based critical-period hypothesis, that is, a critical period that is independent of the age of the learner. While the optimal distance model applies more appropriately to adult learners, it could pertain to children, although less critically so. Because they have not built up years and years of a culture-bound world view (or view of themselves), children have fewer perceptive filters to readjust and therefore move through the stages of acculturation more quickly. They nevertheless move through the same stages, and it is plausible to hypothesize that their recovery stages are also crucial periods of acquisition.

Some research evidence has been gathered in support of the optimal distance construct. In a study of returning Peace Corps volunteers who had remained in their assigned countries for two or more years, Day (1982) garnered some observational evidence of the coinciding of critical leaps in language fluency and cultural anomie. And Svanes (1987, 1988) found that university foreign students studying in Norway appeared to achieve higher language proficiency if they had "a balanced and critical attitude to the host people" (1988: 368) as opposed to uncritical admiration for all aspects of the target culture. The informal testimony of many teachers of ESL in the United States also confirms the plausibility of a motivational tension created by the need to "move along" in the sometimes long and frustrating process of adaptation to a new homeland. Teachers in similar contexts could benefit from a careful assessment of the current cultural stages of learners with due attention to possible optimal periods for language mastery.

CULTURE IN THE CLASSROOM

While most learners can indeed find positive benefits in cross-cultural living or learning experiences, a number of people experience psychological blocks and other inhibiting effects of the second culture. Teachers who follow an experiential or process model (Robinson-Stuart & Nocon 1996) of culture learning in the classroom can help students turn such an experience into one of increased cultural and self-awareness.

Stevick (1976b) cautioned that learners can feel alienation in the process of learning a second language, alienation from people in their home culture, the target culture, and from themselves. In teaching an "alien" language, we need to be sensitive to the fragility of students by using techniques that promote cultural understanding. Donahue and Parsons (1982) examined the use of role-play in ESL classrooms as a means of helping students to overcome cultural "fatigue"; role-play promotes the process of cross-cultural dialog while providing opportunities for oral communication. Numerous other materials and techniques—readings, films, simulation games, culture assimilators, "culture capsules," and "culturgrams"—are available to language teachers to assist them in the process of acculturation in the classroom (Fantini 1997; Ramirez 1995; Levine et al. 1987; McGroarty & Galvan 1985; Kohls 1984).

Perhaps the best model of the combination of second language and second culture learning is found among students who learn a second language in a country where that language is spoken natively. In many countries, thousands of foreign students are enrolled in institutions of higher education and must study the language of the country in order to pursue their academic objectives. Or one might simply consider the multitude of immigrants who enter the educational stream of their new country after having received their early schooling in their previous country. They bring with them the cultural mores and patterns of "good" behavior learned in their home culture, and tend to apply those expectations to their new situation. What is the nature of those students' expectations of behavior in their new educational system?

Consider Kenji, a university student from Japan who is studying at a pre-university language institute in the United States. During his previous twelve years of schooling, he was taught some very specific behaviors. He was taught to give the utmost "respect" to his teacher, which means a number of things: never to contradict the teacher; never to speak in class unless spoken to—always let the teacher initiate communication; let the teacher's wisdom be "poured into" him; never call a teacher by a first name; respect older teachers even more than younger teachers. But in his new U.S. language school, his youngish teachers are friendly and encourage a first-name basis, they ask students to participate in group work, they try to get students to come up with answers to problems, rather than just giving the answer, and so on. Kenji is confused. Why?

Some means of conceptualizing such mismatches in expectations were outlined in a thought-provoking article by Geert Hofstede (1986), who used four different conceptual categories to study the cultural norms of fifty different countries. Each category was described as follows:

1. *Individualism* as a characteristic of a culture opposes *collectivism* (the word is used here in an anthropological, not a political, sense). Individualist cultures assume that any person looks primarily after his/her own interest and the interest of his/her immediate family (husband, wife and children). Collectivist cultures assume that any person through birth and possible later events belongs to one or more tight "in-groups," from which he/she cannot detach him/herself. The "in-group" (whether extended family, clan, or organization) protects the interest of its members, but in turn expects their permanent loyalty. A collectivist society is tightly integrated; an individualist society is loosely integrated.

2. *Power Distance* as a characteristic of a culture defines the extent to which the less powerful persons in a society accept inequality in power and consider it as normal. Inequality exists within any culture, but the degree of it that is tolerated varies between one culture and another. "All societies are unequal, but some are more unequal than others" (Hofstede 1980: 136).

3. *Uncertainty Avoidance* as a characteristic of a culture defines the extent to which people within a culture are made nervous by situations they perceive as unstructured, unclear, or unpredictable, situations which they therefore try to avoid by maintaining strict codes of behavior and a belief in absolute truths. Cultures with a strong uncertainty avoidance are active, aggressive, emotional, compulsive, security-seeking, and intolerant; cultures with a weak uncertainty avoidance are contemplative, less aggressive, unemotional, relaxed, accepting of personal risks, and relatively tolerant.

4. *Masculinity* as a characteristic of a culture opposes *femininity*. The two differ in the social roles associated with the biological fact of the existence of two sexes, and in particular in the social roles attributed to men. The cultures which I labeled as "masculine" strive for maximal distinction between what men are

expected to do and what women are expected to do. They expect men to be assertive, ambitious and competitive, to strive for material success, and to respect whatever is big, strong, and fast. They expect women to serve and to care for the non-material quality of life, for children, and for the weak. Feminine cultures, on the other hand, define relatively overlapping social roles for the sexes, in which men need not be ambitious or competitive, but may go for a different quality of life than material success; men may respect whatever is small, weak, and slow. So, in masculine cultures these political/organizational values stress material success and assertiveness; in feminine cultures they stress other types of quality of life, interpersonal relationships, and concern for the weak.

Table 7.1 shows Hofstede's conception of the manifestation of the first of the above four categories, individualism/collectivism, with particular focus on classroom manifestations of these two factors in contrast.

Teachers who are charged with educating students whose cultural backgrounds differ from their own must of course attend to such factors as those that Hofstede has brought to our attention. The climate for effective classroom language acquisition may be considerably clouded by what students see as contradictory expectations for their participation, and as a result, certain unnecessary blocks stand in the way of their success.

LANGUAGE POLICY AND POLITICS

The relationship between language and society cannot be discussed for long without touching on the political ramifications of language and language policy. Virtually every country has some form of explicit, "official," or implicit, "unofficial," policy affecting the status of its native language(s) and one or more foreign languages. Ultimately those language policies become politicized as special interest groups vie for power and economic gain. Into this mix, English, now the major worldwide *lingua franca*, is the subject of international debate as policy makers struggle over the legitimization of varieties of English. Some strands of research even suggest that English teaching worldwide threatens to form an elitist cultural hegemony, widening the gap between "haves" and "have nots." The surface of these issues will be scratched in this section, with the suggestion that the reader turn to other sources for further enlightenment.

Table 7.1. Differences in teacher/student and student/student interaction related to the individualism versus collectivism dimension (Hofstede 1986: 312)

Collectivist Societies	Individualist Societies
• positive association in society with whatever is rooted in tradition	• positive association in society with whatever is "new"
• the young should learn; adults cannot accept student role	• one is never too old to learn; "permanent education"
• students expect to learn how to do	• students expect to learn how to learn
• individual students will only speak up in class when called upon personally by the teacher	• individual students will speak up in class in response to a general invitation by the teacher
• individuals will only speak up in small groups	• individuals will only speak up in large groups
• large classes split socially into smaller, cohesive subgroups based on particularist criteria (e.g., ethnic affiliation)	• subgroupings in class vary from one situation to the next based on universalist criteria (e.g., the task "at hand")
• formal harmony in learning situations should be maintained at all times	• confrontation in learning situations can be salutary; conflicts can be brought into the open
• neither the teacher nor any student should ever be made to lose face	• face-consciousness is weak
• education is a way of gaining prestige in one's social environment and of joining a higher-status group	• education is a way of improving one's economic worth and self-respect based on ability and competence
• diploma certificates are important and displayed on walls	• diploma certificates have little symbolic value
• acquiring certificates even through [dubious] means is more important than acquiring competence	• acquiring competence is more important than acquiring certificates
• teachers are expected to give preferential treatment to some students (e.g., based on ethnic affiliation or on recommendation by an influential person)	• teachers are expected to be strictly impartial

World Englishes

The rapid growth of English as an international language (EIL) of communication has stimulated interesting but often controversial discussion about the status of English in its varieties of what is now commonly called "world Englishes" (Kachru & Nelson 1996; Kachru 1985, 1992). Learning English in India, for example, really does not involve taking on a new culture since one is acquiring *Indian* English in India. According to Kachru, the "Indianization" of English in India has led to a situation in which English has few if any British cultural attributes. This process of "nativization" or "indigenization" (Richards 1979) of English has spread to an "outer circle" (Kachru 1985) of countries that includes India, Singapore, the Philippines, Nigeria, Ghana, and others. In such contexts English is commonly learned by children at school age and is the medium for most of their primary, secondary, and tertiary education.

The spread and stratification of EIL led Kachru and others who have joined in the debate (Tollefson 1995; Phillipson 1992; Davies 1989; Quirk 1988 for example) to a fresh conceptualization of contexts of English language use.

> The traditional dichotomy between native and non-native is functionally uninsightful and linguistically questionable, particularly when discussing the functions of English in multilingual societies. The earlier distinction of English as a native language (ENL), second (ESL) and foreign (EFL) has come under attack for reasons other than sociolinguistic. (Kachru 1992: 3)

Instead, we are advised to view English in terms of a broad range of its functions and the degree of its penetration into a country's society.

ESL and EFL

The spread of EIL has indeed muddied the formerly clear waters that separated what we still refer to as English as a Second Language (ESL) and English as a Foreign Language (EFL). Learning ESL—English within a culture where English is spoken natively—may be clearly defined in the case of, say, an Arabic speaker learning English in the USA or the UK, but not as easily identified where English is already an accepted and widely used language for education, government, or business within the country (for example, learning English in the Philippines or India). According to Nayar (1997), we need to add yet another ESL context, English in Scandinavia, where English has no official status but occupies such a high profile that virtually every educated person can communicate competently with native speakers of English.

Learning EFL, that is, English in one's own culture with few immediate opportunities to use the language within the environment of that culture (for example, a Japanese learning English in Japan), may at first also appear to be easy to define. Two global developments, however, mitigate the clarity of identifying a simple "EFL" context: (a) the current trend toward immigrant communities establishing themselves within various countries (e.g., Spanish or Chinese or Russian communities in a large city in the United States) provides ready access to users of so-called foreign languages; (b) in the case of English, the penetration of English-based media (especially television, the Internet, and the motion picture industry) provides further ready access to English even in somewhat isolated settings.

The problem with the ESL/EFL terminology, as Nayar (1997: 22) pointed out, is that it "seems to have created a world view that being a native speaker of English will somehow bestow on people not only unquestionable competence in the use and teaching of the language but also expertise in telling others how English ought to be taught." As we saw in earlier chapters, native-speaker models do not necessarily exemplify the idealized competence that was once claimed for them. The multiplicity of contexts for the use of English worldwide demands a careful look at the variables of each situation before making the blanket generalization that one of two possible models, ESL or EFL, applies. By specifying country, language policy, and status of English, we can at least begin to guard against falling prey to the myth that native-speaker models are to be emulated at all costs.

In terms of degrees of acculturation, on the surface one could conclude that second language learning in a culture foreign to one's own potentially involves the deepest form of culture acquisition. Learners must survive in a strange culture as well as learn a language on which they are totally dependent for communication. On the other hand, one should not too quickly dismiss second language learning in the native culture (e.g., Nigerians learning English in Nigeria) from having a potential acculturation factor. In such contexts, the learner could experience considerable culture stress, depending upon the country, the cultural and sociopolitical status of both the native and target language, the purposes for which one is learning the language (career, academic, social), and the intensity of the motivation of the learner.

Linguistic Imperialism and Language Rights

One of the more controversial issues to rear its head in the global spread of EIL is the extent to which the propagation of English as a medium of education, commerce, and government "has impeded literacy in mother tongue languages, has thwarted social and economic progress for those who do not learn it, and has not generally been relevant to the needs of ordinary people in their day-to-day or future lives" (Ricento 1994: 422). Linguistic imperialism, or "linguicism," as this issue has come to be named (Phillipson & Skutnabb-Kangas 1994; Phillipson 1992; Skutnabb-Kangas & Cummins 1988), calls attention to the potential consequences of English teaching worldwide when Eurocentric ideologies are embedded in instruction, having the effect of legitimizing colonial or establishment power and resources, and of reconstituting "cultural inequalities between English and other languages" (Phillipson 1992: 47).

A central issue in the linguistic imperialism debate is the devaluing of native languages through the colonial spread of English. For more than a century, according to Phillipson (1992), there was little or no recognition of the imperialistic effect of the spread of English (and French) in colonial contexts. But in recent years, there have been some signs of hope for the preservation of indigenous languages as seen, for example, in the Council of Europe's 1988 European Charter for Regional and Minority Languages, which assumes a multilingual context and support for minority languages. Likewise, within the United Nations, the Universal Declaration of Linguistic Rights has endorsed the right of all people to develop and promote their own languages and to offer children access to education in their own languages (Ricento 1994).

As teachers venture into the far corners of the earth and teach English, one of our primary tenets should be the highest respect for the languages and cultures of our students. One of the most worthy causes we can espouse is the preservation of diversity among human beings. At every turn in our curricula, we must beware of imposing a foreign value system on our learners for the sake of bringing a common language to all. We can indeed break down barriers of communication with English, but we are reminded that the two-edged sword of EIL carries with it the danger of the imperialistic destruction of a global ecology of languages and cultures.

Language Policy and the "English Only" Debate

Yet another manifestation of the sociopolitical domain of second language acquisition is found in language policies around the world. Questions in this field range from the language of the education of children to the adoption of "official" status for a language (or languages) in a country. The first topic, the language of education, involves the decision by some political entity (e.g., a ministry of education, a state board of education) to offer education in a designated language or languages. Such decisions inevitably require a judgment on the part of the policy-making body on which language(s) is (are) deemed to be of value for the future generation of wage earners (and voters) in that society. We can visualize the potential twists and turns of the arguments that are mounted to justify a particular language policy for education. A tremendous clash of value systems is brought to bear on the ultimate decision: linguistic diversity, cultural pluralism, ethnicity, race, power, status, politics, economics, and the list goes on. In the final analysis, "history indicates that restricting language rights can be divisive and can lead to segregationist tendencies in a society. At the same time, such legislation rarely results in a unified society speaking solely the mandated language(s)" (Thomas 1996: 129).

In the United States, one of the most misunderstood issues in the last decade of the twentieth century was the widespread move to establish English as an "official" language. Noting that the USA had never declared English to be official, proponents of "English only" ballots across many states argued that an official English policy was needed to unify the country and end decades-long debates over bilingual education. The campaigns to pass such ballots, heavily funded by well-heeled right-wing organizations, painted a picture of the unity and harmony of people communicating in a common tongue. What those campaigns did not reveal was the covert agenda of the ultimate devaluing of minority languages and cultures. (See Crawford 1998, Thomas 1996, Tollefson 1995, Auerbach 1995 for further information.) In related legislative debates across the USA, bilingual education was singled out by the same groups as a waste of time and money. In 1998, for example, in the state of California, a well-financed campaign to severely restrict bilingual education programs managed to seduce the public by promoting myths and misunderstandings about language acquisition and multilingualism (Scovel 1999). Once again, those who end up suffering from such moves toward "English only" are the already disenfranchised minority cultures.

LANGUAGE, THOUGHT, AND CULTURE

No discussion about cultural variables in second language acquisition is complete without some treatment of the relationship between language and thought. We saw in the case of first language acquisition that cognitive development and linguistic development go hand in hand, each interacting with and shaping the other. It is commonly observed that the manner in which an idea or "fact" is stated affects the way we conceptualize the idea. Words shape our lives. The advertising world is a prime example of the use of language to shape, persuade, and dissuade. "Weasel words" tend to glorify very ordinary products into those that are "unsurpassed," "ultimate," "supercharged," and "the right choice." In the case of food that has been sapped of most of its nutrients by the manufacturing process, we are told that these products are now "enriched" and "fortified." A foreigner in the United States once remarked that in the United States there are no "small" eggs, only "medium," "large," "extra large," and "jumbo."

Euphemisms abound in American culture where certain thoughts are taboo or certain words connote something less than desirable. We are persuaded by industry, for example, that "receiving waters" are the lakes or rivers into which industrial wastes are dumped and that "assimilative capacity" refers to how much of the waste can be dumped into the river before it starts to show. Garbagemen are "sanitary engineers"; toilets are "rest rooms"; slums are "substandard dwellings." And when it comes to reporting on military conflicts like the Gulf War of 1991 or the Kosovo War of 1999, deaths are referred to as "collateral damage."

Verbal labels can shape the way we store events for later recall. In a classic study, Carmichael, Hogan, and Walter (1932) found that when subjects were briefly exposed to figures like those in Figure 7.1 and later asked to reproduce them, the reproductions were influenced by the labels assigned to the figures.

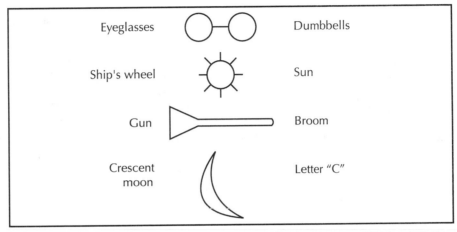

Figure 7.1. Sample stimulus figures used by Carmichael, Hogan, and Walter (1932)

For example, the first drawing tended to be reproduced as something like this if subjects had seen the "eyeglasses" label:

Or like this if they had seen the "dumbbells" label:

Words are not the only linguistic category affecting thought. The way a sentence is structured will affect nuances of meaning. Elizabeth Loftus (1976) discovered that subtle differences in the structure of questions can affect the answer a person gives. For example, after viewing a film of an automobile accident, subjects were asked questions like "Did you see the broken headlight?" in some cases, and in other cases "Did you see a broken headlight?" Questions using "the" tended to produce more false recognition of events. The presence of the definite article led subjects to believe that there was a broken headlight whether they saw it or not. Similar results were found for questions like "Did you see some people watching the accident?" versus "Did you see any people watching the accident?" or even for questions containing a presupposition: "How fast was the car going when it hit the stop sign?" (presupposing both the existence of a stop sign and that the car hit a stop sign whether the subject actually saw it or not).

On the discourse level of language, we are familiar with the persuasiveness of an emotional speech or a well-written novel. How often has a gifted orator swayed opinion and thought? Or a powerful editorial moved one to action or change? These are common examples of the influence of language on our cognitive and affective states.

Culture is really an integral part of the interaction between language and thought. Cultural patterns of cognition and customs are sometimes explicitly coded in language. Conversational discourse styles, for example, may be a factor of culture. Consider the "directness" of discourse of some cultures: in the US, for example, casual conversation is said to be less frank and more concerned about face-saving than conversation in Greece (Kakava 1995), and therefore a Greek conversation may be more confrontational than a conversation in the US. In Japanese, the relationship of one's interlocutor is almost always expressed explicitly, either verbally and/or nonverbally. Perhaps those forms shape one's perception of others in relation to self.

Lexical items may reflect something about the intersection of culture and cognition. Color categorization has been cited as a factor of one's linguistic lexicon. Gleason (1961: 4) noted that the Shona of Rhodesia and the Bassa of Liberia have fewer color categories than speakers of European languages and they break up the spectrum at different points. Of course, the Shona or Bassa are able to perceive and describe other colors, in the same way that an English speaker might describe a "dark bluish green," but according to Gleason the labels that the language provides tend to shape the person's overall cognitive organization of color and to cause varying degrees of color discrimination.

You might be tempted at this point to say, "Ah, yes, and I hear that the Eskimos have many different words for 'snow,' which explains why they are able to discriminate types of snow better than English speakers." This claim is one of the myths about language "that refuses to die" (Scovel 1999: 1), a vocabulary "hoax" (Pullum 1991) perpetuated along with other myths about Eskimos, such as rubbing noses and throwing Grandma out to be eaten by polar bears (Pinker 1994: 64). The problem lies not only in the fact that there is no single language called "Eskimo," but that "languages spoken in northeastern Canada like Inuit do *not* have a disproportionately large number of words for this cold white stuff" (Scovel 1999: 1).

Another popular misconception about language and cognition came from Whorf's (1956) claims about the expression of time in Hopi. Arguing that Hopi contains no grammatical forms that refer to "time," Whorf suggested that Hopi had "no general notion or intuition of time" (Carroll 1956: 57). The suggestion was so enticingly supportive of the linguistic determinism hypothesis (see below) that gradually Whorf's claim became accepted as fact. It is interesting that several decades later, Malotki (1983) showed that Hopi speech does contain tense, metaphors for time, units of time, and ways to quantify units of time!

A tantalizing question emerges from such observations. Does language reflect a cultural world view, or does language actually shape the world view? Drawing on the ideas of Wilhelm von Humboldt (1767–1835), who claimed that language shaped a person's *Weltanschauung*, Edward Sapir and Benjamin Whorf proposed a hypothesis that has now been given several alternative labels: the *Sapir-Whorf hypothesis*, the *Whorfian hypothesis*, *linguistic relativity*, or *linguistic determinism*. Whorf (1956: 212–214) summed up the hypothesis:

> The background linguistic system (in other words, the grammar) of each language is not merely a reproducing instrument for voicing ideas but rather is itself the shaper of ideas, the program and guide for the individual's mental activity, for his analysis of impressions, for his synthesis of his mental stock in trade. Formulation of ideas is not an independent process, strictly rational in the old sense, but is part of a particular grammar and differs, from slightly to greatly, as between different grammars. We dissect nature along lines laid down by our native languages. The categories and types that we isolate from the world of phenomena we do not find there because they stare every observer in the face; on the contrary, the world is presented in a kaleidoscopic flux of impressions which has to be organized by our minds—and this means largely by the linguistic systems in our minds. We cut nature up, organize it into concepts, and ascribe significance as we do, largely because we are parties to an agreement to organize it in this way—an agreement that holds through our speech community and is codified in the patterns of our language. The agreement is, of course, an implicit and unstated one, but its terms are absolutely obligatory; we cannot talk at all except by subscribing to the organization and classification of data which the agreement decrees.

Over the years, the Whorfian hypothesis has unfortunately been overstated and misinterpreted. Guiora (1981: 177) criticized Whorf's claim that the influence of language on behavior was "undifferentiated, all pervasive, permanent and absolute"; Guiora called these claims "extravagant." It would appear that it was Guiora's interpretation that was extravagant, for he put ideas into Whorf's writings that were never there. Clarke, Losoff, McCracken, and Rood (1984: 57), in a careful review of Whorf's writings, eloquently demonstrated that the Whorfian hypothesis was not nearly as monolithic or causal as some would interpret it to be. "The 'extravagant claims' made in the name of linguistic relativity were not made by Whorf, and attributing to him simplistic views of linguistic determination serves only to obscure the usefulness of his insights."

The language teaching profession today has actually subscribed to a more moderate view of the Whorfian hypothesis, if only because of the mounting evidence of the interaction of language and culture. A quarter of a century ago, in the spirit of those who have exposed the mythical nature of many of the claims about linguistic determinism, Ronald Wardhaugh (1976: 74) offered the following alternative to a strong view of the Whorfian hypothesis:

> The most valid conclusion to all such studies is that it appears possible to talk about anything in any language provided the speaker is willing to use some degree of circumlocution. Some concepts are more "codable," that is, easier to express, in some languages than in others. The speaker, of course, will not be aware of the circumlocution in the absence of familiarity with another language that uses a more succinct means of expression. Every natural language provides both a language for talking about every other language, that is, a metalanguage, and an entirely adequate apparatus for making any kinds of observations that need to be made about the world. If such is the case, every natural language must be an extremely rich system which readily allows its speakers to overcome any predispositions that exist.

So, while some aspects of language seem to provide us with potential cognitive mind sets (e.g., in English, the passive voice, the tense system, "weasel words," and lexical items), we can also recognize that through both language and culture, some universal properties bind us all together in one world. The act of learning to think in another language may require a considerable degree of mastery of that language, but a second language learner does not have to learn to think, in general, all over again. As in every other human learning experience, the second language learner can make positive use of prior experiences to facilitate the process of learning by retaining that which is valid and valuable for second culture learning and second language learning.

In the Classroom:
Toward a Principled Approach
to Language Pedagogy

It should be clear from the vignette of the previous chapter that as an "enlightened, eclectic" teacher, you can think in terms of a number of possible methodological options for tailoring classes to particular contexts. Your *approach* to language pedagogy therefore takes on great importance. Your approach to language teaching methodology is your theoretical rationale that underlies everything that you do in the classroom.

Your approach actually draws on most of what is presented in this book—issues, findings, conclusions, and *principles* of language learning and teaching, principles such as:

- Intrinsic motivation is a powerful incentive for learning.
- A moderate to high level of risk-taking behavior is important.
- Language and culture are inextricably intertwined.
- Successful learners make a strategic investment in their learning.
- Self-confidence is an important precursor to success.

Your understanding of these principles forms a set of foundation stones upon which to build curricular plans, lesson designs, and moment-by-moment techniques and activities. (For more on principled approaches to language teaching, see Brown's *Teaching by Principles*, Second Edition, 2000.)

Your approach to language pedagogy is not just a set of static principles, set in stone. It is, in fact, a dynamic composite of energies that changes (or should change, if you are a growing teacher) with your experiences in your own learning and teaching. The way you understand the language learning process—what makes for successful and unsuccessful learning—may be relatively stable across months or years, but it doesn't pay to be too smug. There is far too much that we do not know collectively about this process, and there are far too many new research findings pouring in to assume that you can confidently assert that you know everything you already need to know about language and language learning.

The interaction between your approach and your classroom practice is the key to dynamic teaching. The best teachers always take a few calculated risks in the classroom, trying new activities here and there. The inspiration for such innovation comes from the approach level, but the feedback that they gather from actual implementation then informs their overall understanding of what learning and teaching is. Which, in turn, may give rise to a new insight and more innovative possibilities, and the cycle continues.

Consider an example of this cycle. The language–culture connection, as explained in this chapter, is an important factor in the learning of a second language, potentially a "keystone" in one's approach to language teaching. How does that keystone interact with classroom techniques? In a number of ways, the language–culture connection points toward certain techniques and away from others. The following checklist illustrates how techniques are generated, shaped, and revised according to just this one principle.

Culturally Appropriate Techniques: A Checklist

1. Does the technique recognize the value and belief systems that are presumed to be a part of the culture(s) of the students?
2. Does the technique refrain from any demeaning stereotypes of any culture, including the culture(s) of your students?
3. Does the technique refrain from any possible devaluing of the students' native language(s)?
4. Does the technique recognize varying degrees of willingness of students to participate openly due to factors of collectivism/individualism and power distance?
5. If the technique requires students to go beyond the comfort zone of uncertainty avoidance in their culture(s), does it do so empathetically and tactfully?
6. Is the technique sensitive to the perceived roles of males and females in the culture(s) of your students?
7. Does the technique sufficiently connect specific language features (e.g., grammatical categories, lexicon, discourse) to cultural ways of thinking, feeling, and acting?
8. Does the technique in some way draw on the potentially rich background experiences of the students, including their own experiences in other cultures?

The eight criteria in the checklist represent various facets of the language–culture connection as discussed in this chapter. As each item is applied to a technique that is either being planned or has already been taught, evaluation takes place and the technique thereby becomes a manifestation of a principled approach. All of the principles in your approach could easily lead to similar checklists for the validation of techniques.

In the process of actual teaching in the classroom, it is quite possible that you will be led to modify certain aspects of your approach. For example, suppose you were a secondary school teacher in Bangladesh where boys sat on one side of the room and girls on the other, and you had planned group work that not only grouped boys and girls together but asked them to discuss women's rights. While this is an extreme example, you can see that several items on the checklist (#1, #4, #5, #6) would lead you to change that activity!

Classroom experience then might stir you to further refinement.

As you continue to read this book, you may do well to pay increasing attention to your growing stockpile of language learning/teaching principles that together are forming a composite approach to language learning and teaching. Consider the pedagogical implications and classroom applications of every finding, every issue, every conclusion, and every generalization. In so doing your overall approach will not only be more enlightened but more readily applicable to classroom practice.

TOPICS AND QUESTIONS FOR
STUDY AND DISCUSSION

[Note: (I) individual work; (G) group or pair work; (C) whole-class discussion.]

1. (G) The class should be divided into groups of five or six people per group. Each group is assigned a country; countries should be as widely varying as possible, but at least one of the countries should be geographically close to the country you are now in. First, each group should be warned to suspend their usual tact and diplomacy for the sake of making this activity more enlightening. The task is for each group to brainstorm stereotypes for the people of their assigned country. The stereotypes can be negative and demeaning and/or positive and complimentary.

2. (C) Groups in item 1 now write their list of stereotypes on the blackboard; each group reports on (a) any difficulties they had in agreeing on stereotypes, (b) what the sources of these stereotypes are, (c) any guilty feelings about some of the items on the list and the reasons for the guilt, and (d) comments on any of the other lists. The ultimate objective is to get stereotypes out in the open, discuss their origins, and become sensitive to how oversimplified and demeaning certain stereotypes can be.

3. (C) Anyone in the class who has lived for a year or more in another country (and another language) might share with the class the extent to which he or she experienced any or all of the stages of culture acquisition discussed in this chapter. Were the stages easily identifiable? Was there an optimal period for language breakthrough?

4. (I) Look again at Hofstede's categories: collectivism/individualism, power distance, uncertainty avoidance, masculinity/femininity. Try to find one example of each in your own past experiences in language classrooms (or in any other classroom). What did the teacher do? Was it effective in bridging any gaps? If not, how could you have made a

more effective bridge?

5. (G) In considering so-called "world Englishes," where do you draw the line in recognizing the "legitimacy" of a variety of English? If Indian English, for example, is a legitimate variety of English, is "Singlish" (English in Singapore) in the same category? What about Japanese English ("Japlish")? With a partner, think of other examples and try to arrive at a conclusion.

6. (C) Why is language learning and teaching a political issue? In countries with which you are familiar, discuss in class the extent to which government dictates language policies either in education in particular or in the country in general.

7. (G) In groups of three to five, review Phillipson's (1992) contention that English teaching efforts around the world can be viewed as fostering linguistic imperialism. Do you agree? Provide examples and counterexamples to illustrate your answer. Report your findings back to the whole class.

8. (C) If you are familiar with the "English only" debates in the US or with similar issues in another country, share with others your perceptions of how special interest groups further their cause in their attempts to influence voting.

9. (C) In foreign languages represented in the class, find examples that support the contention that language (specific vocabulary items, perhaps) seems to shape the way the speaker of a language views the world. On the other hand, in what way does the Whorfian hypothesis present yet another chicken-or-egg issue?

SUGGESTED READINGS

Morgan, Carol. 1993. Attitude change and foreign language culture learning. *Language Teaching* 26: 63–75.

Dirven, René and Pütz, Martin. 1993. Intercultural communication. *Language Teaching* 26: 144–156.

Both of these summary surveys offer overviews of research on culture learning and on intercultural communication.

Hofstede, Geert. 1986. Cultural differences in teaching and learning. *International Journal of Intercultural Relations* 10: 301–320.

Hofstede's article covers the perspectives of fifty different countries on collectivism, power distance, uncertainty avoidance, and masculinity. It might be an interesting stimulus to conducting some of your own further research.

Kohls, Robert. 1984. *Survival Kit for Overseas Living.* Yarmouth, ME: Intercultural Press.

This handy manual provides a good practical set of culture learning techniques especially applicable to those traveling outside their own country.

Dresser, Norine. 1996. *Multicultural Manners: New Rules of Etiquette for a Changing Society.* New York: John Wiley & Sons.

Dresser's book is written for the lay audience and humorously discusses a multitude of cross-cultural rules of etiquette, ranging from body language to colors, food, gifts, religion, holidays, and health practices.

Scollon, Ron and Scollon, Suzanne Wong. 1995. *Intercultural Communication: A Discourse Approach.* Cambridge, MA: Blackwell Publishers.

The authors provide a more technical read here on the topic of discourse patterns across cultures.

Fantini, Alvino E. 1997. *New Ways of Teaching Culture.* Alexandria, VA: Teachers of English to Speakers of Other Languages.

A nice collection of practical classroom activities, all categorized into different types and coded for appropriate levels of proficiency, is provided in this volume in TESOL's "New Ways" series of innovative classroom techniques.

Tollefson, James. 1995. *Power and Inequality in Language Education.* Cambridge: Cambridge University Press.

A number of sensitive political issues are covered in this very informative anthology. Topics range from power issues in classrooms all the way up to societal implications.

LANGUAGE LEARNING EXPERIENCE: JOURNAL ENTRY 7

[Note: See pages 18 and 19 of Chapter 1 for general guidelines for writing a journal on a previous or concurrent language learning experience.]

• In your journal, describe any cross-cultural living experiences you have had, even just a brief visit in another country. Describe any feelings of euphoria, uneasiness or stress, and a sense of recovery if you felt such. How did those feeling mesh with any language learning processes?

- Think of one or two languages you're familiar with or you've tried to learn. How do you feel about the people of the culture of that language? Any mixed feelings?
- Look at item 4 on page 203 and write about an example of one or more of Hofstede's categories in your own current or past experiences in language classrooms.
- Do you personally think the spread of English in the colonial era had imperialistic overtones? How can you as an English teacher in this new millennium avoid such cultural imperialism?
- Make a list of words, phrases, or language rules in your foreign language that are good examples of the Whorfian hypothesis. Take two or three of those and write about whether or not you think the language itself shapes the way speakers of that language think or feel.

CHAPTER **8**

CROSS-LINGUISTIC

INFLUENCE AND

LEARNER LANGUAGE

Up to this point in the treatment of principles of second language acquisition, our focus has been on the psychology of language learning.
Psychological principles of second language acquisition form the foundation stones for building a comprehensive understanding of the acquisition
of the linguistic system. In this chapter we will take a different direction as
we begin to examine the most salient component of second language
acquisition: the language itself. This treatment will first consider, in historical progression, an era of preoccupation with studies of contrasts between
the native language and the target language (contrastive analysis) and the
effect of native on target language (now called "cross-linguistic influence").
We will then see how the era of contrastive analysis gave way to an era of
error analysis, with its guiding concept of interlanguage, now also widely
referred to as "learner language." Finally, questions about the effect of classroom instruction and error treatment will be addressed, with some practical implications for the language teacher.

THE CONTRASTIVE ANALYSIS HYPOTHESIS

In the middle of the twentieth century, one of the most popular pursuits
for applied linguists was the study of two languages in contrast. Eventually
the stockpile of comparative and contrastive data on a multitude of pairs of
languages yielded what commonly came to be known as the **Contrastive
Analysis Hypothesis** (CAH). Deeply rooted in the behavioristic and struc-

turalist approaches of the day, the CAH claimed that the principal barrier to second language acquisition is the interference of the first language system with the second language system, and that a scientific, structural analysis of the two languages in question would yield a taxonomy of linguistic contrasts between them which in turn would enable the linguist to predict the difficulties a learner would encounter.

It was at that time considered feasible that the tools of structural linguistics, such as Fries's (1952) slot-filler grammar, would enable a linguist to accurately describe the two languages in question, and to match those two descriptions against each other to determine valid contrasts, or differences, between them. Behaviorism contributed to the notion that human behavior is the sum of its smallest parts and components, and therefore that language learning could be described as the acquisition of all of those discrete units. Moreover, human learning theories highlighted *interfering* elements of learning, concluding that where no interference could be predicted, no difficulty would be experienced since one could *transfer* positively all other items in a language. The logical conclusion from these various psychological and linguistic assumptions was that second language learning basically involved the overcoming of the differences between the two linguistic systems—the native and target languages.

Intuitively the CAH has appeal in that we commonly observe in second language learners a plethora of errors attributable to the negative transfer of the native language to the target language. It is quite common, for example, to detect certain foreign accents and to be able to infer, from the speech of the learner alone, where the learner comes from. Native English speakers can easily identify the accents of English language learners from Germany, France, Spain, and Japan, for example. Such accents can even be represented in the written word. Consider Mark Twain's *The Innocents Abroad* (1869: 111), in which the French-speaking guide introduces himself: "If ze zhentlemans will to me make ze grande honneur to me rattain in hees serveece, I shall show to him everysing zat is magnifique to look upon in ze beautiful Paree. I speaky ze Angleesh parfaitmaw." Or William E. Callahan's Juan Castaniegos, a young Mexican in *Afraid of the Dark*, who says: "Help me to leave from thees place. But, Señor Capitán, me, I'ave do notheeng. Notheeng, Señor Capitán." These excerpts also capture the transfer of vocabulary and grammatical rules from the native language.

Some rather strong claims were made of the CAH by language teaching experts and linguists. One of the strongest was made by Robert Lado (1957: vii) in the preface to *Linguistics Across Cultures*: "The plan of the book rests on the assumption that we can predict and describe the patterns that will cause difficulty in learning, and those that will not cause difficulty, by comparing systematically the language and the culture to be learned with the native language and culture of the student." Then, in the first chapter of the book, Lado continues: "in the comparison between native and foreign language lies the key to ease or difficulty in foreign language learning. . . . Those elements that are similar to [the learner's] native language will be simple for him and those elements that are different will be difficult" (pp. 1–2). An equally strong claim was made by Banathy, Trager, and Waddle (1966: 37): "The change that has to take place in the language behavior of a foreign language student can be equated with the differences between the structure of the student's native language and culture and that of the target language and culture."

Such claims were supported by what some researchers claimed to be an empirical method of prediction. A well-known model was offered by Stockwell, Bowen, and Martin (1965), who posited what they called a **hierarchy of difficulty** by which a teacher or linguist could make a prediction of the relative difficulty of a given aspect of the target language. For phonological systems in contrast, Stockwell and his associates suggested eight possible degrees of difficulty. These degrees were based upon the notions of transfer (positive, negative, and zero) and of optional and obligatory choices of certain phonemes in the two languages in contrast. Through a very careful, systematic analysis of the properties of the two languages in reference to the hierarchy of difficulty, applied linguists were able to derive a reasonably accurate inventory of phonological difficulties that a second language learner would encounter.

Stockwell and his associates also constructed a hierarchy of difficulty for grammatical structures of two languages in contrast. Their grammatical hierarchy included sixteen levels of difficulty, based on the same notions used to construct phonological criteria, with the added dimensions of "structural correspondence" and "functional/semantic correspondence." Clifford Prator (1967) captured the essence of this grammatical hierarchy in six categories of difficulty. Prator's hierarchy was applicable to both grammatical and phonological features of language. The six categories, in ascending order of difficulty, are listed below. Most of the examples are taken from English and Spanish (a native English speaker learning Spanish as a second language); a few examples illustrate other pairs of contrasting languages.

>   **Level 0 — Transfer.** No difference or contrast is present between the two languages. The learner can simply transfer (positively) a sound, structure, or lexical item from the native language to the target language. Examples: English and Spanish cardinal vowels, word order, and certain words *(mortal, inteligente, arte, americanos)*.

Level 1 — Coalescence. Two items in the native language become coalesced into essentially one item in the target language. This requires that learners overlook a distinction they have grown accustomed to. Examples: English third-person possessives require gender distinction *(his/her)*, and in Spanish they do not *(su)*; an English speaker learning French must overlook the distinction between *teach* and *learn*, and use just the one word *apprendre* in French.

Level 2 — Underdifferentiation. An item in the native language is absent in the target language. The learner must avoid that item. Examples: English learners of Spanish must "forget" such items as English *do* as a tense carrier, possessive forms of *wh-* words *(whose)*, or the use of *some* with mass nouns.

Level 3 — Reinterpretation. An item that exists in the native language is given a new shape or distribution. Example: an English speaker learning French must learn a new distribution for nasalized vowels.

Level 4 — Overdifferentiation. A new item entirely, bearing little if any similarity to the native language item, must be learned. Example: an English speaker learning Spanish must learn to include determiners in generalized nominals (Man is mortal/*El hombre es mortal*), or, most commonly, to learn Spanish grammatical gender inherent in nouns.

Level 5 — Split. One item in the native language becomes two or more in the target language, requiring the learner to make a new distinction. Example: an English speaker learning Spanish must learn the distinction between *ser* and *estar* (to be), or the distinction between Spanish indicative and subjunctive moods.

Prator's reinterpretation, and Stockwell and his associates' original hierarchy of difficulty, were based on principles of human learning. The first, or "zero," degree of difficulty represents complete one-to-one correspondence and transfer, while the fifth degree of difficulty was the height of interference. Prator and Stockwell both claimed that their hierarchy could be applied to virtually any two languages and make it possible to predict second language learner difficulties in any language with a fair degree of certainty and objectivity.

FROM THE CAH TO CLI (CROSS-LINGUISTIC INFLUENCE)

Prediction of difficulty by means of contrastive procedures was not without glaring shortcomings. For one thing, the process was oversimplified. Subtle phonetic, phonological, and grammatical distinctions were not carefully accounted for. Second, it was very difficult, even with six categories, to determine exactly which category a particular contrast fit into. For example, when a Japanese speaker learns the English /r/, is it a case of a level 0, 1, or 3 difficulty? A case can be made for all three. The third and most problematic issue centered on the larger question of whether or not predictions of difficulty levels were actually verifiable.

The attempt to predict difficulty by means of contrastive analysis is what Ronald Wardhaugh (1970) called the **strong version** of the CAH, a version that he believed was quite unrealistic and impracticable. Wardhaugh noted (p. 125) that "at the very least, this version demands of linguists that they have available a set of linguistic universals formulated within a comprehensive linguistic theory which deals adequately with syntax, semantics, and phonology." He went on to point out the difficulty (p. 126), already noted, of an adequate procedure, built on sound theory, for actually contrasting the forms of languages: "Do linguists have available to them an overall contrastive system within which they can relate the two languages in terms of mergers, splits, zeroes, over-differentiations, under-differentiations, reinterpretations?" And so, while many linguists claimed to be using a scientific, empirical, and theoretically justified tool in contrastive analysis, in actuality they were operating more out of mentalistic subjectivity.

Wardhaugh noted, however (p. 126), that contrastive analysis had intuitive appeal, and that teachers and linguists had successfully used "the best linguistic knowledge available . . . in order to account for observed difficulties in second language learning." He termed such observational use of contrastive analysis the **weak version** of the CAH. The weak version does not imply the *a priori* prediction of certain degrees of difficulty. It recognizes the significance of interference across languages, the fact that such interference does exist and can explain difficulties, but it also recognizes that linguistic difficulties can be more profitably explained *a posteriori*—after the fact. As learners are learning the language and errors appear, teachers can utilize their knowledge of the target and native languages to understand sources of error.

The so-called weak version of the CAH is what remains today under the label **cross-linguistic influence** (CLI), suggesting that we all recognize the significant role that prior experience plays in any learning act, and that the influence of the native language as prior experience must not be overlooked. The difference between today's emphasis on influence, rather than prediction, is an important one. Aside from phonology, which remains the most reliable linguistic category for predicting learner performance, as illustrated at the beginning of the chapter, other aspects of language present more of a gamble. Syntactic, lexical, and semantic interference show far more variation among learners than psychomotor-based pronunciation interference. Even presumably simple grammatical categories like word order, tense, or aspect have been shown to contain a good deal of variation. For example, one might expect a French speaker who is beginning to learn English to say "I am in New York since January"; however, to predict such an utterance from every French learner of English is to go too far.

The most convincing early criticism of the strong version of the CAH was offered by Whitman and Jackson (1972), who undertook to test empirically the effectiveness of contrastive analysis as a tool for predicting areas of difficulty for Japanese learners of English. The predictions of four separate contrastive analysis rubrics (including that of Stockwell, Bowen, & Martin 1965) were applied to a forty-item test of English grammar to determine, *a priori*, the relative difficulty of the test items for speakers of Japanese. The test was administered to 2500 Japanese learners of English who did not know the relative predicted difficulty of each item. The results of the test were compared with the predictions. The result: Whitman and Jackson found no support for the predictions of the contrastive analyses so carefully worked out by linguists! They concluded (p. 40) that "contrastive analysis, as represented by the four analyses tested in this project, is inadequate, theoretically and practically, to predict the interference problems of a language learner."

Another blow to the strong version of the CAH was delivered by Oller and Ziahosseiny (1970), who proposed what one might call a "subtle differences" version of the CAH on the basis of a rather intriguing study of spelling errors. They found that for learners of English as a second language, English spelling proved to be more difficult for people whose native language used a Roman script (for example, French, Spanish) than for those whose native language used a non-Roman script (Arabic, Japanese). The strong form of the CAH would have predicted that the learning of an entirely new writing system (Level 4 in the hierarchy of difficulty) would be more difficult than reinterpreting (Level 3) spelling rules. Oller and Ziahosseiny (p. 186) found the opposite to be true, concluding that "wherever patterns are minimally distinct in form or meaning in one or more systems, confusion may result."

The learning of sounds, sequences, and meanings will, according to Oller and Ziahosseiny's study, be potentially very difficult where subtle distinctions are required either between the target language and native language or within the target language itself. In the case of their research on spelling English, there were more differences between non-Roman writing and Roman writing, but learners from a non-Roman writing system had to make fewer subtle distinctions than did those from the Roman writing system. Examples of subtle distinctions at the lexical level may be seen in false cognates like the French word *parent*, which in the singular means "relative" or "kin," while only the plural *(parents)* means "parents." Consider the Spanish verb *embarazar*, which commonly denotes "to make pregnant," and has therefore been the source of true "embarrassment" on the part of beginners attempting to speak Spanish! In recent years, research on CLI has uncovered a number of instances of subtle differences causing great difficulty (Sjöholm 1995).

The conclusion that great difference does not necessarily cause great difficulty underscores the significance of **intralingual** (within one language) errors (see subsequent sections in this chapter), which are as much a factor in second language learning as **interlingual** (across two or more languages) errors. The forms within one language are often perceived to be minimally distinct in comparison to the vast differences between the native and target language, yet those intralingual factors can lead to some of the greatest difficulties.

Today we recognize that teachers must certainly guard against *a priori* pigeon-holing of learners before we have even given learners a chance to perform. At the same time, we must also understand that CLI is an important linguistic factor at play in the acquisition of a second language (Jaszczolt 1995). CLI implies much more than simply the effect of one's first language on a second: the second language also influences the first; moreover, subsequent languages in multilinguals all affect each other in various ways. Specialized research on CLI in the form of contrastive lexicology, syntax, semantics, and pragmatics continues to provide insights into SLA that must not be discounted (Sharwood-Smith 1996; Sheen 1996). Sheen (1996) found, for example, that in an ESL course for speakers of Arabic, overt attention to targeted syntactic contrasts between Arabic and English reduced error rates. Indeed, the strong form of the CAH was too strong, but the weak form was also perhaps too weak. CLI research offers a cautious middle ground.

MARKEDNESS AND UNIVERSAL GRAMMAR

Fred Eckman (1977, 1981) proposed a useful method for determining directionality of difficulty. His Markedness Differential Hypothesis (otherwise known as **markedness** theory) accounted for relative degrees of difficulty by means of principles of universal grammar. Celce-Murcia and Hawkins (1985: 66) sum up markedness theory:

> It distinguishes members of a pair of related forms or structures by assuming that the marked member of a pair contains at least one more feature than the unmarked one. In addition, the unmarked (or neutral) member of the pair is the one with a wider range of distribution than the marked one. For example, in the case of the English indefinite articles (*a* and *an*), *an* is the more complex or marked form (it has an additional sound) and *a* is the unmarked form with the wider distribution.

Eckman (1981) showed that marked items in a language will be more difficult to acquire than unmarked, and that degrees of markedness will correspond to degrees of difficulty. Rutherford (1982) used markedness theory to explain why there seems to be a certain order of acquisition of morphemes in English: marked structures are acquired later than unmarked structures. Major and Faudree (1996) found that the phonological performance of native speakers of Korean learning English reflected principles of markedness universals.

In recent years, the attention of some second language researchers has expanded beyond markedness hypotheses alone to the broader framework of linguistic universals in general (Major & Faudree 1996; Eckman 1991; Carroll and Meisel 1990; Comrie 1990; Gass 1989). Some of these arguments focus on the applicability of notions of **universal grammar** (UG) to second language acquisition (White 1990; Schachter 1988; among others). As we saw in Chapter 2, many of the "rules" acquired by children learning their first language are presumed to be universal. By extension, rules that are shared by all languages comprise this UG. Such rules are a set of limitations or **parameters** (Flynn 1987) of language. Different languages set their parameters differently, thereby creating the characteristic grammar for that language. The hope is that by discovering innate linguistic principles that govern what is possible in human languages, we may be better able to understand and describe contrasts between native and target languages and the difficulties encountered by adult second language learners. Research on UG has begun to identify such universal properties and principles, and therefore represents an avenue of some promise.

Markedness theory and UG perspectives provide a more sophisticated understanding of difficulty in learning a second language than we had previously from the early formulations of the CAH, and fit more appropriately into current studies of CLI. But we do well to remember that describing and predicting difficulty amidst all the variables of human learning is still an elusive process. Teachers of foreign languages can benefit from UG and markedness research, but even in this hope-filled avenue of research, an instant map predicting learner difficulties is not right around the corner.

LEARNER LANGUAGE

The CAH stressed the interfering effects of the first language on second language learning and claimed, in its strong form, that second language learning is primarily, if not exclusively, a process of acquiring whatever items are different from the first language. As already noted above, such a narrow view of interference ignored the intralingual effects of learning, among other factors. In recent years researchers and teachers have come more and more to understand that second language learning is a process of the creative construction of a system in which learners are consciously testing hypotheses about the target language from a number of possible sources of knowledge: knowledge of the native language, limited knowledge of the target language itself, knowledge of the communicative functions of language, knowledge about language in general, and knowledge about life, human beings, and the universe. The learners, in acting upon their environment, construct what to them is a legitimate system of language in its own right—a structured set of rules that for the time being bring some order to the linguistic chaos that confronts them.

By the late 1960s, SLA began to be examined in much the same way that first language acquisition had been studied for some time: learners were looked on not as producers of malformed, imperfect language replete with mistakes but as intelligent and creative beings proceeding through logical, systematic stages of acquisition, creatively acting upon their linguistic environment as they encountered its forms and functions in meaningful contexts. By a gradual process of trial and error and hypothesis testing, learners slowly and tediously succeed in establishing closer and closer approximations to the system used by native speakers of the language. A number of terms have been coined to describe the perspective that stresses the legitimacy of learners' second language systems. The best known of these is **interlanguage**, a term that Selinker (1972) adapted from Weinreich's (1953) term "interlingual." Interlanguage refers to the separateness of a second language learner's system, a system that has a structurally intermediate status between the native and target languages.

Nemser (1971) referred to the same general phenomenon in second language learning but stressed the successive approximation to the target language in his term **approximative system**. Corder (1971:151) used the term **idiosyncratic dialect** to connote the idea that the learner's language is unique to a particular individual, that the rules of the learner's language are peculiar to the language of that individual alone. While each of these designations emphasizes a particular notion, they share the concept that second language learners are forming their own self-contained linguistic systems. This is neither the system of the native language nor the system of the target language, but a system based upon the best attempt of learners to bring order and structure to the linguistic stimuli surrounding them. The interlanguage hypothesis led to a whole new era of second language research and teaching and presented a significant breakthrough from the shackles of the CAH.

The most obvious approach to analyzing interlanguage is to study the speech and writing of learners, or what has come to be called **learner language** (Lightbown & Spada 1993; C. James 1990). Production data is publicly observable and is presumably reflective of a learner's underlying competence—production competence, that is. Comprehension of a second language is more difficult to study since it is not directly observable and must be inferred from overt verbal and nonverbal responses, by artificial instruments, or by the intuition of the teacher or researcher.

It follows that the study of the speech and writing of learners is largely the study of the errors of learners. "Correct" production yields little information about the actual linguistic system of learners, only information about the target language system that learners have already acquired. Therefore, our focus in the rest of this chapter will be on the significance of errors in learners' developing systems, otherwise known as **error analysis**.

ERROR ANALYSIS

Human learning is fundamentally a process that involves the making of mistakes. Mistakes, misjudgments, miscalculations, and erroneous assumptions form an important aspect of learning virtually any skill or acquiring information. You learn to swim by first jumping into the water and flailing arms and legs until you discover that there is a combination of movements—a structured pattern—that succeeds in keeping you afloat and propelling you through the water. The first mistakes of learning to swim are giant ones, gradually diminishing as you learn from making those mistakes. Learning to swim, to play tennis, to type, or to read all involve a process in which success comes by profiting from mistakes, by using mistakes to obtain feedback from the environment, and with that feedback to make new attempts that successively approximate desired goals.

Language learning, in this sense, is like any other human learning. We have already seen in the second chapter that children learning their first language make countless "mistakes" from the point of view of adult grammatical language. Many of these mistakes are logical in the limited linguistic system within which children operate, but, by carefully processing feedback from others, children slowly but surely learn to produce what is acceptable speech in their native language. Second language learning is a process that is clearly not unlike first language learning in its trial-and-error nature. Inevitably learners will make mistakes in the process of acquisition, and that process will be impeded if they do not commit errors and then benefit from various forms of feedback on those errors.

Researchers and teachers of second languages came to realize that the mistakes a person made in this process of constructing a new system of language needed to be analyzed carefully, for they possibly held in them some of the keys to the understanding of the process of second language acquisition. As Corder (1967: 167) noted: "A learner's errors . . . are significant in [that] they provide to the researcher evidence of how language is learned or acquired, what strategies or procedures the learner is employing in the discovery of the language."

Mistakes and Errors

In order to analyze learner language in an appropriate perspective, it is crucial to make a distinction between **mistakes** and **errors**, technically two very different phenomena. A mistake refers to a performance error that is either a random guess or a "slip," in that it is a failure to utilize a known system correctly. All people make mistakes, in both native and second language situations. Native speakers are normally capable of recognizing and correcting such "lapses" or mistakes, which are not the result of a deficiency in competence but the result of some sort of temporary breakdown or imperfection in the process of producing speech. These hesitations, slips of the tongue, random ungrammaticalities, and other performance lapses in native-speaker production also occur in second language speech. Mistakes, when attention is called to them, can be self-corrected.

Mistakes must be carefully distinguished from errors of a second language learner, idiosyncrasies in the language of the learner that are direct manifestations of a system within which a learner is operating at the time. An error, a noticeable deviation from the adult grammar of a native speaker, reflects the competence of the learner. Learners of English who ask, "Does John can sing?" are in all likelihood reflecting a competence level in which all verbs require a pre-posed *do* auxiliary for question formation. As such, it is an error, most likely not a mistake, and an error that reveals a portion of the learner's competence in the target language.

Can you tell the difference between an error and a mistake? Not always. An error cannot be self-corrected, according to James (1998: 83), while mistakes can be self-corrected if the deviation is pointed out to the speaker. But the learner's capacity for self-correction is objectively observable only if the learner actually self-corrects; therefore, if no such self-correction occurs, we are still left with no means to identify error vs. mistake. So, can we turn to frequency of a deviant form as a criterion? Sometimes. If, on one or two occasions, an English learner says "John cans sing," but on other occasions says "John can sing," it is difficult to determine whether "cans" is a mistake or an error. If, however, further examination of the learner's speech consistently reveals such utterances as "John wills go," "John mays come," and so forth, with very few instances of correct third-person singular usage of modal auxiliaries, you might safely conclude that "cans," "mays," and other such forms are errors indicating that the learner has not distinguished modals from other verbs. But it is possible, because of the few correct instances of production of this form, that the learner is on the verge of making the necessary differentiation between the two types of verbs. You can thus appreciate the subjectivity of determining the difference between a mistake and an error in learner speech. That undertaking always bears with it the chance of a faulty assumption on the part of a teacher or researcher.

The fact that learners do make errors, and that these errors can be observed, analyzed, and classified to reveal something of the system operating within the learner, led to a surge of study of learners' errors, called **error analysis**. Error analysis became distinguished from contrastive analysis by its examination of errors attributable to all possible sources, not just those resulting from negative transfer of the native language. Error analysis easily superseded contrastive analysis, as we discovered that only *some* of the errors a learner makes are attributable to the mother tongue, that learners do not actually make all the errors that contrastive analysis predicted they should, and that learners from disparate language backgrounds tend to make similar errors in learning one target language. Errors—overt manifestations of learners' systems—arise from several possible general sources: interlingual errors of interference from the native language, intralingual errors within the target language, the sociolinguistic context of communication, psycholinguistic or cognitive strategies, and no doubt countless affective variables.

Errors in Error Analysis

There is a danger in too much attention to learners' errors. While errors indeed reveal a system at work, the classroom language teacher can become so preoccupied with noticing errors that the correct utterances in the second language go unnoticed. In our observation and analysis of errors—for all that they do reveal about the learner—we must beware of placing too much attention on errors and not lose sight of the value of positive reinforcement of clear, free communication. While the diminishing of errors is an important criterion for increasing language proficiency, the ultimate goal of second language learning is the attainment of communicative fluency.

Another shortcoming in error analysis is an overemphasis on production data. Language is speaking *and* listening, writing *and* reading. The comprehension of language is as important as production. It so happens that production lends itself to analysis and thus becomes the prey of researchers, but comprehension data is equally important in developing an understanding of the process of SLA.

Over the years, many studies (James 1998; Tarone 1981; Kleinmann 1977; Schachter 1974) have shown that error analysis fails to account for the strategy of avoidance. A learner who for one reason or another avoids a particular sound, word, structure, or discourse category may be assumed incorrectly to have no difficulty therewith. Schachter (1974) found, for example, that it was misleading to draw conclusions about relative clause errors among certain English learners; native Japanese speakers were largely avoiding that structure and thus not manifesting nearly as many errors as some native Persian speakers. The absence of error therefore does not necessarily reflect nativelike competence because learners may be avoiding the very structures that pose difficulty for them.

Finally, error analysis can keep us too closely focused on specific languages rather than viewing universal aspects of language. Gass (1989) recommended that researchers pay more attention to linguistic elements that are common to all languages. The language systems of learners may have elements that reflect neither the target language nor the native language, but rather a universal feature of some kind. Such assertions are in keeping with the bioprogramming theories referred to in Chapter 2. But there are problems, of course, with the search for universal properties of learner's errors. "It is not at all clear in any precise way when the influence of the universal will appear in the interlanguage of learners rather than a violation of it based on influence from either the source or target language" (Celce-Murcia & Hawkins 1985: 66).

We do well, therefore, in the analysis of learners' errors, to engage in "performance analysis" or "interlanguage analysis" (Celce-Murcia & Hawkins 1985: 64), a less restrictive concept that places a healthy investigation of errors within the larger perspective of the learner's total language performance. While a significant portion of this chapter deals with error analysis, let us nevertheless remember that production errors are only a subset of the overall performance of the learner.

Identifying and Describing Errors

One of the common difficulties in understanding the linguistic systems of both first and second language learners is the fact that such systems cannot be directly observed. They must be inferred by means of analyzing production and comprehension data. What makes the task even thornier is the *instability* of learners' systems. Systems are in a constant state of flux as new information flows in and, through the process of subsumption, causes existing structures to be revised. Repeated observations of a learner will often reveal apparently unpredictable or even contradictory data. In undertaking the task of performance analysis, the teacher and researcher are called upon to infer order and logic in this unstable and variable system.

The first step in the process of analysis is the identification and description of errors. Corder (1971) provided a model for identifying erroneous or idiosyncratic utterances in a second language. That model is schematized in Figure 8.1. According to Corder's model, any sentence uttered by the learner and subsequently transcribed can be analyzed for idiosyncrasies. A major distinction is made at the outset between **overt** and **covert** errors. Overtly erroneous utterances are unquestionably ungrammatical at the sentence level. Covertly erroneous utterances are grammatically well-formed at the sentence level but are not interpretable within the context of communication. Covert errors, in other words, are not really covert at all if you attend to surrounding discourse (before or after the utterance). "I'm fine, thank you" is grammatically correct at the sentence level, but as a response to "Who are you?" it is obviously an error. A simpler and more straightforward set of terms, then, would be "sentence level" and "discourse level" errors.

Corder's model in Figure 8.1 indicates that, in the case of both overt and covert errors, if a plausible interpretation can be made of the sentence, then one should form a reconstruction of the sentence in the target language, compare the reconstruction with the original idiosyncratic sentence, and then describe the differences. If the native language of the learner is known, the model indicates using translation as a possible indicator of native language interference as the source of error. In some cases, of course, no plausible interpretation is possible at all, and the researcher is left with no analysis of the error (OUT_3).

Consider the following examples of idiosyncratic utterances of learners, and let us allow them to be fed through Corder's procedure for error analysis:

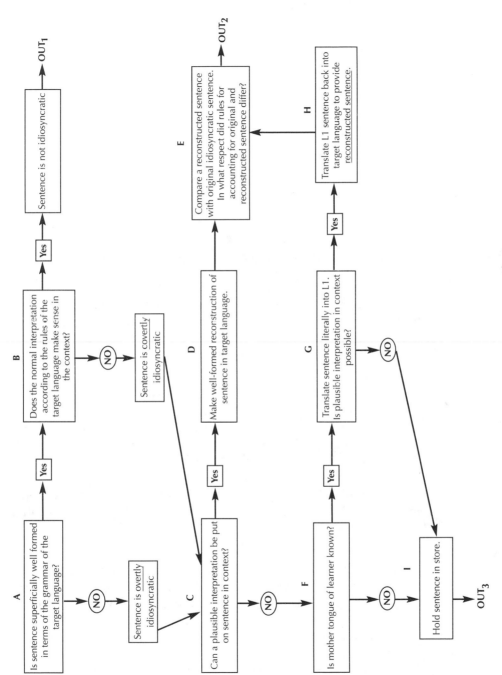

Figure 8.1. Procedure for identifying errors in second language learner production data (Corder 1971)

1. Does John can sing?

   A. NO
   C. YES
   D. Can John sing?
   E. Original sentence contained pre-posed *do* auxiliary applicable to most verbs, but not to verbs with modal auxiliaries. OUT_2

2. I saw their department.

   A. YES
   B. NO (context was in a conversation about living quarters in Mexico)
   C. NO
   F. YES, Spanish.
   G. Yo vi su departamento. YES
   H. I saw their apartment.
   E. *Departamento* was translated to false cognate *department.* OUT_2

3. The different city is another one in the another two.

   A. NO
   C. NO
   F. YES, Spanish.
   G. No plausible translation or interpretation.
   I. No analysis. OUT_3

It can be seen that the model is not complicated and represents a procedure that teachers and researchers might intuitively follow. Of course, once an error is identified, the next step is to describe it adequately, something the above procedure has only begun to accomplish.

A number of different categories for description of errors have been identified in research on learner language (for an overview, see Lennon 1991).

1. The most generalized breakdown can be made by identifying errors of addition, omission, substitution, and ordering, following standard mathematical categories. In English a *do* auxiliary might be added *(Does can he sing?)*, a definite article omitted *(I went to movie)*, an item substituted *(I lost my road)*, or a word order confused *(I to the store went)*. But such categories are clearly very generalized.

2. Within each category, *levels* of language can be considered: phonology or orthography, lexicon, grammar, and discourse.

Often, of course, it is difficult to distinguish different levels of errors. A word with a faulty pronunciation, for example, might hide a syntactic or lexical error. A French learner who says "[zhey] suis allé à l'école" might be mispronouncing the grammatically correct "je," or correctly pronouncing a grammatically incorrect "j'ai."

3. Errors may also be viewed as either *global* or *local* (Burt & Kiparsky 1972). Global errors hinder communication; they prevent the hearer from comprehending some aspect of the message. For example, "Well, it's a great hurry around," in whatever context, may be difficult or impossible to interpret. Local errors do not prevent the message from being heard, usually because there is only a minor violation of one segment of a sentence, allowing the hearer/reader to make an accurate guess about the intended meaning. "A scissors," for example, is a local error. The global-local distinction is discussed in the vignette at the end of this chapter.

4. Finally, Lennon (1991) suggests that two related dimensions of error, *domain* and *extent* should be considered in any error analysis. *Domain* is the rank of linguistic unit (from phoneme to discourse) that must be taken as context in order for the error to become apparent, and *extent* is the rank of linguistic unit that would have to be deleted, replaced, supplied, or reordered in order to repair the sentence. Lennon's categories help to operationalize Corder's overt-covert distinction discussed above. So, in the example just cited above, "a scissors," the domain is the phrase, and the extent is the indefinite article.

Sources of Error

Having examined procedures of error analysis used to identify errors in second language learner production data, our final step in the analysis of erroneous learner speech is that of determining the source of error. Why are certain errors made? What cognitive strategies and styles or even personality variables underlie certain errors? While the answers to these questions are somewhat speculative in that sources must be inferred from available data, in such questions lies the ultimate value of learner language analysis in general. By trying to identify sources we can take another step toward understanding how the learner's cognitive and affective processes relate to the linguistic system and to formulate an integrated understanding of the process of second language acquisition.

Interlingual Transfer

As we have already seen, interlingual transfer is a significant source of error for all learners. The beginning stages of learning a second language are especially vulnerable to interlingual transfer from the native language, or interference. In these early stages, before the system of the second language is familiar, the native language is the only previous linguistic system upon which the learner can draw. We have all heard English learners say "sheep" for "ship," or "the book of Jack" instead of "Jack's book"; French learners may say "Je sais Jean" for "Je connais Jean," and so forth. All these errors are attributable to negative interlingual transfer. While it is not always clear that an error is the result of transfer from the native language, many such errors are detectable in learner speech. Fluent knowledge or even familiarity with a learner's native language of course aids the teacher in detecting and analyzing such errors.

The learning of a **third language** (and subsequent languages) provides an interesting context for research. Depending upon a number of factors, including the linguistic and cultural relatedness of the languages and the context of learning, there are varying degrees of interlingual interference from both the first and second language to the third language, especially if the second and third languages are closely related or the learner is attempting a third language shortly after beginning a second language.

Intralingual Transfer

One of the major contributions of learner language research has been its recognition of sources of error that extend beyond interlingual errors in learning a second language. It is now clear that intralingual transfer (within the target language itself) is a major factor in second language learning. In Chapter 4 we discussed overgeneralization, which is the negative counterpart of intralingual transfer. Researchers (see Jaszczolt 1995; Taylor 1975) have found that the early stages of language learning are characterized by a predominance of interference (interlingual transfer), but once learners have begun to acquire parts of the new system, more and more intralingual transfer—generalization within the target language—is manifested. This of course follows logically from the tenets of learning theory. As learners progress in the second language, their previous experience and their existing subsumers begin to include structures within the target language itself.

Negative intralingual transfer, or overgeneralization, has already been illustrated in such utterances as "Does John can sing?" Other examples abound—utterances like "He goed," "I don't know what time is it," and "Il a tombé." Once again, the teacher or researcher cannot always be certain of the source of an apparent intralingual error, but repeated systematic observations of a learner's speech data will often remove the ambiguity of a single observation of an error.

The analysis of intralingual errors in a corpus of production data can become quite complex. For example, in Barry Taylor's (1975: 95) analysis of English sentences produced by ESL learners, just the class of errors in producing the main verb following an auxiliary yielded nine different types of error:

Table 8.1. Typical English intralingual errors in the use of articles (from Richards 1971: 187)

1. Omission of *THE*

(a) before unique nouns	Sun is very hot
	Himalayas are . . .
(b) before nouns of nationality	Spaniards and Arabs . . .
(c) before nouns made particular in context	At the conclusion of article
	She goes to bazaar every day
	She is mother of that boy
(d) before a noun modified by a participle	Solution given in this article
(e) before superlatives	Richest person
(f) before a noun modified by an *of-phrase*	Institute of Nuclear Physics

2. *THE* Used Instead of Ø

(a) before proper names	The Shakespeare, the Sunday
(b) before abstract nouns	The friendship, the nature, the science
(c) before nouns behaving like abstract nouns	After the school, after the breakfast
(d) before plural nouns	The complex structures are still developing
(e) before *some*	The some knowledge

3. *A* Used Instead of *THE*

(a) before superlatives	a worst, a best boy in the class
(b) before unique nouns	a sun becomes red

4. *A* Instead of Ø

(a) before a plural noun qualified by an adjective	a holy places, a human beings, a bad news
(b) before uncountables	a gold, a work
(c) before an adjective	. . . taken as a definite

5. Omission of *A*

before class nouns defined by adjectives	he was good boy
	he was brave man

1. Past-tense form of verb following a modal
2. Present-tense -s on a verb following a modal
3. -ing on a verb following a modal
4. are (for be) following will
5. Past-tense form of verb following do
6. Present-tense -s on a verb following do
7. -ing on a verb following do
8. Past-tense form of a verb following be (inserted to replace a modal or do)
9. Present-tense -s on a verb following be (inserted to replace a modal or do)

And of course these are limited to the particular data that Taylor was analyzing and are therefore not exhaustive within a grammatical category. Moreover, they pertain only to errors of overgeneralization, excluding another long list of categories of errors that he found attributable to interlingual transfer. Similarly, Jack C. Richards (1971:185–187) provided a list of typical English intralingual errors in the use of articles (see Table 8.1 on page 225). These are not exhaustive either, but are examples of some of the errors commonly encountered in English learners from disparate native language backgrounds. Both Taylor's and Richards's lists are restricted to English, but clearly their counterparts exist in other languages.

Context of Learning

A third major source of error, although it overlaps both types of transfer, is the context of learning. "Context" refers, for example, to the classroom with its teacher and its materials in the case of school learning or the social situation in the case of untutored second language learning. In a classroom context the teacher or the textbook can lead the learner to make faulty hypotheses about the language, what Richards (1971) called "false concepts" and what Stenson (1974) termed "induced errors." Students often make errors because of a misleading explanation from the teacher, faulty presentation of a structure or word in a textbook, or even because of a pattern that was rotely memorized in a drill but improperly contextualized. Two vocabulary items presented contiguously—for example, *point at* and *point out*—might in later recall be confused simply because of the contiguity of presentation. Or a teacher may provide incorrect information—not an uncommon occurrence—by way of a misleading definition, word, or grammatical generalization. Another manifestation of language learned in classroom contexts is the occasional tendency on the part of learners to give uncontracted and inappropriately formal forms of language. We have all experienced foreign learners whose "bookish" language gives them away as classroom language learners.

The sociolinguistic context of natural, untutored language acquisition can give rise to certain dialect acquisition that may itself be a source of error. Corder's term "idiosyncratic dialect" applies especially well here. For example, a Japanese immigrant who lived in a predominantly Mexican-American area of a U.S. city produced a learner language that was an interesting blend of Mexican-American English and the standard English to which he was exposed in the university, colored by his Japanese accent.

Communication Strategies

In Chapter 5, communication strategies were defined and related to learning styles. Learners obviously use production strategies in order to enhance getting their messages across, but at times these techniques can themselves become a source of error. Once an ESL learner said, "Let us work for the well done of our country." While it exhibited a nice little twist of humor, the sentence had an incorrect approximation of the word *welfare*. Likewise, word coinage, circumlocution, false cognates (from Tarone 1981), and prefabricated patterns can all be sources of error.

STAGES OF LEARNER LANGUAGE DEVELOPMENT

There are many different ways to describe the progression of learners' linguistic development as their attempts at production successively approximate the target language system. Indeed, learners are so variable in their acquisition of a second language that stages of development defy description. Borrowing some insights from an earlier model proposed by Corder (1973), I have found it useful to think in terms of four stages, based on observations of what the learner does in terms of errors alone.

1. The first is a stage of **random errors**, a stage that Corder called "presystematic," in which the learner is only vaguely aware that there is some systematic order to a particular class of items. The written utterance "The different city is another one in the another two" surely comes out of a random error stage in which the learner is making rather wild guesses at what to write. Inconsistencies like "John cans sing," "John can to sing," and "John can singing," all said by the same learner within a short period of time, might indicate a stage of experimentation and inaccurate guessing.

2. The second, or **emergent**, stage of learner language finds the

learner growing in consistency in linguistic production. The learner has begun to discern a system and to internalize certain rules. These rules may not be correct by target language standards, but they are nevertheless legitimate in the mind of the learner. This stage is characterized by some "backsliding," in which the learner seems to have grasped a rule or principle and then regresses to some previous stage. In general the learner is still, at this stage, unable to correct errors when they are pointed out by someone else. Avoidance of structures and topics is typical. Consider the following conversation between a learner (L) and a native speaker (NS) of English:

> **L:**   I go New York.
> **NS:**   You're going to New York?
> **L:**   [doesn't understand] What?
> **NS:**   You will go to New York?
> **L:**   Yes.
> **NS:**   When?
> **L:**   1972.
> **NS:**   Oh, you went to New York in 1972.
> **L:**   Yes, I go 1972.

Such a conversation is reminiscent of those mentioned in Chapter 2 where children in first language situations could not discern any error in their speech.

3. A third stage is a truly **systematic** stage in which the learner is now able to manifest more consistency in producing the second language. While those rules that are stored in the learner's brain are still not all well-formed, they are more internally self-consistent and, of course, they more closely approximate the target language system. The most salient difference between the second and third stage is the ability of learners to correct their errors when they are pointed out—even very subtly—to them. Consider the English learner who described a popular fishing-resort area.

> **L:**   Many fish are in the lake. These fish are serving in the restaurants near the lake.
> **NS:**   [laughing] The *fish* are serving?
> **L:**   [laughing] Oh, no, the fish are *served* in the restaurants!

4. A final stage, which I will call the **stabilization** stage, in the

development of learner language systems is akin to what Corder (1973) called a "postsystematic" stage. Here the learner has relatively few errors and has mastered the system to the point that fluency and intended meanings are not problematic. This fourth stage is characterized by the learner's ability to self-correct. The system is complete enough that attention can be paid to those few errors that occur and corrections be made without waiting for feedback from someone else. At this point learners can stabilize too fast, allowing minor errors to slip by undetected, and thus manifest **fossilization** of their language, a concept that will be defined and discussed later in this chapter (see Selinker and Lamendella 1979).

It should be made clear that the four stages of systematicity outlined above do not describe a learner's total second language system. We would find it hard to assert, for example, that a learner is in an emergent stage, globally, for all of the linguistic subsystems of language. One might be in a second stage with respect to, say, the perfect tense system, and in the third or fourth stage when it comes to simple present and past tenses. Nor do these stages, which are based on error analysis, adequately account for sociolinguistic, functional, pragmatic (see Kasper 1998), or nonverbal strategies, all of which are important in assessing the total competence of the second language learner. Finally, we need to remember that production errors alone are inadequate measures of overall competence. They happen to be salient features of second language learners' interlanguage and present us with grist for error-analysis mills, but correct utterances warrant our attention and, especially in the teaching-learning process, deserve positive reinforcement.

VARIABILITY IN LEARNER LANGUAGE

Lest you be tempted to assume that all learner language is orderly and systematic, a caveat is in order. A great deal of attention has been given to the *variability* of interlanguage development (Bayley & Preston 1996; James 1990; Tarone 1988; Ellis 1987; Littlewood 1981). Just as native speakers of a language vacillate between expressions like "It has to be you" and "It must be you," learners also exhibit variation, sometimes within the parameters of acceptable norms, sometimes not. Some variability in learner language can be explained by what Gatbonton (1983) described as the "gradual diffusion" of incorrect forms of language in emergent and systematic stages of development. First, incorrect forms coexist with correct; then, the incorrect are expunged. Context has also been identified as a source of variation. In classrooms, the type of task can affect variation (Tarone & Parrish 1988).

And variability can be affected, in both tutored and untutored learning, by the exposure that a learner gets to norms.

While one simply must expect a good proportion of learner language data to fall beyond our capacity for systematic categorization, one of the more controversial current debates in SLA theory centers on the extent to which variability can indeed be systematically explained. The essence of the problem is that learners can and do exhibit a tremendous degree of variation in the way they speak (and write) second languages. Is that variation predictable? Can we explain it? Or do we dismiss it all as "free variation"?

Notable among models of variability are Elaine Tarone's (1988) **capability continuum paradigm** and Rod Ellis's (1994, 1986) **variable competence model**, both of which have inspired others to carry out research on the issue (see Foster & Skehan 1996; Bayley & Preston 1996; Preston 1996; Crookes 1989; Adamson 1988; Young 1988; for example).

Tarone (1988) granted that non-systematic free variation and individual variation do indeed exist, but chose to focus her research on *contextual* variability, that is, the extent to which both linguistic and situational contexts may help to systematically describe what might otherwise appear simply as unexplained variation. Tarone suggested four categories of variation:

1. variation according to linguistic context
2. variation according to psychological processing factors
3. variation according to social context
4. variation according to language function

The emphasis on context led us to look carefully at the conditions under which certain linguistic forms vary. For example, suppose a learner at one point in time says (a) "He must paid for the insurance," and at another time says (b) "He must pay the parking fee." An examination of the linguistic (and conceptual) context (the first of Tarone's categories) might explain the variation. In this case, sentence (a) was uttered in the context of describing an event in the past, and sentence (b) referred to the present moment. Thus the apparent free variation of the main verb form in a modal auxiliary context is explained.

One of the most fruitful areas of learner language research has focused on the variation that arises from the disparity between *classroom* contexts and *natural* situations outside language classes. As researchers have examined instructed second language acquisition (Ellis 1990b, 1997; Doughty 1991; Buczowska & Weist 1991), it has become apparent not only that instruction makes a difference in learners' success rates but also that the classroom context itself explains a great deal of variability in learners' output.

Rod Ellis (1994b, 1986) has drawn a more "internal" picture of the learner in his variable competence model. Drawing on Bialystok's (1978) earlier work, Ellis hypothesized a storehouse of "variable interlanguage rules" (p. 269) depending on how automatic and how analyzed the rules are. He drew a sharp distinction between planned and unplanned discourse in order to examine variation. The former implies less automaticity, and therefore requires the learner to call upon a certain category of learner language rules, while the latter, more automatic production, predisposes the learner to dip into another set of rules.

Both models garnered criticism. Gregg (1990) quarreled with both Tarone's and Ellis's rejection of Chomsky's "homogeneous competence paradigm" (see the discussion in Chapter 2 of this book about competence and performance). "Why should the fact that a learner's competence changes over time lead us to reject the standard concept of competence?" argued Gregg (1990: 367). It would appear from Ellis's arguments that Chomsky's "performance variables" may be better thought of as part of one's "variable competence" and therefore not attributable to mere "slips" in performance. Such arguments and counter-arguments (see responses to Gregg by Ellis 1990a and Tarone 1990) will continue, but one lesson we are learning in all this is apparent: even the tiniest of the bits and pieces of learner language, however random or "variable" they may appear to be at first blush, could be quite "systematic" if we only keep on looking. It is often tempting as a teacher or as a researcher to dismiss a good deal of learners' production as a mystery beyond our capacity to explain. Short of engaging in an absurd game of straining at gnats, we must guard against yielding to that temptation.

FOSSILIZATION

It is quite common to encounter in a learner's language various erroneous features that persist despite what is otherwise a reasonably fluent command of the language. This phenomenon is most saliently manifested phonologically in "foreign accents" in the speech of many of those who have learned a second language after puberty, as we saw in Chapter 3. We also frequently observe syntactic and lexical errors persisting in the speech of those who have learned a language quite well. The relatively permanent incorporation of incorrect linguistic forms into a person's second language competence has been referred to as **fossilization**. Fossilization is a normal and natural stage for many learners, and should not be viewed as some sort of terminal illness, in spite of the forbidding metaphor that suggests an unchangeable situation etched in stone. A better metaphor might be something like "cryogenation"—the process of freezing matter at very low temperatures; we would then have a picture of a situation that could be reversed (given some warmth, of course!).

How do items become fossilized? Fossilization can be seen as consistent with principles of human learning already discussed in this book: conditioning, reinforcement, need, motivation, self-determination, and others. Vigil and Oller (1976) provided a formal account of fossilization as a factor of positive and negative affective and cognitive feedback. They noted that there are two kinds of information transmitted between sources (learners) and audiences (in this case, native speakers): information about the *affective* relationship between source and audience, and *cognitive* information—facts, suppositions, beliefs. Affective information is primarily encoded in terms of kinesic mechanisms such as gestures, tone of voice, and facial expressions, while cognitive information is usually conveyed by means of linguistic devices (sounds, phrases, structures, discourse). The feedback learners get from their audience can be either positive, neutral, somewhere in between, or negative. The two types and levels of feedback are charted below:

Affective Feedback:
Positive: Keep talking; I'm listening.
Neutral: I'm not sure I want to maintain this conversation.
Negative: This conversation is over.

Cognitive Feedback:
Positive: I understand your message; it's clear.
Neutral: I'm not sure if I correctly understand you or not.
Negative: I don't understand what you are saying; it's not clear.

Various combinations of the two major types of feedback are possible. For example, a person can indicate positive affective feedback ("I affirm you and value what you are trying to communicate") but give neutral or negative cognitive feedback to indicate that the message itself is unclear. Negative affective feedback, however, regardless of the degree of cognitive feedback, will likely result in the abortion of the communication. This is, of course, consistent with the overriding affective nature of human interaction: if people are not at least affirmed in their attempts to communicate, there is little reason for continuing. So, one of the first requirements for meaningful communication, as has been pointed out in earlier chapters, is an affective affirmation by the other person.

Vigil and Oller's model thus holds that a positive affective response is imperative to the learner's desire to continue attempts to communicate. Cognitive feedback then determines the degree of internalization. Negative or neutral feedback in the cognitive dimension will, with the prerequisite positive affective feedback, encourage learners to try again, to restate, to reformulate, or to draw a different hypothesis about a rule. Positive feedback in the cognitive dimension will potentially result in reinforcement of the forms used and a conclusion on the part of learners that their speech is well-formed. Fossilized items, according to this model, are those deviant items in the speech of a learner that first gain positive affective feedback ("Keep talking") then positive cognitive feedback ("I understand"), reinforcing an incorrect form of language.

It is interesting that this internalization of incorrect forms takes place by means of the same processes as the internalization of correct forms. We refer to the latter, of course, as "learning," but the same elements of input, interaction, and feedback are present. When correct forms are produced, feedback that says "I understand you perfectly" reinforces those forms.

Having discussed Vigil and Oller's model in some detail, we need to exercise caution in its interpretation. While it is most helpful, for example, in understanding models of error correction, as we shall see in the next section, there are flaws in attributing such importance to feedback alone. Selinker and Lamendella (1979) noted that Vigil and Oller's model relied on the notion of *extrinsic* feedback, and that other factors internal to the learner affect fossilization. Learners are not merely pawns at the mercy of bigger pieces in the chess game of language learning. Successful language learners tend to take charge of their own attainment, proactively seeking means for acquisition. So, fossilization could be the result of the presence or absence of internal motivating factors, of seeking interaction with other people, of consciously focusing on forms, and of one's strategic investment in the learning process. As teachers, we may, and rightly, attach great importance to the feedback we give to students, but we must recognize that there are other forces at work in the process of internalizing a second language.

FORM-FOCUSED INSTRUCTION

As the focus of classroom instruction has shifted over the past few decades from an emphasis on language forms to attention to functional language within communicative contexts, the question of the place of what has come to be called "form-focused instruction" (FFI) has become more and more important. What do we mean, exactly, by FFI? A number of varying definitions have emerged (Doughty & Williams 1998), but for the sake of simplifying a complex pedagogical issue, let us rely on Spada's nicely worded definition: "any pedagogical effort which is used to draw the learners' attention to language form either implicitly or explicitly" (1997: 73). Implied in the definition is a range of approaches to form. On one side of a long continuum are explicit, discrete-point metalinguistic explanations and discussions of rules and exceptions, or curricula governed and sequenced by grammatical or phonological categories. On the other end of the continuum are (a) implicit, peripheral references to form; (b) **noticing** (Ellis 1997: 119), that is, the learner's paying attention to specific linguistic features in input; and (c) the incorporation of forms into communicative tasks, or what Ellis (1997) calls **grammar consciousness raising**.

The research on this issue (Doughty & Williams 1998; Long & Robinson 1998; Spada 1997; Ellis 1997; Lightbown & Spada 1990; Long 1988, to cite only a few sources) addresses a number of questions that must be answered before one can conclude whether or not FFI is beneficial:

1. Are some types of FFI more beneficial than others?
2. Is there an optimal time to provide FFI?
3. Are particular linguistic features more affected by FFI?
4. Do particular students benefit more from FFI?

It is difficult to generalize the diverse findings on FFI over the years, but it may be reasonable to conclude the following:

1a. Most of the research suggests that FFI can indeed increase learners' levels of attainment, but that the "Neanderthal" (Long 1988: 136) practices (grammatical explanations, discussion of rules, rote practice) of bygone years is clearly not justified. Error treatment and focus on language forms appear to be most effective when incorporated into a communicative, learner-centered curriculum, and least effective when error correction is a dominant pedagogical feature, occupying the focal attention of students in the classroom.

2a. Very few research studies have been able to identify particular stages in which learners are more ready than others to internalize FFI. A more important question (Spada 1997: 80) is perhaps "whether there are more propitious pedagogical moments to draw learners' attention to language form." Should a teacher interrupt learners in the middle of an attempt to communicate? One study (Lightbown & Spada 1990) suggested the answer to this question is "no." Should FFI come before or after communicative practice? Tomasello and Herron (1989) found evidence to support giving corrective feedback after a communicative task.

3a. The possible number of linguistic features in a language and the many potential contexts of learning make this question impossible to answer. One tantalizingly suggestion, however, was supported in DeKeyser's (1995) finding that explicit instruction was more appropriate for easily stated grammar rules and implicit instruction was more successful for more complex rules.

4a. The wide-ranging research on learner characteristics, styles, and strategies supports the conclusion that certain learners clearly benefit more than others from FFI. Analytic, field-independent, left-brain-oriented learners internalize explicit FFI better than relational, field-dependent, right-brain-oriented learners (Jamieson 1992). Visual input will favor visual learners (Reid 1987). Students who are "Js" and "Ts" on the Myers-Briggs scale will more readily be able to focus on form (Ehrman 1989).

ERROR TREATMENT

One of the major issues involved in carrying out FFI is the manner in which teachers deal with student errors. Should errors be treated? How should they be treated? When? For a tentative answer to these questions, as they apply to spoken (not written) errors, let us first look again at the feedback model offered by Vigil and Oller (1976). Figure 8.2 metaphorically depicts what happens in that model.

The "green light" of the affective feedback mode allows the sender to continue attempting to get a message across; a "red light" causes the sender to abort such attempts. (The metaphorical nature of such a chart is evident in the fact that affective feedback does not precede cognitive feedback, as this chart may lead you to believe; both modes can take place simultaneously.) The traffic signal of cognitive feedback is the point at which error correction enters. A green light here symbolizes noncorrective feedback that says "I understand your message." A red light symbolizes corrective feedback that takes on a myriad of possible forms (outlined below) and causes the learner to make some kind of alteration in production. To push the metaphor further, a yellow light could represent those various shades of color that are interpreted by the learner as falling somewhere in between a complete green light and a red light, causing the learner to adjust, to alter, to recycle, to try again in some way. Note that fossilization may be the result of too many green lights when there should have been some yellow or red lights.

The most useful implication of Vigil and Oller's model for a theory of error treatment is that cognitive feedback must be optimal in order to be effective. Too much negative cognitive feedback—a barrage of interruptions, corrections, and overt attention to malformations—often leads learners to shut off their attempts at communication. They perceive that so much is wrong with their production that there is little hope to get anything right. On the other hand, too much positive cognitive feedback—willingness of the teacher-hearer to let errors go uncorrected, to indicate understanding when understanding may not have occurred—serves to reinforce the errors of the speaker-learner. The result is the persistence, and perhaps the eventual fossilization, of such errors. The task of the teacher is to discern the optimal tension between positive and negative cognitive feedback: providing enough green lights to encourage continued communication, but not so many that crucial errors go unnoticed, and providing enough red lights to call attention to those crucial errors, but not so many that the learner is discouraged from attempting to speak at all.

We do well to recall at this point the application of Skinner's operant conditioning model of learning discussed in Chapter 4. The affective and cognitive modes of feedback are reinforcers to speakers' responses. As speakers perceive "positive" reinforcement, or the "green lights" of Figure 8.2, they will be led to internalize certain speech patterns. Corrective feedback can still be "positive" in the Skinnerian sense, as we shall see below. However, ignoring erroneous behavior has the effect of a positive reinforcer; therefore teachers must be very careful to discern the possible reinforcing consequences of neutral feedback. What we must avoid at all costs is the administration of punitive reinforcement, or correction that is viewed by learners as an affective red light—devaluing, dehumanizing, or insulting them.

Against this theoretical backdrop we can evaluate some possibilities of when and how to treat errors in the language classroom. Long (1977: 288) suggested that the question of when to treat an error (that is, which errors to provide some sort of feedback on) has no simple answer.

Having noticed an error, the first (and, I would argue, crucial) decision the teacher makes is whether or not to treat it at all. In order to make the decision the teacher may have recourse to fac-

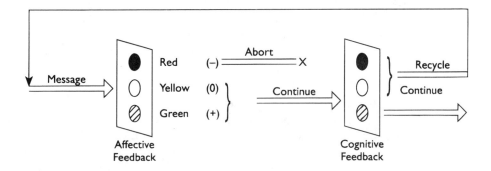

Figure 8.2. Affective and cognitive feedback

tors with immediate, temporary bearing, such as the importance of the error to the current pedagogical focus of the lesson, the teacher's perception of the chance of eliciting correct performance from the student if negative feedback is given, and so on. Consideration of these ephemeral factors may be preempted, however, by the teacher's beliefs (conscious or unconscious) as to what a language is and how a new one is learned. These beliefs may have been formed years before the lesson in question.

In a very practical article on error treatment, Hendrickson (1980) advised teachers to try to discern the difference between **global** and **local** errors, already described earlier in this chapter. Once, a learner of English was describing a quaint old hotel in Europe and said, "There is a French widow in every bedroom." The local error is clearly, and humorously, recognized. Hendrickson recommended that local errors usually need not be corrected since the message is clear and correction might interrupt a learner in the flow of productive communication. Global errors need to be treated in some way since the message may otherwise remain garbled. "The different city is another one in the another two" is a sentence that would certainly need treatment because it is incomprehensible as is. Many utterances are not clearly global or local, and it is difficult to discern the necessity for corrective feedback. A learner once wrote, "The grammar is the basement of every language." While this witty little proclamation may indeed sound more like Chomsky than Chomsky does, it behooves the teacher to ascertain just what the learner meant here (no doubt "basis" rather than "basement"), and to provide some feedback to clarify the difference between the two. The bottom line is that we simply must not stifle our students' attempts at production by smothering them with corrective feedback.

The matter of *how* to correct errors is exceedingly complex. Research on error correction methods is not at all conclusive about the most effective method or technique for error correction. It seems quite clear that students in the classroom generally want and expect errors to be corrected (Cathcart & Olsen 1976). Nevertheless, some methods recommend no direct treatment of error at all (Krashen & Terrell 1983). In "natural," untutored environments, non-native speakers are usually corrected by native speakers on only a small percentage of errors that they make (Chun et al. 1982); native speakers will attend basically only to global errors and then usually not in the form of interruptions but at transition points in conversations (Day et al. 1984). Balancing these various perspectives, I think we can safely conclude that a sensitive and perceptive language teacher should make the language classroom a happy optimum between some of the over-politeness of the real world and the expectations that learners bring with them to the classroom.

Error treatment options can be classified in a number of possible ways (see Gaies 1983; Long 1977), but one useful taxonomy was recommended by Bailey (1985), who drew from the work of Allwright (1975). Seven "basic options" are complemented by eight "possible features" within each option (Bailey 1985: 111).

Basic Options:

1. To treat or to ignore
2. To treat immediately or to delay
3. To transfer treatment [to, say, other learners] or not
4. To transfer to another individual, a subgroup, or the whole class
5. To return, or not, to original error maker after treatment
6. To permit other learners to initiate treatment
7. To test for the efficacy of the treatment

Possible Features:

1. Fact of error indicated
2. Location indicated
3. Opportunity for new attempt given
4. Model provided
5. Error type indicated
6. Remedy indicated
7. Improvement indicated
8. Praise indicated

All of the basic options and features within each option are conceivably viable modes of error correction in the classroom. The teacher needs to develop the intuition, through experience and solid eclectic theoretical foundations, for ascertaining which option or combination of options is appropriate at a given moment. Principles of optimal affective and cognitive feedback, of reinforcement theory, and of communicative language teaching all combine to form those theoretical foundations.

At least one general conclusion that can be drawn from the study of errors in the linguistic systems of learners is that learners are indeed creatively operating on a second language—constructing, either consciously or subconsciously, a system for understanding and producing utterances in the language. That system should not necessarily be treated as an imperfect system; it is such only insofar as native speakers compare their own knowledge of the language to that of the learners. It should rather be looked upon as a variable, dynamic, approximative system, reasonable to a great degree in the mind of the learners, albeit idiosyncratic. Learners are processing language on the basis of knowledge of their own interlanguage, which, as a system lying between two languages, ought not to have the value judgments of either language placed upon it. The teacher's task is to value learners, prize their attempts to communicate, and then provide optimal feedback for the system to evolve in successive stages until learners are communicating meaningfully and unambiguously in the second language.

In the Classroom: A Model for Error Treatment

In these end-of-chapter vignettes, an attempt has been made to provide some pedagogical information of historical or implicational interest. This chapter has focused strongly on the concept of error in the developing learner language of students of second languages, and the last sections above honed in on error treatment in form-focused instruction. Therefore, one more step will be taken here: to offer a conceptual model of error treatment that incorporates some of what has been covered in the chapter.

Figure 8.3 illustrates what I would claim are the split-second series of decisions that a teacher makes when a student has uttered some deviant form of the foreign language in question. In those few nanoseconds, information is accessed, processed, and evaluated, with a decision forthcoming on what the teacher is going to do about the deviant form. Imagine that you are the teacher and let me walk you through the flow chart.

Some sort of deviant utterance is made by a student. Instantly, you run this speech event through a number of nearly simultaneous screens: (1) You identify the type of deviation (lexical, phonological, etc.), and (2) often, but not always, you identify its source, the latter of which will be useful in determining how you might treat the deviation. (3) Next, the complexity of the deviation may determine not only whether to treat or ignore, but how to treat if that is your decision. In some cases a deviation may require so much explanation, or so much interruption of the task at hand, that it isn't worth treating. (4) Your most crucial and possibly the very first decision among these ten factors is to quickly decide whether the utterance is interpretable (local) or not (global). Local errors can sometimes be ignored for the sake of maintaining a flow of communication. Global errors by definition very often call for some sort of treatment, even if only in the form of a clarification request. Then, from your previous knowledge of this student, (5) you make a guess at whether it is a performance slip (mistake) or a competence error. This is not always easy to do, but you may be surprised to know that a teacher's intuition on this factor will often be correct. Mistakes

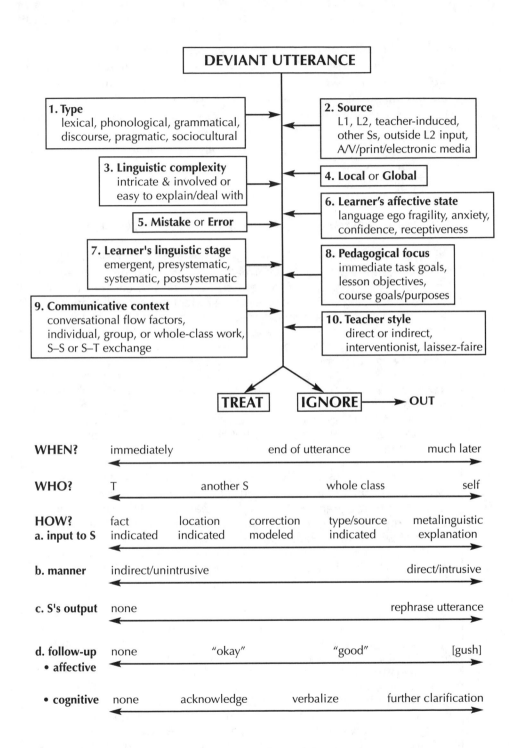

Figure 8.3. A model for classroom treatment of speech errors

rarely call for treatment, while errors more frequently demand some sort of teacher response.

All the above information is quickly stored as you perhaps simultaneously run through the next five possible considerations. (6) From your knowledge about this learner, you make a series of instant judgments about the learner's language ego fragility, anxiety level, confidence, and willingness to accept correction. If, for example, the learner rarely says anything at all, shows high anxiety and low confidence when attempting to speak, you may, on this count alone, decide to ignore the deviant utterance. (7) Then, the learner's linguistic stage of development, which you must discern within this little microsecond, will tell you something about how to treat the deviation. (8) Your own pedagogical focus at the moment (Is this a form-focused task to begin with? Does this lesson focus on the form that was deviant? What are the overall objectives of the lesson or task?) will help you to decide whether or not to treat. (9) The communicative context of the deviation (Was the student in the middle of a productive flow of language? How easily could you interrupt?) is also considered. (10) Somewhere in this rapid-fire processing, your own style as a teacher comes into play: Are you generally an interventionist? laissez-faire? If, for example, you tend as a rule to make very few error treatments, a treatment now on a minor deviation would be out of character, and possibly interpreted by the student as a response to a grievous shortcoming.

You are now ready to decide whether to treat or ignore the deviation! If you decide to do nothing, then you simply move on. But if you decide to do something in the way of treatment, you have a number of treatment options, as discussed earlier. You have to decide when to treat, who will treat, and how to treat, and each of those decisions offers a range of possibilities as indicated in the chart. Notice that you, the teacher, do not always have to be the person who provides the treatment. Manner of treatment varies according to the input to the student, the directness of the treatment, the student's output, and your follow-up.

After one very quick deviant utterance by a student, you have made an amazing number of observations and evaluations that go into the process of error treatment. New teachers will find such a prospect daunting, perhaps, but with experience, many of these considerations will become automatic.

TOPICS AND QUESTIONS FOR
STUDY AND DISCUSSION

[Note: (I) individual work; (G) group or pair work; (C) whole-class discussion.]

1. (C) Pick several languages with which students in the class are familiar, and think about the phonological features of those languages that are most salient in "foreign-accented" English. List the features and, using the hierarchy of difficulty on pages 209 and 210, discuss the possible reasons for the saliency of those features (why particular features get mapped onto English speech performance, and not others).

2. (I) What is the difference between the CAH and CLI? How does the subtle-differences principle (Oller & Ziahosseiny 1970) move away from the notion that difficulty can be predicted? How does the weak version of the CAH compare to your understanding of what is meant by CLI?

3. (G) In groups of three or four, compile examples, in languages that members of your group know, of (a) mistakes vs. errors, (b) global vs. local errors, and (c) overt vs. covert errors. Share your examples with the rest of the class.

4. (C) For a challenging class discussion, try to come up with examples of errors in four different cells: overt/global, overt/local, covert/global, and covert/local.

5. (C) If possible, secure an audiotape of a few minutes of the language of an advanced-beginning learner of English. As the class listens to the tape, listen the first time for the general gist. The second time, students should write down errors (phonological, grammatical, lexical, discourse) they hear. Then, in class discussion, identify the source of each error. Such an exercise should offer a sense of the "messiness" of real language.

6. (C) Has anyone in the class learned, or attempted to learn, a third or fourth language? Those students could share some of the difficulties they encountered, and the extent to which there was L1–L3, L2–L3, etc., cross-linguistic influence.

7. (I) Fossilization and learning are actually the result of the same cognitive processes at work. Explain this. Then, try to think of factors other than feedback that could cause or contribute to fossilization. Once a language form is fossilized, can it ever be corrected?

8. (G) Divide into groups such that each group has at least two people in it who have learned or studied a foreign language. Members of the group should share experiences with form-focused instruction (FFI).

Try to decide as a group what the features are of the most and least effective FFI.

9. (C) Look at the error treatment model in the vignette at the very end of the chapter. Using examples posed to the class, discuss the specific steps that a teacher goes through in determining whether to treat or ignore a deviant utterance, and in the case of a decision to treat, what the treatment should be.

SUGGESTED READINGS

Jaszczolt, Katarzyna. 1995. Typology of contrastive studies: Specialization, progress, and applications. *Language Teaching* 28: 1–15.

This state-of-the-art article offers a comprehensive update and summary of research on cross-linguistic influence.

James, Carl. 1998. *Errors in Language Learning and Use: Exploring Error Analysis.* Harlow, UK: Addison Wesley Longman.

This book is an excellent overview of several decades of research on the field of error analysis, a topic that continues to draw the attention of researchers.

Bayley, Robert and Preston, Dennis (Eds.). 1996. *Second Language Acquisition and Linguistic Variation.* Philadelphia: John Benjamins Publishing Company.

Variability models accounting for learner language are scrutinized in detail in Bayley and Preston's anthology. The reading is very technical, and therefore would be difficult for the first-level graduate student.

Doughty, Catherine and Williams, Jessica. 1998. *Focus on Form in Classroom Second Language Acquisition.* New York: Cambridge University Press.

Spada, Nina. 1997. "Form-focussed instruction and second language acquisition: A review of classroom and laboratory research." *Language Teaching* 30:73–87.

Two comprehensive sources on form-focused instruction that are suitable for newcomers in the field of SLA are to be found in the above works. The first is an anthology of chapters, some written by well-known leaders in the field (Long, DeKeyser, Swain, Harley, and Lightbown), and the second is another state-of-the-art synthesis of research.

LANGUAGE LEARNING EXPERIENCE:
JOURNAL ENTRY 8

[Note: See pages 18 and 19 of Chapter 1 for general guidelines for writing a journal on a previous or concurrent language learning experience.]

- Make a list of some of the specific contrasts between your native and target languages that have been or still are difficult for you. Can you analyze why they are difficult, using the information in this chapter?
- In your list above, are there examples of "subtle differences" which nevertheless present some difficulty for you? Analyze those differences.
- Think about some of the errors you are making (made) in learning a foreign language. List as many as you can, up to ten or so, being as descriptive as possible (e.g., the French subjunctive mood, Japanese honorifics, English definite articles, separable two-word verbs). Now, analyze where those errors came from. If they did not come from your native language, what other sources are possible?
- Have you ever reached a stage of fossilization, or in milder form, a "plateau" of progress where you seemed to just stall for weeks or months? If so, describe that experience. Then tell about what, if anything, propelled you out of those doldrums, or determine what might have helped you if you stayed there or are still there.
- Describe your language teacher's error treatment style. Does/Did your teacher overcorrect or undercorrect? To what extent does/did your teacher follow the model at the end of the chapter?

CHAPTER 9

COMMUNICATIVE

COMPETENCE

THE PREVIOUS chapter and this one follow the historical development of research on applied linguistics and related second language pedagogy. The middle part of the twentieth century was characterized by a zeal for the scientific, linguistic analysis of the structures of languages with a focus on how languages differed from each other. This was followed by a cognitive/rationalistic period of research into the processes of cognition and affect and the resulting developing linguistic systems of learners, with a focus on errors as important keys to understanding the makeup of those systems. Both of those strains of research continue to be important as we now begin the twenty-first century. But, as noted in Chapter 1, a new wave of interest characterized the last couple of decades of the twentieth century, a social constructivist wave that found the discipline focusing less on individual development and more on the effect of learners' interactions with others.

Social constructivist perspectives drew our attention to language as communication across individuals. Researchers looked at discourse, interaction, pragmatics, and negotiation, among other things. Teachers and materials writers treated the language classroom as a locus of meaningful, authentic exchanges among users of a language. Foreign language learning started to be viewed not just as a potentially predictable developmental process but also as the creation of meaning through interactive negotiation among learners. "Communicative competence" became a household word in SLA, and still stands as an appropriate term to capture current trends in teaching and research.

DEFINING COMMUNICATIVE COMPETENCE

The term **communicative competence** was coined by Dell Hymes (1967, 1972), a sociolinguist who was convinced that Chomsky's (1965) notion of competence (see Chapter 2) was too limited. Chomsky's "rule-governed creativity" that so aptly described a child's mushrooming grammar at the age of three or four did not, according to Hymes, account sufficiently for the social and functional rules of language. So Hymes referred to communicative competence as that aspect of our competence that enables us to convey and interpret messages and to negotiate meanings interpersonally within specific contexts. Savignon (1983: 9) noted that "communicative competence is relative, not absolute, and depends on the cooperation of all the participants involved." It is not so much an intrapersonal construct as we saw in Chomsky's early writings but rather a dynamic, interpersonal construct that can be examined only by means of the overt performance of two or more individuals in the process of communication.

In the 1970s, research on communicative competence distinguished between *linguistic* and *communicative* competence (Hymes 1967; Paulston 1974) to highlight the difference between knowledge "about" language forms and knowledge that enables a person to communicate functionally and interactively. In a similar vein, James Cummins (1979, 1980) proposed a distinction between **cognitive/academic language proficiency** (CALP) and **basic interpersonal communicative skills** (BICS). CALP is that dimension of proficiency in which the learner manipulates or reflects upon the surface features of language outside of the immediate interpersonal context. It is what learners often use in classroom exercises and tests that focus on form. BICS, on the other hand, is the communicative capacity that all children acquire in order to be able to function in daily interpersonal exchanges. Cummins later (1981) modified his notion of CALP and BICS in the form of **context-reduced** and **context-embedded** communication, where the former resembles CALP and the latter BICS, but with the added dimension of considering the context in which language is used. A good share of classroom, school-oriented language is context-reduced, while face-to-face communication with people is context-embedded. By referring to the context of our use of language, then, the distinction becomes more feasible to operationalize.

Seminal work on defining communicative competence was carried out by Michael Canale and Merrill Swain (1980), now the reference point for virtually all discussions of communicative competence vis-à-vis second language teaching. In Canale and Swain's and later in Canale's (1983) definition, four different components, or subcategories, make up the construct of communicative competence. The first two subcategories reflect the use of the linguistic system itself; the last two define the functional aspects of communication.

1. **Grammatical** competence is that aspect of communicative competence that encompasses "knowledge of lexical items and of rules of morphology, syntax, sentence-grammar semantics, and phonology" (Canale & Swain 1980: 29). It is the competence that we associate with mastering the linguistic code of a language, the "linguistic" competence of Hymes and Paulston, referred to above.

2. The second subcategory is **discourse** competence, the complement of grammatical competence in many ways. It is the ability we have to connect sentences in stretches of discourse and to form a meaningful whole out of a series of utterances. Discourse means everything from simple spoken conversation to lengthy written texts (articles, books, and the like). While grammatical competence focuses on sentence-level grammar, discourse competence is concerned with intersentential relationships.

3. **Sociolinguistic** competence is the knowledge of the sociocultural rules of language and of discourse. This type of competence "requires an understanding of the social context in which language is used: the roles of the participants, the information they share, and the function of the interaction. Only in a full context of this kind can judgments be made on the appropriateness of a particular utterance" (Savignon 1983: 37).

4. The fourth subcategory is **strategic** competence, a construct that is exceedingly complex. Canale and Swain (1980: 30) described strategic competence as "the verbal and nonverbal communication strategies that may be called into action to compensate for breakdowns in communication due to performance variables or due to insufficient competence." Savignon (1983: 40) paraphrases this as "the strategies that one uses to compensate for imperfect knowledge of rules—or limiting factors in their application such as fatigue, distraction, and inattention." In short, it is the competence underlying our ability to make repairs, to cope with imperfect knowledge, and to sustain communication through "paraphrase, circumlocution, repetition, hesitation, avoidance, and guessing, as well as shifts in register and style" (pp. 40–41).

Strategic competence occupies a special place in an understanding of communication. Actually, definitions of strategic competence that are limited to the notion of "compensatory strategies" fall short of encompassing the full spectrum of the construct. In a follow-up to the previous (Canale &

Swain 1980) article, Swain (1984: 189) amended the earlier notion of strategic competence to include "communication strategies that may be called into action either to enhance the effectiveness of communication or to compensate for breakdowns." Similarly, Yule and Tarone (1990: 181) referred to strategic competence as "an ability to select an effective means of performing a communicative act that enables the listener/reader to identify the intended referent." So, all communication strategies—such as those discussed in Chapter 5—may be thought of as arising out of a person's strategic competence. In fact, strategic competence is the way we manipulate language in order to meet communicative goals. An eloquent speaker possesses and uses a sophisticated strategic competence. A salesman utilizes certain strategies of communication to make a product seem irresistible. A friend persuades you to do something extraordinary because he or she has mustered communicative strategies for the occasion.

Canale and Swain's (1980) model of communicative competence has undergone some other modifications over the years. These newer views are perhaps best captured in Lyle Bachman's (1990) schematization of what he simply calls "language competence," as shown in Figure 9.1. Bachman places grammatical and discourse (renamed "textual") competence under one node, which he appropriately calls **organizational** competence: all those rules and systems that dictate what we can do with the forms of language, whether they be sentence-level rules (grammar) or rules that govern how we "string" sentences together (discourse). Canale and Swain's sociolinguistic competence is now broken down into two separate pragmatic categories: functional aspects of language (**illocutionary** competence, or, pertaining to sending and receiving intended meanings) and sociolinguistic aspects (which deal with such considerations as politeness, formality, metaphor, register, and culturally related aspects of language). And, in keeping with current waves of thought, Bachman adds strategic competence as an entirely separate element of communicative language ability (see Figure 9.2). Here, strategic competence almost serves an "executive" function of making the final "decision," among many possible options, on wording, phrasing, and other productive and receptive means for negotiating meaning.

LANGUAGE FUNCTIONS

In the Bachman model, illocutionary competence consists of the ability to manipulate the **functions** of language, a component that Canale and Swain subsume under discourse and sociolinguistic competence. Functions are essentially the purposes that we accomplish with language, e.g., stating, requesting, responding, greeting, parting, etc. Functions cannot be accom-

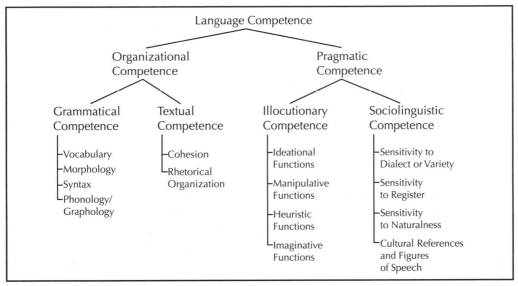

Figure 9.1. Components of language competence (Bachman 1990: 87)

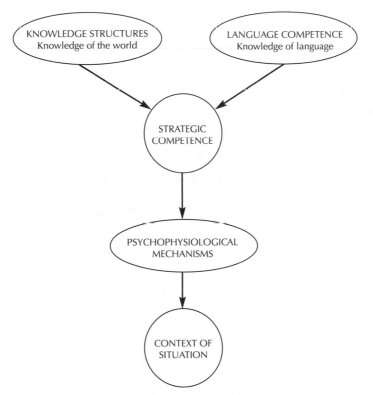

Figure 9.2. Components of communicative language ability in communicative language use
        (Bachman 1990: 85)

plished, of course, without the **forms** of language: morphemes, words, grammar rules, discourse rules, and other organizational competencies. While forms are the outward manifestation of language, functions are the realization of those forms.

Functions are sometimes directly related to forms. "How much does that cost?" is usually a form functioning as a question, and "He bought a car" functions as a statement. But linguistic forms are not always unambiguous in their function. "I can't find my umbrella," uttered in a high-pitched voice by a frustrated adult who is late for work on a rainy day may be a frantic request for all in the household to join in a search. A child who says "I want some ice cream" is rarely stating a simple fact or observation but requesting ice cream in her own intimate register. A sign on the street that says "one way" functions to guide traffic in only one direction. A sign in a church parking lot in a busy downtown area was subtle in form but direct in function: "We forgive those who trespass against us, but we also tow them"; that sign functioned effectively to prevent unauthorized cars from parking there!

Communication may be regarded as a combination of acts, a series of elements with purpose and intent. Communication is not merely an event, something that happens; it is functional, purposive, and designed to bring about some effect—some change, however subtle or unobservable—on the environment of hearers and speakers. Communication is a series of communicative acts or **speech acts**, to use John Austin's (1962) term, which are used systematically to accomplish particular purposes. Austin stressed the importance of consequences, the **perlocutionary** force, of linguistic communication. Researchers have since been led to examine communication in terms of the effect that utterances achieve. That effect has implications for both the production and comprehension of an utterance; both modes of performance serve to bring the communicative act to its ultimate purpose. Second language learners need to understand the purpose of communication, developing an awareness of what the purpose of a communicative act is and how to achieve that purpose through linguistic forms.

The functional approach to describing language is one that has its roots in the traditions of British linguist J.R. Firth, who viewed language as interactive and interpersonal, "a way of behaving and making others behave" (quoted by Berns 1984a: 5). Since then the term "function" has been variously interpreted. Michael Halliday (1973), who provided one of the best expositions of language functions, used the term to mean the purposive nature of communication, and outlined seven different functions of language.

1. The **instrumental** function serves to manipulate the environment, to cause certain events to happen. Sentences like "This
court finds you guilty," "On your mark, get set, go!" or "Don't touch
the stove" have an instrumental function; they are communicative
acts that have a specific perlocutionary force; they bring about a
particular condition.

2. The **regulatory** function of language is the control of events.
While such control is sometimes difficult to distinguish from the
instrumental function, regulatory functions of language are not so
much the "unleashing" of certain power as the maintenance of
control. "I pronounce you guilty and sentence you to three years
in prison" serves an instrumental function, but the sentence
"Upon good behavior, you will be eligible for parole in ten
months" serves more of a regulatory function. The regulations of
encounters among people—approval, disapproval, behavior control, setting laws and rules—are all regulatory features of language.

3. The **representational** function is the use of language to make
statements, convey facts and knowledge, explain, or report—that
is, to "represent" reality as one sees it. "The sun is hot," "The presi-
dent gave a speech last night," or even "The world is flat" all serve
representational functions, although the last representation may
be highly disputed.

4. The **interactional** function of language serves to ensure social
maintenance. "Phatic communion," Malinowski's term referring to
the communicative contact between and among human beings
that simply allows them to establish social contact and to keep
channels of communication open, is part of the interactional function of language. Successful interactional communication requires
knowledge of slang, jargon, jokes, folklore, cultural mores, politeness and formality expectations, and other keys to social
exchange.

5. The **personal** function allows a speaker to express feelings, emotions, personality, "gut-level" reactions. A person's individuality is
usually characterized by his or her use of the personal function of
communication. In the personal nature of language, cognition,
affect, and culture all interact.

6. The **heuristic** function involves language used to acquire knowledge, to learn about the environment. Heuristic functions are
often conveyed in the form of questions that will lead to answers.
Children typically make good use of the heuristic function in

their incessant "why" questions about the world around them. Inquiry is a heuristic method of eliciting representations of reality from others.

7. The **imaginative** function serves to create imaginary systems or ideas. Telling fairy tales, joking, or writing a novel are all uses of the imaginative function. Poetry, tongue twisters, puns, and other instances of the pleasurable uses of language also fall into the imaginative function. Through the imaginative dimensions of language we are free to go beyond the real world to soar to the heights of the beauty of language itself, and through that language to create impossible dreams if we so desire.

These seven different functions of language are neither discrete nor mutually exclusive. A single sentence or conversation might incorporate many different functions simultaneously. Yet it is the understanding of how to use linguistic forms to achieve these functions of language that comprises the crux of second language learning. A learner might acquire correct word order, syntax, and lexical items, but not understand how to achieve a desired and intended function through careful selection of words, structure, intonation, nonverbal signals, and astute perception of the context of a particular stretch of discourse.

FUNCTIONAL SYLLABUSES

The most apparent practical classroom application of functional descriptions of language was found in the development of functional syllabuses, more popularly **notional-functional syllabuses** ("syllabus," in this case, is a term used mainly in the United Kingdom to refer to what is commonly known as a "curriculum" in the United States). Beginning with the work of the Council of Europe (Van Ek & Alexander 1975) and later followed by numerous interpretations of "notional" syllabuses (Wilkins 1976), notional-functional syllabuses attended to functions as organizing elements of a foreign language curriculum. Grammar, which was the primary element in the historically preceding **structural syllabus**, was relegated to a secondary focus. "Notions" referred both to abstract concepts such as existence, space, time, quantity, and quality and to what we also call "contexts" or "situations," such as travel, health, education, shopping, and free time.

The "functional" part of the notional-functional syllabus corresponded to what we have defined above as language functions. Curricula were organized around such functions as identifying, reporting, denying, declining an invitation, asking permission, apologizing, etc. Van Ek and Alexander's (1975) exhaustive list of language functions became a basic reference for notional-functional syllabuses, now simply referred to as **functional syllabuses**. Functional syllabuses remain today in modified form. A typical current language textbook will list a sequence of communicative functions that are covered. For example, the following functions are covered in the first several lessons of an advanced-beginner's textbook, *New Vistas 1* (Brown 1999):

1. Introducing self and other people
2. Exchanging personal information
3. Asking how to spell someone's name
4. Giving commands
5. Apologizing and thanking
6. Identifying and describing people
7. Asking for information

A typical unit in this textbook includes an eclectic blend of conversation practice with a classmate, interactive group work, role-plays, grammar and pronunciation focus exercises, information-gap techniques, Internet activities, and extra-class interactive practice.

In the early days of functional syllabuses, there was some controversy over their effectiveness. Some language courses, as Campbell (1978: 18) wryly observed, could turn out to be "structural lamb served up as notional-functional mutton." And Berns (1984b: 15) echoed some of Widdowson's (1978a) earlier complaints when she warned teachers that textbooks that claim to have a functional base may be "sorely inadequate and even misleading in their representation of language as interaction." She went on to show how *context* is the real key to giving meaning to both form and function, and therefore just because a function is "covered" does not mean that learners have internalized it for authentic, unrehearsed use in the real world. Communication is qualitative and infinite; a syllabus is quantitative and finite.

DISCOURSE ANALYSIS

The analysis of the relationship between forms and functions of language is commonly called **discourse analysis**, which encompasses the notion that language is more than a sentence-level phenomenon. A single sentence can seldom be fully analyzed without considering its context. We use language in stretches of discourse. We string many sentences together in interrelated, cohesive units. In most oral language, our discourse is marked by exchanges with another person or several persons in which a few sentences spoken by one participant are followed and built upon by sentences spoken by another. Both the production and comprehension of language are a factor of our ability to perceive and process stretches of discourse, to formulate representations of meaning not just from a single sentence but from referents in both previous sentences and following sentences.

Consider the following:

1. **A:**   Got the time?
   B: Ten fifteen.
2. **Waiter:**   More coffee?
   Customer: I'm okay.
3. **Parent:**   Dinner!
   Child: Just a minute!

In so many of our everyday exchanges, a single sentence sometimes contains certain presuppositions or entailments that are not overtly manifested in surrounding sentence-level surface structure, but that are clear from the total context. All three of the above conversations contained such presuppositions (how to ask what time of day it is; how to say "no more coffee"; how to announce dinner and then indicate one will be there in a minute). So, while linguistic science in the middle of the twentieth century centered on the sentence for the purpose of analysis, in the last quarter of a century trends in linguistics have increasingly emphasized the importance of intersentential relations in discourse. In written language, similar intersentential discourse relations hold true as the writer builds a network of ideas or feelings and the reader interprets them.

Without the pragmatic contexts of discourse, our communications would be extraordinarily ambiguous. A stand-alone sentence such as "I didn't like that casserole" could, depending on context, be agreement, disagreement, argument, complaint, apology, insult, or simply a comment. A second language learner of English might utter such a sentence with perfect pronunciation and grammar, but fail to achieve the communicative function of, say, apologizing to a dinner host or hostess, and instead be taken as an unrefined boor who most certainly would not be invited back!

With the increasing communicative emphasis on the discourse level of language in classrooms, we saw that approaches that emphasized only the formal aspects of learner language overlooked important discourse functions. Wagner-Gough (1975), for example, noted that acquisition by a learner of the *-ing* morpheme of the present progressive tense does not necessarily mean acquisition of varying functions of the morpheme: to indicate present action, action about to occur immediately, future action, or repeated actions. Formal approaches have also tended to shape our conception of the whole process of second language learning. Evelyn Hatch (1978a: 404) spoke of the dangers.

> In second language learning the basic assumption has been . . . that one first learns how to manipulate structures, that one gradually builds up a repertoire of structures and then, somehow, learns how to put the structures to use in discourse. We would like to consider the possibility that just the reverse happens. One learns how to do conversation, one learns how to interact verbally, and out of this interaction syntactic structures are developed.

Of equal interest to second language researchers is the discourse of the written word, and the process of acquiring reading and writing skills. The last few years have seen a great deal of work on second language reading strategies. Techniques in the teaching of reading skills have gone far beyond the traditional passage, comprehension questions, and vocabulary exercises. Text attack skills now include sophisticated techniques for recognizing and interpreting cohesive devices (for example, reference and ellipsis), discourse markers *(then, moreover, therefore)*, rhetorical organization, and other textual discourse features (Nuttall 1996). Cohesion and coherence are common terms that need to be considered in teaching reading. Likewise the analysis of writing skills has progressed to a recognition of the full range of pragmatic and organizational competence that is necessary to write effectively in a second language.

Conversation Analysis

The above comments on the significance of acquiring literacy competence notwithstanding, conversation still remains one of the most salient and significant modes of discourse. Conversations are excellent examples of the interactive and interpersonal nature of communication. "Conversations are cooperative ventures" (Hatch & Long 1980: 4). What are the rules that govern our conversations? How do we get someone's attention? How do we initiate topics? terminate topics? avoid topics? How does a person interrupt, correct, or seek clarification? These questions relate to an area of linguistic competence possessed by every adult native speaker of a language, yet few foreign language curricula traditionally deal with these important aspects of communicative competence. Once again our consideration of conversation rules will be general, since specific languages differ.

Very early in life, children learn the first and essential rule of conversation: **attention getting**. If you wish linguistic production to be functional and to accomplish its intended purpose, you must of course have the attention of your audience. The attention-getting conventions within each language—both verbal and nonverbal—need to be carefully assimilated by learners. Without knowledge and use of such conventions, second language learners may be reluctant to participate in a conversation because of their own inhibitions, or they may become obnoxious in securing attention in ways that "turn off" their hearer to the topic they wish to discuss.

Once speakers have secured the hearer's attention, their task becomes one of **topic nomination**. Rules for nominating topics in conversation, which involve both verbal and nonverbal cues, are highly contextually constrained. It is odd that only in recent years have language curricula included explicit instruction on how to secure the attention of an audience. Typical classroom activities in English include teaching students verbal gambits like "Excuse me," "Say," "Oh, sir," "Well, I'd like to ask you something" and nonverbal signals such as eye contact, gestures, and proxemics (see a discussion of these categories later in this chapter).

Once a topic is nominated, participants in a conversation then embark on **topic development**, using conventions of **turn-taking** to accomplish various functions of language. Allwright (1980) showed how students of English as a second language failed to use appropriate turn-taking signals in their interactions with each other and with the teacher. Turn-taking is another culturally oriented sets of rules that require finely tuned perceptions in order to communicate effectively. Aside from turn-taking itself, topic development, or maintenance of a conversation, involves **clarification**, **shifting**, **avoidance**, and **interruption**. Topic clarification manifests itself in various forms of heuristic functions. In the case of conversations between second language learners and native speakers, topic clarification often involves seeking or giving *repair* of linguistic forms that contain errors. Repair, as we saw in Chapter 8, involves a continuum of possibilities ranging from indirect signals to outright correction. It is what Canale and Swain (1980) labeled "strategic competence," and comprises a part of what Bachman (1990) included in strategic competence. Topic shifting and avoidance may be effected through both verbal and nonverbal signals. Interruptions, a form of attention getting, are a typical feature of all conversations. Rules governing appropriate, acceptable interruption vary widely across cultures and languages.

Topic termination is an art that even native speakers of a language have difficulty in mastering at times. We commonly experience situations in which a conversation has ensued for some time and neither participant seems to know how to terminate it. Usually, in American English, conversations are terminated by various interactional functions—a glance at a watch, a polite smile, or a "Well, I have to be going now." Each language has verbal and nonverbal signals for termination. It is important for teachers to be acutely aware of the rules of conversation in the second language and to aid learners to both perceive those rules and follow them in their own conversations.

H.P. Grice (1967) once noted that certain conversational "maxims" enable the speaker to nominate and maintain a topic of conversation:

1. Quantity: Say only as much as is necessary for understanding the communication.
2. Quality: Say only what is true.
3. Relevance: Say only what is relevant.
4. Manner: Be clear.

Grice's maxims have been widely used as criteria for analyzing why speakers are sometimes ineffective in conversations, and as suggestions for improvement of one's "power" over others through conversation.

One aspect of the acquisition of conversation competence is the recognition and production of conventions for accomplishing certain functions. Second language researchers have studied such varied functions as apologizing (Olshtain & Cohen 1983), complimenting (Wolfson 1981), disapproving (D'Amico-Reisner 1983), inviting (Wolfson, D'Amico-Reisner, & Huber 1983), and even "how to tell when someone is saying 'no'" (Rubin 1976). There is no end to the possibility for research on such topics. The applications to teaching are equally numerous, apparent in a perusal of the many foreign language textbooks now aimed at focusing on conversational discourse.

PRAGMATICS

Implicit in the above discussions of language functions, discourse analysis, and conversation rules is the importance of **pragmatics** in conveying and interpreting meaning. Pragmatic constraints on language comprehension and production may be loosely thought of as the effect of *context* on strings of linguistic events. Consider the following conversation:

> [Phone rings, a ten-year-old child picks up the phone]
> **Stefanie:** Hello.
> **Voice:** Hi, Stef, is your Mom there?
> **Stefanie:** Just a minute. [cups the phone, and yells] Mom! Phone!
> **Mom:** [from upstairs] I'm in the tub!
> **Stefanie:** [returning to the phone] She can't talk now. Wanna leave a message?
> **Voice:** Oh, [pause] I'll call back later. Bye.

Pragmatic considerations allowed all three participants to interpret what would otherwise be ambiguous sentences. "Is your Mom there?" is not, in a telephone context, a question that requires a yes or no answer. Stefanie's "Just a minute" confirmed to the caller that her mother was indeed home, and let the caller know that she would either (a) check to see if she was home, and/or (b) get her to come to the phone. Then, Stefanie's "Mom! Phone!" was easily interpreted by her mother as "Someone is on the phone who wants to talk with you." Mom's response, otherwise a rather worthless bit of information, in fact informed Stefanie that she couldn't come to the phone, which was then conveyed to the caller. The caller didn't explicitly respond "no" to Stefanie's offer to take a message, but implicitly did so with "I'll call back later."

Second language acquisition becomes an exceedingly difficult task when these **sociopragmatic** or **pragmalinguistic** constraints are brought to bear. Kasper (1998), LoCastro (1997), Turner (1995, 1996), Scollon and Scollon (1995), Kasper and Blum-Kulka (1993), Harlow (1990), and Holmes and Brown (1987) have all demonstrated the difficulty of such conventions because of subtle cross-cultural contrasts. Variations in politeness and formality are particularly touchy:

American:	What an unusual necklace. It's beautiful!
Samoan:	Please take it. (Holmes & Brown 1987: 526)

American teacher:	Would you like to read?
Russian student:	No, I would not. (Harlow 1990: 328)

In both cases the non-native English speakers misunderstood the **illocutionary force** (intended meaning) of the utterance within the contexts.

Learning the organizational rules of a second language are almost simple when compared to the complexity of catching on to a seemingly never-ending list of pragmatic constraints. Pragmatic conventions from a learner's first language can transfer both positively and negatively. Apologizing, complimenting, thanking, face-saving conventions, and conversational cooperation strategies (Turner 1995) often prove to be difficult for second language learners to acquire. Japanese learners of English may express gratitude by saying "I'm sorry," a direct transfer from "Sumimasen," which in Japanese commonly conveys a sense of gratitude, especially to persons of higher status (Kasper 1998: 194). Cooperation principles are especially difficult to master: the difference between "Rake the leaves" and "Don't you think you could rake the leaves?" (Turner 1996: 1) is an example of how, in English, cooperation is sometimes given precedence over directness.

Language and Gender

One of the major pragmatic factors affecting the acquisition of communicative competence in virtually every language, and one that has received considerable attention recently, is the effect of one's sex on both production and reception of language. Differences between the way males and females speak have been noted for some time now (Tannen 1990, 1996; Holmes 1989, 1991; Nilsen et al. 1977; Lakoff 1975). Among American English speakers, girls have been found to produce more "standard" language than boys, a pattern that continues on through adulthood. Women appear to use language that expresses more uncertainty (hedges, tag questions, rising intonation on declaratives, etc.) than men, suggesting less confidence in what they say. Men have been reported to interrupt more than women, and to use stronger expletives, while the latter use more polite forms. Tannen (1996) and others have found that males place more value, in conversational interaction, on status and report talk, competing for the floor, while females value connection and rapport, fulfilling their role as more "cooperative and facilitative conversationalists, concerned for their partner's positive face needs" (Holmes 1991: 210).

These studies of language and gender, which were conducted in English-speaking cultures, do not even begin to deal with some of the more overtly formal patterns for men's and women's talk in other languages. Among the Carib Indians in the Lesser Antilles, for example, males and females must use entirely different gender markings for abstract nouns. In several languages males and females use different syntactic and phonological variants. In Japanese, women's and men's language is differentiated by formal (syntactic) variants, intonation patterns, and nonverbal expression. It is not uncommon for American men who learned Japanese from a female native-speaking Japanese teacher to inadvertently "say things like a woman" when, say, conducting business with Japanese men, much to their embarrassment.

In English, another twist on the language and gender issue has been directed toward "sexist" language: language that either calls unnecessary attention to gender or is demeaning to one gender. Writers are cautioned to refrain from using what we used to call the "generic" *he* and instead to pluralize or to use *he* or *she*. What used to be *stewardesses, chairmen,* and *policemen* are now more commonly called *flight attendants, chairs,* and *police officers*. Words/phrases like *broads, skirtchasers, the wife,* etc., are now marked as demeaning perpetuations of negative stereotypes of women. The list of sexist terms, phrases, and metaphors goes on and on. Fortunately, the research of linguists like Janet Holmes, Robin Lakoff, and Deborah Tannen has called the attention of the public to such sexism, and we are seeing signs of the decline of this sort of language. All these factors are subtleties that a second language learner must contend with. They all form a significant, intricately interwoven tapestry in our sociopragmatic competence.

STYLES AND REGISTERS

Another important issue in describing communicative competence is the way we use language in different **styles** depending on the context of a communicative act in terms of subject matter, audience, occasion, shared experience, and purpose of communication. A style is not a social or regional dialect, but a variety of language used for a specific purpose. Styles vary considerably within a single language user's idiolect. When you converse informally with a friend, you use a different style than you use in an interview for a job with a prospective employer. Native speakers, as they mature into adulthood, learn to adopt appropriate styles for widely different contexts. An important difference between a child's and an adult's fluency in a native language is the degree to which an adult is able to vary styles for different occasions and persons. Adult second language learners must acquire stylistic adaptability in order to be able to encode and decode the discourse around them correctly.

Martin Joos (1967) provided one of the most common classifications of speech styles using the criterion of **formality**, which tends to subsume subject matter, audience, and occasion. Joos described five levels of formality.

1. An **oratorical** style is used in public speaking before a large audience; wording is carefully planned in advance, intonation is somewhat exaggerated, and numerous rhetorical devices are appropriate.
2. A **deliberative** style is also used in addressing audiences, usually audiences too large to permit effective interchange between speaker and hearers, although the forms are normally not as polished as those in an oratorical style. A typical university classroom lecture is often carried out in a deliberative style.
3. A **consultative** style is typically a dialogue, though formal enough that words are chosen with some care. Business transactions, doctor-patient conversations, and the like are usually consultative in nature.
4. **Casual** conversations are between friends or colleagues or sometimes members of a family; in this context words need not be guarded and social barriers are moderately low.
5. An **intimate** style is one characterized by complete absence of social inhibitions. Talk with family, loved ones, and very close

friends, where the inner self is revealed, is usually in an intimate style.

Categories of style can apply to written discourse as well. Most writing is addressed to readers who cannot respond immediately; that is, long stretches of discourse—books, essays, even letters—are read from beginning to end before the reader gives a response. Written style is therefore usually more deliberative with the exception of friendly letters, notes, or literature intended to capture a more personal style. Even the latter, however, often carry with them reasonably carefully chosen wording with relatively few performance variables.

Styles are manifested by both verbal and nonverbal features. Differences in style can be conveyed in body language, gestures, eye contact, and the like—all very difficult aspects of "language" for the learner to acquire. (Nonverbal communication is discussed below.) Verbal aspects of style are difficult enough to learn. Syntax in many languages is characterized by contractions and other deletions in intimate and casual styles. Lexical items vary, too. Bolinger (1975) gave a somewhat tongue-in-cheek illustration of lexical items that have one semantic meaning but represent each of the five styles: *on the ball, smart, intelligent, perceptive,* and *astute*—from intimate to frozen, respectively. He of course recognized other meanings besides those of style that intervene to make the example somewhat overstated. Style distinctions in pronunciation are likely to be most noticeable in the form of hesitations and other misarticulations, phonological deletion rules in informal speech, and perhaps a more affected pronunciation in formal language.

Related to stylistic variation is another factor called "register," sometimes incorrectly used as a synonym for style. Registers are commonly identified by certain phonological variants, vocabulary, idioms, and other expressions that are associated with different occupational or socioeconomic groups. Registers sometimes enable people to identify with a particular group and to maintain solidarity. Colleagues in the same occupation or profession will use certain jargon to communicate with each other, to the exclusion of eavesdroppers. Truckers, airline pilots, salespersons, and farmers, for example, use words and phrases unique to their own group. Register is also sometimes associated with social class distinctions, but here the line between register and dialect is difficult to define (see Wardhaugh 1992 and Chaika 1989 for further comments).

The acquisition of styles and registers poses no simple problem for second language learners. Cross-cultural variation is a primary barrier—that is, understanding cognitively and affectively what levels of formality are appropriate or inappropriate. North American culture generally tends to accept more informal styles for given occasions than some other cultures.

Some English learners in the United States consequently experience difficulty in gauging appropriate formality distinctions and tend to be overly formal. Such students are often surprised by the level of informality expressed by their American professors. The acquisition of both styles and registers thus combines a linguistic and culture-learning process.

NONVERBAL COMMUNICATION

We communicate so much information nonverbally in conversations that often the verbal aspect of the conversation is negligible. This is particularly true for interactive language functions in which social contact is of key importance and in which it is not *what* you say that counts but *how* you say it—what you convey with body language, gestures, eye contact, physical distance, and other nonverbal messages. Nonverbal communication, however, is so subtle and subconscious in a native speaker that verbal language seems, by comparison, quite mechanical and systematic. Language becomes distinctly human through its nonverbal dimension, or what Edward Hall (1959) called the "silent language." The expression of culture is so bound up in nonverbal communication that the barriers to culture learning are more nonverbal than verbal. Verbal language requires the use of only one of the five sensory modalities: hearing. But there remain in our communicative repertoire three other senses by which we communicate every day, if we for the moment rule out taste as falling within a communicative category (though messages are indeed sent and received through the taste modality). We will examine each of these.

Kinesics

Every culture and language uses body language, or **kinesics**, in unique but clearly interpretable ways. "There was speech in their dumbness, language in their very gesture," wrote Shakespeare in *The Winter's Tale*. All cultures throughout the history of humankind have relied on kinesics for conveying important messages. Books like Dresser's *Multicultural Manners* (1996) join a long string of manuals (e.g., Fast 1970; Hall 1959, 1966) offering light-hearted but provocative insights on the use of kinesics in North American and other cultures. Today, virtually every book on communication explains how you communicate—and miscommunicate—when you fold your arms, cross your legs, stand, walk, move your eyes and mouth, and so on.

But as universal as kinesic communication is, there is tremendous variation cross-culturally and cross-linguistically in the specific interpretations of gestures. Human beings all move their heads, blink their eyes, move their arms and hands, but the significance of these movements varies from society to society. Consider the following categories and how you would express them in American culture.

1. Agreement, "yes"
2. "No!"
3. "Come here"
4. Lack of interest, "I don't know"
5. Flirting signals, sexual signals
6. Insults, obscene gestures

There are conventionalized gestural signals to convey these semantic categories. Are those signals the same in another language and culture? Sometimes they are not. And sometimes a gesture that is appropriate in one culture is obscene or insulting in another. Nodding the head, for example, means "yes" among most European language speakers. But among the Ainu of Japan, "yes" is expressed by bringing the arms to the chest and waving them. The pygmy Negritos of interior Malaya indicate "yes" by thrusting the head sharply forward, and people from the Punjab of India throw their heads sharply backward. The Ceylonese curve their chins gracefully downward in an arc to the left shoulder, whereas Bengalis rock their heads rapidly from one shoulder to the other.

Eye Contact

Is eye contact appropriate between two participants in a conversation? When is it permissible not to maintain eye contact? What does eye contact or the absence thereof signal? Cultures differ widely in this particular visual modality of nonverbal communication. In American culture it is permissible, for example, for two participants of unequal status to maintain prolonged eye contact. In fact, an American might interpret lack of eye contact as discourteous lack of attention, while in Japanese culture eye contact might be considered rude. Intercultural interference in this nonverbal category can lead to misunderstanding.

Not only is eye contact itself an important category, but the gestures, as it were, of the eyes are in some instances keys to communication. Eyes can signal interest, boredom, empathy, hostility, attraction, understanding, misunderstanding, and other messages. The nonverbal language of each culture has different ways of signaling such messages. An important aspect of unfettered and unambiguous conversation in a second language is the acquisition of conventions for conveying messages by means of eye signals.

Proxemics

Physical proximity, or **proxemics**, is also a meaningful communicative category. Cultures vary widely in acceptable distances for conversation. Edward Hall (1966) calculated acceptable distances for public, social-consultative, personal, and intimate discourse. He noted, for example, that Americans feel that a certain personal space "bubble" has been violated if a stranger stands closer than twenty to twenty-four inches away unless space is restricted, such as in a subway or an elevator. However, a typical member of a Latin American culture would feel that such a physical distance would be too great. The interesting thing is that neither party is specifically aware of what is wrong when the distance is not right. They merely have vague feelings of discomfort or anxiety.

Sometimes objects—desks, counters, other furniture—serve to maintain certain physical distances. Such objects tend to establish both the overall register and relationship of participants. Thus, a counter between two people maintains a consultative mood. Similarly, the presence of a desk or a computer monitor will set the tone of a conversation. Again, however, different cultures interpret different messages in such objects. In some cultures, objects might enhance the communicative process, but in other cases they impede it.

Artifacts

The nonverbal messages of clothing and ornamentation are also important aspects of communication. Clothes often signal a person's sense of self-esteem, socioeconomic class, and general character. Jewelry also conveys certain messages. In a multicultural conversation group, such artifacts, along with other nonverbal signals, can be a significant factor in lifting barriers, identifying certain personality characteristics, and setting a general mood.

Kinesthetics

Touching, sometimes referred to as **kinesthetics**, is another culturally loaded aspect of nonverbal communication. How we touch others and where we touch them is sometimes the most misunderstood aspect of nonverbal communication. Touching in some cultures signals a very personal or intimate register, while in other cultures extensive touching is commonplace. Knowing the limits and conventions is important for clear and unambiguous communication.

Olfactory Dimensions

Our noses also receive sensory nonverbal messages. The olfactory modality is of course an important one for the animal kingdom, but for the human race, too, different cultures have established different dimensions of olfactory communication. The twentieth century has created in most technological societies a penchant for perfumes, lotions, creams, and powders as acceptable and even necessary; natural human odors, especially perspiration, are thought to be undesirable. In some societies, of course, the smell of human perspiration is quite acceptable and even attractive. Second language and especially second culture learners need to be aware of the accepted mores of other cultures in the olfactory modality.

We cannot underestimate the importance of nonverbal communication in second language learning and in conversational analysis (see Kellerman 1992). Communicative competence includes nonverbal competence—knowledge of all the varying nonverbal semantics of the second culture, and an ability both to send and receive nonverbal signals unambiguously.

We have seen in this chapter alone that communicative competence is such an intricate web of psychological, sociocultural, physical, and linguistic features that it is easy to become entangled in just one part of that web. But some of the distinctive features of human discourse are becoming clearer, and language teaching methodology has demonstrated our steadily improving capacity to teach communication in the classroom. I believe we are moving in positive and creative directions. The language teacher and researcher, in dialog with each other, can be a part of that creative event by fashioning an integrated and cohesive understanding of how learners acquire the ability to communicate clearly and effectively in a second language.

In the Classroom:
Communicative Language Teaching

As the field of second language pedagogy has developed and matured over the past few decades, we have experienced a number of reactions and counter-reactions in methods and approaches to language teaching. We can look back over a century of foreign language teaching and observe the trends as they came and went. How will we look back 100 years from now and characterize the present era? Almost certainly the answer lies in our recent efforts to engage in **communicative language teaching** (CLT). The "push toward communication" (Higgs & Clifford 1982) has been relentless. Researchers have defined and redefined the construct of communicative competence. They have explored the myriad functions of language that learners must be able to accomplish. They have described spoken and written discourse and pragmatic conventions. They have examined the nature of styles and nonverbal communication. With this storehouse of knowledge we have valiantly pursued the goal of learning how best to teach communication.

One glance at current journals in second language teaching reveals quite an array of material on CLT. Numerous textbooks for teachers and teacher trainers expound on the nature of communicative approaches and offer techniques for varying ages and purposes. In short, wherever you look in the literature today, you will find reference to the communicative nature of language classes.

CLT is best understood as an *approach*, not a method. (For some comments on the difference between a method and an approach, see Brown 2000 and the vignette at the end of Chapter 6.) It is therefore a unified but broadly based theoretical position about the nature of language and of language learning and teaching. It is nevertheless difficult to synthesize all of the various definitions that have been offered. From the earlier seminal works in CLT (Savignon 1983; Breen & Candlin 1980; Widdowson 1978b) up to more recent teacher education textbooks (Brown 2000; Richard-Amato 1996), we have definitions enough to send us reeling. For the sake of simplicity and directness, I offer the following four interconnected characteristics as a definition of CLT.

1. Classroom goals are focused on all of the components of communicative competence and not restricted to grammatical or linguistic competence.
2. Language techniques are designed to engage learners in the pragmatic, authentic, functional use of language for meaningful purposes. Organizational language forms are not the central focus but rather aspects of language that enable the learner to accomplish those purposes.
3. Fluency and accuracy are seen as complementary principles underlying communicative techniques. At times fluency may

have to take on more importance than accuracy in order to keep learners meaningfully engaged in language use.

4. In the communicative classroom, students ultimately have to use the language, productively and receptively, in unrehearsed contexts.

These four characteristics underscore some major departures from earlier approaches. In some ways those departures were a gradual product of outgrowing the numerous methods (CLL, the Natural Approach, etc.—see vignette at the end of Chapter 4) that characterized a long stretch of history. In other ways those departures were radical. Structurally (grammatically) sequenced curricula were a mainstay of language teaching for centuries. CLT suggests that grammatical structure might better be subsumed under various functional categories. In CLT we pay considerably less attention to the overt presentation and discussion of grammatical rules than we traditionally did. A great deal of use of authentic language is implied in CLT, as we attempt to build fluency (Chambers 1997). It is important to note, however, that fluency should never be encouraged at the expense of clear, unambiguous, direct communication. Finally, much more spontaneity is present in communicative classrooms: students are encouraged to deal with unrehearsed situations under the guidance, but not control, of the teacher.

The fourth characteristic of CLT often makes it difficult for a non-native speaking teacher who is not very proficient in the second language to teach effectively. Dialogs, drills, rehearsed exercises, and discussions (in the first language) of grammatical rules are much simpler for some non-native speaking teachers to contend with. This drawback should not deter one, however, from pursuing communicative goals in the classroom. Technology (video, television, audiotapes, the Internet, computer software) can come to the aid of such teachers. Moreover, in the last decade or so, we have seen a marked increase in English teachers' proficiency levels around the world. As educational and political institutions in various countries become more sensitive to the importance of teaching foreign languages for communicative purposes (not just for the purpose of fulfilling a "requirement" or of "passing a test"), we may be better able, worldwide, to accomplish the goals of communicative language teaching.

TOPICS AND QUESTIONS FOR STUDY AND DISCUSSION

[Note: (I) Individual work; (G) group or pair work; (C) whole-class discussion.]

1. (G) With a partner, look at Figure 9.1, which describes language competence, and quickly come up with one example in a current or previous foreign language learning experience of each of the little items on the bottom line of the chart. Share these with the rest of the class.

2. (G) In groups, talk about your current or previous foreign language classes in terms of the extent to which CALP and/or BICS is the primary focus of your class. Identify which activities seem to promote CALP and which promote BICS.

3. (I) Review the discussion of strategic competence. Explain the relationship of strategic competence to language competence. What is the relationship between "compensatory" strategies and "executive" strategies? Finally, how do the learning and communication strategies discussed in Chapter 5 fit into strategic competence as defined here?

4. (C) Hatch suggested (page 255) that in second language learning, one should learn how to do conversation and interact verbally first, and out of this interaction will emerge grammatical structures. Does this mean that language classes for adults should somehow teach conversation rules and gambits before teaching basic grammatical or phonological structures? If not, how would you see Hatch's suggestion playing out in a foreign language course?

5. (G) To illustrate conversation rules and conventions in action, try this: In groups of five to six, appoint two people to be observers only. The rest of the group then engages in a discussion of a controversial topic: abortion, women's rights, nonviolence, race, a current political issue, or whatever. The observers should note on a piece of paper specifically what linguistic (verbal) and nonverbal features members of the group used to accomplish the following: (a) attention getting, (b) interrupting, (c) turn-taking, (d) clarification, (e) topic changing. Observers might also take note of cooperation, face-saving, and politeness conventions that were used. Observers can then report their findings to the rest of the class.

6. (C) The class is invited to offer specific examples of verbal and nonverbal features in Joos's five styles. What are some surface linguistic manifestations of differences in style? nonverbal manifestations? How do styles vary cross-culturally? How many styles are appropriate to teach in a foreign language class?

7. (C) Compare English with other languages that members of the class are familiar with, in terms of gender issues. Are there differences in the way one addresses women and men? in the the way women and men talk? in gender-differentiated grammatical (or morphological) forms? Do other languages reflect sexism, as English does?

8. (G) Arrange groups of four or five people in such a way that each group has members that are familiar with a variety of languages/cultures. (Alternative: arrange homogeneous groups which then share differences afterward.) Using the categories in this chapter, compare

nonverbal expressions in English-speaking culture with those of another language/culture. How might such differences be taught in a foreign language class?

9. (C) Illustrate from your own foreign language classes how the principles of CLT (pages 266 and 267) have been applied—or misapplied.

SUGGESTED READINGS

Canale, Michael and Swain, Merrill. 1980. "Theoretical bases of communicative approaches to second language teaching and testing." *Applied Linguistics* 1:1–47.

The seminal work on communicative competence by Canale and Swain is important reading for the serious student of SLA. It was, appropriately, the inaugural article in the first issue of Applied Linguistics.

Angelis, Paul and Henderson, Thelma (Eds.). 1989. Selected papers from the proceedings of the BAAL/AAAL joint seminar "Communicative Competence Revisited." *Applied Linguistics* 10 (June).

A decade later, Applied Linguistics *devoted a whole issue to "revisiting" communicative competence research.*

Bachman, Lyle. 1990. *Fundamental Considerations in Language Testing.* New York: Oxford University Press.

Yule, George and Tarone, Elaine. "Eliciting the performance of strategic competence." In Scarcella, Andersen, and Krashen (1990).

These two sources, especially the second, offer a good deal of detail on the subject of strategic competence.

Turner, Ken. 1995. "The principal principles of pragmatic inference: Cooperation." *Language Teaching* 28: 67–76.

Turner, Ken. 1996. "The principal principles of pragmatic inference: Politeness." *Language Teaching* 29: 1–13.

The two pragmatic issues of cooperation and politeness are covered along with an overview of other issues in these two state-of-the-art articles in Language Teaching.

Holmes, Janet. 1991. "Language and gender." *Language Teaching* 24: 207–220.

The language and gender issue presents some important challenges to researchers and teachers alike. A summary of research through

1991 is available in this article, yet another of the very accessible state-of-the-art summaries in Language Teaching.

Dresser, Norine. 1996. *Multicultural Manners: New Rules of Etiquette for a Changing Society.* New York: John Wiley & Sons.

For a popular treatment of the topic of nonverbal communication, Dresser's guide is informative easy reading.

LANGUAGE LEARNING EXPERIENCE: JOURNAL ENTRY 9

[Note: See pages 18 and 19 of Chapter 1 for general guidelines for writing a journal on a previous or concurrent language learning experience.]

- In your foreign language, would you say you are "communicatively competent"? Defend your response using some of the categories discussed in the first part of this chapter.
- Make two lists: activities your teacher uses (used) to promote (a) CALP and (b) BICS. Do you agree with the proportion of one to the other, given the purposes of your class?
- Are you satisfied with your progress in acquiring some of the discourse features, conversation rules, and pragmatic conventions of your foreign language? Describe what you think you can "do," in your language, in these domains.
- Is your foreign language gender-loaded in any way? Describe.
- Describe the verbal and nonverbal manifestations of different styles (from intimate to oratorical) in your foreign language.
- Does your teacher engage in CLT? Evaluate the methodology of your class on the basis of the four principles of CLT.

CHAPTER 10

THEORIES OF SECOND

LANGUAGE ACQUISITION

Tʜᴇ ᴘʀɪɴᴄɪᴘᴀʟ purpose of this book is to offer teachers and future teachers information for developing an integrated understanding of the principles of second language acquisition (SLA) that underlie the pedagogical process. That purpose has necessarily involved theoretical considerations. A theory, as I noted in the first chapter, is an extended definition. We have examined essential components of an extended definition of SLA. That is, we have attempted to answer the perplexing question "What is SLA?" And we have seen that SLA is, among other things, not unlike first language acquisition, is a subset of general human learning, involves cognitive variations, is closely related to one's personality type, is interwoven with second culture learning, and involves interference, the creation of new linguistic systems, and the learning of discourse and communicative functions of language. All of these categories and the many subcategories subsumed under them form the basis for structuring an integrated theory of SLA.

Is there such an integrated, unified theory of SLA, a standard set of constructs to which large numbers of researchers and teachers predominantly subscribe? The answer is, not exactly. As surely as competing models are typical of all disciplines that attempt to give explanatory power to complex phenomena, so this field has its fair share of claims and hypotheses, each vying for credibility and validity. We can be quite content with this state of affairs, for it reflects the intricacy of the acquisition process itself and the variability of individuals and contexts. On the other hand, we have discovered a great deal about SLA in many contexts, across proficiency levels, and within many specific purposes. We need not be apologetic, therefore, about the remaining unanswered questions, for many of the questions posed in the last, say, five decades, have been effectively answered.

In this chapter we will critically examine a number of current generalizations, hypotheses, and models of SLA. Remember that such "opinion" about SLA may represent one view of that metaphorical mountain of factors we talked about in Chapter 1. From such varied perspectives we should be able to place a large number of variables (which have been defined and discussed in this book) into a reasonably consistent tapestry of factors. That self-constructed system of variables is one's theory of SLA.

BUILDING A THEORY OF SLA

To say that second language learning is a complex process is obviously trite. The pages of this book alone bear testimony to that complexity. But complexity means that there are so many separate but interrelated factors within one intricate entity that it is exceedingly difficult to bring order and simplicity to that "chaos" (Larsen-Freeman 1997). We must nevertheless pursue the task of theory building (Long 1990a; Spolsky 1988). Consider, for a few moments, some of the domains and generalizations that describe the skeletal structure of a theory.

Domains and Generalizations

First, take a look at a taxonomy that was proposed several decades ago (Yorio 1976), represented in Figure 10.1. This list of factors begins to give you an idea of the many different domains of inquiry that must be included in a theory of SLA.

Certain factors subsumed in the chapter topics of this book are also a set of domains of consideration in a theory of SLA:

1. A theory of SLA includes an understanding, in general, of what language is, what learning is, and for classroom contexts, what teaching is.
2. Knowledge of children's learning of their first language provides essential insights to an understanding of SLA.
3. However, a number of important differences between adult and child learning and between first and second language acquisition must be carefully accounted for.
4. Second language learning is a part of and adheres to general principles of human learning and intelligence.
5. There is tremendous variation across learners in cognitive style and within a learner in strategy choice.

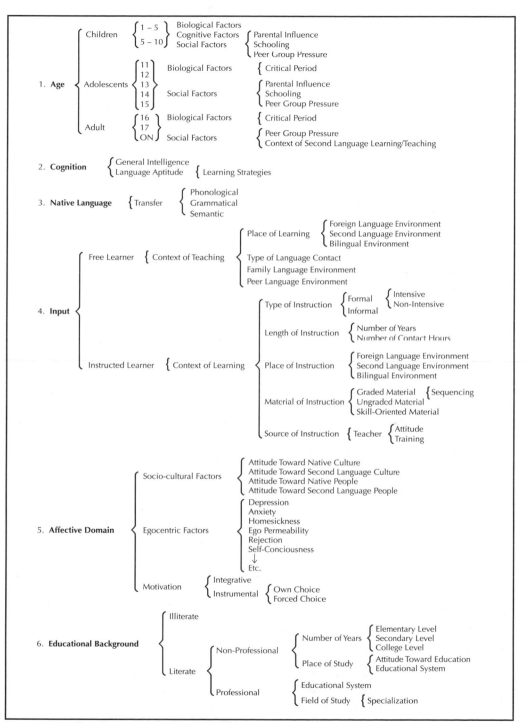

Figure 10.1. Classification of learner variables (Yorio 1976: 61)

6. Personality, the way people view themselves and reveal themselves in communication, will affect both the quantity and quality of second language learning.
7. Learning a second culture is often intricately intertwined with learning a second language.
8. The linguistic contrasts between the native and target language form one source of difficulty in learning a second language. But the creative process of forming an interlanguage system involves the learner in utilizing many facilitative sources and resources. Inevitable aspects of this process are errors, from which learners and teachers can gain further insight.
9. Communicative competence, with all of its subcategories, is the ultimate goal of learners as they deal with function, discourse, register, and nonverbal aspects of human interaction and linguistic negotiation.

However general those nine statements are, they, along with taxonomies such as Yorio's, constitute a framework for a theory of SLA. That framework has had substance built into it in the course of each chapter of this book. The interrelationships within that framework have been dealt with. One cannot, for example, engage in contrastive analysis and draw implications from it without knowledge of the place of interference in human learning in general. In comparing and contrasting first and second language acquisition, it is impossible to ignore affective and cultural variables and differences between adult and child cognition. Determining the source of a second language learner's error inevitably involves consideration of cognitive strategies and styles, group dynamics, and even the validity of data-gathering procedures. No single component of this "theory" is sufficient alone: the interaction and interdependence of the other components are necessary.

Hypotheses and Claims

A theory of SLA is really an interrelated set of hypotheses and/or claims about how people become proficient in a second language. In a summary of research findings on SLA, Lightbown (1985: 176–180) made the following claims:

1. Adults and adolescents can "acquire" a second language.
2. The learner creates a systematic interlanguage that is often characterized by the same systematic errors as [those of] the child learning the same language as the first language, as well as others that appear to be based on the learner's own native language.

3. There are predictable sequences in acquisition so that certain structures have to be acquired before others can be integrated.
4. Practice does not make perfect.
5. Knowing a language rule does not mean one will be able to use it in communicative interaction.
6. Isolated explicit error correction is usually ineffective in changing language behavior.
7. For most adult learners, acquisition stops—"fossilizes"—before the learner has achieved nativelike mastery of the target language.
8. One cannot achieve nativelike (or near-nativelike) command of a second language in one hour a day.
9. The learner's task is enormous because language is enormously complex.
10. A learner's ability to understand language in a meaningful context exceeds his or her ability to comprehend decontextualized language and to produce language of comparable complexity and accuracy.

A similar set of statements was made by Lightbown and Spada (1993) outlining some myths about SLA—what one should not conclude to be necessarily a correct generalization. Certain claims about SLA demand caution; our response to them might be prefaced with a "Well, it depends" sort of caveat. Following are some of those "popular ideas" that may not be supported by research (Lightbown & Spada 1993: 111–116):

1. Languages are learned mainly through imitation.
2. Parents usually correct young children when they make errors.
3. People with high IQs are good language learners.
4. The earlier a second language is introduced in school programs, the greater the likelihood of success in learning.
5. Most of the mistakes that second language learners make are due to interference from their first language.
6. Learners' errors should be corrected as soon as they are made in order to prevent the formation of bad habits.

We have seen in this book that the above statements—if they are not downright false—require considerable expansion, contextualization, and modification before we can claim their veracity.

Unlike Yorio's (1976) list and the nine items that synopsized the chapter topics of this book, most of Lightbown's generalizations and myths do more than define a domain. They hypothesize directionality within a domain, and are therefore the subject of debate. Item 6 in the first

(Lightbown 1985) list, for example, stems from studies that fail to show that explicit error correction causes a permanent change in language production. Such a claim, however, may be mitigated by many teachers who have gathered observational evidence of the positive effects of error treatment in the classroom. Nevertheless, all such claims are the beginnings of theory building. As we carefully examine each claim, add others to it, and then refine them into sets of tenable hypotheses, we begin to build a theory.

Criteria for a Viable Theory

How do we know if we have the appropriate components of a theory of SLA? One answer to this question may lie in an examination of **chaos/complexity theory**. Diane Larsen-Freeman (1997), outlining similarities between chaos theory and SLA, argued that SLA is as much a dynamic, complex, nonlinear system as are physics, biology, and other sciences. The pathway that one learner takes in order to achieve success is different, and sometimes markedly so, from another's. Like predicting the patterns of flocking birds or the course of droplets of water in a waterfall, certain laws are axiomatic, but the sheer number and complexity of the variables involved make SLA exceedingly difficult to predict *a priori*.

Larsen-Freeman (1997) suggested several lessons from chaos theory that can help us to design a theory of SLA. I have synthesized her comments below.

1. Beware of false dichotomies. Look for complementarity, inclusiveness, and interface. We have examined a number of continua in this book; it is important to see them just as that, and not as dichotomies.

2. Beware of linear, causal approaches to theorizing. The "butterfly effect" in chaos theory reminds us that the fluttering wing of a butterfly in the Amazonian forest can have a chain of reactions and interreactions that extend all the way to the path of a hurricane in Hawaii. SLA is so complex with so many interacting factors that to state that there is a single cause for a SLA effect is to go too far.

3. Beware of overgeneralization. Pay attention to details. The smallest, apparently most insignificant of factors in learning a second language may turn out to be important! But on the other hand,

4. Beware of reductionist thinking. It is very tempting, with any chaotic, complex system, to oversimplify by taking some little part of the whole and extracting it from the whole system.

If a theory avoids just these four pitfalls, then perhaps it is on its way to achieving adequacy.

Michael Long (1990a: 659–660) also tackled the problem of theory building in a number of suggestions about "the least" a theory of SLA needs to explain. He offered eight criteria for a comprehensive theory of SLA:

1. Account for universals.
2. Account for environmental factors.
3. Account for variability in age, acquisition rate, and proficiency level.
4. Explain both cognitive and affective factors.
5. Account for form-focused learning, not just subconscious acquisition.
6. Account for other variables besides exposure and input.
7. Account for cognitive/innate factors which explain interlanguage systematicity.
8. Recognize that acquisition is not a steady accumulation of generalizations.

The process of theory building may be best illustrated in the form of several models of SLA that have appeared in recent history. These correspond to the schools of thought introduced in Chapter 1 and reintroduced throughout the book. While there is no viable behavioristic model of SLA (it would be far too limiting), we can identify a major innatist model, two cognitive models, and a social constructivist theory. As you read on, look back at Larsen-Freeman's and Long's lists here and decide for yourself the extent to which each model fulfills the criteria. We begin with Krashen's innatist, or creative construction, model of SLA.

AN INNATIST MODEL: KRASHEN'S INPUT HYPOTHESIS

One of the most controversial theoretical perspectives in SLA in the last quarter of the twentieth century was offered by Stephen Krashen (1977, 1981, 1982, 1985, 1992, 1993, 1997) in a host of articles and books. Krashen's hypotheses have had a number of different names. In the earlier years the "Monitor Model" and the "Acquisition-Learning Hypothesis" were more popular terms; in recent years the "Input Hypothesis" has come to identify what is really a set of five interrelated hypotheses. These five hypotheses are summarized below.

1. The Acquisition-Learning Hypothesis. Krashen claimed that adult second language learners have two means for internalizing the target language. The first is "acquisition," a subconscious and intuitive process of constructing the system of a language, not unlike the process used by a child to "pick up" a language. The second means is a conscious "learning" process in which learners attend to form, figure out rules, and are generally aware of their own process. According to Krashen, "fluency in second language performance is due to what we have acquired, not what we have learned" (1981a: 99). Adults should, therefore, do as much acquiring as possible in order to achieve communicative fluency; otherwise, they will get bogged down in rule learning and too much conscious attention to the forms of language and to watching their own progress.

Moreover, for Krashen (1982), our conscious learning processes and our subconscious acquisition processes are mutually exclusive: learning cannot "become" acquisition. This claim of "no interface" between acquisition and learning is used to strengthen the argument for recommending large doses of acquisition activity in the classroom, with only a very minor role assigned to learning.

2. The Monitor Hypothesis. The "monitor" is involved in learning, not in acquisition. It is a device for "watchdogging" one's output, for editing and making alterations or corrections as they are consciously perceived. Only once fluency is established should an optimal amount of monitoring, or editing, be employed by the learner (Krashen 1981a).

3. The Natural Order Hypothesis. Following the earlier morpheme order studies of Dulay and Burt (1974b, 1976) and others, Krashen has claimed that we acquire language rules in a predictable or "natural" order.

4. The Input Hypothesis. The Input Hypothesis claims that an important "condition for language acquisition to occur is that the acquirer *understand* (via hearing or reading) input language that contains structure 'a bit beyond' his or her current level of competence. . . . If an acquirer is at stage or level *i*, the input he or she understands should contain $i + 1$" (Krashen 1981: 100). In other words, the language that learners are exposed to should be just far enough beyond their current competence that they can understand most of it but still be challenged to make progress. The corollary to this is that input should neither be so far beyond their reach that they are overwhelmed (this might be, say, $i + 2$), nor so close to their current stage that they are not challenged at all $(i + 0)$.

An important part of the Input Hypothesis is Krashen's recommendation that speaking not be taught directly or very early in the language classroom. Speech will "emerge" once the acquirer has built up enough comprehensible input $(i + 1)$, as we saw in Chapter 4 in a discussion of the Natural Approach.

5. The Affective Filter Hypothesis. Krashen has further claimed that the best acquisition will occur in environments where anxiety is low and defensiveness absent, or, in Krashen's terms, in contexts where the "affective filter" is low.

The first two of Krashen's hypotheses have intuitive appeal to teachers in the field. Who can deny that we should have less "learning" in our classrooms than traditional language programs offer? Who in their right mind would refute the importance of learners engaging in somewhat unmonitored meaningful communication in the classroom? And the natural order hypothesis is, after all, supported in some research (Larsen-Freeman & Long 1991). Finally, the effectiveness of providing a reasonable challenge *(i + 1)* to students in a supportive, low-anxiety environment can hardly be denied by any teacher.

It is unfortunate that SLA is not as simply defined as Krashen would claim, and therefore his assumptions have been hotly disputed (e.g., de Bot 1996; Swain & Lapkin 1995; Brumfit 1992; White 1987; Gregg 1984; McLaughlin 1978, to name but a few). McLaughlin (1978, 1990a), a psychologist, sharply criticized Krashen's rather fuzzy distinction between subconscious (acquisition) and conscious (learning) processes. Psychologists are still in wide disagreement in their definitions of "the notoriously slippery notion" (Odlin 1986: 138) of consciousness. McLaughlin (1990a: 627) commented:

> My own bias . . . is to avoid use of the terms conscious and unconscious in second language theory. I believe that these terms are too laden with surplus meaning and too difficult to define empirically to be useful theoretically. Hence, my critique of Krashen's distinction between learning and acquisition—a distinction that assumes that it is possible to differentiate what is conscious from what is unconscious.

In McLaughlin's view, then, a language acquisition theory that appeals to conscious/subconscious distinctions is greatly weakened by our inability to identify just what that distinction is.

A second criticism of Krashen's views arose out of the claim that there is no interface—no overlap—between acquisition and learning. We have already seen over and over again in this book that so-called dichotomies in human behavior almost always define the end-points of a continuum, and not mutually exclusive categories. As Gregg (1984: 82) pointed out,

> Krashen plays fast and loose with his definitions. . . . If unconscious knowledge is capable of being brought to consciousness,

and if conscious knowledge is capable of becoming unconscious—and this seems to be a reasonable assumption—then
there is no reason whatever to accept Krashen's claim, in the
absence of evidence. And there is an absence of evidence.

Second language learning clearly is a process in which varying degrees
of learning and of acquisition can both be beneficial, depending upon the
learner's own styles and strategies. Swain (1998), Doughty and Williams
(1998), Buczowska and Weist (1991), Doughty (1991), Ellis (1990b),
Lightbown and Spada 1990, and Long (1983, 1988) have all shown, in a
number of empirical research studies, that Krashen's "zero option" (don't
ever teach grammar) (see Ellis 1997: 47) is not supported in the literature.
Instruction in conscious rule learning and other types of form-focused
instruction, as we saw in Chapter 8, can indeed aid in the attainment of successful communicative competence in a second language.

A third difficulty in Krashen's Input Hypothesis is found in his explicit
claim (1986: 62) that "comprehensible input is the only causative variable
in second language acquisition." In other words, success in a foreign language can be attributed to input alone. Such a theory ascribes little credit
to learners and their own active engagement in the process. Moreover, it is
important to distinguish between input and **intake**. The latter is the subset
of all input that actually gets assigned to our long-term memory store. Just
imagine, for example, reading a book, listening to a conversation, or
watching a movie—in any language. This is your input. But your intake is
what you take with you over a period of time and can later remember.
Krashen (1983) did suggest that input gets converted to intake through a
learner's process of linking forms to meaning and noticing "gaps" between
the learner's current internalized rule system and the new input. Others
have noted, however, that these processes "are not clearly operationalized
or consistently proposed" (Mitchell & Myles 1998: 126). So, we are still left
with a theory that paints a picture of learners at the mercy of the input that
others offer.

Seliger (1983) offered a much broader conceptualization of the role of
input that gives learners more credit (and blame) for eventual success.
Certain learners are what he called **High Input Generators** (HIGs),
people who are good at initiating and sustaining interaction, or "generating" input from teachers, fellow learners, and others. **Low Input
Generators** (LIGs) are more passive learners who do little to stick their
necks out to get input directed toward them. In two studies of second language learners, Seliger found that "learners who maintained high levels of
interaction [HIGs] in the second language, both in the classroom and outside, progressed at a faster rate than learners who interacted little [LIGs] in
the classroom" (p. 262).

Such studies, coupled with a great deal of intuitive observation of successful learners, suggest that Krashen's comprehensible input must at the very least be complemented by a significant amount of output that gives credit to the role of the learner's production. While Krashen (1997: 7) staunchly maintained that in the language classroom "output is too scarce to make any important impact on language development," Swain and Lapkin (1995) offered convincing evidence that their **Output Hypothesis** was at least as significant as input, if not more so, in explaining learner success. In a review of the Output Hypothesis, de Bot (1996: 529) argued that "output serves an important role in second language acquisition ... because it generates highly specific input the cognitive system needs to build up a coherent set of knowledge."

Finally, it is important to note that the notion of *i + 1* is nothing new. It is a reiteration of a general principle of learning that we have already discussed in this book (Chapter 4). Meaningfulness, or "subsumability" in Ausubel's terms, is that which is relatable to existing cognitive structures, neither too far beyond the structures *(i + 2)*, nor the existing structures themselves *(i + 0)*. But Krashen presents the *i + 1* formula as if we are actually able to define *i* and *1*, and we are not, as Gregg (1984), White (1987), and others have pointed out. Furthermore, the notion that speech will "emerge" in a context of comprehensible input sounds promising, and for some learners (bright, highly motivated, outgoing learners), speech will indeed emerge. But we are left with no significant information from Krashen's theories on what to do about the other half (or more) of our language students for whom speech does not "emerge" and for whom the "silent period" might last forever.

Krashen's innatist model of SLA has had wide appeal to teachers who cry for something simple and concrete on which to base their methodology. It is easy to see its appeal since, on the surface, the claims that are made seem to reflect accepted principles of SLA. But in their oversimplicity, the claims have been exaggerated. Nevertheless, in the final analysis, oddly enough, I feel we owe a debt of gratitude to Krashen for his bold, if brash, insights. They have spurred many a researcher to look very carefully at what we do know, what the research evidence is, and then in the process of refutation to propose plausible alternatives. We continue now with several of these alternative theoretical perspectives.

COGNITIVE MODELS

It is quite tempting, with Krashen, to conceptualize SLA in terms of conscious and subconscious processes. In explaining the difference between a child's and an adult's second language acquisition, our first appeal is to children's "knack" for "picking up" a language, which, in everyday terms, appears to refer to what we think of as subconscious. But there are two problems with such an appeal: (a) as both McLaughlin (1990a) and Schmidt (1990) agreed, "consciousness" is a tricky term, and (b) younger (child language acquisition) is not necessarily better (Scovel 1999).

McLaughlin's Attention-Processing Model

So, if we rule out a consciousness continuum in constructing a viable theory of SLA, and we do not hold child first language acquisition up as the ideal model of language acquisition, we must look elsewhere for the foundation stones of a theory. A more sound heuristic for conceptualizing the language acquisition process, one that did indeed avoid any direct appeal to a consciousness continuum, was proposed by Barry McLaughlin and his colleagues (McLaughlin 1978; McLaughlin, Rossman, & McLeod 1983; McLeod & McLaughlin 1986; McLaughlin 1987, 1990b). Their model juxtaposes processing mechanisms (**controlled** and **automatic**) and categories of **attention** to form four cells (see Table 10.1).

Controlled processes are "capacity limited and temporary," and automatic processes are a relatively permanent" (McLaughlin et al. 1983: 142). We can think of controlled processing as typical of anyone learning a brand new skill in which only a very few elements of the skill can be retained.

When you first learn to play tennis, for example, you can only manage the elements of, say, making contact between ball and racquet, getting the

Table 10.1. Possible second language performance as a function of information-processing procedures and attention to formal properties of language (McLaughlin et al. 1983)

ATTENTION TO
FORMAL PROPERTIES
OF LANGUAGE

| | **INFORMATION PROCESSING** | |
	Controlled	**Automatic**
Focal	(Cell A) Performance based on formal rule learning	(Cell B) Performance in a test situation
Peripheral	(Cell C) Performance based on implicit learning or analogic learning	(Cell D) Performance in communication situations

ball over the net, and hitting the ball into the green space on the other side of the net. Everything else about the game is far too complex for your capacity-limited ability.

Automatic processes, on the other hand, refer to processing in a more accomplished skill, where the "hard drive" (to borrow a computer metaphor) of your brain can manage hundreds and thousands of bits of information simultaneously. The automatizing of this multiplicity of data is accomplished by a process of **restructuring** (McLeod & McLaughlin 1986; McLaughlin 1987, 1990b) in which "the components of a task are coordinated, integrated, or reorganized into new units, thereby allowing the . . . old components to be replaced by a more efficient procedure" (McLaughlin 1990b: 118). Restructuring is conceptually synonymous with Ausubel's construct of subsumption discussed in Chapter 4.

Both ends of this continuum of processing can occur with either **focal** or **peripheral** attention to the task at hand; that is, focusing attention either centrally or simply on the periphery. It is easy to fall into the temptation of thinking of focal attention as "conscious" attention, but such a pitfall must be avoided. Both focal and peripheral attention to some task may be quite conscious (Hulstijn 1990). When you are driving a car, for example, your focal attention may center on cars directly in front of you as you move forward; but your peripheral attention to cars beside you and behind you, to potential hazards, and of course to the other thoughts "running through your mind," is all very much within your conscious awareness.

While many controlled processes are focal, some, like child first language learning or the learning of skills without any instruction, can be peripheral. Similarly, many automatic processes are peripheral, but some can be focal, as in the case of an accomplished pianist performing in a concert or an experienced driver paying particular attention to the road on a foggy night. It is very important to note that in virtually every act of performing something, focal and peripheral attention actually occur simultaneously, and the question is: What, specifically, occupies a person's focal and peripheral attention? So, for example, a very young child who says to a parent "Nobody don't like me" is undoubtedly focally attending to conveying emotion, mental anguish, or loneliness, and peripherally attending to words and morphemes that underlie the central meaning. Other factors that garner attention somewhere in between centrally focal and extremely peripheral may be reading the parent's facial features, mental recall of an uncomfortable incident of rejection, awareness of a sibling overhearing the communication, and even such peripheral nonlinguistic, noncognitive factors as the temperature in the room at the moment, a light in the background, the smell of dinner cooking, or the warmth of the parent's arms enfolding the child. All of these perceptions, from highly focal to very peripheral, are within the *awareness* of the child. McLaughlin (1990a) noted that the literature in experimental psychology indicates that there is no long-term learning (of new material) without awareness, an observation well documented by Loew (1997) and Schmidt (1990) for second language learning in particular. A cognitive perspective of SLA entirely obviates the need to distinguish conscious and subconscious processing.

How does McLaughlin's model apply to practical aspects of learning a second language? I have attempted to "demystify" some of the rather complex constructs of the attention-processing model in Table 10.2. It is important to note that these cells are described in terms of one's processing of and attention to language forms (grammatical, phonological, discourse rules and categories, lexical choices, etc.). If, for example, peripheral attention is given to language forms in a more advanced language classroom, focal attention is no doubt being given to meaning, function, purpose, or person. Child second language learning may consist almost exclusively of peripheral (cells C and D) attention to language forms. Most adult second language learning of language forms in the classroom involves a movement from cell A through a combination of C and B, to D (DeKeyser 1997). Peripheral, automatic attention-processing of the bits and pieces of language is thus an ultimate communicative goal for language learners.

Table 10.2. Practical applications of McLaughlin's attention-processing model

	CONTROLLED: new skill, capacity limited	**AUTOMATIC:** well trained, practiced skill capacity is relatively <u>un</u>limited
FOCAL intentional attention	**A** • grammatical explanation of a specific point • word definition • copy a written model • the <u>first</u> stages of "memorizing" a dialog • prefabricated patterns • various discrete-point exercises	**B** • "keeping an eye out" for something • advanced L2 learner focuses on modals, clause formation, etc. • monitoring oneself while talking or writing • scanning • editing, peer-editing
PERIPHERAL	**C** • simple greetings • the later stages of "memorizing" a dialog • TPR/Natural Approach • new L2 learner successfully completes a <u>brief</u> conversation	**D** • open-ended group work • rapid reading, skimming • free writes • normal conversational exchanges of some length

Implicit and Explicit Models

Another set of constructs for conceptualizing the varied processes of second language learning is found in models that make a distinction between explicit and implicit linguistic knowledge. In the **explicit** category are the facts that a person knows about language and the ability to articulate those facts in some way. Explicit processing differs from McLaughlin's focal attention in that explicit signals one's knowledge about language. **Implicit** knowledge is information that is automatically and spontaneously used in language tasks. Children implicitly learn phonological, syntactic, semantic, and pragmatic rules for language, but do not have access to an explanation, explicitly, of those rules. Implicit processes enable a learner to perform language but not necessarily to cite rules governing the performance.

Among those who have proposed models of SLA using the implicit/explicit distinction are Ellen Bialystok (1978, 1982, 1990a), Rod Ellis (1994a, 1997), and Nick Ellis (1994a). Bialystok's (1978) diagrammatic conception of SLA (see Figure 10.2) featured a flow chart showing implicit and explicit processing as central to the total act of learning a second language. Bialystok later (1982: 183) equated implicit and explicit with the

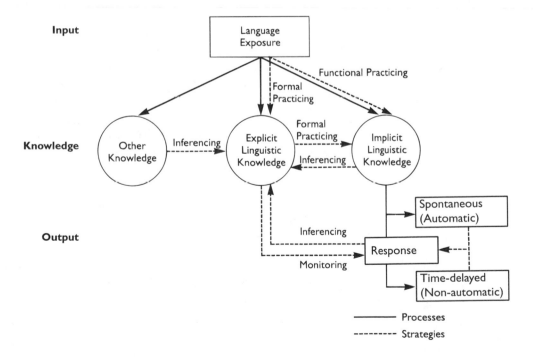

Figure 10.2. Model of second language learning (adapted from Bialystok 1978: 71)

synonymous terms **unanalyzed** and **analyzed** knowledge: "Unanalyzed knowledge is the general form in which we know most things without being aware of the structure of that knowledge"; on the other hand, learners are overtly aware of the structure of analyzed knowledge. For example, at the unanalyzed extreme of this knowledge dimension, learners have little awareness of language rules, but at the analyzed end, learners can verbalize complex rules governing language.

These same models feature a distinction between **automatic** and **non-automatic** processing, building on McLaughlin's conception of automaticity. Automaticity refers to the learner's relative access to the knowledge. Knowledge that can be retrieved easily and quickly is automatic. Knowledge that takes time and effort to retrieve is non-automatic. As was true for the McLaughlin model, both forms of attention can be either analyzed or unanalyzed. An important dimension of this distinction is *time*. Processing time is a significant factor in second language performance, one that has pedagogical salience in the classroom. The length of time that a learner takes before oral production performance, for example, can be indicative of the perceived complexity of certain language forms in a task. Mehnert (1998) found that planning time had a significant effect on the accuracy and fluency of second language learners' production.

The constructs of automaticity/nonautomaticity and of explicit/implicit knowledge have drawn the attention of numerous researchers over the past decade or so. On the one hand, arguments were raised about the identification of just what we mean by implicit and explicit (Hulstijn 1990; Robinson 1994, 1995, 1997), and responses offered (see Bialystok 1990b, for example). On the other hand, some useful applications have emerged in Rod Ellis's (1994, 1997: 107–133; Han & Ellis 1998) proposals of a theory of classroom instruction using implicit/explicit continua. Here, we are given some suggestions for grammar consciousness raising, for example, in which some explicit attention to language form is blended with implicit communicative tasks.

A SOCIAL CONSTRUCTIVIST MODEL: LONG'S INTERACTION HYPOTHESIS

The preceding two general theoretical positions, Krashen's Input Hypothesis and the cognitive models of SLA, both focus to a considerable extent on the learner. As such, they represent what Firth and Wagner (1997: 288) called "SLA's general preoccupation with the *learner*, at the expense of other potentially relevant social identities." The social constructivist perspectives that are associated with more current approaches to both first and second language acquisition emphasize the dynamic nature of the interplay between learners and their peers and their teachers and others with whom they interact. The interpersonal context in which a learner operates takes on great significance, and therefore, the interaction between learners and others is the focus of observation and explanation.

One of the most widely discussed social constructivist positions in the field emerged from the work of Michael Long (1985, 1996). Taking up where in a sense Krashen left off, Long posits, in what has come to be called the **interaction hypothesis**, that comprehensible input is the result of **modified interaction**. The latter is defined as the various modifications that native speakers and other interlocutors create in order to render their input comprehensible to learners. As we saw in Chapter 2, in first language contexts parents modify their speech to children (Mother to baby: "Mommy go bye bye now"). Native speakers often slow down speech to second language learners, speaking more deliberately. Modifications also include comprehension checks: "Go down to the subway—do you know the word 'subway'?"; clarification/repair requests: "Did you say 'to the right'?"; or paraphrases: "I went to a New Year's Eve party, you know, January 1st, I mean, December 31st, the night before the first day of the new year."

In Long's view, interaction and input are two major players in the process of acquisition. In a radical departure from an old paradigm in which second language classrooms might have been seen as contexts for "practicing" grammatical structures and other language forms, conversation and other interactive communication are, according to Long, the basis for the development of linguistic rules. While Gass and Varonis (1994) ably pointed out that such a view is not subscribed to by all, nevertheless a number of studies have supported the link between interaction and acquisition (Swain & Lapkin 1998; Gass, Mackey, & Pica 1998; van Lier 1996; Jordens 1996; Loschky 1994; Gass & Varonis 1994; Pica 1987). In a strong endorsement of the power of interaction in the language curriculum, van Lier (1996: 188) devoted a whole book to "the curriculum as interaction." Here, principles of awareness, autonomy, and authenticity lead the learner into Vygotsky's (1978) **zone of proximal development** (ZPD) (see Chapter 2), where learners construct the new language through socially mediated interaction.

Lest you assume that this genre of research and teaching possesses unquestionably final answers to dilemmas of how best to teach and learn second languages, a word of precaution is in order. Interactionist research has just begun, and it has begun mostly in the context of Western cultural settings. The studies that are so far available are fragmentary with regard to pinpointing specific linguistic features, stages of learner development, pragmatic contexts, and pedagogical settings. And, as always, one side of the second language mountain of research must be compared with other perspectives. A broadly based theory of SLA must encompass models of learner-internal processing (such as those previously discussed) as well as the socially constructed dynamics of interpersonal communication. (See Table 10.3 for a summary of the previously discussed perspectives.)

The other side of the story is that Long's Interaction Hypothesis has pushed pedagogical research on SLA into a new frontier. It centers us on the language classroom not just as a place where learners of varying abilities and styles and backgrounds mingle, but as a place where the contexts for interaction are carefully designed. It focuses materials and curriculum developers on creating the optimal environments and tasks for input and interaction such that the learner will be stimulated to create his or her own learner language in a socially constructed process. Further, it reminds us that the many variables at work in an interactive classroom should prime teachers to expect the unexpected and to anticipate the novel creations of learners engaged in the process of discovery.

FROM THEORY TO PRACTICE

The field of second language learning and teaching has for many decades now been plagued by debates about the relationship between theory and practice. People might say, "Well, how do I apply so-and-so's theory in my classroom?" Or, as Krashen (1983: 261) once said, "When we [Krashen] provide theory, we provide them [teachers] with the underlying rationale for methodology in general." Typically, theories are constructed by professors and researchers who spend lots of time hypothesizing, describing, measuring, and concluding things about learners and learning. Just as typically, practitioners are thought of as teachers who are out there in classrooms every day stimulating, encouraging, observing, and assessing real-live learners.

Table 10.3. Theories and models of SLA

Innatist	Cognitive	Constructivist
[Krashen] • subconscious acquisition superior to "learning" and "monitoring" • comprehensible input *(i + 1)* • low affective filter • natural order of acquisition • "zero option" for grammar instruction	[McLaughlin/Bialystok] • controlled/automatic processing (McL) • focal/peripheral attention (McL) • restructuring (McL) • implicit vs. explicit (B) • unanalyzed vs. analyzed knowledge (B) • form-focused instruction	[Long] • interaction hypothesis • intake through social interaction • output hypothesis (Swain) • HIGs (Seliger) • authenticity • task-based instruction

The last century of language teaching history, operating within this theory-practice, researcher-teacher dichotomy, has not been completely devoid of dialog between the two sides. The cycles that are represented in the In the Classroom vignettes throughout this book were the result of the interplay between in-class practice and beyond-class research. We moved in and out of paradigms (Kuhn 1970) as inadequacies of the old ways of doing things were replaced by better ways. These trends in language teaching were partly the result of teachers and researchers communicating with each other. As pedagogical approaches and techniques were conceived and developed, essential data were provided for the stimulation of research, which in turn suggested more effective ways of teaching and learning, and the interdependent cycle continued.

These historical mileposts notwithstanding, the custom of leaving theory to researchers and practice to teachers has become, in Clarke's (1994) words, "dysfunctional." The unnecessary stratification of laborers in the same vineyard, a dysfunction that has been perpetuated by both sides, has accorded higher status to a researcher/theorist than to a practitioner/teacher. The latter is made to feel that he or she is the recipient of the former's findings and prognostications, with little to offer in return. What is becoming clearer in this profession now is the importance of viewing the process of language instruction as a cooperative dialog among many technicians, each endowed with special skills. Technicians' skills vary widely: program developing, textbook writing, observing, measuring variables of acquisition, teacher educating, synthesizing others' findings, in-class facilitating, designing experiments, assessing, applying technology to teaching, counseling, and the list goes on. There is no set of technical skills here that gets uniquely commissioned to create theory or another set allocated to "practicing" something.

We are all practitioners and we are all theorists. We are all charged with developing a broadly based conceptualization of the process of language learning and teaching. We are all responsible for understanding as much as we can how to create contexts for optimal acquisition among learners. Whenever that understanding calls for putting together diverse bits and pieces of knowledge, you are doing some theory building. Let's say you have some thoughts about the relevance of age factors, cognitive style variations, intercultural communication, and strategic competence to a set of learners and tasks; then you are constructing theory. Or, if you have observed some learners in classrooms and you discern common threads of process among them, you have created a theory. And whenever you, in the role of a teacher, ask pertinent questions about SLA, you are beginning the process of research that can lead to a theoretical statement.

So, the ages-old theory–practice debate can be put aside. Instead, all technicians in the various subfields of SLA are called upon to assume the responsibility for synthesizing the myriad findings and claims and hypotheses—and, yes, the would-be theories—into a coherent under-standing of what SLA is and how learners can be successful in fulfilling their classroom goals. This means you, perhaps as a novice in this field, can indeed formulate an integrated understanding of SLA. You can take the information that has been presented in this book and create a rationale for language teaching. In due course of time, as you engage in professional dis-course with your teammates in the field, you will be a part of a community of theory builders that talk with each other in pursuit of a better theory.

How do you begin to join this community of theory builders? Here are some suggestions:

1. Play both the believing game and the doubting game.

Throughout this book, we have seen that truth is neither unitary nor uni-dimensional. We have seen that definitions and extended definitions are never simple. Just as a photographer captures many facets of the same mountain by circling around it, truth presents itself to us in many forms, and sometimes those forms seem to conflict.

This elusive nature of truth was addressed by Peter Elbow (1973), who noted that most scholarly traditions are too myopically involved in what he called the "doubting game" of truth-seeking: trying to find something wrong with someone's claim or hypothesis. The doubting game is seen, incor-rectly, as rigorous, disciplined, rational, and tough-minded. But Elbow con-tended that we need to turn such conceptions upside down, to look at the other end of the continuum and recognize the importance of what he called the "believing game." In the believing game you try to find truths, not errors; you make acts of self-insertion and self-involvement, not self-extrication. "It helps to think of it as trying to get inside the head of someone who saw things this way. Perhaps even constructing such a person for yourself. Try to have the experience of someone who made this assertion" (Elbow 1973: 149). Elbow was careful to note the interdepend-ence of the believing game and the doubting game. "The two games are interdependent. . . .The two games are only halves of a full cycle of thinking" (p. 190).

If you were to try to unify or to integrate everything that every second language researcher concluded, or even everything listed in the previous sections, you could not do so through the doubting game. But by balancing your perspective with a believing attitude toward those elements that are not categorically ruled out, you can maintain a sense of perspective. If someone were to tell you, for example, that your class of adult learners will without question experience difficulty because of the critical period hypothesis ("the younger the better"), you might first play the believing game by embracing the statement in a genuine dialog with the claimant. After a discussion of context, learner variables, methodology, and other factors, it is quite likely that both of you will become clearer about the claim and will reach a more balanced perspective. The alternative of quickly dismissing the claim as so much balderdash leaves little room open for an intelligent exchange.

2. *Appreciate both the art and science of SLA.*

Not unrelated to balancing believing games and doubting games is the notion that SLA can be seen as both an art and a science. Several decades ago, Ochsner (1979) made a plea for a "poetics" of SLA research in which we use two research traditions to draw conclusions. One tradition is a **nomothetic** tradition of empiricism, scientific methodology, and prediction; this is the behavioristic school of thought referred to in Chapter 1. On the other hand, a **hermeneutic** (or, in Chapter 1, the cognitive/rationalistic) tradition provides us with a means for interpretation and understanding in which we do not look for absolute laws. "A poetics of second language acquisition lets us shift our perspectives," according to Ochsner (p. 71), who sounded very much like he had been reading Peter Elbow!

Schumann (1982a) adopted a similar point of view in recommending that we see both the "art" and the "science" of SLA research. Noting that Krashen and McLaughlin have had two different experiences themselves in learning a second language, Schumann suggests that "Krashen's and McLaughlin's views can co-exist as two different paintings of the language learning experience—as reality symbolized in two different ways" (p. 113). His concluding remarks, however, lean toward viewing our research as art, advantageous because such a view reduces the need of closure and allows us to see our work in a larger perspective with less dogmatism and ego involvement. In short, it frees us to play the believing game more ardently and more fruitfully.

The artful side of theory building will surely involve us in the creative use of metaphor as we seek to describe that which cannot always be empirically defined. Some scholars caution against using metaphor in describing SLA because it gives us "license to take one's claims as something less than serious hypotheses" (Gregg 1993: 291). But Lantolf (1996) made a plea for the legitimacy of metaphor in SLA theory building. Much of our ordinary language is metaphorical, whether we realize it or not, and a good many of our theoretical statements utilize metaphor. Think of some of the terms used in this book: transfer, distance, filter, monitor, equilibration, automatic, device. How would we describe SLA without such terms? (I have pushed the metaphorical envelope in the vignette at the end of this chapter.) It would appear that as long as one recognizes the limitations of metaphors, then they have the power to maintain the vibrancy of theory.

3. *Trust (to some extent) your intuition.*

Teachers generally want to "know" that a method is "right," that it will work successfully. We want finely tuned programs that map the pathways to successful learning. In other words, we tend to be born doubters. But the believing game provides us with a contrasting principle, intuition. Psychological research on cognitive styles has shown us that people tend to favor either an **intuitive** approach or an **analytical** approach to a problem. Ewing (1977: 69) noted that analytical or "systematic" thinkers "generally excel in problems that call for planning and organization, as when one set of numbers must be worked out before another can be analyzed." On the other hand, he went on, "intuitive thinkers are likely to excel if the problem is elusive and difficult to define. They keep coming up with different possibilities, follow their hunches, and don't commit themselves too soon." Sternberg and Davidson (1982) found that "insight"—making inductive leaps beyond the given data—is an indispensable factor of what we call "intelligence," much of which is traditionally defined in terms of analysis.

All this suggests that intuition forms an essential component of our total intellectual endeavor. In looking at the contrasting role of intuition and analysis in educational systems in general, Bruner and Clinchy (1966: 71) said, "Intuition is less rigorous with respect to proof, more visual or 'iconic,' more oriented to the whole problem than to particular parts, less verbalized with respect to justification, and based on a confidence in one's ability to operate with insufficient data."

One of the important characteristics of intuition is its nonverbalizability; often, persons are not able to give much verbal explanation of why they have made a particular decision or solution. The implications for teaching are clear. We daily face problems in language teaching that have no ready analysis, no available language or metalanguage to capture the essence of why a particular decision was made. Many good teachers cannot verbalize why they do what they do, in a specific and analytical way, yet they remain good teachers.

Intuition involves a certain kind of risk-taking. As we saw in Chapter 6, language learners need to take risks willingly. Language teachers must be willing to risk techniques or assessments that have their roots in a "gut feeling," a hunch, that they are right. In our universe of complex theory, we still perceive vast black holes of unanswerable questions about how people best learn second languages. Intuition, "the making of good guesses in situations where one has neither an answer nor an algorithm for obtaining it" (Baldwin 1966: 84), fills the void.

There is ample evidence that good language teachers have developed good intuition. In an informal study of cognitive styles among ESL learners a few years ago, I asked their teachers to predict the TOEFL score that each of their students would attain when they sat for the TOEFL the following week. The teachers had been with their students for only one semester, yet their predicted scores and the actual TOEFL results yielded the highest (+.90) correlations in the whole study.

How do you "learn" intuition? There is no simple answer to this question, yet some ingredients of a rationale are apparent:

1. First, you need to internalize essential theoretical foundations like those we have been grappling with throughout this book. Intuition is not developed in a vacuum. It is the product, in part, of a firm grounding in what is known, in analytical terms, about how people learn languages and why some people do not learn languages.

2. Second, there is no substitute for the experience of standing on your own two feet (or sitting down!) in the presence of real learners in the real world. Intuitions are formed at the crossroads of knowledge and experience. As you face those day-by-day, or even minute-by-minute, struggles of finding out who your learners are, deciding what to teach them, and designing ways to teach, you learn by trial, by error, and by success. You cannot be a master teacher the first time you teach a class. Your failures, near failures, partial successes, and successes all teach you intuition. They teach you to sense what will work and what will not work.

3. A third principle of intuition learning follows from the second. You must be a willing risk-taker yourself. Let the creative juices within you flow freely. The wildest and craziest ideas should be entertained openly and valued positively. In so doing, intuition will be allowed to germinate and to grow to full fruition.

Our search for an adequate theory of SLA can become thwarted by overzealous attempts to find analytical solutions. We may be looking too hard to find the ultimate system. As Schumann (1982a) said, at times we need to feel, ironically, that our own ideas are unimportant. That way we avoid the panicky feeling that what we do today in class is somehow going to be permanently etched in the annals of foreign language history. The relevance of theory can be perceived by adopting an essential attitude of self-confidence in our ability to form hunches that will probably be "right." We teachers are human. We are not fail-safe, preprogrammed robots. We therefore need to become willing risk-takers.

Out on a Limb:
The Ecology of Language Acquisition

This final end-of-chapter vignette is not directed, in the usual fashion, toward classroom methodology. Rather, it is simply the product of some of my right-brain musings as I have struggled over the years with the complexities of the kinds of models of SLA that have been described in this chapter. Such models, in their graphic or flow chart form (Bialystok's model in Figure 10.2 on page 285, for example), always appear to be so mechanical. Some of them more closely resemble the wiring diagrams pasted on the back of electric stoves than what I like to imagine the human brain must "look" like. Or certainly than the way our *organic* world operates!

So, heeding my sometimes rebellious spirit, I was moved one day in a SLA class I was teaching to create a different "picture" of language acquisition: one that responded not so much to rules of logic, mathematics, and physics, as to botany and ecology. The germination (pun intended) of my picture was the metaphor once used by Derek Bickerton in a lecture at the University of Hawaii about his contention that human beings are "bioprogrammed" for language (see Bickerton's [1981] *The Roots of Language*), perhaps not unlike the bioprogram of a flower seed, whose genetic makeup predisposes it to deliver, in successive stages, roots, stem, branches, leaves, and flowers. In a burst of wild artistic energy, I went out on a limb to extend the flower-seed metaphor to language acquisition. My picture of the "ecology" of language acquisition is in Figure 10.3.

At the risk of overstating what may already be obvious, I will nevertheless indulge in a few comments. The rain clouds of input stimulate seeds of predisposition (innate, genetically transmitted processes). But the potency of that input is dependent on the appropriate styles and strategies that a person puts into action (here represented as soil). Upon the germination of language abilities (notice not all the seeds of predisposition are effectively activated), networks of competence (which, like underground roots, cannot be observed from above the ground) build and grow stronger as the organism actively engages in comprehension and production of language. The resulting root system (inferred competence) is what we commonly call intake. Notice that several factors distinguish input from intake. Through the use of further strategies and affective abilities, coupled with the feedback we receive from others (note the tree trunk), we ultimately develop full-flowering communicative abilities. The fruit of our performance (or output) is of

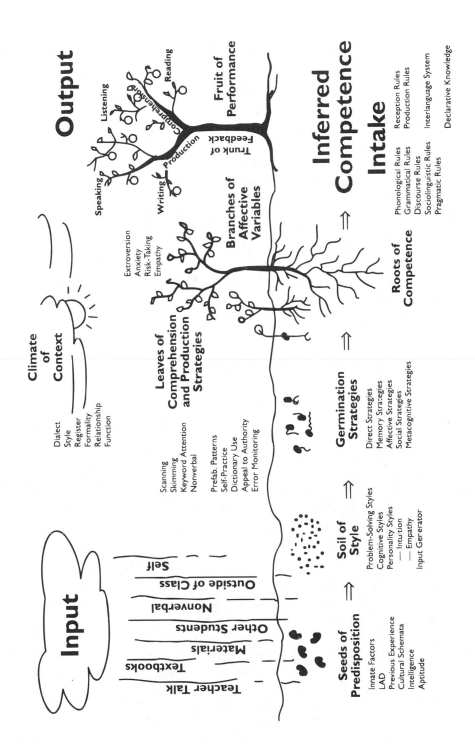

Figure 10.3. The ecology of language acquisition (Brown 1991)

course conditioned by the climate of innumerable contextual variables.

At any point the horticulturist (teacher) can irrigate to create better input, apply fertilizers for richer soil, encourage the use of effective strategies and affective enhancers, and, in the greenhouses of our classrooms, control the contextual climate for optimal growth!

No, this is not the kind of extended metaphor that one can "prove" or verify through empirical research. But, lest you scoff at such outlandish depictions, think about how many factors in SLA theory are conceptualized and described metaphorically: language acquisition *device, pivot* and *open* words, Piaget's *equilibration, cognitive pruning,* Ausubel's *subsumption, transfer, social distance, global* and *local errors, monitoring, affective filter, automatic* and *controlled* processing. If a metaphor enables us to describe a phenomenon clearly and to apply it wisely, then we can surely entertain it—as long as we understand that these word-pictures are usually subject to certain breakdowns when logically extended too far. (For comments about metaphor in SLA theory, see Lantolf 1996)

So, while you might exercise a little caution in drawing a tight analogy between Earth's botanical cycles and language learning, you might just allow yourself to think of second language learners as budding flowers—as plants needing your nurture and care. When the scientific flow charts and technical terminology of current second language research become excruciatingly painful to understand, try creating your own metaphors, perhaps! Play the believing game, and enjoy it.

TOPICS AND QUESTIONS FOR STUDY AND DISCUSSION

[Note: (I) Individual work; (G) group or pair work; (C) whole-class discussion.]

1. (G) In the first part of this chapter on pages 274 and 275, Lightbown's (1985) ten generalizations about SLA are listed. In pairs or small groups (if numbers permit) assign one generalization to each pair/group with the task of (a) explaining the generalization further, (b) offering any caveats or "it depends" statements about it, and (c) citing an example or two of the generalization in the language classroom.
2. (G) Likewise (see item 1 above), look at the six "myths" (page 275). In small groups, figure out (a) why it is a myth, (b) caveats or comments that qualify the statement, and (c) some examples or counter-examples in the language classroom.
3. (I) Review the major tenets of the three schools of thought outlined in Chapter 1 and referred to throughout the book: structuralism–behav-

iorism, rationalism–cognitivism, constructivism. Do Krashen's Input Hypothesis and the cognitive models of people like McLaughlin and Bialystok and Ellis fit the second school of thought? How so? Ask the same questions about Long's Interaction Hypothesis for the third school.

4. (C) Review the five tenets of Krashen's Input Hypothesis. Which ones are most plausible? least plausible? How would you take the "best" of his theories and apply them in the classroom and yet still be mindful of the various problems inherent in his ideas about SLA? How do Larsen-Freeman's caveats about chaos theory and Long's criteria (pages 276 and 277) enlighten your evaluation of Krashen's model?

5. (G) In pairs, each assigned to one topic below, think of examples in learning a foreign language (inside or outside a classroom) that illustrate: (a) HIGs and LIGs, (b) McLaughlin's focal and peripheral processes, (c) McLaughlin's controlled and automatic stages, (d) implicit and explicit linguistic knowledge, (e) interaction as the basis of acquisition.

6. (I/G/C) If you have quite a bit of time, try devising a "model" of SLA that doesn't use prose as much as a visual, graphic, or kinesthetic metaphor. For example, you might create an SLA board game in which players have to throw dice and pass through the "pits of puberty," the "mire of mistakes," the "falls of fossilization," and so on. Or, you could create a chart something like Bialystok's (Figure 10.2, page 285) model. Do this individually, or in pairs/groups, for "homework," then share your creation with the rest of the class. Try to defend your model on the basis of at least some of the criteria for a viable theory presented by Larsen-Freeman or Long (pages 276 and 277).

7. (G/C) Suppose you have been invited to an international symposium on SLA, the goal of which is to devise a theory of SLA. Each person can bring three and only three tenets or generalizations to be included in the theory. In groups or pairs, decide on three such tenets (or, at least, domains of consideration) that you consider the most important to include. Defend your three on the basis of Larsen-Freeman's or Long's lists, if appropriate, found on pages 276 and 277. Share findings with the class and see if the class can create a composite picture of the most important features of a theory of SLA.

8. (I) Consider some of the controversies that have been discussed in this book: innateness, defining intelligence, the Whorfian hypothesis, the strong version of the Contrastive Analysis Hypothesis, Krashen's Input Hypothesis, and others. Play the believing game with what might be labeled the "unpopular side" of the controversy. How does it feel? How does it help to put things into balance? In what way are both games necessary for ultimate understanding?

9. (I) Go back to the definitions of language, learning, and teaching that

you formulated at the beginning of this book. How might you revise those definitions now?

10. (G) Pairs or groups should each make a list of characteristics of a "successful language teacher." What steps do you think you could take to train yourself to be more successful? That is, what are your weaknesses and strengths, and how might you work on those weaknesses from what you know so far about foreign language teaching?

SUGGESTED READINGS

TESOL Quarterly, Winter 1990 issue.

This issue was entirely given over to the scope and form of theories of SLA. Articles by leading theorists (McLaughlin, Bialystok, Long, Schumann, Spolsky, and others) provided a good sense of issues in theory-making.

Krashen, Stephen. 1997. *Foreign Language Education: The Easy Way.* Culver City, CA: Language Education Associates.

For a quick, popularized version of Krashen's ideas about SLA, pick up this little 62-page tract written for classroom teachers.

Ellis, Rod. 1997. *SLA Research and Language Teaching.* Oxford: Oxford University Press.

Ellis, Rod. 1994. "A theory of instructed second language acquisition." In Ellis, Nick (Ed.). 1994b. *Implicit and Explicit Learning of Language.* London: Academic Press. (pp. 79–114).

Rod Ellis's proposal for a theory of instructed second language acquisition gives a good picture of his view of the role of input and interaction and implicit and explicit knowledge in SLA. An earlier version of his theory is presented in the 1994 article.

Modern Language Journal, Fall 1998 issue.

This issue consists of six articles on the topic of input and interaction in second language acquisition. Most of these are not difficult, technical reading. The lead article by Gass, Mackey, and Pica offers an informative overview.

Lantolf, James P. 1996. "SLA theory building: Letting all the flowers bloom!" *Language Learning* 46: 713–749.

Lantolf presents some tough but rewarding reading on the place of metaphor in SLA theories, with a balanced perspective on theories in SLA and other disciplines.

LANGUAGE LEARNING EXPERIENCE: FINAL JOURNAL ENTRY

[Note: See pages 18 and 19 of Chapter 1 for general guidelines for writing a journal on a previous or concurrent language learning experience.]

- At the beginning of the chapter, nine statements were made that correspond to the previous nine chapters in this book. Choose two or three of those nine (more if you have time), and write about your own language learning experience in relation to the topic.
- What do you think, in your own experience as a language learner, is the most useful aspect of Krashen's Input Hypothesis, and what is the least useful?
- Think of an example in your own learning of each of McLaughlin's four cells: (1) Focal-controlled; (2) Peripheral-controlled; (3) Focal-automatic; (4) Peripheral-automatic. Write them in your journal in a chart format and comment.
- If you didn't do item 5 on page 297 for class, take on that assignment of creating a largely nonverbal model of SLA.
- Given everything you now know about learning a second language, what are the characteristics of a successful teacher? How did your own foreign language teacher measure up?
- What did you like the most about writing this journal? the least? What benefit did you gain from the journal-writing process?

BIBLIOGRAPHY

Abraham, Roberta G. 1981. The relationship of cognitive style to the use of grammatical rules by Spanish-speaking ESL students in editing written English. Unpublished doctoral dissertation, University of Illinois at Champaign-Urbana.

Abraham, Roberta G. 1985. Field independence-dependence and the teaching of grammar. *TESOL Quarterly 19:* 689–702.

Acton, William. 1979. Second language learning and perception of difference in attitude. Unpublished doctoral dissertation, University of Michigan.

Adamson, H.D. 1988. *Variation Theory and Second Language Acquisition.* Washington, DC: Georgetown University Press.

Adler, Peter S. 1972. Culture shock and the cross cultural learning experience. *Readings in Intercultural Education, Volume 2.* Pittsburgh: Intercultural Communication Network.

Alatis, James E. (Ed.). 1990. *Georgetown University Round Table on Languages and Linguistics 1990.* Washington, DC: Georgetown University Press.

Alatis, James (Ed.). 1993. *Strategic Interaction and Language Acquisition: Theory, Practice, and Research.* Washington, DC: Georgetown University Press.

Alderson, J. Charles. 1991. Language testing in the 1990s: How far have we come? How much further do we have to go? In Anivan 1991.

Allwright, Richard L. 1975. Problems in the study of teachers' treatment of learner error. In Burt & Dulay 1975.

Allwright, Richard L. 1980. Turns, topics, and tasks: Patterns of participation in language learning and teaching. In Larsen-Freeman 1980.

Alpert, R. and Haber, R. 1960. Anxiety in academic achievement situations. *Journal of Abnormal and Social Psychology 61:* 207–215.

Alptekin, C. and Atakan. S. 1990. Field dependence-independence and hemisphericity as variables in L2 achievement. *Second Language Research 6:* 135–149.

American Council on the Teaching of Foreign Languages (ACTFL). 1982. *ACTFL Provisional Proficiency Guidelines.* Hastings-on-Hudson, NY: *ACTFL.*

Andersen, Roger W. 1978. An implicational model for second-language research. *Language Learning 28:* 221–282.

Andersen, Roger W. 1979. Expanding Schumann's pidginization hypothesis. *Language Learning 29:* 105–119.

Andersen, Roger W. (Ed.). 1981. *New Dimensions in Second Language Acquisition Research.* Rowley, MA: Newbury House.

Andersen, Roger W. 1982. Determining the linguistic attributes of language attrition. In Lambert & Freed 1982.

Anderson, Neil J. 1991. Individual differences in strategy use in second language reading and testing. *Modern Language Journal 75:* 460–472.

Anderson, Richard C. and Ausubel, David A. (Eds.). 1965. *Readings in the Psychology of Cognition.* New York: Holt, Rinehart & Winston.

Andrés, Verónica. 1999. Self-esteem in the classroom or the metamorphosis of butterflies. In Arnold 1999.

Angelis, Paul and Henderson, Thelma (Eds.). 1989. Selected papers from the proceedings of the BAAL/AAAL joint seminar "Communicative Competence Revisited." *Applied Linguistics 10* (June).

Anivan, S. (Ed.). 1991. *Current Developments in Language Testing.* Singapore: SEAMEO Regional Language Center.

Anthony, Edward M. 1963. Approach, method and technique. *English Language Teaching 17:* 63–67.

Armstrong, Thomas. 1993. *Seven Kinds of Smart.* New York: Penguin Books.

Armstrong, Thomas. 1994. *Multiple Intelligences in the Classroom.* Philadelphia: Association for Curriculum Development.

Arnold, Jane (Ed.). 1999. *Affect in Language Learning.* Cambridge: Cambridge University Press.

Asher, James. 1977. *Learning Another Language Through Actions: The Complete Teacher's Guidebook.* Los Gatos, CA: Sky Oaks Productions.

Au, S.Y. 1988. A critical appraisal of Gardner's social-psychological theory of second language learning. *Language Learning 38:* 75–100.

Auerbach, Elsa. 1995. The politics of the ESL classroom: Issues of power in pedagogical choices. In Tollefson 1995.

Augustine, St. 1838. *Confessions.* Translated by Edward B. Pusey. Oxford: J.C. Parker Company.

Austin, John L. 1962. *How to Do Things with Words.* Cambridge: Harvard University Press.

Ausubel, David A. 1963. Cognitive structure and the facilitation of meaningful verbal learning. *Journal of Teacher Education 14:* 217–221.

Ausubel, David A. 1964. Adults vs. children in second language learning: Psychological considerations. *Modern Language Journal 48:* 420–424.

Ausubel, David A. 1965. Introduction to part one. In Anderson & Ausubel 1965.

Ausubel, David A. 1968. *Educational Psychology: A Cognitive View.* New York: Holt, Rinehart & Winston.

Bachman, Lyle F. 1982. The trait structure of cloze test scores. *TESOL Quarterly 16:* 61–70.

Bachman, Lyle F. 1984. The TOEFL as a measure of communicative competence. Paper delivered at the Second TOEFL Invitational Conference, Educational Testing Service, Princeton, NJ, October 1984.

Bachman, Lyle F. 1988. Problems in examining the validity of the ACTFL oral proficiency interview. *Studies in Second Language Acquisition 10:* 149–164.

Bachman, Lyle F. 1990. *Fundamental Considerations in Language Testing.* New York: Oxford University Press.

Bachman, Lyle F. 1991. What does language testing have to offer? *TESOL Quarterly 25:* 671–704.

Bachman, Lyle F. and Palmer, Adrian. 1981. The construct validation of the FSI oral interview. *Language Learning 31:* 67–86.

Bachman, Lyle F. and Palmer, Adrian. 1982. The construct validation of some components of communicative proficiency. *TESOL Quarterly 16:* 449–465.

Bacon, Susan M. 1992. The relationship between gender, comprehension, processing strategies, and cognitive and affective response in foreign language listening. *Modern Language Journal 76:* 160–178.

Bailey, Kathleen M. 1983. Competitiveness and anxiety in adult second language learning: Looking at and through the diary studies. In Seliger & Long 1983.

Bailey, Kathleen M. 1985. Classroom-centered research on language teaching and learning. In Celce-Murcia 1985.

Bailey, Kathleen M. 1986. Class lecture, Spring 1986. Monterey Institute of International Studies.

Baldwin, Alfred. 1966. The development of intuition. In Bruner 1966a.

Banathy, Bela, Trager, Edith C., and Waddle, Carl D. 1966. The use of contrastive data in foreign language course development. In Valdman 1966.

Bandura, Albert and Walters, Richard H. 1963. *Social Learning and Personality Development.* New York: Holt, Rinehart & Winston.

Bar Adon, A. and Leopold, Werner F. (Eds.). 1971. *Child Language: A Book of Readings.* Englewood Cliffs, NJ: Prentice-Hall.

Bateson, Gregory. 1972. *Steps to an Ecology of Mind.* New York: Ballantine Books.

Bayley, Robert and Preston, Dennis (Eds.). 1996. *Second Language Acquisition and Linguistic Variation.* Philadelphia and Amsterdam: John Benjamins Publishing Company.

Beebe, Leslie M. 1983. Risk-taking and the language learner. In Seliger & Long 1983.

Beebe, Leslie M. (Ed.). 1988. *Issues in Second Language Acquisition: Multiple Perspectives.* New York: Newbury House.

Bellugi, Ursula and Brown, Roger (Eds.). 1964. *The Acquisition of Language.* Monographs of the Society for Research in Child Development, Number 29 (Serial Number 92).

Berko, Jean. 1958. The child's learning of English morphology. *Word 14:* 150–177.

Berko-Gleason, Jean. 1982. Insights from child acquisition for second language loss. In Lambert & Freed 1982.

Berko-Gleason, Jean. 1985. *The Development of Language.* New York: Charles E. Merrill.

Berko-Gleason, Jean. 1988. Language and socialization. In Kessel 1988.

Berns, Margie S. 1984a. Functional approaches to language and language teaching: Another look. In Savignon & Berns 1984.

Berns, Margie S. 1984b. Review of Finocchiaro and Brumfit 1983. *TESOL Quarterly 18:* 325–329.

Berns, Margie S. 1990. *Contexts of Competence: Social and Cultural Considerations in Communicative Language Teaching.* New York: Plenum Press.

Bialystok, Ellen. 1978. A theoretical model of second language learning. *Language Learning 28:* 69–83.

Bialystok, Ellen. 1981. Some evidence for the integrity and interaction of two knowledge sources. In Andersen 1981.

Bialystok, Ellen. 1982. On the relationship between knowing and using linguistic forms. *Applied Linguistics 3:* 181–206.

Bialystok, Ellen. 1983. Inferencing: Testing the "hypothesis testing" hypothesis. In Seliger & Long 1983.

Bialystok, Ellen. 1985. The compatibility of teaching and learning strategies. *Applied Linguistics 6:* 255–262.

Bialystok, Ellen. 1990a. *Communication Strategies: A Psychological Analysis of Second Language Use.* Oxford: Blackwell.

Bialystok, Ellen. 1990b. The dangers of dichotomy: A reply to Hulstijn. *Applied Linguistics 11:* 46–52.

Bialystok, Ellen. 1997. The structure of age: In search of barriers to second language acquisition. *Second Language Research 13:* 116–137.

Bialystok, Ellen and Bouchard-Ryan, E. 1985. A metacognitive framework for the development of first and second language skills. In Forrest-Pressley et al. 1985.

Bialystok, Ellen and Mitterer, J. 1987. Metalinguistic differences among three kinds of readers. *Journal of Educational Psychology 79:* 147–153.

Bickerton, Derek. 1981. *Roots of Language.* Ann Arbor, MI: Karoma Publishers.

Bierce, Ambrose. 1967. *The Devil's Dictionary.* New York: Doubleday.

Blair, Robert W. (Ed.). 1982. *Innovative Approaches to Language Teaching.* Rowley, MA: Newbury House.

Blatchford, Charles H. and Schachter, Jacqueline (Eds.). 1978. *On TESOL 78: EFL Policies, Programs, Practices.* Washington, DC: Teachers of English to Speakers of Other Languages.

Bley-Vroman, Robert. 1988. The fundamental character of foreign language learning. In Rutherford & Sharwood-Smith 1988.

Bloom, Lois. 1971. Why not pivot grammar? *Journal of Speech and Hearing Disorders 36:* 40–50.

Bloom, Lois (Ed.). 1978. *Readings in Language Development.* New York: John Wiley & Sons.

Bolinger, Dwight. 1975. *Aspects of Language.* Second Edition. New York: Harcourt Brace Jovanovich.

Bongaerts, Theo and Poulisse, Nanda. 1989. Communication strategies in L1 and L2: Same or different? *Applied Linguistics 10:* 253-268.

Bongaerts, Theo, Planken, Brigitte, and Schils, Erik. 1995. Can late starters attain a native accent in a foreign language? A test of the critical period hypothesis. In Singleton & Lengyel 1995.

Bowen, J. Donald. 1975. *Patterns of English Pronunciation.* Rowley, MA: Newbury House.

Bowen, J. Donald, Madsen, Harold, and Hilferty, Ann. 1985. *TESOL Techniques and Procedures.* Rowley, MA: Newbury House.

Braine, Martin D.S. 1965. On the basis of phrase structure: A reply to Bever, Fodor, and Weksel. *Psychological Review 72:* 153-159.

Breen, Michael P. and Candlin, Christopher N. 1980. The essentials of a communicative curriculum in language teaching. *Applied Linguistics 1:* 89-112.

Briere, Eugene J. and Hinofotis, Frances B. 1979. *Concepts in Language Testing: Some Recent Studies.* Washington, DC: Teachers of English to Speakers of Other Languages.

Brodkey, Dean and Shore, Howard. 1976. Student personality and success in an English language program. *Language Learning 26:* 153-159.

Brown, H. Douglas. 1970. English relativization and sentence comprehension in child language. Unpublished doctoral dissertation, University of California, Los Angeles.

Brown, H. Douglas. 1971. Children's comprehension of relativized English sentences. *Child Development 42:* 1923-1936.

Brown, H. Douglas. 1972. Cognitive pruning and second language acquisition. *Modern Language Journal 56:* 218-222.

Brown, H. Douglas. 1973. Affective variables in second language acquisition. *Language Learning 23:* 231-244.

Brown, H. Douglas (Ed.). 1976a. Papers in second language acquisition. *Language Learning, Special Issue Number 4.* Ann Arbor, MI: Research Club in Language Learning.

Brown, H. Douglas. 1976b. What is applied linguistics? In Wardhaugh & Brown 1976.

Brown, H. Douglas. 1977a. Cognitive and affective characteristics of good language learners. In Henning 1977.

Brown, H. Douglas. 1977b. Some limitations of C-L/CLL models of second language teaching. *TESOL Quarterly 11:* 365-372.

Brown, H. Douglas. 1980. The optimal distance model of second language acquisition. *TESOL Quarterly 14:* 157-164.

Brown, H. Douglas. 1989. *A Practical Guide to Language Learning.* New York: McGraw-Hill.

Brown, H. Douglas. 1990. M & Ms for language classrooms? Another look at motivation. In Alatis 1990.

Brown, H. Douglas. 1991. *Breaking the Language Barrier.* Yarmouth, ME: Intercultural Press.

Brown, H. Douglas. 1994. *Teaching by Principles: An Interactive Approach to Language Pedagogy.* Englewood Cliffs, NJ: Prentice Hall Regents. Second Edition: White Plains, NY: Longman, forthcoming.

Brown, H. Douglas. 1998. *New Vistas* series: *Getting Started.* 1999, *Books 1 and 2:* Upper Saddle River, NJ: Prentice Hall Regents. 2000, *Book 3.* White Plains, NY: Longman. *Book 4*, forthcoming.

Brown, H. Douglas. 1999. *New Vistas: Getting Started, Books 1* and *2. Teacher's Resource Manuals.* Upper Saddle River, NJ: Prentice Hall Regents.

Brown, H. Douglas. In press. *Strategies for Success: A Practical Guide.* White Plains, NY: Longman.

Brown, H. Douglas, Yorio, Carlos A., and Crymes, Ruth H. (Eds.). 1977. *Teaching and Learning English as a Second Language: Trends in Research and Practice. On TESOL* 77. Washington, DC: Teachers of English to Speakers of Other Languages.

Brown, James D. and Bailey, Kathleen M. 1984. A categorical instrument for scoring second language writing skills. *Language Learning 34:* 21–42.

Brown, Roger. 1966. The "tip of the tongue" phenomenon. *Journal of Verbal Learning and Verbal Behavior 5:* 325–337.

Brown, Roger. 1973. *A First Language: The Early Stages.* Cambridge: Harvard University Press.

Brown, Roger and Bellugi, Ursula. 1964. Three processes in the child's acquisition of syntax. *Harvard Educational Review 34:* 133–151.

Brown, Roger and Hanlon, C. 1970. Derivational complexity and order of acquisition in child speech. In Hayes 1970.

Brumfit, Christopher. 1992. Review of Stephen Krashen's *Language Acquisition and Language Education* (1989). *Applied Linguistics 13:* 123–125.

Bruner, Jerome (Ed.). 1966a. *Learning About Learning.* Washington, DC: U. S. Government Printing Office.

Bruner, Jerome S. 1966b. *Toward a Theory of Instruction.* New York: W. W. Norton.

Bruner, Jerome and Clinchy, Blythe. 1966. Towards a disciplined intuition. In Bruner 1966a.

Bruner, Jerome S., Olver, Rose, and Greenfield, P. (Eds.). 1966. *Studies in Cognitive Growth.* New York: John Wiley & Sons.

Buczowska, Ewa and Weist, Richard M. 1991. The effects of formal instruction on the second language acquisition of temporal location. *Language Learning 41:* 535–554.

Budwig, N. 1995. *A Developmental-Functionalist Approach to Child Language.* Mahwah, NJ: Lawrence Erlbaum Associates.

Burling, Robbins. 1970. *Man's Many Voices.* New York: Holt, Rinehart & Winston.

Burt, Marina K. 1975. Error analysis in the adult EFL classroom. *TESOL Quarterly 9:* 53–63.

Burt, Marina K. and Dulay, Heidi. 1975. *New Directions in Second Language Learning, Teaching, and Bilingual Education. On TESOL '75.* Washington, DC: Teachers of English to Speakers of Other Languages.

Burt, Marina K. and Kiparsky, Carol. 1972. *The Gooficon: A Repair Manual for English.* Rowley, MA: Newbury House.

Burt, Marina K., Dulay, Heidi C., and Finocchiaro, Mary (Eds.). 1977. *Viewpoints on English as a Second Language.* New York: Regents Publishing Company.

Busch, Deborah. 1982. Introversion-extroversion and the EFL proficiency of Japanese students. *Language Learning 32:* 109-132.

Byrnes, Heidi. 1998. *Learning Foreign and Second Languages: Perspectives in Research and Scholarship.* New York: The Modern Language Association of America.

Cairns, E. and Cammock, T. 1989. The 20-item matching familiar figures test: Technical data. Unpublished manuscript, University of Ulster, Coleraine.

California State Department of Education. 1986. *Schooling and Language Minority Students: A Theoretical Framework.* Sacramento, CA: Department of Education.

Campbell, D.T. and Fiske, D.W. 1959. Convergent and discriminant validation by the multitrait/multimethod matrix. *Psychological Bulletin 56:* 81-105.

Campbell, Russell. 1978. Notional-functional syllabuses 1978: Part I. In Blatchford & Schachter 1978.

Canale, Michael. 1983. From communicative competence to communicative language pedagogy. In Richards & Schmidt 1983.

Canale, Michael. 1984. Considerations in the testing of reading and listening proficiency. *Foreign Language Annals 17:* 349-357.

Canale, Michael and Swain, Merrill. 1980. Theoretical bases of communicative approaches to second language teaching and testing. *Applied Linguistics 1:* 1-47.

Carmichael, L., Hogan, H.P., and Walter, A.A. 1932. An experimental study of the effect of language on visually perceived form. *Journal of Experimental Psychology 15:* 73-86.

Carrell, Patricia L. 1982. Cohesion is not coherence. *TESOL Quarterly 16:* 479-488.

Carrell, Patricia L. 1986. A view of the written text as communicative interaction: Implications for reading in a second language. In Devine et al. 1986.

Carrell, Patricia, Prince, Moneta S., and Astika, Gusti G. 1996. Personality types and language learning in an EFL context. *Language Learning 46:* 75-99.

Carroll, David W. 1994. *Psychology of Language.* Pacific Grove, CA: Brooks/Cole Publishing Company.

Carroll, John B. (Ed.). 1956. *Language, Thought, and Reality: Selected Writings of Benjamin Lee Whorf.* Cambridge: M.I.T. Press.

Carroll, John B. 1961. *Fundamental Considerations in Testing for English Language Proficiency of Foreign Students.* Washington, DC: Center for Applied Linguistics.

Carroll, John B. and Sapon, Stanley M. 1958. *Modern Language Aptitude Test.* New York: The Psychological Corporation.

Carroll, Lewis. 1872. *Through the Looking Glass.* Boston: Lee & Shepard.

Carroll, Susanne and Meisel, Jurgen M. 1990. Universals and second language acquisition: Some comments on the state of current theory. *Studies in Second Language Acquisition 12:* 201–208.

Cathcart, Ruth L. and Olsen, Judy E.W.B. 1976. Teachers' and students' preferences for correction of classroom conversation errors. In Fanselow & Crymes 1976.

Celce-Murcia, Marianne (Ed.). 1985. *Beyond Basics: Issues and Research in TESOL.* Rowley, MA: Newbury House.

Celce-Murcia, Marianne (Ed.). 1991. *Teaching English as a Second or Foreign Language.* Second Edition. New York: Newbury House.

Celce-Murcia, Marianne and Hawkins, Barbara. 1985. Contrastive analysis, error analysis, and interlanguage analysis. In Celce-Murcia 1985.

Celce-Murcia, Marianne and McIntosh, Lois. 1979. *Teaching English as a Second or Foreign Language.* Rowley, MA: Newbury House.

Chaika, Elaine. 1989. *Language: The Social Mirror.* New York: Newbury House.

Chambers, Francine. 1997. What do we mean by fluency? *System 25:* 535–544.

Chamot, Anna U. and McKeon, Denise. 1984. *Second Language Teaching.* Rosslyn, VA: National Clearinghouse for Bilingual Education.

Chamot, Anna Uhl and O'Malley, Michael. 1986. *A Cognitive Academic Language Learning Approach: An ESL Content-based Curriculum.* Wheaton, MD: National Clearinghouse for Bilingual Education.

Chamot, Anna Uhl and O'Malley, Michael. 1987. The cognitive academic language learning approach: A bridge to the mainstream. *TESOL Quarterly 21:* 227–249.

Chamot, Anna Uhl, O'Malley, Michael, and Kupper, Lisa. 1992. *Building Bridges: Content and Learning Strategies for ESL. Books 1, 2, 3.* New York: Heinle & Heinle.

Chamot, Anna Uhl; Barnhart, Sarah; El-Dinary, Pamela Beard; and Robbins, Jill. 1999. *The Learning Strategies Handbook.* White Plains, NY: Longman.

Chapelle, Carol A. 1983. The relationship between ambiguity tolerance and success in acquiring English as a second language in adult learners. Unpublished doctoral dissertation, University of Illinois.

Chapelle, Carol. 1992. Disembedding "Disembedded Figures in the Landscape . . .": An appraisal of Griffiths and Sheen's "reappraisal of L2 research on field dependence/independence." 1992. *Applied Linguistics 13:* 375–384.

Chapelle, Carol and Abraham, Roberta G. 1990. Cloze method: What difference does it make? *Language Testing 7:* 121–146.

Chapelle, Carol and Green, Pat. 1992. Field independence/dependence in second language acquisition research. *Language Learning 42:* 47–83.

Chapelle, Carol A. and Roberts, Cheryl. 1986. Ambiguity tolerance and field independence as predictors of proficiency in English as a second language. *Language Learning 36:* 27–45.

Chesterfield, Ray and Chesterfield, Kathleen B. 1985. Natural order in children's use of second language learning strategies. *Applied Linguistics 6:* 45–59.

Chihara, Tetsuro and Oller, John W. 1978. Attitudes and proficiency in EFL: A sociolinguistic study of adult Japanese speakers. *Language Learning 28:* 55–68.

Chomsky, Noam. 1959. A review of B.F. Skinner's *Verbal Behavior. Language 35:* 26–58.

Chomsky, Noam. 1964. Current issues in linguistic theory. In Fodor & Katz 1964.

Chomsky, Noam. 1965. *Aspects of the Theory of Syntax.* Cambridge: M.I.T. Press.

Chomsky, Noam. 1966. Linguistic theory. In Mead 1966.

Chun, Ann E.; Day, Richard R.; Chenoweth, N. Ann; and Luppescu, Stuart. 1982. Types of errors corrected in native-nonnative conversations. *TESOL Quarterly 16:* 537–547.

Clark, Herbert H. and Clark, Eve V. 1977. *Psychology and Language: An Introduction to Psycholinguistics.* New York: Harcourt Brace Jovanovich.

Clark, John L.D. 1983. Language testing: Past and current status—directions for the future. *Modern Language Journal 67:* 431–443.

Clarke, Mark A. 1976. Second language acquisition as a clash of consciousness. *Language Learning 26:* 377–390.

Clarke, Mark A. 1982. On bandwagons, tyranny, and common sense. *TESOL Quarterly 16:* 437–448.

Clarke, Mark. 1990. Some cautionary observations on liberation education. *Language Arts 67:* 388–398.

Clarke, Mark. 1994. The dysfunctions of the theory/practice discourse. *TESOL Quarterly 28:* 9–26.

Clarke, Mark A. and Handscombe, Jean. 1982. *Pacific Perspectives on Language Learning and Teaching. On TESOL '82.* Washington, DC: Teachers of English to Speakers of Other Languages.

Clarke, Mark; Losoff, Ann; McCracken, Margaret Dickenson; and Rood, David S. 1984. Linguistic relativity and sex/gender studies: Epistemological and methodological considerations. *Language Learning 34:* 47–67.

Coffey, Margaret Pogemiller. 1983. *Fitting In: A Functional/Notional Text for Learners of English.* Englewood Cliffs, NJ: Prentice-Hall.

Cohen, Andrew. 1998. *Strategies in Learning and Using a Second Language.* New York: Addison Wesley Longman.

Cohen, Andrew D. and Aphek, Edna. 1981. Easifying second language learning. *Studies in Second Language Acquisition 3:* 221–236.

Coleman, Algernon. 1929. *The Teaching of Modern Foreign Languages in the United States: A Report Prepared for the Modern Language Study.* New York: Macmillan Company.

Comrie, Bernard. 1990. Second language acquisition and language universals research. *Studies in Second Language Acquisition 12:* 209–218.

Concise Columbia Encyclopedia. Third Edition. 1994. New York: Columbia University Press.

Condon, E.C. 1973. *Introduction to Cross Cultural Communication.* New Brunswick, NJ: Rutgers University Press.

Cook, Vivian. 1969. The analogy between first and second language learning. *International Review of Applied Linguistics 7:* 207–216.

Cook, Vivian. 1973. Comparison of language development in native children and foreign adults. *International Review of Applied Linguistics 11:* 13–28.

Cook, Vivian. 1993. *Linguistics and Second Language Acquisition.* New York: St. Martin's Press.

Cook, Vivian. 1995. Multi-competence and the effects of age. In Singleton & Lengyel 1995.

Cook, V. and Newson, M. 1996. *Chomsky's Universal Grammar: An Introduction.* Oxford: Blackwell.

Coopersmith, Stanley. 1967. *The Antecedents of Self-Esteem.* San Francisco: W.H. Freeman.

Corder, S. Pit. 1967. The significance of learners' errors. *International Review of Applied Linguistics 5:* 161–170.

Corder, S. Pit. 1971. Idiosyncratic dialects and error analysis. *International Review of Applied Linguistics 9:* 147–159.

Corder, S. Pit. 1973. *Introducing Applied Linguistics.* Harmondsworth, UK: Penguin Books.

Crawford, James. 1998. English only for the children? *TESOL Matters 8:* 20–21.

Croft, Kenneth (Ed.). 1980. *Readings on English as a Second Language.* Second Edition. Cambridge, MA: Winthrop Publishers.

Crookes, Graham. 1989. Planning and interlanguage variation. *Studies in Second Language Acquisition 11:* 367–384.

Crookes, Graham and Schmidt, Richard W. 1991. Motivation: Reopening the research agenda. *Language Learning 41:* 469–512.

Cummins, James. 1979. Cognitive/academic language proficiency, linguistic interdependence, the optimal age question and some other matters. *Working Papers on Bilingualism 19:* 197–205.

Cummins, James. 1980. The cross-lingual dimensions of language proficiency: Implications for bilingual education and the optimal age issue. *TESOL Quarterly 14:* 175–187.

Cummins, James. 1981. *The Role of Primary Language Development in Promoting Educational Success for Language Minority Students.* Sacramento: California State Department of Education, Office of Bilingual Bicultural Education.

Curran, Charles A. 1972. *Counseling-Learning: A Whole Person Model for Education.* New York: Grune & Stratton.

Curran, Charles A. 1976. *Counseling-Learning in Second Languages.* Apple River, IL: Apple River Press.

Curtiss, Susan. 1977. *Genie: A Psycholinguistic Study of a Modern-Day "Wild Child."* New York: Academic Press.

Cziko, Gary A. 1982. Improving the psychometric, criterion-referenced, and practical qualities of integrative language tests. *TESOL Quarterly 16:* 367–379.

D'Amico-Reisner, Lynne. 1983. An analysis of the surface structure of disapproval exchanges. In Wolfson & Judd 1983.

Danesi, Marcel. 1988. Neurological bimodality and theories of language teaching. *Studies in Second Language Acquisition 10:* 13–31.

Davidson, Fred, Hudson, Thom, and Lynch, Brian. 1985. Language testing: Operationalization in classroom measurement and L2 research. In Celce-Murcia 1985.

Davies, Alan. 1989. Is international English an interlanguage? *TESOL Quarterly 23:* 447–467.

Davies, Alan. 1990. *Principles of Language Testing.* Oxford: Blackwell.

Day, Cathy. 1982. The optimal distance model of acculturation and success in second language learning. Unpublished doctoral dissertation, University of Illinois, Champaign-Urbana.

Day, Richard R.; Chenoweth, N. Ann; Chun, Ann E.; and Luppescu, Stuart. 1984. Corrective feedback in native-nonnative discourse. *Language Learning 34:* 19–45.

de Bot, Kees. 1996. The psycholinguistics of the output hypothesis. *Language Learning 46:* 529–555.

Deci, Edward L. 1975. *Intrinsic Motivation.* New York: Plenum Press.

DeKeyser, Robert. 1995. Learning L2 grammar rules: An experiment with a miniature linguistic system. *Studies in Second Language Acquisition 17:* 379–410.

DeKeyser, Robert. 1997. Beyond explicit rule learning: Automatizing second language morphosyntax. *Studies in Second Language Acquisition 19:* 195–221.

De Vito, Joseph A. 1971. *Psycholinguistics.* Indianapolis: Bobbs-Merrill.

Devine, Joanne, Carrell, Patricia L., and Eskey, David E. (Eds.). 1986. *Research in Reading ESL.* Washington, DC: Teachers of English to Speakers of Other Languages.

Dewaele, J.-M. and Furnham, A. 1998. Extraversion: The unloved variable in applied linguistic research. Unpublished manuscript.

Dewey, John. 1910. *How We Think.* Boston: D.C. Heath Company.

Dieterich, Thomas G., Freeman, Cecilia, and Crandall, Jo Ann. 1979. A linguistic analysis of some English proficiency tests. *TESOL Quarterly 13:* 535–550.

Diller, Karl C. 1978. *The Language Teaching Controversy.* Rowley, MA: Newbury House.

Diller, Karl C. (Ed.). 1981. *Individual Differences and Universals in Language Learning Aptitude.* Rowley, MA: Newbury House.

Dirven, René and Pütz, Martin. 1993. Intercultural communication. *Language Teaching 26:* 144–156.

Dixon, T.R. and Horton, D.L. (Eds.). 1968. *Verbal Behavior and General Behavior Theory.* Englewood Cliffs, NJ: Prentice Hall.

Donahue, Meghan and Parsons, Adelaide Heyde. 1982. The use of roleplay to overcome cultural fatigue. *TESOL Quarterly 16:* 359–365.

Donne, John. 1624. *Devotions upon Emergent Occasions.* (Edited, with commentary by Anthony Raspa). 1975. Montreal: McGill-Queen's University Press.

Dörnyei, Zoltán. 1995. On the teachability of communication strategies. *TESOL Quarterly 29:* 55–84.

Dörnyei, Zoltán. 1998. Motivation in second and foreign language learning. *Language Teaching 31:* 117–135.

Dörnyei, Zoltán and Csizér, Kata. 1998. Ten commandments for motivating language learners: Results of an empirical study. *Language Teaching Research 2:* 203–229.

Doron, Sandra. 1973. Reflectivity-impulsivity and their influence on reading for inference for adult students of ESL. Unpublished manuscript, University of Michigan.

Doughty, Catherine. 1991. Second language instruction does make a difference: Evidence from an empirical study of SL relativization. *Studies in Second Language Acquisition 13:* 431–469.

Doughty, Catherine and Williams, Jessica. 1998. *Focus on Form in Classroom Second Language Acquisition.* New York: Cambridge University Press.

Douglas, Dan. 1988. Testing listening comprehension in the context of the ACTFL proficiency guidelines. *Studies in Second Language Acquisition 10:* 245–261.

Drach, K. 1969. The language of the parent: A pilot study. Working Paper Number 14, Language Behavior Research Laboratory, University of California, Berkeley.

Dresser, Norine. 1996. *Multicultural Manners: New Rules of Etiquette for a Changing Society.* New York: John Wiley & Sons.

Dufeu, B. 1994. *Teaching Myself.* Oxford: Oxford University Press.

Dulay, Heidi C. and Burt, Marina K. 1972. Goofing: An indicator of children's second language learning strategies. *Language Learning 22:* 235–252.

Dulay, Heidi C. and Burt, Marina K. 1974a. Errors and strategies in child second language acquisition. *TESOL Quarterly 8:* 129–136.

Dulay, Heidi C. and Burt, Marina K. 1974b. Natural sequences in child second language acquisition. *Language Learning 24:* 37–53.

Dulay, Heidi C. and Burt, Marina K. 1976. Creative construction in second language learning and teaching. *Language Learning, Special Issue Number 4:* 65–79.

Dulay, Heidi C., Burt, Marina K., and Hernandez-Ch., Eduardo. 1975. *Bilingual Syntax Measure.* New York: Harcourt Brace Jovanovich.

Dunn, Rita, Beaudry, Jeffrey S., and Klavas, Angela. 1989. Survey of research on learning styles. *Educational Leadership 32:* 50–58.

Duran, Richard P., with Canale, Michael; Penfield, Joyce; Stansfield, Charles W.; and Liskin-Gasparro, Judith E. 1985. TOEFL from a communicative viewpoint on language proficiency: A working paper. Princeton, NJ: Educational Testing Service.

Durkheim, Emile. 1897. *Le suicide.* Paris: F. Alcan.

Eckman, Fred R. 1977. Markedness and the contrastive analysis hypothesis. *Language Learning 27:* 315–330.

Eckman, Fred R. 1981. On the naturalness of interlanguage phonological rules. *Language Learning 31:* 195–216.

Eckman, Fred R. 1991. The structural conformity hypothesis and the acquisition of consonant clusters in the interlanguage of ESL learners. *Studies in Second Language Acquisition 13:* 23–41.

Edwards, Betty. 1979. *Drawing on the Right Side of the Brain.* Los Angeles: J.P. Tarcher/St. Martin's.

Ehrman, Madeline. 1989. Ants, grasshoppers, badgers, and butterflies: Qualitative and quantitative investigation of adult language learning styles and strategies. Unpublished doctoral dissertation, Union Institute.

Ehrman, Madeline. 1990. The role of personality type in adult language learning: An ongoing investigation. In Parry & Stansfield 1990.

Ehrman, Madeline E. 1993. Ego boundaries revisited: Toward a model of personality and learning. In Alatis 1993.

Ehrman, Madeline. 1996. *Understanding Second Language Learning Difficulties.* Thousand Oaks, CA: Sage Publications.

Ehrman, Madeline. 1999. Ego boundaries and tolerance of ambiguity in second language learning. In Arnold 1999.

Ehrman, Madeline and Oxford, Rebecca. 1989. Effects of sex differences, career choice, and psychological type on adult language learning strategies. *Modern Language Journal 73:* 1-13.

Ehrman, Madeline and Oxford, Rebecca. 1990. Adult language learning styles and strategies in an intensive training setting. *Modern Language Journal 74:* 311-327.

Ehrman, Madeline and Oxford, Rebecca L. 1995. Cognition plus: Correlates of language proficiency. *Modern Language Journal 79:* 67-89.

Elbow, Peter. 1973. *Writing Without Teachers.* New York: Oxford University Press. (Appendix Essay: "The doubting game and the believing game: An analysis of the intellectual enterprise.")

Elliott, A. Raymond. 1995a. Field independence/dependence, hemispheric specialization, and attitude in relation to pronunciation accuracy in Spanish as a foreign language. *Modern Language Journal 79:* 356-371.

Elliott, A. Raymond. 1995b. Foreign language phonology: Field independence, attitude, and the success of formal instruction in Spanish pronunciation. *Modern Language Journal 79:* 530-542.

Ellis, Gail and Sinclair, Barbara. 1989. *Learning to Learn English: A Course in Learner Training.* Cambridge: Cambridge University Press.

Ellis, Nick. 1994a. Implicit and explicit language learning: An overview. In Nick Ellis 1994b.

Ellis, Nick. 1994b. *Implicit and Explicit Learning of Language.* London: Academic Press.

Ellis, Rod. 1986. *Understanding Second Language Acquisition.* Oxford: Oxford University Press.

Ellis, Rod. 1987. *Second Language Acquisition in Context.* New York: Prentice-Hall.

Ellis, Rod. 1989. Sources of intra-learner variability in language use and their relationship to second language acquisition. In Gass et al. 1989.

Ellis, Rod. 1990a. A response to Gregg. *Applied Linguistics 11:* 384-391.

Ellis, Rod. 1990b. *Instructed Second Language Acquisition: Learning in the Classroom.* Cambridge, MA: Basil Blackwell.

Ellis, Rod. 1994a. A theory of instructed second language acquisition. In Nick Ellis 1994b.

Ellis, Rod. 1994b. *The Study of Second Language Acquisition.* Oxford: Oxford University Press.

Ellis, Rod. 1997. *SLA Research and Language Teaching.* Oxford: Oxford University Press.

Ely, Christopher M. 1986. An analysis of discomfort, risktaking, sociability, and motivation in the L2 classroom. *Language Learning 36:* 1–25.

Ervin-Tripp, Susan. 1974. Is second language learning like the first? *TESOL Quarterly 8:* 111–127.

Ewing, David W. 1977. Discovering your problem solving style. *Psychology Today 11:* 69–73.

Faerch, Claus and Kasper, Gabriele. 1983a. Plans and strategies in foreign language communication. In Faerch & Kasper 1983b.

Faerch, Claus and Kasper, Gabriele (Eds.). 1983b. *Strategies in Interlanguage Communication.* London: Longman.

Faerch, Claus and Kasper, Gabrielle. 1984. Two ways of defining communication strategies. *Language Learning 34:* 45–63.

Fanselow, John F. and Crymes, Ruth H. (Eds.). 1976. *On TESOL 76.* Washington, DC: Teachers of English to Speakers of Other Languages.

Fantini, Alvino E. 1997. *New Ways of Teaching Culture.* Alexandria, VA: Teachers of English to Speakers of Other Languages.

Farhady, Hossein. 1979. The disjunctive fallacy between discrete-point and integrative tests. *TESOL Quarterly 13:* 347–357.

Farhady, Hossein. 1982. Measures of language proficiency from the learner's perspective. *TESOL Quarterly 16:* 43–59.

Fast, Julius. 1970. *Body Language.* New York: M. Evans Company.

Fersh, Seymour (Ed.). 1974. *Learning About People and Cultures.* Evanston, IL: McDougal, Littel.

Finocchiaro, Mary. 1964. *English as a Second Language: From Theory to Practice.* New York: Simon & Schuster.

Finocchiaro, Mary and Brumfit, Christopher. 1983. *The Functional–Notional Approach: From Theory to Practice.* New York: Oxford University Press.

Firth, Alan and Wagner, Johannes. 1997. On discourse, communication, and (some) fundamental concepts in SLA research. *Modern Language Journal 81:* 285–300.

Flege, James E. 1981. The phonological basis of foreign accent: A hypothesis. *TESOL Quarterly 15:* 443–455.

Flege, James Emil. 1987. A critical period for learning to pronounce foreign languages? *Applied Linguistics 8:* 162–177.

Flynn, Suzanne. 1987. Contrast and construction in a parameter-setting model of L2 acquisition. *Language Learning 37:* 19–62.

Fodor, Jerry A. and Katz, Jerrold J. (Eds.). 1964. *The Structure of Language: Readings in the Philosophy of Language.* Englewood Cliffs, NJ: Prentice-Hall.

Forrest-Pressley, D.L., MacKinnon, G.E., and Waller, T.G. (Eds.). 1985. *Metacognition, Cognition, and Human Performance. Volume 1.* New York: Academic Press.

Foster, George M. 1962. *Traditional Cultures.* New York: Harper & Row.

Foster P. and Skehan, P. 1996. The influence of planning and task type on second language performance. *Studies in Second Language Acquisition 18:* 299–323.

Fotos, Sandra S. 1991. The cloze test as an integrative measure of EFL proficiency: A substitute for essays on college entrance examinations? *Language Learning 41:* 313–336.

Freire, Paolo. 1970. *Pedagogy of the Oppressed.* New York: Seabury Press.

Freud, Sigmund. 1920. *A General Introduction to Psychoanalysis.* New York: Liveright.

Fries, Charles C. 1945. *Teaching and Learning English as a Foreign Language.* Ann Arbor: University of Michigan Press.

Fries, Charles C. 1952. *The Structure of English.* New York: Harcourt, Brace, & World.

Gage, Nathan (Ed.). 1964. *Handbook of Research on Teaching.* Chicago: Rand McNally.

Gagné, Robert M. 1965. *The Conditions of Learning.* New York: Holt, Rinehart & Winston.

Gaies, Stephen J. 1983. Learner feedback: An exploratory study of its role in the second language classroom. In Seliger & Long 1983.

Ganschow, Leonore and Sparks, Richard L. 1996. Anxiety about foreign language learning among high school women. *Modern Language Journal 80:* 199–212.

Ganschow, Leonore; Sparks, Richard L.; Anderson, Reed; Jovorshy, James; Skinner, Sue; and Patton, Jon. 1994. Differences in language performance among high-, average-, and low-anxious college foreign language learners. *Modern Language Journal 78:* 41–55.

Gardner, Howard. 1983. *Frames of Mind: The Theory of Multiple Intelligences.* New York: Basic Books.

Gardner, Robert C. 1982. Social factors in language retention. In Lambert & Freed 1982.

Gardner, Robert C. 1985. *Social Psychology and Second Language Learning: The Role of Attitudes and Motivation.* London: Edward Arnold.

Gardner, Robert C. and Lambert, Wallace E. 1972. *Attitudes and Motivation in Second Language Learning.* Rowley, MA: Newbury House.

Gardner, Robert C. and MacIntyre, Peter D. 1991. An instrumental motivation in language study: Who says it isn't effective? *Studies in Second Language Acquisition 13:* 57–72.

Gardner, Robert C. and MacIntyre, Peter D. 1992. A student's contributions to second language learning. Part I: Cognitive variables. *Language Teaching 25:* 211–220.

Gardner, Robert C. and MacIntyre, Peter D. 1993a. A student's contributions to second language learning. Part II: Affective variables. *Language Teaching 26:* 1–11.

Gardner, Robert C. and MacIntyre, Peter D. 1993b. On the measurement of affective variables in second language learning. *Language Learning 43:* 157–194.

Gardner, Robert C., Day, J.B., and MacIntyre, Peter D. 1992. Integrative motivation, induced anxiety, and language learning in a controlled environment. *Studies in Second Language Acquisition 14:* 197–214.

Gass, Susan. 1989. Language universals and second language acquisition. *Language Learning 39:* 497–534.

Gass, Susan and Madden, Carolyn (Eds.). 1985. *Input in Second Language Acquisition.* Rowley, MA: Newbury House.

Gass, Susan and Selinker, Larry (Eds.). 1983. *Language Transfer in Language Learning.* Rowley, MA: Newbury House.

Gass, Susan and Varonis, Evangeline Marlos. 1994. Input, interaction, and second language production. *Studies in Second Language Acquisition 16:* 283–302.

Gass, Susan M., Mackey, Alison, and Pica, Teresa. 1998. The role of input and interaction in second language acquisition. *Modern Language Journal 82:* 299–305.

Gass, Susan; Madden, Carolyn; Preston, Dennis; and Selinker, Larry (Eds.). 1989. *Variation in Second Language Acquisition: Psycholinguistic Issues.* Clevedon, UK: Multilingual Matters.

Gatbonton, Elisabeth. 1983. Patterned phonetic variability in second language speech: A gradual diffusion model. In Robinett & Schachter 1983.

Gathercole, Virginia C. 1988. Some myths you may have heard about first language acquisition. *TESOL Quarterly 22:* 407–435.

Gattegno, Caleb. 1972. *Teaching Foreign Languages in Schools: The Silent Way.* Second Edition. New York: Educational Solutions.

Gattegno, Caleb. 1976. *The Common Sense of Teaching Foreign Languages.* New York: Educational Solutions.

Genesee, Fred. 1982. Experimental neuropsychological research on second language processing. *TESOL Quarterly 16:* 315–322.

Geschwind, Norman. 1970. The organization of language and the brain. *Science 170:* 940–944.

Gibbons, John. 1985. The silent period: An examination. *Language Learning 35:* 255–267.

Gleason, Henry A. 1961. *An Introduction to Descriptive Linguistics.* Revised Edition. New York: Holt, Rinehart & Winston.

Gleitman, Lila R. and Wanner, Eric. 1982. Language acquisition: The state of the state of the art. In Wanner & Gleitman 1982.

Goleman, Daniel. 1995. *Emotional Intelligence.* New York: Bantam Books.

Goodman, Kenneth S. 1970. Reading: A psycholinguistic guessing game. In Singer & Ruddell 1970.

Gouin, François. 1880. *L'art d'enseigner et d'étudier les langues.* Paris: Librairie Fischbacher.

Graham, C.R. 1984. Beyond integrative motivation: The development and influence of assimilative motivation. Paper presented at the TESOL Convention, Houston, TX, March 1984.

Greenberg, Joseph H. (Ed.). 1963. *Universals of Language.* Cambridge: M.I.T. Press.

Greenberg, Joseph H. 1966. *Language Universals.* The Hague: Mouton Publishers.

Gregg, Kevin R. 1984. Krashen's monitor and Occam's razor. *Applied Linguistics 5:* 79-100.

Gregg, Kevin R. 1990. The variable competence model of second language acquisition and why it isn't. *Applied Linguistics 11:* 364-383.

Gregg, Kevin. 1993. Taking explanation seriously: Or, let a couple of flowers bloom. *Applied Linguistics 14:* 276-294.

Grice, H.P. 1967. Logic and conversation. Unpublished manuscript, University of California, Berkeley.

Griffiths, Roger and Sheen, Ronald. 1992. Disembedded figures in the landscape: A reappraisal of L2 research on field dependence-independence. *Applied Linguistics 13:* 133-148.

Guidelines for the Preparation of Teachers of English to Speakers of Other Languages in the United States. 1975. Washington, DC: Teachers of English to Speakers of Other Languages.

Guiora, Alexander Z. 1981. Language, personality and culture, or the Whorfian hypothesis revisited. In Hines & Rutherford 1981.

Guiora, Alexander Z.; Acton, William R.; Erard, Robert; and Strickland, Fred W. 1980. The effects of benzodiazepine (Valium) on permeability of ego boundaries. *Language Learning 30:* 351-363.

Guiora, Alexander Z.; Beit Hallami, Benjamin; Brannon, Robert C.; Dull, Cecelia Y.; and Scovel, Thomas. 1972a. The effects of experimentally induced changes in ego states on pronunciation ability in second language: An exploratory study. *Comprehensive Psychiatry 13.*

Guiora, Alexander Z., Brannon, Robert C., and Dull, Cecilia Y. 1972b. Empathy and second language learning. *Language Learning 22:* 111-130.

Hakuta, Kenji. 1974. Prefabricated patterns and the emergence of structure in second language acquisition. *Language Learning 24:* 287-297.

Hakuta, Kenji. 1976. A case study of a Japanese child learning English as a second language. *Language Learning 26:* 326-351.

Hall, Edward. 1959. *The Silent Language.* New York: Doubleday.

Hall, Edward. 1966. *The Hidden Dimension.* New York: Doubleday.

Hall, Edward. 1974. Making sense without words. In Fersh 1974.

Halliday, Michael. 1973. *Explorations in the Functions of Language.* London: Edward Arnold.

Hammerly, Hector. 1985. *An Integrated Theory of Language Teaching.* Blaine, WA: Second Language Publications.

Han, Youngju and Ellis, Rod. 1998. Implicit knowledge, explicit knowledge, and general language proficiency. *Language Teaching Research 2:* 1-23.

Hansen, Jacqueline and Stansfield, Charles. 1981. The relationship of field dependent-independent cognitive styles to foreign language achievement. *Language Learning 31:* 349-367.

Hansen, Lynne. 1984. Field dependence-independence and language testing: Evidence from six Pacific island cultures. *TESOL Quarterly 18:* 311-324.

Hansen-Bede, Lynn. 1975. A child's creation of a second language. *Working Papers on Bilingualism 6:* 103-126.

Harley, Birgit and Hart, Doug. 1997. Language aptitude and second language proficiency in classroom learners of different starting ages. *Studies in Second Language Acquisition 19:* 379–400.

Harlow, Linda L. 1990. Do they mean what they say? Sociopragmatic competence and second language learners. *Modern Language Journal 74:* 328–351.

Hartnett, Dayle D. 1985. Cognitive style and second language learning. In Celce-Murcia 1985.

Hatch, Evelyn. 1978a. Discourse analysis and second language acquisition. In Hatch 1978b.

Hatch, Evelyn (Ed.). 1978b. *Second Language Acquisition.* Rowley, MA: Newbury House.

Hatch, Evelyn and Long, Michael H. 1980. Discourse analysis, what's that? In Larsen-Freeman 1980.

Hayes, J. (Ed.). 1970. *Cognition and the Development of Language.* New York: John Wiley & Sons.

Hendrickson, James M. 1980. Error correction in foreign language teaching: Recent theory, research, and practice. In Croft 1980.

Henning, Carol A. (Ed.). 1977. *Proceedings of the Los Angeles Second Language Research Forum.* Los Angeles: University of California at Los Angeles.

Heyde, Adelaide. 1979. The relationship between self-esteem and the oral production of a second language. Unpublished doctoral dissertation, University of Michigan.

Higgs, Theodore V. 1982. *Curriculum, Competence, and the Foreign Language Teacher.* ACTFL Foreign Language Education Series. Lincolnwood, IL: National Textbook Company.

Higgs, Theodore V. and Clifford, Ray. 1982. The push toward communication. In Higgs 1982.

Hilgard, Ernest. 1963. Motivation in learning theory. In Koch 1963.

Hill, Brian. 1994. Self-managed learning. *Language Teaching 27:* 213–223.

Hill, Jane. 1970. Foreign accents, language acquisition, and cerebral dominance revisited. *Language Learning 20:* 237–248.

Hill, Joseph. 1972. *The Educational Sciences.* Detroit: Oakland Community College.

Hines, Mary and Rutherford, William. 1981. *On TESOL '81.* Washington, DC: Teachers of English to Speakers of Other Languages.

Hladik, Ellen G. and Edwards, Harold T. 1984. A comparative analysis of mother-father speech in the naturalistic home environment. *Journal of Psycholinguistic Research 13:* 321–332.

Hoffman, Suzanne Q. 1997. Field dependence/independence in second language acquisition and implications for educators and instructional designers. *Foreign Language Annals 30:* 221–234.

Hofstede, Geert. 1986. Cultural differences in teaching and learning. *International Journal of Intercultural Relations 10:* 301–320.

Hogan, Robert. 1969. Development of an empathy scale. *Journal of Consulting and Clinical Psychology 33:* 307–316.

Holmes, Janet. 1989. Sex differences and apologies: One aspect of communicative competence. *Applied Linguistics 10:* 194–213.

Holmes, Janet. 1991. Language and gender. *Language Teaching 24:* 207–220.

Holmes, Janet. 1995. *Women, Men and Politeness.* White Plains, NY: Longman.

Holmes, Janet and Brown, Dorothy F. 1987. Teachers and students learning about compliments. *TESOL Quarterly 21:* 523–546.

Holzman, Mathilda. 1984. Evidence for a reciprocal model of language development. *Journal of Psycholinguistic Research 13:* 119–146.

Holzman, Mathilda. 1998. *The Language of Children.* Second Edition. Cambridge, MA: Blackwell.

Horstein, N. and Lightfoot, D. (Eds.). 1981. *Explanations in Linguistics: The Logical Problem of Language Acquisition.* New York: Longman.

Horwitz, Elaine K. 1990. Attending to the affective domain in the foreign language classroom. In Magnan 1990.

Horwitz, Elaine K. and Young, Dolly Jesusita (Eds.). 1991. *Language Anxiety: From Theory and Research to Classroom Implications.* Englewood Cliffs, NJ: Prentice-Hall.

Horwitz, E.K., Horwitz, M.B., and Cope, J. 1986. Foreign language classroom anxiety. *Modern Language Journal 70:* 125–132.

Huang, Xiao-hua and Van Naerssen, Margaret. 1987. Learning strategies for oral communication. *Applied Linguistics 8:* 287–307.

Hughes, Arthur. 1989. *Testing for Language Teachers.* Cambridge: Cambridge University Press.

Hulstijn, Jan H. 1990. A comparison between the information-processing and the analysis/control approaches to language learning. *Applied Linguistics 11:* 30–45.

Hymes, Dell. 1967. On communicative competence. Unpublished manuscript, University of Pennsylvania.

Hymes, Dell. 1972. On communicative competence. In Pride & Holmes 1972.

Hymes, Dell. 1974. *Foundations in Sociolinguistics: An Ethnographic Approach.* Philadelphia: University of Pennsylvania Press.

Jacobs, Bob. 1988. Neurological differentiation of primary and secondary language acquisition. *Studies in Second Language Acquisition 10:* 303–337.

Jacobs, Bob and Schumann, John. 1992. Language acquisition and the neurosciences: Towards a more integrative perspective. *Applied Linguistics 13:* 282–301.

Jakobovits, Leon. 1968. Implications of recent psycholinguistic developments for the teaching of a second language. *Language Learning 18:* 89–109.

James, Carl. 1990. Learner language. *Language Teaching 23:* 205–213.

James, Carl. 1998. *Errors in Language Learning and Use: Exploring Error Analysis.* Harlow, UK: Addison Wesley Longman.

James, William. 1890. *The Principles of Psychology. Volume 1.* New York: Henry Holt (Dover Publications 1950).

Jamieson, Joan. 1992. The cognitive styles of reflection/impulsivity and field independence and ESL success. *Modern Language Journal 76:* 491–501.

Jamieson, Joan and Chapelle, Carol. 1987. Working styles on computers as evidence of second language learning strategies. *Language Learning 37:* 523–544.

Jaszczolt, Katarzyna. 1995. Typology of contrastive studies: Specialization, progress, and applications. *Language Teaching 28:* 1–15.

Jenkins, James and Palermo, David. 1964. Mediation processes and the acquisition of linguistic structure. In Bellugi & Brown 1964.

Jesperson, Otto. 1904. *How to Teach a Foreign Language.* Translated by Sophia Yhlen-Olsen Bertelsen. London: Allen & Unwin.

Jesperson, Otto. 1933. *Essentials of English Grammar.* London: Allen & Unwin.

Johnson, Jacqueline S. 1992. Critical period effects in second language acquisition: The effect of written versus auditory materials on the assessment of grammatical competence. *Language Learning 42:* 217–248.

Jonz, Jon. 1990. Another turn in the conversation: What does cloze measure? *TESOL Quarterly 24:* 61–83.

Joos, Martin. 1967. *The Five Clocks.* New York: Harcourt, Brace & World.

Jordens, Peter. 1996. Input and instruction in second language acquisition. In Jordens & Lalleman 1996.

Jordens, Peter and Lalleman, Josine (Eds.). 1996. *Investigating Second Language Acquisition.* Berlin: Mouton de Gruyter.

Judd, Elliot. 1983. The problem of applying sociolinguistic findings to TESOL: The case of male/female language. In Wolfson & Judd 1983.

Jung, Carl. 1923. *Psychological Types.* New York: Harcourt Brace.

Kachru, Braj B. 1965. The Indianness in Indian English. *Word 21:* 391–410.

Kachru, Braj B. 1976. Models of English for the third world: White man's linguistic burden or language pragmatics? *TESOL Quarterly 10:* 221–239.

Kachru, Braj B. 1977. New Englishes and old models. *English Language Forum,* July.

Kachru, Braj B. 1985. Standards, codification, and sociolinguistic realism: The English language in the outer circle. In Quirk & Widdowson 1988.

Kachru, Braj B. 1992. World Englishes: Approaches, issues, and resources. *Language Teaching 25:* 1–14.

Kachru, Braj B. and Nelson, Cecil L. 1996. World Englishes. In McKay & Hornberger 1996.

Kagan, Jerome. 1965. Reflection-impulsivity and reading ability in primary grade children. *Child Development 36:* 609–628.

Kagan, Jerome, Pearson, L., and Welch, Lois. 1966. Conceptual impulsivity and inductive reasoning. *Child Development 37:* 583–594.

Kakava, Christina. 1995. An analysis of Greek and English discourse features. Paper delivered at San Francisco State University, March 1995.

Kaplan, Robert, Jones, Randall L., and Tucker, G. Richard. 1981. *Annual Review of Applied Linguistics.* Rowley, MA: Newbury House.

Kasper, Gabrielle. 1998. Interlanguage pragmatics. In Byrnes 1998.

Kasper, Gabrielle and Blum-Kulka, Shoshana (Eds.). 1993. *Interlanguage Pragmatics.* New York: Oxford University Press.

Keefe, J.W. 1979. *Student Learning Styles: Diagnosing and Prescribing Programs.* Reston, VA: National Association of Secondary School Principals.

Keirsey, David and Bates, Marilyn. 1984. *Please Understand Me: Character and Temperament Types.* Del Mar, CA: Prometheus Nemesis Book Company.

Keller, J.M. 1983. Motivational design of instruction. C.M. Reigelruth (Ed.), *Instructional Design Theories and Models: An Overview of Their Current Status.* Hillsdale, NJ: Lawrence Erlbaum Associates.

Kellerman, Susan. 1992. "I see what you mean": The role of kinesic behaviour in listening, and implications for foreign and second language learning. *Applied Linguistics 13:* 239-258.

Kessel, Frank S. (Ed.). 1988. *The Development of Language and Language Researchers: Essays in Honor of Roger Brown.* Hillsdale, NJ: Lawrence Erlbaum Associates.

Kimble, Gregory A. and Garmezy, Norman. 1963. *Principles of General Psychology.* Second Edition. New York: The Ronald Press.

Kitao, S. Kathleen. Linguistic pragmatics and English language learning. *Cross Currents 17:* 15-22.

Kleinmann, Howard. 1977. Avoidance behavior in adult second language acquisition. *Language Learning 27:* 93-107.

Koch, S. (Ed.). 1963. *Psychology: A Study of Science, Volume 5.* New York: McGraw-Hill.

Kohls, Robert L. 1984. *Survival Kit for Overseas Living.* Yarmouth, ME: Intercultural Press.

Krasegnor, Norman A.; Rumbaugh, Duane M.; Schliefelbusch, Richard L.; and Studdert-Kennedy, Michael (Eds.). 1991. *Biological and Behavioral Determinants of Language Development.* Hillsdale, NJ: Lawrence Erlbaum Associates.

Krashen, Stephen. 1973. Lateralization, language learning, and the critical period: Some new evidence. *Language Learning 23:* 63-74.

Krashen, Stephen. 1976. Formal and informal linguistic environments in language acquisition and language learning. *TESOL Quarterly 10:* 157-168.

Krashen, Stephen. 1977. The monitor model for adult second language performance. In Burt et al. 1977.

Krashen, Stephen. 1981. *Second Language Acquisition and Second Language Learning.* Oxford: Pergamon Press.

Krashen, Stephen. 1982. *Principles and Practice in Second Language Acquisition.* Oxford: Pergamon Press.

Krashen, Stephen. 1983. Newmark's ignorance hypothesis and current second language acquisition theory. In Gass & Selinker 1983.

Krashen, Stephen. 1985. *The Input Hypothesis.* London: Longman.

Krashen, Stephen D. 1986. Bilingual education and second language acquisition theory. In California State Department of Education 1986.

Krashen, Stephen. 1992. Under what conditions, if any, should formal grammar instruction take place? *TESOL Quarterly 26:* 409-411.

Krashen, Stephen. 1994. The effect of formal grammar teaching: Still peripheral. *TESOL Quarterly 27:* 722-725.

Krashen, Stephen. 1997. *Foreign Language Education: The Easy Way.* Culver City, CA: Language Education Associates.

Krashen, Stephen and Terrell, Tracy D. 1983. *The Natural Approach: Language Acquisition in the Classroom.* Oxford: Pergamon Press.

Krashen, Stephen, Seliger, Herbert, and Hartnett, Dayle. 1974. Two studies in adult second language learning. *Kritikon Literarum 3:* 220–228.

Krathwohl, David R., Bloom, Benjamin, and Masia, Bertram B. 1964. *Taxonomy of Educational Objectives. Handbook H: Affective Domain.* New York: David McKay.

Kuczaj, Stan A. (Ed.). 1984. *Discourse Development: Progress in Cognitive Development Research.* New York: Springer-Verlag.

Kuhn, Thomas. 1970. *The Structure of Scientific Revolutions.* Chicago: University of Chicago Press.

Labov, William. 1970. The study of language in its social context. *Studium Generale 23:* 30–87.

Lado, Robert. 1957. *Linguistics Across Cultures.* Ann Arbor: University of Michigan Press.

Lado, Robert. 1961. *Language Testing: The Construction and Use of Foreign Language Tests.* London: Longman Group, Ltd.

LaForge, Paul. 1971. Community language learning: A pilot study. *Language Learning 21:* 45–61.

Lakoff, Robin. 1975. *Language and Woman's Place.* New York: Harper Colophon.

Lakoff, Robin. 1976. Language and society. In Wardhaugh & Brown 1976.

Lakshmanan, Usha. 1995. Child second language acquisition of syntax. *Studies in Second Language Acquisition 17:* 301–329.

Lambert, Richard D. and Freed, Barbara F. 1982. *The Loss of Language Skills.* Rowley, MA: Newbury House.

Lambert, Wallace E. 1963. Psychological approaches to the study of language. *Modern Language Journal 47:* 51–62, 114–121.

Lambert, Wallace E. 1967. A social psychology of bilingualism. *The Journal of Social Issues 23:* 91–109.

Lambert, Wallace E. 1972. *Language, Psychology, and Culture: Essays by Wallace E. Lambert.* Palo Alto, CA: Stanford University Press.

Landes, James. 1975. Speech addressed to children: Issues and characteristics of parental input. *Language Learning 25:* 355–379.

Langacker, Ronald W. 1973. *Language and Its Structure.* Second Edition. New York: Harcourt Brace Jovanovich.

Lange, Dale and Lowe, Pardee. 1986. Testing the transfer of the ACTFL/ETS/ILR reading proficiency scales to academia. Paper presented at the TESOL Testing Colloquium, Monterey, CA, March 1986.

Langi, Uinise T. 1984. The natural approach: Approach, design, and procedure. *TESL Reporter 17:* 11–18.

Lantolf, James P. 1996. SLA theory building: "Letting all the flowers bloom!" *Language Learning 46:* 713–749.

Larsen-Freeman, Diane. 1976. An explanation for the morpheme acquisition order of second language learners. *Language Learning 26:* 125–134.

Larsen-Freeman, Diane (Ed.). 1980. *Discourse Analysis in Second Language Research.* Rowley, MA: Newbury House.

Larsen-Freeman, Diane. 1986. *Techniques and Principles in Language Teaching.* New York: Oxford University Press.

Larsen-Freeman, Diane. 1991. Teaching grammar. In Celce-Murcia 1991.

Larsen-Freeman, Diane. 1997. Chaos/complexity science and second language acquisition. *Applied Linguistics 18:* 141–165.

Larsen-Freeman, Diane and Long, Michael H. 1991. *An Introduction to Second Language Acquisition Research.* New York: Longman.

Larson, Donald N. and Smalley, William A. 1972. *Becoming Bilingual: A Guide to Language Learning.* New Canaan, CN: Practical Anthropology.

Lawrence, Gordon. 1984. *People Types and Tiger Stripes: A Practical Guide to Learning Styles.* Gainesville, FL: Center for Applications of Psychological Type.

Leech, Gregory and Svartvik, Jan. 1975. *A Communicative Grammar of English.* London: Longman Group, Ltd.

Lenneberg, Eric H. 1964. The capacity for language acquisition. In Fodor & Katz 1964.

Lenneberg, Eric H. 1967. *The Biological Foundations of Language.* New York: John Wiley & Sons.

Lennon, Paul. 1991. Error: Some problems of definition, identification, and distinction. *Applied Linguistics 12:* 180–196.

Leopold, Werner F. 1949. *Speech Development of a Bilingual Child: A Linguist's Record.* Evanston, IL: Northwestern University Press.

Leopold, Werner F. 1954. A child's learning of two languages. *Georgetown University Round Table on Language and Linguistics 7:* 19–30.

Lett, John A. and O'Mara, Francis E. 1990. Predictors of success in an intensive foreign language learning context: Correlates of language learning at the Defense Language Institute Foreign Language Center. In Parry & Stansfield 1990.

Levine, Deena R., Baxter, Jim, and McNulty, Piper. 1987. *The Culture Puzzle.* New York: Prentice-Hall.

Lightbown, Patsy M. 1985. Great expectations: Second language acquisition research and classroom teaching. *Applied Linguistics 6:* 173–189.

Lightbown, Patsy and Spada, Nina. 1990. Focus-on-form and corrective feedback in communicative language teaching: Effects on second language learning. *Studies in Second Language Acquisition 12:* 429–448.

Lightbown, Patsy and Spada, Nina. 1993. *How Languages Are Learned.* Oxford: Oxford University Press.

Littlewood, W.T. 1981. Language variation and second language acquisition theory. *Applied Linguistics 2:* 150–158.

LoCastro, Virginia. 1997. Politeness and pragmatic competence in foreign language education. *Language Teaching Research 1:* 239–267.

Lock, Andrew. 1991. The role of social interaction in early language development. In Krasegnor et al. 1991.

Loew, Ronald P. 1997. Attention, awareness, and foreign language behavior. *Language Learning 47:* 467–505.

Loftus, Elizabeth F. 1976. Language memories in the judicial system. Paper presented at the NWAVE Conference, Georgetown University.

Long, Michael H. 1977. Teacher feedback on learner error: Mapping cognitions. In Brown, et al. 1977.

Long, Michael H. 1983. Does second language instruction make a difference? A review of research. *TESOL Quarterly 17:* 359–382.

Long, Michael H. 1985. Input and second language acquisition theory. In Gass & Madden 1985.

Long, Michael H. 1988. Instructed interlanguage development. In Beebe 1988.

Long, Michael H. 1990a. The least a second language acquisition theory needs to explain. *TESOL Quarterly 24:* 649–666.

Long, Michael H. 1990b. Maturational constraints on language development. *Studies in Second Language Acquisition 12:* 251–285.

Long, Michael H. 1996. The role of the linguistic environment in second language acquisition. In Ritchie & Bhatia 1996.

Long, Michael H. and Porter, Patricia. 1985. Group work, interlanguage talk, and second language acquisition. *TESOL Quarterly 19:* 207–228.

Long, Michael and Robinson, Peter. 1998. Focus on form: Theory, research, and practice. In Doughty & Williams 1998.

Loschky, Lester. 1994. Comprehensible input and second language acquisition: What is the relationship? *Studies in Second Language Acquisition 16:* 303–323.

Loup, Georgette; Boustagui, Elizabeth; El Tigi, Manal; and Moselle, Martha. 1994. Reexaming the critical period hypothesis: A case study of successful adult SLA in a naturalist environment. *Studies in Second Language Acquisition 16:* 73–98.

Lowe, Pardee and Stansfield, Charles W. (Eds.). 1988. *Second Language Proficiency Assessment: Current Issues.* Englewood Cliffs, NJ: Prentice-Hall Regents.

Lowenberg, Peter (Ed.). 1988. *Georgetown University Round Table on Languages and Linguistics: 1987.* Washington, DC: Georgetown University Press.

Lozanov, Georgi. 1979. *Suggestology and Outlines of Suggestopedy.* New York: Gordon and Breach Science Publishers.

Lukmani, Yasmeen. 1972. Motivation to learn and language proficiency. *Language Learning 22:* 261–274.

MacCorquodale, Kenneth. 1970. On Chomsky's review of Skinner's *Verbal Behavior. Journal of the Experimental Analysis of Behavior 13:* 83–99.

MacIntyre, Peter D. and Gardner, Robert C. 1988. The measurement of anxiety and applications to second language learning: An annotated bibliography. *Research Bulletin #672.* London, Ontario: The University of Western Ontario.

MacIntyre, Peter D. and Gardner, Robert C. 1989. Anxiety and second language learning: Toward a theoretical clarification. *Language Learning 39:* 251–275.

MacIntyre, Peter D. and Gardner, Robert C. 1991a. Investigating language class anxiety using the focused essay technique. *Modern Language Journal 75:* 296–304.

MacIntyre, Peter D. and Gardner, Robert C. 1991b. Language anxiety: Its relationship to other anxieties and to processing in native and second languages. *Language Learning 41:* 513-534.

MacIntyre, Peter D. and Gardner, Robert C. 1991c. Methods and results in the study of anxiety and language learning: A review of the literature. *Language Learning 41:* 85-117.

MacIntyre, Peter D. and Gardner, Robert C. 1994. The subtle effects of language anxiety on cognitive processing in the second language. *Language Learning 44:* 283-305.

MacIntyre, Peter D. and Noels, Kimberly A. 1996. Using social-psychological variables to predict the use of language learning strategies. *Foreign Language Annals 29:* 373-386. MacIntyre, Peter D., Noels, Kimberly A., and Clément, Richard. 1997. Biases in self-ratings of second language proficiency: The role of anxiety. *Language Learning 47:* 265-287.

MacIntyre, Peter D.; Dörnyei, Zoltán; Clément, Richard; and Noels, Kimberly. 1998. Conceptualizing willingness to communicate in a L2: A situational model of L2 confidence and affiliation. *Modern Language Journal 82:* 545-562.

Maclay, Howard and Osgood, Charles E. 1959. Hesitation phenomena in spontaneous English speech. *Word 15:* 19-44.

Macnamara, John. 1973. The cognitive strategies of language learning. In Oller & Richards 1973.

Macnamara, John. 1975. Comparison between first and second language learning. *Working Papers on Bilingualism 7:* 71-94.

Madsen, Harold S. 1982. Determining the debilitative impact of test anxiety. *Language Learning 32:* 133-143.

Madsen, Harold S. 1983. *Techniques in Testing.* New York: Oxford University Press.

Magnan, S.S. (Ed.). 1990. *Shifting the Instructional Focus to the Learner.* Middlebury, VT: Northeast Conference on the Teaching of Foreign Languages.

Major, Roy C. and Faudree, Michael C. 1996. Markedness universals and acquisition of voicing contrasts by Korean speakers of English. *Studies in Second Language Acquisition 18:* 69-90.

Malinowski, Bronislaw. 1923. The problem of meaning in primitive languages. In Ogden & Richards 1923.

Malotki, E. 1983. *Hopi Time: A Linguistic Analysis of Temporal Concepts in the Hopi Language.* Berlin: Mouton and Company.

Maratsos, Michael. 1988. Crosslinguistic analysis, universals, and language acquisition. In Kessel 1988.

Marckwardt, Albert D. 1972. Changing winds and shifting sands. *MST English Quarterly 21:* 3-11.

Marshall, Terry. 1989. *The Whole World Guide to Language Learning.* Yarmouth, ME: Intercultural Press.

Maslow, Abraham H. 1970. *Motivation and Personality.* Second Edition. New York: Harper & Row.

McDonough, Steven H. 1999. Learner strategies. *Language Teaching 32:* 1-18.

McGroarty, Mary. 1984. Some meanings of communicative competence for second language students. *TESOL Quarterly 18:* 257–272.

McGroarty, Mary and Galvan, Jose L. 1985. Culture as an issue in second language teaching. In Celce-Murcia 1985.

McKay, Sandra Lee and Hornberger, Nancy H. 1996. *Sociolinguistics and Language Teaching.* Cambridge: Cambridge University Press.

McLaughlin, Barry. 1978. The monitor model: Some methodological considerations. *Language Learning 28:* 309–332.

McLaughlin, Barry. 1987. *Theories of Second Language Learning.* London: Edward Arnold.

McLaughlin, Barry. 1990a. "Conscious" versus "unconscious" learning. *TESOL Quarterly 24:* 617–634.

McLaughlin, Barry. 1990b. Restructuring. *Applied Linguistics 11:* 113–128.

McLaughlin, Barry, Rossman, Tammi, and McLeod, Beverly. 1983. Second language learning: An information-processing perspective. *Language Learning 33:* 135–158.

McLeod, Beverly and McLaughlin, Barry. 1986. Restructuring or automaticity? Reading in a second language. *Language Learning 36:* 109–123.

McNeill, David. 1966. Developmental psycholinguistics. In Smith & Miller 1966.

McNeill, David. 1968. On the theories of language acquisition. In Dixon & Horton 1968.

McTear, Michael F. 1984. Structure and process in children's conversational development. In Kuczaj 1984.

Mead, Robert C. (Ed.). 1966. *Reports of the Working Committee.* New York: Northeast Conference on the Teaching of Foreign Languages.

Mehnert, Uta. 1998. The effects of different lengths of time for planning on second language performance. *Studies in Second Language Acquisition 20:* 83–108.

Menyuk, Paula. 1971. *The Acquisition and Development of Language.* Englewood Cliffs, NJ: Prentice-Hall.

Milhollan, Frank and Forisha, B.E. 1972. *From Skinner to Rogers: Contrasting Approaches to Education.* Lincoln, NE: Professional Educators Publications.

Miller, George A. 1956. The magical number seven, plus or minus two: Some limits on our capacity for processing information. *Psychological Review 63:* 81–97.

Miller, W.R. 1963. The acquisition of formal features of language. *American Journal of Orthopsychiatry 34:* 862–867.

Milon, J. 1974. The development of negation in English by a second language learner. *TESOL Quarterly 8:* 137–143.

Minnis, Noel (Ed.). 1971. *Linguistics at Large.* New York: Viking Press.

Mitchell, Rosamond and Myles, Florence. 1998. *Second Language Learning Theories.* New York: Oxford University Press.

Moerk, Ernst L. 1985. Analytic, synthetic, abstracting, and word-class defining aspects of verbal mother-child interactions. *Journal of Psycholinguistic Research 14:* 263–287.

Montgomery, Carol and Eisenstein, Miriam. 1985. Real reality revisited: An experimental communicative course in ESL. *TESOL Quarterly 19:* 317–334.

Moody, R. 1988. Personality preferences and foreign language learning. *Modern Language Journal 72:* 389–401.

Moore, Frank W. 1961. *Readings in Cross Cultures.* New Haven, CN: HRAF Press.

Morgan, Carol. 1993. Attitude change and foreign language culture learning. *Language Teaching 26:* 63–75.

Morley, Joan (Ed.). 1986. *Current Perspectives on Pronunciation: Practices Anchored in Theory.* Washington, DC: Teachers of English to Speakers of Other Languages.

Morris, Beth S.K. and Gerstman, Louis J. 1986. Age contrasts in the learning of language-relevant materials: Some challenges to critical period hypotheses. *Language Learning 36:* 311–352.

Moyer, Alene. 1999. Ultimate attainment in L2 phonology: The critical factors of age, motivation, and instruction. *Studies in Second Language Acquisition 21:* 81–108.

Murdock, George Peter. 1961. The cross-cultural survey. In Moore 1961.

Myers, Isabel. 1962. *The Myers-Briggs Type Indicator.* Palo Alto, CA: Consulting Psychologists Press.

Naiman, Neil; Fröhlich, Maria; Stern, H.H.; and Todesco, Angie. 1978. *The Good Language Learner.* Toronto: Ontario Institute for Studies in Education. Reprinted 1996 by Multilingual Matters, Clevedon, UK.

Natalicio, D.S. and Natalicio, L.F.S. 1971. A comparative study of English pluralization by native and non-native English speakers. *Child Development 42:* 1302–1306.

Nattinger, James R. 1984. Communicative language teaching: A new metaphor. *TESOL Quarterly 18:* 391–407.

Nayar, P. Bhaskaran. 1997. ESL/EFL dichotomy today: Language politics or pragmatics? *TESOL Quarterly 31:* 9–37.

Neapolitan, Denise M., Pepperberg, Irene M., and Schinke-Llano, Linda. 1988. Second language acquisition: Possible insights from studies on how birds acquire song. *Studies in Second Language Acquisition 10:* 1–11.

Nemser, W. 1971. Approximative systems of foreign language learners. *International Review of Applied Linguistics 9:* 115–123.

Neufeld, Gerald G. 1977. Language learning ability in adults: A study on the acquisition of prosodic and articulatory features. *Working Papers on Bilingualism 12:* 45–60.

Neufeld, Gerald G. 1979. Towards a theory of language learning ability. *Language Learning 29:* 227–241.

Neufeld, Gerald G. 1980. On the adult's ability to acquire phonology. *TESOL Quarterly 14:* 285–298.

New Standard Encyclopedia. 1940. Edited by Frank Vizetelly. New York: Funk & Wagnalls.

Ney, James and Pearson, Bethyl A. 1990. Connectionism as a model of language learning: Parallels in foreign language teaching. *Modern Language Journal 74:* 474–482.

Nilsen, Aileen Pace; Bosmajian, Haig; Gershuny, H. Lee; and Stanley, Julia P. 1977. *Sexism and Language.* Urbana, IL: National Council of Teachers of English.

Nunan, David. 1991a. Communicative tasks and the language curriculum. *TESOL Quarterly 25:* 279–295.

Nunan, David. 1991b. *Language Teaching Methodology: A Textbook for Teachers.* New York: Prentice-Hall.

Nuttall, Christine. 1982. *Teaching Reading Skills in a Foreign Language.* Oxford: Heinemann. Reprinted 1996.

Nyikos, Martha and Hashimoto, Reiko. 1997. Constructivist theory applied to collaborative learning in teacher education: In search of ZPD. *Modern Language Journal 81:* 506–517.

O'Grady, William. 1996. Language acquisition without Universal Grammar: A general nativist proposal for L2 learning. *Second Language Research 12:* 374–397.

O'Grady, William, Dobrovolsky, Michael, and Aronoff, Michael. 1989. *Contemporary Linguistics.* New York: St. Martin's Press.

O'Malley, Michael and Chamot, Anna Uhl. 1990. *Learning Strategies in Second Language Acquisition.* New York: Cambridge University Press.

O'Malley, Michael, Chamot, Anna Uhl, and Kupper, Lisa. 1989. Listening comprehension strategies in second language acquisition. *Applied Linguistics 10:* 418–437.

O'Malley, J. Michael, Russo, Rocco P., and Chamot, Anna U. 1983. A review of the literature on learning strategies in the acquisition of English as a second language: The potential for research applications. Rosslyn, VA: InterAmerica Research Associates.

O'Malley, Michael, Chamot, Anna Uhl, and Walker, C. 1987. Some applications of cognitive theory to second language acquisition. *Studies in Second Language Acquisition 9:* 287–306.

O'Malley, J. Michael; Chamot, Anna U.; Stewner-Manzanares, Gloria; Kupper, Lisa; and Russo, Rocco P. 1985a. Learning strategies used by beginning and intermediate ESL students. *Language Learning 35:* 21–46.

O'Malley, J. Michael; Chamot, Anna U.; Stewner-Manzanares, Gloria; Russo, Rocco P.; and Kupper, Lisa. 1985b. Learning strategy applications with students of English as a second language. *TESOL Quarterly 19:* 557–584.

Obler, Lorraine K. 1981. Right hemisphere participation in second language acquisition. In Diller 1981.

Obler, Lorraine K. 1982. Neurolinguistic aspects of language loss as they pertain to second language acquisition. In Lambert & Freed 1982.

Ochsner, Robert. 1979. A poetics of second language acquisition. *Language Learning 29:* 53–80.

Odlin, Terence. 1986. On the nature and use of explicit knowledge. *International Review of Applied Linguistics 24:* 123–144.

Ogden, Charles K. and Richards, I.A. (Eds.). 1923. *The Meaning of Meaning.* London: Kegan Paul.

Ohio State University. 1991. *Language Files.* Columbus: Ohio State University Press.

Oller, John W. 1976. A program for language testing research. *Language Learning, Special Issue Number 4:* 141–165.

Oller, John W. 1979. *Language Tests at School: A Pragmatic Approach.* London: Longman Group, Ltd.

Oller, John W. 1981a. Language as intelligence? *Language Learning 31:* 465–492.

Oller, John W. 1981b. Research on the measurement of affective variables: Some remaining questions. In Andersen 1981.

Oller, John W. 1982. Gardner on affect: A reply to Gardner. *Language Learning 32:* 183–189.

Oller, John W. (Ed.). 1983. *Issues in Language Testing Research.* Rowley, MA: Newbury House.

Oller, John W. and Perkins, Kyle (Eds.). 1980. *Research in Language Testing.* Rowley, MA: Newbury House.

Oller, John W. and Richards, Jack C. (Eds.). 1973. *Focus on the Learner: Pragmatic Perspectives for the Language Teacher.* Rowley, MA: Newbury House.

Oller, John W. and Streiff, Virginia. 1975. Dictation: A test of grammar based on expectancies. *English Language Teaching 30:* 25–36.

Oller, John W. and Ziahosseiny, Seid M. 1970. The contrastive analysis hypothesis and spelling errors. *Language Learning 20:* 183–189.

Oller, John W., Baca, Lori L., and Vigil, Alfredo. 1978. Attitudes and attained proficiency in ESL: A sociolinguistic study of Mexican-Americans in the Southwest. *TESOL Quarterly 11:* 173–183.

Oller, John W., Hudson, A., and Liu, Phyllis F. 1977. Attitudes and attained proficiency in ESL: A sociolinguistic study of native speakers of Chinese in the United States. *Language Learning 27:* 1–27.

Olshtain, Elite. 1989. Is second language attrition the reversal of second language acquisition? *Studies in Second Language Acquisition 11:* 151–165.

Olshtain, Elite and Cohen, Andrew D. 1983. Apology: A speech-act set. In Wolfson & Judd 1983.

Omaggio, Alice C. 1981. *Helping Learners Succeed: Activities for the Foreign Language Classroom.* Washington, DC: Center for Applied Linguistics.

Osgood, Charles E. 1953. *Method and Theory in Experimental Psychology.* New York: Oxford University Press.

Osgood, Charles E. 1957. *Contemporary Approaches to Cognition.* Cambridge: Harvard University Press.

Ostrander, Sheila and Schroeder, Lynn. 1979. *Superlearning.* New York: Dell.

Oxford, Rebecca. 1990a. *Language Learning Strategies: What Every Teacher Should Know.* New York: Newbury House.

Oxford, Rebecca. 1990b. Styles, strategies, and aptitude: Connections for language learning. In Parry & Stansfield 1990.

Oxford, Rebecca (Ed.). 1996. *Learning Strategies Around the World: Cross-Cultural Perspectives.* Honolulu: University of Hawaii Press.

Oxford, Rebecca L. 1999. Anxiety and the language learner: New insights. In Arnold 1999.

Oxford, Rebecca and Anderson, Neil J. 1995. A crosscultural view of learning styles. *Language Teaching 28:* 201–215.

Oxford, Rebecca and Crookall, David. 1989. Research on language learning strategies: Methods, findings, and instructional issues. *Modern Language Journal 73:* 404–419.

Oxford, Rebecca and Ehrman, Madeline. 1988. Psychological type and adult language learning strategies: A pilot study. *Journal of Psychological Type 16:* 22–32.

Paribakht, Tahereh. 1984. The relationship between the use of communication strategies and aspects of target language proficiencies: A study of ESL students. Quebec: International Center for Research on Bilingualism.

Paribakht, Tahereh. 1985. Strategic competence and language proficiency. *Applied Linguistics 6:* 132–146.

Parry, Thomas and Child, James R. 1990. Preliminary investigation of the relationship between VORD, MLAT, and language proficiency. In Parry & Stansfield 1990.

Parry, Thomas S. and Stansfield, Charles W. (Eds.). 1990. *Language Aptitude Reconsidered.* New York: Prentice-Hall Regents.

Patkowski, Mark S. 1990. Age and accent in a second language: A reply to James Emil Flege. *Applied Linguistics 11:* 73–89.

Paulston, Christina B. 1974. Linguistic and communicative competence. *TESOL Quarterly 8:* 347–362.

Pei, Mario. 1966. *Glossary of Linguistic Terminology.* New York: Anchor Books.

Pemberton, Richard. 1996. *Taking Control: Autonomy in Language Learning.* Hong Kong: Hong Kong University Press.

Peters, Ann M. 1981. Language learning strategies: Does the whole equal the sum of the parts? In Diller 1981.

Phillips, Elaine M. 1992. The effects of language anxiety on students' oral test performance and attitudes. *Modern Language Journal 76:* 14–26.

Phillipson, Robert. 1992. *Linguistic Imperialism.* London: Oxford University Press.

Piaget, Jean. 1972. *The Principles of Genetic Epistemology.* New York: Basic Books.

Piaget, Jean and Inhelder B. 1969. *The Psychology of the Child.* New York: Basic Books.

Pica, Teresa. 1987. Second language acquisition, social interaction, and the classroom. *Applied Linguistics 8:* 3–21.

Pike, Kenneth. 1967. *Language in Relation to a Unified Theory of the Structure of Human Behavior.* The Hague: Mouton Publishers.

Pimsleur, Paul. 1966. *Pimsleur Language Aptitude Battery.* New York: Harcourt, Brace & World.

Pinker, Stephen. 1994. *The Language Instinct: How the Mind Creates Language.* New York: William Morrow.

Prator, Clifford H. 1967. Hierarchy of difficulty. Unpublished classroom lecture, University of California, Los Angeles.

Prator, Clifford H. 1972. *Manual of American English Pronunciation. Diagnostic Passage.* New York: Holt, Rinehart & Winston.

Prator, Clifford H. and Celce-Murcia, Marianne. 1979. An outline of language teaching approaches. In Celce-Murcia & McIntosh 1979.

Preston, Dennis. 1996. Variationist perspectives on second language acquisition. In Bayley & Preston 1996.

Pride, J.B. and Holmes, J. (Eds.). 1972. *Sociolinguistics.* Harmondsworth, UK: Penguin Books.

Pullum, G.K. 1991. *The Great Eskimo Vocabulary Hoax and Other Irreverent Essays on the Study of Language.* Chicago: University of Chicago Press.

Purpura, James Enos. 1997. An analysis of the relationships between test takers' cognitive and metacognitive strategy use and second language test performance. *Language Learning 47:* 289-325.

Quirk, R. 1988. The question of standard in the international use of English. In Lowenberg 1988.

Quirk, R. and Widdowson, Henry. 1988. *English in the World: Teaching and Learning the Language and Literatures.* Cambridge: Cambridge University Press.

Raimes, Ann. 1983. Tradition and revolution in ESL teaching. *TESOL Quarterly 17:* 535-552.

Ramage, Katherine. 1990. Motivational factors and persistence in foreign language study. *Language Learning 40:* 189-219.

Ramirez, Arnulfo G. 1995. *Creating Contexts for Second Language Acquisition: Theory and Methods.* White Plains, NY: Longman.

Random House Dictionary of the English Language. 1966. New York: Random House.

Ravem, Roar. 1968. Language acquisition in a second language environment. *International Review of Applied Linguistics 6:* 175-185.

Reid, Joy M. 1987. The learning style preferences of ESL students. *TESOL Quarterly 21:* 87-111.

Reid, Joy. 1995. *Learning Styles in the ESL/EFL Classroom.* Boston: Heinle & Heinle.

Reynolds, Allan G. 1991. The cognitive consequences of bilingualism. *ERIC/CLL News Bulletin 14:* 1-8.

Rice, M. 1980. *Cognition to Language: Categories, Word Meanings, and Training.* Baltimore: University Park Press.

Ricento, Thomas. 1994. Review of Phillipson 1992. *TESOL Quarterly 28:* 421-427.

Richard-Amato, Patricia. 1996. *Making It Happen: Interaction in the Second Language Classroom: From Theory to Practice.* White Plains, NY: Addison-Wesley.

Richards, Jack. 1971. A non-contrastive approach to error analysis. *English Language Teaching 25:* 204-219.

Richards, Jack C. 1974. *Error Analysis: Perspectives on Second Language Acquisition.* London: Longman Group, Ltd.

Richards, Jack C. 1975. Simplification: A strategy in the adult acquisition of a foreign language: An example from Indonesian/Malay. *Language Learning 25:* 115-126.

Richards, Jack C. 1976. Second language learning. In Wardhaugh & Brown 1976.

Richards, Jack C. 1979. Rhetorical styles and communicative styles in the new varieties of English. *Language Learning 29:* 1-25.

Richards, Jack C. 1984. The secret life of methods. *TESOL Quarterly 18:* 7–23.

Richards, Jack C. and Rodgers, Theodore S. 1982. Method: Approach, design, and procedure. *TESOL Quarterly 16:* 153–168.

Richards, Jack C. and Rodgers, Theodore S. 1986. *Approaches and Methods in Language Teaching.* Cambridge: Cambridge University Press.

Richards, Jack C. and Schmidt, Richard (Eds.). 1983. *Language and Communication.* London: Longman Group, Ltd.

Ritchie, William C. and Bhatia, T.K. (Eds.). 1996. *Handbook of Second Language Acquisition.* San Diego: Academic Press.

Rivers, Wilga M. 1964. *The Psychologist and the Foreign Language Teacher.* Chicago: University of Chicago Press.

Rivers, Wilga M. 1981. *Teaching Foreign Language Skills.* Second Edition. Chicago: University of Chicago Press.

Roberts, Cheryl. 1983. Field independence as a predictor of second language learning for adult ESL learners in the United States. Unpublished doctoral dissertation, University of Illinois.

Robinett, B.J. and Schachter, Jacquelyn (Eds.). 1983. *Second Language Learning: Contrastive Analysis, Error Analysis, and Related Aspects.* Ann Arbor: University of Michigan Press.

Robinson, Peter. 1994. Implicit knowledge, second language learning, and syllabus construction. *TESOL Quarterly 28:* 161–166.

Robinson, Peter. 1995. Attention, memory, and the "noticing" hypothesis. *Language Learning 45:* 283–331.

Robinson, Peter. 1997. Individual differences and the fundamental similarity of implicit and explicit adult second language learning. *Language Learning 47:* 45–99.

Robinson-Stuart, Gail and Nocon, Honorine. 1996. Second culture acquistion: Ethnography in the foreign language classroom. *Modern Language Journal 80:* 431–449.

Rogers, Carl. 1951. *Client-Centered Therapy.* Boston: Houghton Mifflin.

Rogers, Carl R. 1983. *Freedom to Learn for the Eighties.* Columbus, OH: Charles E. Merrill.

Rosansky, Ellen J. 1975. The critical period for the acquisition of language: Some cognitive developmental considerations. *Working Papers on Bilingualism 6:* 92–102.

Rosansky, Ellen J. 1976. Methods and morphemes in second language acquisition research. *Language Learning 26:* 409–425.

Ross, Steven and Berwick, Richard. 1992. The discourse of accommodation in oral proficiency interviews. *Studies in Second Language Acquisition 14:* 159–176.

Rost, Michael and Ross, Steven. 1991. Learner use of strategies in interaction: Typology and predictability. *Language Learning 41:* 235–273.

Rubin, Joan. 1975. What the "good language learner" can teach us. *TESOL Quarterly 9:* 41–51.

Rubin, Joan. 1976. How to tell when someone is saying "no." *Topics in Culture Learning. Volume 4.* Honolulu: East-West Culture Learning Institute. Reprinted in Wolfson & Judd 1983.

Rubin, Joan and Thompson, Irene. 1982. *How to Be a More Successful Language Learner.* Boston: Heinle & Heinle. Second Edition, 1994.

Rutherford, William. 1982. Markedness in second language acquisition. *Language Learning 32:* 85–108.

Rutherford, William and Sharwood-Smith, Michael (Eds.). 1988. *Grammar and Second Language Teaching: A Book of Readings.* New York: Newbury House.

Saleemi, A. 1992. *Universal Grammar and Language Learnability.* Cambridge: Cambridge University Press.

Sasaki, Miyuki. 1993a. Relationships among second language proficiency, foreign language aptitude, and intelligence: A structural equation modeling approach. *Language Learning 43:* 313–344.

Sasaki, Miyuki. 1993b. Relationships among second language proficiency, foreign language aptitude, and intelligence: A protocol analysis. *Language Learning 43:* 469–505.

Saussure, Ferdinand de. 1916. *Cours de linguistique générale* (Course in General Linguistics). Translated by Wade Baskin. New York: McGraw-Hill, 1959.

Savignon, Sandra J. 1972. *Communicative Competence: An Experiment in Foreign Language Teaching.* Philadelphia: Center for Curriculum Development.

Savignon, Sandra J. 1982. Dictation as a measure of communicative competence in French as a second language. *Language Learning 32:* 33–51.

Savignon, Sandra J. 1983. *Communicative Competence: Theory and Classroom Practice.* Reading, MA: Addison-Wesley.

Savignon, Sandra J. and Berns, Margie S. 1984. *Initiatives in Communicative Language Teaching: A Book of Readings.* Reading, MA: Addison-Wesley.

Saville-Truike, Muriel. 1976. *Foundations for Teaching English as a Second Language.* Englewood Cliffs, NJ: Prentice-Hall.

Scarcella, Robin C., Andersen, Elaine S., and Krashen, Stephen D. (Eds.). 1990. *Developing Communicative Competence in a Second Language.* New York: Newbury House.

Schachter, Jacqueline. 1974. An error in error analysis. *Language Learning 24:* 205–214.

Schachter, Jacquelyn. 1988. Second language acquisition and its relationship to Universal Grammar. *Applied Linguistics 9:* 219–235.

Schinke-Llano, Linda. 1989. Early childhood bilingualism. *Studies in Second Language Acquisition 11:* 223–240.

Schinke-Llano, Linda. 1993. On the value of a Vygotskian framework for SLA theory. *Language Learning 43:* 121–129.

Schmidt, Richard W. 1983. Interaction, acculturation, and the acquisition of communicative competence: A case study of an adult. In Wolfson & Judd 1983.

Schmidt, Richard W. 1990. The role of consciousness in second language learning. *Applied Linguistics 11:* 129–158.

Schultz, Renate. 1991. Second language acquisition theories and teaching practice: How do they fit? *Modern Language Journal 75:* 17–26.

Schumann, John H. 1975. Affective factors and the problem of age in second language acquisition. *Language Learning 25:* 209–235.

Schumann, John H. 1976a. Second language acquisition: The pidginization hypothesis. *Language Learning 26:* 391–408.

Schumann, John H. 1976b. Second language acquisition research: Getting a more global look at the learner. *Language Learning, Special Issue Number 4:* 15–28.

Schumann, John H. 1976c. Social distance as a factor in second language acquisition. *Language Learning 26:* 135–143.

Schumann, John H. 1978. *The Pidginization Process: A Model for Second Language Acquisition.* Rowley, MA: Newbury House.

Schumann, John H. 1982a. Art and science in second language acquisition research. In Clarke & Handscombe 1982.

Schumann, John H. 1982b. Simplification, transfer, and relexification as aspects of pidginization and early second language acquisition. *Language Learning 32:* 337–366.

Schumann, John H. 1990. Extending the scope of the acculturation/pidginization model to include cognition. *TESOL Quarterly 24:* 667–684.

Schumann, John H. 1997. *The Neurobiology of Affect in Language.* Cambridge, MA: Blackwell.

Schumann, John H. 1998. The neurobiology of affect in language. *Language Learning 48, Supplement 1,* Special Issue.

Schumann, John H. 1999. A neurobiological perspective on affect and methodology in second language learning. In Arnold 1999.

Schumann, John H. and Stenson, Nancy (Eds.). 1974. *New Frontiers of Second Language Learning.* Rowley, MA: Newbury House.

Schumann, John H.; Holroyd, Jean; Campbell, Russell N.; and Ward, Frederick A. 1978. Improvement of foreign language pronunciation under hypnosis: A preliminary study. *Language Learning 28:* 143–148.

Schwartz, Joan. 1980. The negotiation for meaning: Repair in conversations between second language learners of English. In Larsen-Freeman 1980.

Sciarone, A.G. and Schoorl, J.J. 1989. The cloze test: Or why small isn't always beautiful. *Language Learning 39:* 415–438.

Scollon, Ron and Scollon, Suzanne Wong. 1995. *Intercultural Communication: A Discourse Approach.* Cambridge, MA: Blackwell.

Scovel, Thomas. 1969. Foreign accents, language acquisition, and cerebral dominance. *Language Learning 19:* 245–254.

Scovel, Thomas. 1978. The effect of affect on foreign language learning: A review of the anxiety research. *Language Learning 28:* 129–142.

Scovel, Thomas. 1979. Review of *Suggestology and Outlines of Suggestopedy,* by Georgi Lozanov. *TESOL Quarterly 13:* 255–266.

Scovel, Thomas. 1982. Questions concerning the application of neurolinguistic research to second language learning/teaching. *TESOL Quarterly 16:* 323–331.

Scovel, Thomas. 1984. A time to speak: Evidence for a biologically based critical period for language acquisition. Paper presented at San Francisco State University, January 19.

Scovel, Thomas. 1988. *A Time to Speak: A Psycholinguistic Inquiry into the Critical Period for Human Speech.* New York: Newbury House.

Scovel, Thomas. 1997. Review of Singleton & Lengyel's (1995) *The Age Factor in Second Language Acquisition. Modern Language Journal 81:* 118–119.

Scovel, Thomas. 1999. "The younger the better" myth and bilingual education. In Gonzalez, Roseann, and Melis, Ildiko (Eds.). *Language Ideologies: Critical Perspectives on the English Only Movement.* Urbana, IL: National Council of Teachers of English.

Sebuktekin, Hikmet. 1975. *An Outline of English-Turkish Contrastive Phonology: Segmental Phonemes.* Istanbul: Bogazici University.

Seliger, Herbert W. 1982. On the possible role of the right hemisphere in second language acquisition. *TESOL Quarterly 16:* 307–314.

Seliger, Herbert W. 1983. Learner interaction in the classroom and its effects on language acquisition. In Seliger & Long 1983.

Seliger, Herbert W. and Long, Michael H. 1983. *Classroom Oriented Research in Second Language Acquisition.* Rowley, MA: Newbury House.

Selinker, Larry. 1972. Interlanguage. *International Review of Applied Linguistics 10:* 201–231.

Selinker, Larry and Lamendella, John. 1979. The role of extrinsic feedback in interlanguage fossilization: A discussion of "Rule fossilization: A tentative model." *Language Learning 29:* 363–375.

Sharwood-Smith, Michael. 1996. Crosslinguistic influence with special reference to the acquisition of grammar. In Jordens & Lalleman 1996.

Shatz, Marilyn and McCloskey, Laura. 1984. Answering appropriately: A developmental perspective on conversational knowledge. In Kuczaj 1984.

Sheen, Ronald. 1996. The advantage of exploiting contrastive analysis in teaching and learning a foreign language. *International Review of Applied Linguistics 34:* 183–197.

Shohamy, Elana. 1988. A proposed framework for testing the oral language of second/foreign language learners. *Studies in Second Language Acquisition 10:* 165–180.

Sinclair, J.M. and Coulthard, R.M. 1975. *Towards an Analysis of Discourse: The English Used by Teachers and Pupils.* Oxford: Oxford University Press.

Singleton, David and Lengyel, Zsolt (Eds.). 1995. *The Age Factor in Second Language Acquisition.* Clevedon, UK: Multilingual Matters.

Singer, H. and Ruddell, R.B. (Eds.). 1970. *Theoretical Models and Processes of Reading.* Newark, DE: International Reading Association.

Sjöholm, Kaj. 1995. *The Influence of Crosslinguistic, Semantic, and Input Factors in the Acquisition of English Phrasal Verbs: A Comparison Between Finnish and Swedish Learners at an Intermediate and Advanced Level.* Abo, Finland: Abo Akademi University Press.

Skehan, Peter. 1988. Language testing: Part I. *Language Teaching 21:* 211–221.

Skehan, Peter. 1989a. *Individual Differences in Second Language Learning.* London: Edward Arnold.

Skehan, Peter. 1989b. Language testing: Part II. *Language Teaching 22:* 1–13.

Skehan, Peter. 1991. Individual differences in second language learning. *Studies in Second Language Acquisition 13:* 275–298.

Skehan, Peter. 1998. *A Cognitive Approach to Language Learning.* Oxford: Oxford University Press.

Skinner, B.F. 1938. *Behavior of Organisms: An Experimental Analysis.* New York: Appleton-Century-Crofts.

Skinner, B.F. 1953. *Science and Human Behavior.* New York: Macmillan.

Skinner, B.F. 1957. *Verbal Behavior.* New York: Appleton-Century-Crofts.

Skinner, B.F. 1968. *The Technology of Teaching.* New York: Appleton-Century-Crofts.

Skutnabb-Kangas, Tove. 1988. Multilingualism and the education of minority children. In Skutnabb-Kangas & Cummins 1988.

Skutnabb-Kangas, Tove and Cummins, James (Eds.). 1988. *Minority Education: From Shame to Struggle.* Clevedon, UK: Multilingual Matters.

Skutnabb-Kangas, Tove and Phillipson, Robert (Eds.). 1994. *Linguistic Human Rights: Overcoming Linguistic Determination.* Berlin: Mouton de Gruyter.

Slavoff, Georgina R. and Johnson, Jacqueline. 1995. The effects of age on the rate of learning a second language. *Studies in Second Language Acquisition 17:* 1–16.

Slobin, Dan. I. 1971. *Psycholinguistics.* Glenview, IL: Scott, Foresman.

Slobin, Dan I. (Ed.). 1986. *The Crosslinguistic Study of Language Acquisition. Volumes 1 & 2.* Hillsdale, NJ: Lawrence Erlbaum Associates.

Slobin, Dan I. (Ed.). 1992. *The Crosslinguistic Study of Language Acquisition. Volume 3.* Hillsdale, NJ: Lawrence Erlbaum Associates.

Smith, Frank. 1975. *Comprehension and Learning: A Conceptual Framework for Teachers.* New York: Holt, Rinehart & Winston.

Smith, Frank and Miller, George A. (Eds.). 1966. *The Genesis of Language: A Psycholinguistic Approach.* Cambridge: M.I.T. Press.

Smith, Stephen M. 1984. *The Theater Arts and the Teaching of Second Languages.* Reading, MA: Addison-Wesley.

Snow, Marguerite A. and Shapira, Rina G. 1985. The role of social-psychological factors in second language learning. In Celce-Murcia 1985.

Sokolik, M.E. 1990. Learning without rules: PDP and a resolution of the adult language learning paradox. *TESOL Quarterly 24:* 685–696.

Sorenson, Arthur. 1967. Multilingualism in the Northwest Amazon. *American Anthropologist 69:* 670–684.

Spada, Nina. 1997. Form-focused instruction and second language acquisition: A review of classroom and laboratory research. *Language Teaching 30:* 73–87.

Spivey, N.N. 1997. *The Constructivist Metaphor: Reading, Writing, and the Making of Meaning.* San Diego: Academic Press.

Spolsky, Bernard. 1969. Attitudinal aspects of second language learning. *Language Learning 19:* 271–283.

Spolsky, Bernard. 1970. Linguistics and language pedagogy—applications or implications. Monograph on Languages and Linguistics 22. Report of the 20th Annual Round Table Meeting, Georgetown University.

Spolsky, Bernard (Ed.). 1978a. *Approaches to Language Testing.* Arlington, VA: Center for Applied Linguistics.

Spolsky, Bernard. 1978b. Linguists and language testers. In Spolsky 1978a.

Spolsky, Bernard. 1988. Bridging the gap: A general theory of second language learning. *TESOL Quarterly 22:* 377-396.

Spolsky, Bernard. 1989. Communicative competence, language proficiency, and beyond. *Applied Linguistics 10:* 138-156.

Spolsky, Bernard. 1990. Introduction to a colloquium: The scope and form of a theory of second language learning. *TESOL Quarterly 24:* 609-616.

Stansfield, Charles and Hansen, Jacqueline. 1983. Field dependence independence as a variable in second language cloze test performance. *TESOL Quarterly 17:* 29-38.

Stansfield, Charles W. and Kenyon, Dorry Mann. 1992. The development and validation of a simulated oral proficiency interview. *Modern Language Journal 76:* 129-141.

Stauble, Ann-Marie E. 1978. The process of decreolization: A model for second language development. *Language Learning 28:* 29-54.

Stenson, Nancy. 1974. Induced errors. In Schumann & Stenson 1974.

Stern, H.H. 1970. *Perspectives on Second Language Teaching.* Toronto: Ontario Institute for Studies in Education.

Stern, H.H. 1975. What can we learn from the good language learner? *Canadian Modern Language Review 34:* 304-318. Reprinted in Croft 1980.

Sternberg, Robert J. 1985. *Beyond IQ: A Triarchic Theory of Human Intelligence.* New York: Cambridge University Press.

Sternberg, Robert J. 1988. *The Triarchic Mind: A New Theory of Human Intelligence.* New York: Viking Press.

Sternberg, Robert J. and Davidson, Janet E. 1982. The mind of the puzzler. *Psychology Today 16:* 6: 37-44.

Stevick, Earl. 1974. The meaning of drills and exercises. *Language Learning 24:* 1-22.

Stevick, Earl. 1976a. *Memory, Meaning and Method.* Rowley, MA: Newbury House.

Stevick, Earl. 1976b. English as an alien language. In Fanselow & Crymes 1976.

Stevick, Earl. 1982. *Teaching and Learning Languages.* New York: Cambridge University Press.

Stevick, Earl W. 1989. *Success with Foreign Languages: Seven Who Achieved It and What Worked for Them.* New York: Prentice-Hall.

Stockwell, Robert, Bowen, J. Donald, and Martin, John W. 1965. *The Grammatical Structures of English and Spanish.* Chicago: University of Chicago Press.

Stubbs, M. 1996. *Text and Corpus Analysis.* Oxford: Blackwell.

Sullivan, Edmund V. 1967. *Piaget and the School Curriculum: A Critical Appraisal.* Toronto: Ontario Institute for Studies in Education.

Svanes, Bjorg. 1987. Motivation and "cultural distance" in second language acquisition. *Language Learning 37:* 341-359.

Svanes, Bjorg. 1988. Attitudes and "cultural distance" in second language acquisition. *Applied Linguistics 9:* 357-371.

Swain, Merrill. 1977. Future directions in second language research. In Henning 1977.

Swain, Merrill. 1984. Large-scale communicative language testing. In Savignon & Berns 1984.

Swain, Merrill. 1990. The language of French immersion students: Implications for theory and practice. In Alatis 1990.

Swain, Merrill. 1998. Focus on form through conscious reflection. In Doughty & Williams 1998.

Swain, Merrill and Lapkin, Sharon. 1995. Problems in output and the cognitive process they generate: A step towards second language learning. *Applied Linguistics 16:* 371–391.

Swain, Merrill and Lapkin, Sharon. 1998. Interaction and second language learning: Two adolescent French immersion students working together. *Modern Language Journal 82:* 320–337.

Tannen, Deborah. 1986. *That's Not What I Meant! How Conversational Style Makes or Breaks Your Relations with Others.* New York: William Morrow.

Tannen, Deborah. 1990. *You Just Don't Understand: Women and Men in Conversation.* New York: William Morrow.

Tannen, Deborah. 1996. *Gender and Discourse.* New York: Oxford University Press.

Tarone, Elaine. 1979. Interlanguage as chameleon. *Language Learning 29:* 181–191.

Tarone, Elaine. 1981. Some thoughts on the notion of communication strategy. *TESOL Quarterly 15:* 285–295.

Tarone, Elaine. 1983. Some thoughts on the notion of "communication strategy." In Faerch & Kasper 1983b.

Tarone, Elaine. 1988. *Variation in Interlanguage.* London: Edward Arnold.

Tarone, Elaine. 1990. On variation in interlanguage: A response to Gregg. *Applied Linguistics 11:* 392–400.

Tarone, Elaine and Parrish, B. 1988. Task related variation in interlanguage: The case of articles. *Language Learning 38:* 21–44.

Tarone, Elaine, Frauenfelder, Uli, and Selinker, Larry. 1976. Systematicity/variability and stability/instability in interlanguage systems. In H.D. Brown 1976a.

Taylor, Barry P. 1974. Toward a theory of language acquisition. *Language Learning 24:* 23–35.

Taylor, Barry P. 1975. The use of overgeneralization and transfer learning strategies by elementary and intermediate students in ESL. *Language Learning 25:* 73–107.

Taylor, Barry P. 1983. Teaching ESL: Incorporating a communicative, student-centered component. *TESOL Quarterly 17:* 69–88.

Taylor, David S. 1988. The meaning and use of the term "competence" in linguistics and applied linguistics. *Applied Linguistics 9:* 148–168.

Thomas, Lee. 1996. Language as power: A linguistic critique of U.S. English. *Modern Language Journal 80:* 129–140.

Thompson, Irene. 1991. Foreign accents revisited: The English pronunciation of Russian immigrants. *Language Learning 41:* 177–204.

Thompson, Irene and Rubin, Joan. 1996. Can strategy instruction improve listening comprehension? *Foreign Language Annals 29:* 331–342.

Tollefson, James. 1995. *Power and Inequality in Language Education.* Cambridge: Cambridge University Press.

Tomasello, Michael and Herron, Carol. 1989. Feedback for language transfer errors: The garden path technique. *Studies in Second Language Acquisition 15:* 385-395.

Torrance, E. Paul. 1980. *Your Style of Learning and Thinking, Forms B and C.* Athens: University of Georgia Press.

Trayer, Marie. 1991. Learning style differences: Gifted vs. regular language students. *Foreign Language Annals 24:* 419-425.

Turner, Ken. 1995. The principal principles of pragmatic inference: Cooperation. *Language Teaching 28:* 67-76.

Turner, Ken. 1996. The principal principles of pragmatic inference: Politeness. *Language Teaching 29:* 1-13.

Twaddell, Freeman. 1935. *On Defining the Phoneme.* Language Monograph Number 166.

Twain, Mark. 1869. *The Innocents Abroad. Volume 1.* New York: Harper & Brothers.

Twain, Mark. 1880. *A Tramp Abroad.* Hartford, CT: American Publishing Company.

Upshur, John A. 1976. Discussion of "A program for language testing research." *Language Learning, Special Issue Number 4:* 167-174.

Upshur, John A. and Homburg, T.J. 1983. Some relations among language tests as successive ability levels. In Oller 1983.

Valdman, Albert (Ed.). 1966. *Trends in Language Teaching.* New York: McGraw-Hill.

Valdman, Albert (Ed.). 1988. The assessment of foreign language oral proficiency. *Studies in Second Language Acquisition 10* (June).

Van Buren, Paul. 1996. Are there principles of Universal Grammar that do not apply to second language acquisition? In Jordens & Lalleman 1996.

Van Ek, J.A. and Alexander, L.G. 1975. *Threshold Level English.* Oxford: Pergamon Press.

Van Ek, J.A., Alexander, L.G., and Fitzpatrick, M.A. 1977. *Waystage English.* Oxford: Pergamon Press.

Van Lier, Leo. 1989. Reeling, writhing, drawling, and fainting in coils: Oral proficiency interviews as conversation. *TESOL Quarterly 23:* 489-508.

Van Lier, Leo. 1996. *Interaction in the Language Curriculum: Awareness, Autonomy and Authenticity.* London: Longman.

Vann, Roberta J. and Abraham, Roberta G. 1990. Strategies of unsuccessful language learners. *TESOL Quarterly 24:* 177-198.

Varadi, T. 1973. Strategies of target language learner communication: Message adjustment. Paper presented at the Sixth Conference of the Romanian-English Linguistics Project. Reprinted 1980 in the *International Review of Applied Linguistics 18:* 59-71.

Vigil, Neddy A. and Oller, John W. 1976. Rule fossilization: A tentative model. *Language Learning 26:* 281-295.

Vogely, Anita Jones. 1998. Listening comprehension anxiety: Students' reported sources and solutions. *Foreign Language Annals 31:* 67-80.

Vygotsky, Lev S. 1962. *Thought and Language.* Cambridge: MIT Press.

Vygotsky, Lev S. 1978. *Mind in Society: The Development of Higher Psychological Processes.* Cambridge: Harvard University Press.

Wagner-Gough, Judy. 1975. Comparative studies in second language learning. *CAL-ERIC/CLL Series on Languages and Linguistics 26.*

Walsh, Terence M. and Diller, Karl C. 1981. Neurolinguistic considerations on the optimum age for second language learning. In Diller 1981.

Wanner, Eric and Gleitman, Lila R. 1982. *Language Acquisition: The State of the Art.* Cambridge: Cambridge University Press.

Wardhaugh, Ronald. 1970. The contrastive analysis hypothesis. *TESOL Quarterly 4:* 123–130.

Wardhaugh, Ronald. 1971. Theories of language acquisition in relation to beginning reading instruction. *Language Learning 21:* 1–26.

Wardhaugh, Ronald. 1972. *Introduction to Linguistics.* New York: McGraw-Hill.

Wardhaugh, Ronald. 1974. *Topics in Applied Linguistics.* Rowley, MA: Newbury House.

Wardhaugh, Ronald. 1976. *The Contexts of Language.* Rowley, MA: Newbury House.

Wardhaugh, Ronald. 1977. *Introduction to Linguistics.* Second Edition. Rowley, MA: Newbury House.

Wardhaugh, Ronald. 1992. *An Introduction to Sociolinguistics.* Second Edition. Cambridge, MA: Basil Blackwell.

Wardhaugh, Ronald and Brown, H. Douglas (Eds.). 1976. *A Survey of Applied Linguistics.* Ann Arbor: University of Michigan Press.

Watkins, David, Biggs, John, and Regmi, Murari. 1991. Does confidence in the language of instruction influence a student's approach to learning? *Instructional Science 20:* 331–339.

Watson, John B. 1913. Psychology as the behaviorist views it. *Psychological Review 20:* 158–177.

Webster's New International Dictionary of the English Language. 1934. Edited by W.A. Neilson. Springfield, MA: G. and C. Merriam Company.

Weinreich, Uriel. 1953. *Languages in Contact: Findings and Problems.* New York: Publication Number 1 of the Linguistic Circle of New York.

Weir, Cyril J. 1988. *Communicative Language Testing.* New York: Prentice-Hall.

Weir, Ruth H. 1962. *Language in the Crib.* The Hague: Mouton Publishers.

Weissenborn, Jurgen, Goodluck, Helen, and Roeper, Thomas. 1991. *Theoretical Issues in Language Acquisition: Continuity and Change in Development.* Hillsdale, NJ: Lawrence Erlbaum Associates.

Weltens, Bert. 1987. The attrition of foreign language skills: A literature review. *Applied Linguistics 8:* 22–38.

Weltens, Bert and Cohen, Andrew D. 1989. Language attrition research: An introduction. *Studies in Second Language Acquisition 11:* 127–133.

Wenden, Anita L. 1985. Learner strategies. *TESOL Newsletter 19:* 1–7.

Wenden, Anita. 1992. *Learner Strategies for Learner Autonomy.* Englewood Cliffs, NJ: Prentice-Hall Regents.

Wesche, Marjorie B. 1983. Communicative testing in a second language. *Modern Language Journal 67:* 41–55.

White, Lydia. 1987. Against comprehensible input: The input hypothesis and the development of second language competence. *Applied Linguistics 8:* 95-110.

White, Lydia. 1990. Second language acquisition and universal grammar. *Studies in Second Language Acquisition 12:* 121-133.

Whitman, Randal. 1970. Contrastive analysis: Problems and procedures. *Language Learning 20:* 191-197.

Whitman, Randal and Jackson, Kenneth L. 1972. The unpredictability of contrastive analysis. *Language Learning 22:* 29-41.

Whorf, Benjamin. 1956. Science and linguistics. In Carroll 1956.

Widdowson, Henry G. 1978a. Notional-functional syllabuses 1978: Part IV. In Blatchford & Schachter 1978.

Widdowson, Henry G. 1978b. *Teaching Language as Communication.* Oxford: Oxford University Press.

Wilkins, David A. 1976. *Notional Syllabuses.* London: Oxford University Press.

Williams, Marion and Burden, Robert L. 1997. *Psychology for Language Teachers: A Social Constructivist Approach.* Cambridge: Cambridge University Press.

Witkin, Herman A.; Oltman, Philip K.; Raskin, Evelyn; and Karp, Stephen. 1971. *Embedded Figures Test. Manual for the Embedded Figures Test.* Palo Alto, CA: Consulting Psychologists Press.

Wolfson, Nessa. 1981. Compliments in cross-cultural perspective. *TESOL Quarterly 15:* 117-124.

Wolfson, Nessa and Judd, Elliot (Eds.). 1983. *Sociolinguistics and Language Acquisition.* Rowley, MA: Newbury House.

Wolfson, Nessa, D'Amico-Reisner, Lynne, and Huber, Lisa. 1983. How to arrange for social commitments in American English: The invitation. In Wolfson & Judd 1983.

Wong, Rita F. 1986. Instructional considerations in teaching pronunciation. In Morley 1986.

Wong, Rita F. 1987. *Teaching Pronunciation: Focus on Rhythm and Intonation.* Washington, DC: Center for Applied Linguistics.

Yorio, Carlos. 1976. Discussion of "Explaining sequence and variation in second language acquisition." *Language Learning, Special Issue Number 4:* 59-63.

Young, Dolly Jesusita. 1991. Creating a low anxiety classroom environment: What does language anxiety research suggest? *Modern Language Journal 75:* 426-439.

Young, Dolly Jesusita. 1992. Language anxiety from the foreign language specialist's perspective: Interviews with Krashen, Omaggio-Hadley, Terrell, and Rardin. *Foreign Language Annals 25:* 157-172.

Young, Richard. 1988. Variation and the interlanguage hypothesis. *Studies in Second Language Acquisition 10:* 281-302.

Yule, George and Tarone, Elaine. 1990. Eliciting the performance of strategic competence. In Scarcella, Andersen, & Krashen 1990.

Zangwill, Oliver. 1971. The neurology of language. In Minnis 1971.

Zobl, Helmut and Liceras, Juana. 1994. Functional categories and acquisition orders. *Language Learning 44:* 159-180.

INDEX

Names

Abraham, R., 116, 121, 124

Acton, W., 186–87

Adamson, H. D., 230

Adler, P., 184–85

Alexander, L. G., 252

Allwright, R., 238, 256

Alpert, R., 151

Alptekin, C., 116

Andersen, R., 69, 88

Anderson, R., 80, 83, 124, 127

Andrés, V., 147

Angelis, P., 269

Anthony, E., 169

Aphek, E., 130

Armstrong, T., 102, 110

Arnold, J., 142, 174

Asher, J., 107

Atakan, S., 116

Au, S. Y., 163

Auerbach, E., 196

Austin, J., 250

Ausubel, D., 10, 51, 61, 79, 80, 83–89, 91, 114, 155, 160

Baca, L. L., 181

Bachman, L., 248–49, 256, 269

Bacon, S., 124

Bailey, K., 90, 152, 165, 238

Baldwin, A., 293

Banathy, B., 209

Bates, M., 158, 174

Bayley, R., 37, 229, 230, 243

Beebe, L., 149, 150

Bellugi, U., 31, 41

Berko, J., 25, 37

Berko-Gleason, J., 29, 42

Berlitz, C., 45, 169

Berns, M., 250, 253

Bialystok, E., 54, 127, 131, 231, 285–86, 288

Bickerton, D., 35, 47, 53, 294

Biggs, J., 146

Binet, A., 100

Bley-Vroman, R., 71

Bloom, B., 143–44

Bloom, L., 28, 29

Bloomfield, L., 8

Bolinger, D., 261

Bongaerts, T., 59, 60, 127

Bowen, J., 74, 209, 212

Breen, M., 266

Briggs, K., 156–59

Brodkey, D., 146

Brown, H. D., 14, 18, 39, 87, 98, 117, 124, 131, 135, 141, 164, 188, 201, 253, 266, 295

Brown, R., 31, 40, 41, 69

Brumfit, C., 279

Bruner, J., 37, 165, 292

Buczowska, E., 230, 280

Budwig, N., 29

Burden, R., 17, 161

Burt, M., 67, 68, 223, 278

Busch, D., 155

Cairns, E., 121
Cammock, T., 121
Campbell, R., 167, 253
Canale, M., 246–48, 256, 269
Candlin, C. N., 266
Carmichael, L., 197
Carrell, P., 158
Carroll, D., 47, 214
Carroll, J., 98, 199
Carroll, L., 28
Cathcart, R., 237
Celce-Murcia, M., 15, 74, 214, 219
Chaika, E., 261
Chambers, F., 267
Chamot, A., 106, 124, 135
Chapelle, C., 116, 117, 120
Chesterfield, B., 130
Chesterfield, R., 130
Chihara, T., 181
Child, J. R., 99
Chomsky, N., 9, 10, 23, 24, 25, 31, 231, 246
Chun, A., 237
Clarke, M., 90, 200, 289
Clifford, R., 266
Clinchy, B., 292
Cohen, A., 87, 99, 114, 124, 130, 140, 257
Coleman, A., 74
Comrie, B., 214
Condon, E. C., 177, 180, 182
Cook, V., 25, 36, 47, 51, 60, 67, 71, 72, 77
Coopersmith, S., 145
Corder, S., 215, 217, 220–21, 227–29
Coulthard, R. M., 42
Crawford, J., 196
Crookall, D., 127
Crookes, G., 164, 230
Cummins, J., 194, 246

Curran, C., 89, 103
Curtiss, S., 52

D'Amico-Reisner, L., 257
Danesi, M., 118
Davies, A., 193
Day, C., 188
Day, R., 237
DeBot, K., 279
Deci, E., 164
DeKeyser, R., 234
Dewaele, J. M., 156
Diller, K. C., 47, 56
Dirven, R., 204
Donahue, M., 189
Donne, J., 176
Dörnyei, Z., 127, 128, 160, 164, 165, 174
Doron, S., 121
Doughty, C., 230, 233, 234, 243, 280
Drach, K., 41
Dresser, N., 205, 262, 270
Dufeu, B., 150
Dulay, H., 67, 68, 278
Durkheim, E., 184

Eckman, F., 213–14
Ehrman, M., 64, 99, 114, 147, 148, 152, 158, 159, 160, 235
Elbow, P., 290
Elliott, A. R., 116
Ellis, G., 131
Ellis, N., 285, 286
Ellis, R., 72, 229, 230, 231, 234, 280, 285, 298
Ely, C. M., 150
Ervin-Tripp, S., 67
Ewing, D., 121, 292

Faerch, C., 127
Fantini, A., 189, 205
Fast, J., 262
Firth, A., 286

Firth, J. R., 33, 250
Flege, J., 58
Flynn, S., 214
Foster, G., 230
Freed, B. F., 87
Freire, P., 90
Fries, C., 8, 74, 208

Gagné, R., 91
Gaies, S., 238
Galvan, J., 189
Ganschow, L., 151
Gardner, H., 100
Gardner, R. C., 87, 140, 146, 151, 162–63, 167, 174, 181
Garmezy, N., 7
Gass, S., 214, 219, 287
Gatbonton, E., 229
Gathercole, V. C., 34
Gattegno, C., 106
Genesee, F., 57
Gerstman, L. J., 58
Gibbons, J., 108
Gleason, H. A., 198
Gleitman, L., 28
Goleman, D., 101
Goodman, K., 121
Gouin, F., 43–44, 169
Graham, C. R., 164
Green, P., 116, 117
Greenberg, J., 35
Gregg, K., 231, 279, 281, 291
Grice, H. P., 257
Griffiths, R., 117
Guiora, A. Z., 55, 64, 117, 147, 148, 153, 154, 199

Haber, R., 151
Hall, E., 183, 262, 264
Halliday, M., 33, 250–52
Han, Y., 286
Hanlon, C., 40
Hansen, L., 115, 116

Hansen-Bede, L., 67, 68
Harley, B., 99
Harlow, L. L., 258
Hart, D., 99
Hartnett, D., 118
Hashimoto, R., 11
Hatch, E., 255
Hawkins, B., 214, 219
Henderson, T., 269
Hendrickson, J., 237
Heyde, A., 146
Higgs, T., 266
Hilgard, E., 142
Hill, B., 114, 124
Hill, J., 57
Hladik, E., 41
Hockett, C., 8
Hoffman, S., 116, 117
Hofstede, G., 190–91, 192, 204
Hogan, R., 153, 154, 197
Holmes, J., 42, 258, 259, 269
Holzman, M., 29, 36, 47
Horwitz, E. K., 151, 152
Horwitz, M. B., 151
Huang, X-H., 130
Hulstijn, J. H., 283, 286
Hymes, D., 246

Inhelder, B., 28
Ioup, G., 60

Jackson, K., 212
Jacobs, B., 54
James, C., 219, 243
James, W., 85
Jamieson, J., 121, 235
Jaszczolt, K., 213, 224, 243
Jenkins, J., 23
Joos, M., 260
Jordens, P., 287
Jung, C., 156

Kachru, B., 163, 193
Kagan, J., 121
Kakava, C., 198
Kasper, G., 127, 229, 258
Keefe, J. W., 114
Keirsey, D., 158, 174
Keller, J., 160
Kellerman, S., 265
Kimble, G. A., 7
Kiparsky, C., 223
Kleinmann, H., 219
Kohls, R. L., 189, 205
Krashen, S., 55, 108, 117, 118, 165, 237, 277–81, 288, 298
Krathwohl, D., 143–44
Kuczaj, S., 29
Kuhn, T., 4, 13, 18, 289
Küpper, L., 124, 131

Labov, W., 41
Lado, R., 208
LaForge, P., 104
Lakoff, R., 259
Lakshmanan, U., 71
Lambert, W., 67, 87, 146, 162–63, 181, 184, 187
Lamendella, J., 229, 233
Landes, J., 41
Lantolf, J., 291, 299
Lapkin, S., 279, 281, 287
Larsen-Freeman, D., 69, 94, 272, 276, 279
Larson, D., 176
Lawrence, G., 158, 174
Lengyel, Z., 54, 55, 60, 77
Lenneberg, E., 24, 53, 55
Lennon, P., 222, 223
Leopold, W., 35
Lett, J. A., 99
Levine, D. R., 189
Lierres, F., 178
Lightbown, P., 110, 216, 234, 274–75, 276, 280
Littlewood, W. T., 229

LoCastro, V., 258
Lock, A., 29
Locke, J., 80
Loew, R., 284
Loftus, E., 197
Long, M., 58, 59, 234, 236, 238, 255, 272, 277, 279, 280, 287–88
Loschky, L., 287
Losoff, A., 200
Lozanov, G., 105
Lukmani, Y., 163

MacCorquodale, K., 23
MacIntyre, P., 131, 140, 146, 151, 162–63, 167, 174
Mackey, A., 287
Macnamara, J., 66
Major, R., 214
Malinowski, B., 145
Malotki, E., 199
Maratsos, M., 35
Marckwardt, A., 13
Marshall, T., 124
Martin, J. W., 209, 212
Masia, B. B., 143–44
Maslow, A., 161, 165
McCloskey, L., 42
McCracken, M. D., 200
McDonough, S., 124, 127, 130
McGroarty, M., 189
McKeon, D., 106
McLaughlin, B., 279, 282–84, 288
McLeod, B., 282, 283
McNeill, D., 24, 25, 39, 40–41
McTear, M., 42
Mehnert, U., 286
Miller, G., 85
Miller, W. R., 33
Milon, J., 67

Mitchell, R., 17, 25, 110, 280
Moerk, E., 41
Morgan, C., 204
Morris, B., 58
Moyer, A., 59
Myers, I., 156–59
Myles, F., 17, 25, 110, 280

Naiman, N., 115, 120, 124, 154, 155
Natalicio, D., 67
Nayar, P. B., 193–94
Neapolitan, D. M., 55
Nemser, W., 215
Neufeld, G., 59
Newson, M., 47
Ney, J., 27
Nilsen, A. P., 259
Noels, K., 131
Nunan, D., 14, 103
Nuttall, C., 255
Nyikos, M., 11

O'Grady, W., 71
O'Malley, J. M., 124, 125, 131
O'Mara, E. E., 99
Obler, L., 56, 57, 87
Ochsner, R., 291
Odlin, T., 279
Oller, J., 102, 167, 181, 212, 232–33, 235
Olsen, J., 237
Olshtain, E., 88, 257
Omaggio, A., 131
Osgood, C., 9, 23
Ostrander, S., 105
Oxford, R., 99, 127, 131, 132–33, 135, 140, 151, 152, 158, 160

Palermo, D., 23
Parry, T., 99
Parsons, A. H., 189

Patkowski, M., 58
Paulston, C. B., 246
Pavlov, I., 79–80, 91
Pearson, L., 27, 121
Pemberton, R., 127
Peters, A., 97
Phillips, E. M., 151
Phillipson, R., 193, 194, 195
Piaget, J., 11, 28, 37, 61, 62, 164
Pica, T., 287
Pike, K., 144
Pimsleur, P., 99
Pinker, S., 5, 47, 198
Poulisse, N., 127
Prator, C. H., 15, 74, 209–10
Preston, D., 37, 72, 229, 230, 243
Pullum, G. K., 198
Purpura, J. E., 124
Pütz, M., 204

Quirk, R., 193

Ramage, K., 165
Ramirez, A., 189
Ravem, R., 67
Regmi, M., 146
Reid, J., 99, 114, 122, 235
Reynolds, A. G., 67
Rice, M., 34
Ricento, T., 194, 195
Richard-Amato, P., 14, 18, 266
Richards, J. C., 14, 16, 18, 45, 106, 169–70, 193, 225–26
Rivers, W., 75
Roberts, C., 116, 120
Robinson, P., 234, 286
Robinson-Stuart, G., 178, 182, 189

Rodgers, T., 14, 16, 18, 45, 106, 169–70
Rogers, C., 79, 89–91, 104
Rood, D., 200
Rosansky, E., 61, 69
Ross, S., 127, 130
Rossman, T., 282
Rost, M., 127, 130
Rubin, J., 98, 123, 124, 131, 149, 150, 257
Rutherford, W., 214

Saleemi, A., 36, 47
Sapir, E., 8, 199
Sapon, S. M., 98
Sasaki, M., 99
Saussure, F. de, 10
Savignon, S., 246, 247, 266
Saville-Troike, M., 179
Schachter, J., 51, 52, 214, 219
Schinke-Llano, L., 38, 67
Schmidt, R., 164, 282, 284
Schroeder, L., 105
Schumann, J. H., 54, 148, 166–67, 174, 185–86, 291
Scollon, R., 178, 205, 258
Scollon, S., 178, 205, 258
Scovel, T., 52, 54–57, 59, 60, 69, 76, 105, 118, 147, 151, 196, 198, 282
Seliger, H., 57, 118, 280
Selinker, L., 215, 229, 233
Sharwood-Smith, M., 213
Shatz, M., 42
Sheen, R., 117
Sheen, R., 213
Shore, H., 146
Sinclair, J. M., 42, 131
Singleton, D., 54, 55, 60, 77

Sjöholm, K., 213
Skehan, P., 17, 99, 110, 114, 171*n*, 230
Skinner, B. F., 7, 9–10, 22, 23, 29, 79, 80–82, 91
Skutnabb-Kangas, T., 194
Slavoff, R., 60
Slobin, D., 28, 29, 35
Smalley, W. A., 176
Smith, F., 85
Sokolik, M. E., 27
Sorenson, A., 57
Spada, N., 110, 216, 233, 234, 243, 275, 280
Spivey, N. N., 11
Spolsky, B., 26, 272
Stansfield, C., 116
Stenson, N., 226
Stern, H. H., 50, 51, 123
Sternberg, R., 101, 292
Stevick, E., 118, 124, 134, 149, 189
Stockwell, R., 209, 212
Stubbs, M., 33
Sullivan, E., 62
Svanes, B., 188
Swain, M., 246–48, 256, 269, 279, 280, 287

Tannen, D., 42, 259
Tarone, E., 33, 37, 72, 127, 219, 229, 230, 231, 248, 269
Taylor, B., 224–25
Terrell, T., 108, 237
Thomas, L., 196
Thompson, I., 98, 123, 124, 131, 149
Tollefson, J., 193, 196, 205
Tomasello, M., 234
Torrance, E., 118
Trager, E. C., 209
Turner, K., 258, 269
Twaddell, F., 8, 17

Twain, M., 178, 179, 208

Van Buren, P., 71
Van Ek, J. A., 252
Van Naerssen, M., 130
van Lier, L., 287
Vann, R., 124
Varadi, T., 127
Vigil, N., 232–33, 235
Vogely, A. J., 151
von Humboldt, W., 199
Vygotsky, L., 11, 12, 37, 38, 89, 287

Waddle, C. D., 209
Wagner-Gough, J., 254
Walsh, T. M., 56
Walter, A. A., 197
Wanner, E., 28
Wardhaugh, R., 41, 200, 211, 261
Watkins, D., 146
Watson, J. B., 80
Weinreich, U., 215
Weir, R., 40
Weist, R. M., 230, 280
Welch, L., 121
Weltens, B., 87
Wenden, A., 124, 130
White, L., 214, 279, 281
Whitman, R., 212
Whorf, B., 199–200
Widdowson, H., 253, 266
Wilkins, D., 252
Williams, J., 233, 234, 243, 280
Williams, M., 17, 161
Witkin, H., 154
Wolfson, N., 257
Wong, R., 98

Yorio, C., 272–74, 275
Young, D. J., 151, 152, 230
Yule, G., 248, 269

Zangwill, O., 54
Ziahosseiny, S. M., 212
Zobl, H., 69

Subject
Accent, 58–60
Acculturation, 182–85
Acquisition-Learning Hypothesis, 278
Advance organizers, 125
Affective domain, 64–66, 143–44
Affective factors, measurement of, 167–68
Affective feedback, 232, 235–39
Affective filter, 279
Alcohol and pronunciation, 147–48
Ambiguity tolerance, 119–20
Analytical processes, 292
Analyzed (and unanalyzed) knowledge, 286
Anomie, 184
Anxiety, 150–52
Anxiety, state and trait, 151
Appeal to authority, 126, 128, 130
Applied linguistics, 1–14
Approach, 14
Approach to language pedagogy, 201–3, 266
Approximation, 128
Approximative systems, 215
Aptitude, 98–99
Army Specialized Training Program (ASTP), 74
Artifacts, 264

Assimilative orientations, 164

Attention, focal and peripheral, 282–84

Attention-Processing Model, 282–85

Attitudes, 180–81

Attrition of language, 87

Audiolingual Method (ALM), 13, 51, 73–75, 88

Auditory style, 122

Authenticity, of accent, 58–59

Automatic (and non-automatic) processes, 286

Autonomy, 164

Avoidance strategies, 128–29

Backsliding, 228

Basic interpersonal communicative skills (BICS), 246

Behaviorism, 8–9, 22–24, 80–83, 91, 160

Believing game, 290–91

Bilingualism: compound and coordinate, 67

Bioprogramming, 294

Birdsong, acquisition of, 55–56

Body language, 262–63

Brain, in language acquisition, 54–55, 56–57

Capability continuum paradigm, 230

Casual style, 260

Chaining, 80, 92–93

Chaos/complexity theory, 276–77

Circumlocution, 128

Classical behaviorism, classical conditioning, 80

Classical Method, 15–16. *See also* Grammar Translation Method

Code switching, 67, 128–29

Cognitive development, 28–29, 60–63

Cognitive feedback, 232–33

Cognitive learning theory, 91

Cognitive strategies, 124–26

Cognitive styles, 113–14

Cognitive/academic language proficiency (CALP), 246

Collectivism, 190

Communication strategies, 122–23, 127–30, 227

Communicative competence, 246–48

Communicative language teaching, 14, 266–67

Community language learning, 103–5

Compensatory strategies, 127–30, 132

Competence, 10, 30–33, 70

Compound bilingualism, 67, 72

Comprehension, 33–34, 70

Conditioned response, 80

Connectionism, 27

Constructivism, 11–12, 91, 161

Constructivism, social, 287–88

Consultative style, 260–61

Context-embedded language, 99

Context-reduced language, 99

Contrastive analysis hypothesis (CAH), 207–11
    strong. vs. weak form of, 211–13
    subtle-differences version of, 212

Conversation analysis and rules, 255–57

Coordinate bilingualism, 67, 72

Counseling-learning model of education, 103–5

Creative construction process, 68–69

Critical period hypothesis, 53–54

Cross-linguistic influence, 211–13

Cultural stereotypes, 178–80

Culture, and language and thought, 196–200

Culture conflict, shock, stress, 183–85

Culture in the classroom, 189–91

Debilitative anxiety, 151–52

Deductive reasoning, 97, 126

Defensive learning, 91

Deliberative style, 260

Difficulty, hierarchy of, 209–10

Direct Method, 13

Discourse, 29, 42–43

Discourse analysis, 253–57
Discourse competence, 247
Doubting game, 290–91

Eclecticism, 14
Ecology of second language acquisition, 294–96
Ego enhancement, 161
Egocentricity, 63–66
Elicited response, 81
Embedded Figures Test, 114
Emitted response, 81
Emotional intelligence (EQ), 101
Empathy, 152–54
Empiricism, 9
English as a foreign language (EFL), 193–94
English as a second language (ESL), 193–94
English as International Language (EIL), 192–93
English Only, 195–96
Equilibration, 62
Error(s)
    analysis of, 216–20
    correction of, 235–41
    covert, 220
    distinction between mistakes and, 217–18
    global, 223, 237
    identifying and describing, 220–23
    interlingual, 224
    intralingual, 224–26
    local, 223, 237
    overt, 220

sources of, 223–27
Ethnocentrism, 180
Explicit knowledge, 285–86
Extrinsic motivation, 164–65
Extroversion, 154–56
Eye contact, 263

Facilitative anxiety, 151–52
Feedback, affective, cognitive, corrective, 232–33, 235–39
Femininity, 190–91
Field dependence (field sensitivity), 114–18
Field independence, 114–18
First language acquisition, 21–45
Foreign language anxiety, 151
Foreign language learning (vs. second language learning), 192–93
Forgetting, systematic, 86–89
Form, vs. function, 250
Form-focused instruction, 233–35
Fossilization, 229, 231–33
Frequency, of input, 40
Function, vs. form, 29, 250
Functional approaches in first language acquisition, 27–30
Functional syllabuses, 252–53

Gender and language, 259–60

Generative-transformational linguistics, 9–10
Gestures, 262–63
Good language learners, 123–24
Grammar consciousness-raising, 234
Grammar Translation Method, 13, 15–16. *See also* Classical Method
Grammatical competence, 247

Hermeneutic tradition, 291
Heuristic function, of language, 251–52
Hierarchy of difficulty, 209–10
High Input Generators (HIGs), 280
Hogan's Empathy Scale, 154
Human learning, 78–103
Humanistic psychology, 89–91

$i + 1$, 278–79, 281
Idiosyncratic dialect, 215
Illocutionary force, 248–49, 258
Imaginative function, of language, 252
Imitation in first language acquisition, 38–39, 72
Implicit and explicit attention, 234
Implicit knowledge, 285–86
Impulsivity, 121–22
Individualism, 190
Induced errors, 226
Inductive reasoning, 97

Inhibition, proactive and
retroactive, 86
Inhibitions, 64, 86,
147-49
Innateness, 24, 34-35
Input, in first language
acquisition, 41-42, 73
Input hypothesis, 277-81
Instrumental function, of
language, 251
Instrumental orientation,
162-64
Intake (vs. input), 280
Integrative orientation,
162-64
Intellectual
development, 54-55,
61-63
Intelligence, and second
language learning,
98-102
Interaction hypothesis,
287-88
Interactional function, of
language, 23, 251
Interference, 67-68,
94-96, 126
Interlanguage, 215
Interlingual errors,
transfer, 94-95, 213,
223-24
Intimate style, 260-61
Intralingual errors,
transfer, 94-95, 213,
224-26
Intrinsic motivation,
164-65
Intuition, 158-59,
292-93
Intuitive style, 119
IQ, 99-101

Keywords, 126
Kinesics, 262-63
Kinesthetics, 264

Kissinger, Henry, effect,
59-60

Language acquisition
device (LAD), 24-25,
71
Language ego, 64-65,
147-48
Language policy, 195-96
Language rights, 194-95
Language, definition of,
5-6
Lateralization, 54-55
Learner language,
215-16
Learner strategy training.
See Strategies-based
instruction
Learning, definition of, 7
Learning, types of, 91-94
Learning strategies, 117,
122-27
Learning styles, 113, 135
Learning versus
Acquisition, 277-78
Left- and right-brain
functioning, 54-57,
118-19
Lingua franca, 191
Linguistic competence,
246
Linguistic determinism,
199
Linguistic imperialism,
194-95
Linguistic relativity, 199
Linguistic universals,
35-36
Long-term memory,
85-86, 88
Low Input Generators
(LIGs), 280

Markedness Differential
Hypothesis, 213-15

Masculinity, 190-91
Matching Familiar
Figures Test, 121
Meaningful (vs. rote)
learning, 83-85
Mediation theory, 23
Memory, 85-89, 100
Mentalism, 23
Message abandonment,
128
Metacognitive strategies,
124-25, 133
Methods of language
teaching, 13-14,
168-72
Micro-Momentary
Expression (MME)
test, 154
Mistakes, distinction
between errors and,
217-18
Mnemonic devices, 85
Modern Language
Aptitude Test, 98-99
Monitor hypothesis, 278
Motivation, 160-66
Multiple intelligences,
100-102
Myers-Briggs character
types, 156-60

Nativist approach, to first
language acquisition,
24-27
Natural approach, 108
Natural order
hypothesis, 278
Nature/nurture
controversy, 34-35, 71
Negative transfer, 94-95
Neobehaviorism, 80
Neurobiology of affect,
166-67

Neurological considerations, in language acquisition, 54–58, 118

Nomothetic tradition, 291

Nonverbal communication, 262–65

Noticing, 234

Notional-functional syllabuses, 252–53

Olfactory dimensions, 265

Operant conditioning, 22–23, 80–82

Optimal distance model, 187–88

Optimal perceived social distance, 187

Oratorical style, 260

Organizational competence, 248–49

Output hypothesis, 281

Overgeneralization, 95–97

Parallel distributed processing (PDP) model, 26–27

Pavlovian conditioning, 80, 91

Perceived social distance, 186

Perlocutionary force (of an utterance), 250

Personal function of language, 251

Personality factors, 156–60

Phatic communion, 145

Phonological avoidance, 129

Pimsleur Language Aptitude Battery, 98–99

Pivot grammar, 26

Pop-go-weasel effect, 31

Positive transfer, 94–96

Power distance, 190

Pragmalinguistic constraints, 258

Pragmatic competence, 248–49

Pragmatics, 257–59

Prefabricated patterns, 128–29

Proactive inhibition, 86

Process (vs. style and strategy), 113

Production, 33–35

Professed Difference in Attitude Questionnaire (PDAQ), 187

Programmed instruction, 82

Pronunciation, accent, 58–60

Proxemics, 264

Pruning, cognitive, 87

Psychology, 7–13

Punishment, 82

Rationalistic approach, 10

Reading approach, 45

Reflectivity, 121–22

Registers, 261–62

Regulatory function, of language, 251

Reinforcement, 82

Representational function, of language, 251

Request for clarification strategy, 126, 130

Respondent conditioning, 81

Restructuring, 283

Retroactive inhibition, 86

Right- and left-brain functioning, 118–19

Risk-taking, 149–50

Rote (vs. meaningful) learning, 83–85

Sapir-Whorf hypothesis, 199

Scientific method, 9, 27

Second culture learning, 182–85

Selective attention, 125

Self-actualization, 161

Self-esteem, 145–47

Self-monitoring, 125

Series Method, 43–44

Signal learning, 92–93

Silent Way, 106

Social distance, perceived and optimal, 186–87

Social interaction, and first language acquisition, 29–30

Socioaffective strategies, 124–26

Sociobiological critical period, 55–56

Sociocultural factors, 176–81

Sociolinguistic competence, 247, 249

Sociopolitical considerations, 191–96

Sociopragmatic competence, 258

Speech acts, 250

Speech styles, 260–62

Stages of second language development, 227

State anxiety, 151

Stereotyping, 178–80

Stimulus-response learning, 22–24, 80–81, 92–93

Strategic competence, 247–48

Strategies, 113, 122–34

Strategies-based instruction, 127, 130–39

Structural linguistics, 8, 12

Structural syllabuses, 252

Styles, cognitive. *See* Cognitive styles

Styles, speech, 260–62

Subsumer, 92

Subsumption theory, 84, 88

Subtractive bilingualism, 87

Suggestopedia, 105

Superlearning, 105

Surface-structure imitation, 38–39

Sympathy, 153. *See also* Empathy

Systematic forgetting, 84, 86–87

Systematicity, 25, 37, 229

Tabula rasa, 22

Talk-to-self strategy, 130

Teaching, definition of, 7

Telegraphic utterances, 21

Textual competence, 249

Theory vs. practice debate, 289–90

Third language learning, 224

Thought, culture, language and, 196–200

Tolerance of ambiguity. *See* Ambiguity tolerance

Topic avoidance, 128–29

Topic nomination, etc., in conversation, 256

Total Physical Response, 107

Trait anxiety, 151

Transfer, 94

Transfer, inter- and intralingual, 126, 223–24

Truth value, 39

Turn-taking, 256

Uncertainty avoidance, 190–91

Universal Grammar (UG), 25, 35–36

Universal grammar, 214

Universals, 35–36, 71

Valium and pronunciation, 148

Variability in learner language development, 229–31

Variability, 37

Variable competence model, 230

Visual style, 122

Weasel words, 196

Weltanschauung, 179, 199

Whorfian hypothesis, 199–200

Word coinage, 128

World Englishes, 192–93

Zone of proximal development, 38